DR. IBNU

We in Indonesia are engaged in a great effort to develop our economy so as to improve the welfare of all of our people. We welcome those from other countries who desire to work with us toward this objective. Hopefully this book will contribute to increased understanding of Indonesia and its oil industry.

This is the story of the development of one of our most important national industries. It has been an achievement in which we Indonesians can take pride. We are grateful to the many men who have helped build our oil industry and our national oil company. Thousands have participated in this effort, both Indonesians and foreign. Of these, one man deserves our special gratitude. More than any other single man, Lt. General Dr. H. Ibnu Sutowo deserves credit for the success of PERTAMINA. The Indonesian oil industry today is in large part the product of his vision of what a truly national oil company should be, and his dynamic leadership and tireless efforts to implement that vision.

SUMANTRI BRODJONEGORO
Prof. Dr. Ir.

Minister of Mines—
Republic of Indonesia
President of the University
of Indonesia

MENTERI PERTAMBANGAN
REPUBLIK INDONESIA

PERTAMINA

PERTAMINA

INDONESIAN NATIONAL OIL

ANDERSON G. BARTLETT III
ROBERT JOHN BARTON
JOE CALVIN BARTLETT
GEORGE ANDERSON FOWLER, JR.
CHARLES FRANCIS HAYS

AMERASIAN LTD.
DJAKARTA * SINGAPORE * TULSA

AMERASIAN LTD.

Djalan Subang 3A, Djakarta, Indonesia
26J Tomlinson Road, Republic of Singapore 10
P.O. Box 7307, Tulsa Oklahoma, U.S.A.

Library of Congress Catalog Card Number: 72–941851

PRINTED AND BOUND BY:
MCGRAW-HILL FAR EASTERN PUBLISHERS (S) LTD. JURONG, SINGAPORE

Contents

Foreword

**PRESIDEN
REPUBLIK INDONESIA**

Upon the request of the authors I am happy to write a few words welcoming the publication of their book.

This is a book about oil. But much more important it also illustrates some of the zeal, efforts and success achieved by the Indonesian people in building their nation to form a new, stable, modern and prosperous Indonesia based on social justice. To accomplish this requires our utmost diligence and with an unswerving determination we will face the challenges and responsibilities. However, cooperations with other nations, based on equality and mutual benefit, are also important.

It is hoped that this book will serve as a media to help enrich other people's knowledge about Indonesia in general and its oil in particular, whether their interest lies in helping us with our development or just in wanting to know more about us.

Undeniably this book is of great importance for the Indonesians themselves to read. It is a success story of an important industry a vital one which plays a very significant role in the development of Indonesia. We are proud of the fact. Although it certainly does not mean that we have already completed our tasks or reached all our objectives nor are devoid of any errors. We must, therefore, learn from the experiences of PERTAMINA so as to facilitate further development of our oil industry as well as other sectors in the years to come.

We acknowledge with full appreciation the diligence and efforts of the authors in writing this book.

Jakarta,
October 9, 1972.

PRESIDENT OF THE REPUBLIC OF INDONESIA,

SOEHARTO

PRESIDEN
REPUBLIK INDONESIA

KATA SAMBUTAN

Dengan gembira saya memenuhi permintaan para penulis untuk memberikan kata sambutan pada buku ini.

Buku ini menyangkut soal minyak. Lebih dari itu, buku ini juga mengungkapkan sebahagian daripada semangat, usaha dan hasil yang dicapai oleh bangsa Indonesia untuk membangun dirinya sendiri, membangun Indonesia baru yang kokoh, maju, sejahtera dan berkeadilan sosial. Usaha kearah itu pasti merupakan tugas yang sangat besar, yang tanpa ragu-ragu kami bersedia menghadapi tantangan dan memikul bebannya. Akan tetapi kami juga memandang bermanfaat adanya kerjasama dengan bangsa-bangsa lain atas dasar persamaan derajat dan saling menguntungkan.

Untuk itu kiranya buku ini dapat membantu memperdalam pengetahuan bangsa-bangsa lain tentang Indonesia, khususnya minyaknya, baik bagi mereka yang ingin bersama-sama kami membangun Indonesia maupun bagi mereka yang ingin mengetahui lebih banyak mengenai kami.

Bagi orang Indonesia sendiri membaca buku ini sangat banyak gunanya. Ia merupakan kisah yang berhasil dari suatu industri penting, yang sangat vital, yang makin besar peranannya bagi pembangunan Indonesia. Bangsa Indonesia merasa bangga karenanya. Ini tidak berarti bahwa tugas telah selesai atau tidak banyak lagi yang harus ditangani, atau bahwa tidak terdapat kekeliruan-kekeliruan. Yang perlu kita pungut adalah segala pengalaman dari sejarah PERTAMINA itu sehingga kita dapat memperlancar kelanjutan pembangunan industri minyak itu sendiri maupun pembangunan dibidang lain dimasa kedepan.

Ketekunan para penulis yang telah menyelesaikan buku ini patut kita hargai.

Jakarta, 9 Oktober 1972
PRESIDEN REPUBLIK INDONESIA,

S O E H A R T O
JENDERAL TNI

Preface

The idea for this book started one evening in February 1971 when I was having dinner in the home of Tirto Utomo, of Pertamina's Legal, Foreign Relations, and Foreign Marketing division. Tirto and I first met in December 1968, and as both of us are attorneys connected with the oil business, frequently we spend time discussing legal points, as we had earlier in the evening. After dinner the conversation turned to some general writing problems. Tirto formerly was a journalist and I had previously edited a quarterly magazine. When I mentioned to him that I hoped to write some articles and possibly a book about Indonesia, the ebullient Tirto immediately suggested a book about Pertamina and began talking about his two favorite topics —his boss, Dr. Ibnu, and his company, Pertamina. In two hours I learned more about the history and development of Indonesia's national oil company than I had in the previous two years. It was a fascinating story of the fight against colonialism and communism and the fight for political and economic independence. In this regard, Pertamina symbolized a whole nation's successful struggle.

The idea of actually writing a book slowly took shape over the next few months. I felt a team of writers would be required to do the research, including some who spoke the language, so I began talking to several friends to see if they would be interested in such a project. The result was five co-authors, which became known as "Team Sedjarah" (History Team).

In May, Tirto arranged an interview with Dr. Ibnu to discuss the book. Several authors had already approached Dr. Ibnu with the idea of writing such a book, but they only wanted to spend a month or two in Indonesia and thereafter write the book in New York or London. Dr. Ibnu was most enthusiastic about our team approach, provided we were willing to spend enough time learning about the Indonesian oil industry. To further this, he agreed that

Pertamina would extend full use of their facilities, guest houses, and transportation services to travel throughout Indonesia. His suggestion was: "Study our history, study our people and our struggles. Go everywhere and ask everybody questions. Keep an open mind and draw your own conclusions."

Our purpose in writing about the Indonesian national company, Pertamina, is to present a story about a part of the oil industry from the perspective of nationalism. After fourteen months' research, travel, and above all, listening, we have decided that Pertamina provides an important answer to the question around which wars and revolutions have been fought: Who deserves how much from, and who will control, the development of the vital natural resource, oil. In this regard we are recording a story of how nationalism became tempered by realism and about changed attitudes within the international oil industry.

With almost no existing written materials on the subject of Pertamina and its predecessors, we relied greatly on interviews. In the course of gathering material, we held well over two hundred formal interviews, some lasting four hours and some extending over sixty hours, and visited every major oil producing area in the country.

Our interviews were generally held in English without the use of an interpreter, since most of the people we spoke to were fluent in the language. Occasionally, while visiting the "old cracks" of the oil industry, George and Charlie interviewed entirely in Bahasa Indonesia.

We have discussed oil history and politics with Indonesians and with many of the expatriates who played an active role in the recent years of oil developments in Indonesia. We were fortunate to be able to meet with some of the most respected figures in the nation; their thoughts and advice were invaluable to our understanding of the Indonesian perspective and the national environment in which Pertamina developed.

In our opinion, the personal impact of Dr. Ibnu is the prime reason for Pertamina's success. Some of his accomplishments no doubt relate to the fact that he has the energy of three men. He is a medical doctor, an army officer, an oil man, a family man with seven children, and a sportsman —an avid golfer and former president of the tennis association. The interviews with and about Dr. Ibnu took us to Djajapura, West Irian; Denpasar, Bali; Menado, Sulawesi; Balikpapan, Kalimantan; Singapore, Tokyo, London and Los Angeles. We often suspected that he played golf in order to give his staff a chance to rest.

This is not an official book although it has been researched with the full cooperation of Pertamina and the Ministry of Mines. Nor, on the other hand, is it totally objective. The spirit of nation building which permeates the entire Pertamina organization has deeply impressed us. We enjoyed living and working in Indonesia; we greatly admire the men we interviewed and respect their accomplishments; and we have made many friends in Indonesia. No doubt our personal feelings will thus be conveyed in the book; in fact, in chapters dealing with the history of oil developments, we have consciously tried to present the story from the Indonesian point of view. We have not attempted to advance any radically different views in the historical framework. Here, we relied heavily on secondary source materials such as those of George M.T. Kahin, Arnold Brackman, Justus van der Kroeft, O.G. Roeder, and former United States Ambassador to Indonesia, Howard P. Jones, to name but a few.

As Team Sedjarah, we would like to warmly thank three honorary members, Miss Leslie Keith, Miss Anne Cashin and Miss Chew Wee Khoon who diligently typed our manuscripts, complained about our handwriting, scoffed at our nevermet schedules, and whose presence made our work day much more pleasant. To them: "Terima kasih banjak."

To our many Indonesian friends, we offer this personalized history as a token of our admiration.

DJAKARTA, OCTOBER 6, 1972

ANDERSON G. BARTLETT III,
for *Team Sedjarah*

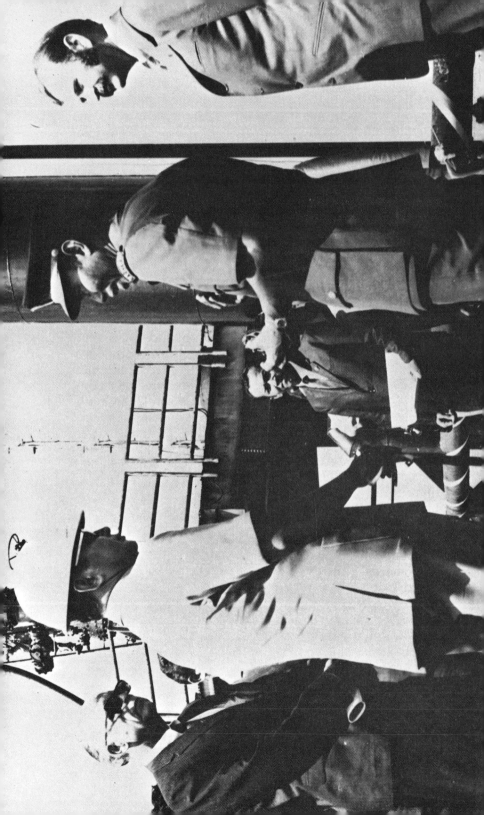

CHAPTER 1

Oil To Build a Nation

Between the morning of Indonesia's declaration of independence and the eve of its twenty-first anniversary, when a new form of oil contract was signed, Indonesia moved from colonial concessions to full control and management of its most important natural resource.

Indonesia has passed through periods of Dutch colonialism, World War II and Japanese imperialism, the fight for independence and emerging nationalism, a courtship with communism, and a move, today, to what may be termed independent national pragmatism. The fortunes of politics and the fortune of oil have been closely intertwined during these periods.

Indonesian oil production is both old and new. Within oil industry history it was one of the world's earliest major producing areas, the first home of the Royal Dutch/Shell group. The search for oil in Indonesia began in 1871, only twelve years after the world's first oil well was drilled in Pennsylvania. First commercial production began in 1885, and by the turn of the century, oil was being produced and refined in north and south Sumatra, central and east Java, and in Kalimantan. Standard Oil of New Jersey entered Indonesia in 1912, and later merged its interests in the Far East with those of Mobil to form Stanvac. Standard Oil of California entered in the 1930s and in 1936 merged its Asian interests with those of Texaco to form Caltex. Thus, in a combination usually referred to as the Big Three, there were five international companies active in Indonesia in 1940. In that year Indonesia's total production ranked fifth in the world.

DR. IBNU WELCOMES PRES. SOEHARTO ABOARD THE IIAPCO CINTA FIELD PRODUCTION PLATFORM, OCT. 23, 1970. LEFT TO RIGHT: U.S. AMBASSADOR FRANCIS J. GALBRAITH, PRES. SOEHARTO, DR. IBNU, DONALD TODD.

Twenty-five years later, only one other leading international company had joined the search and, in spite of an absolute increase in production, Indonesia had fallen to twelfth place in world standing. The period had seen World War II and the fight for independence which precluded new exploration; a ten-year legislative ban on granting new exploration rights; and increasingly chaotic economic conditions, all of which discouraged new entrants. By 1965, the main search for oil was being made in other countries and Indonesia's potential was largely being ignored. Two of the Big Three were negotiating to sell their interests in Indonesia.

Yet by 1970, Indonesia was back in the forefront of world oil development. Pertamina, the national oil company, was overseeing the activities of over twenty international companies that were working under the terms of the new Production Sharing Contracts. These contracts, pioneered by Pertamina, broke new ground in the world oil industry. By the end of 1971, thirty companies had entered into forty-one Production Sharing Contracts with Pertamina for exploration throughout the archipelago.

Indonesia is one of the few countries which operates a fully integrated oil company completely and solely under its own national management. From drilling rigs to computers, from tankers to helicopters, refineries to service stations, Pertamina's divisions and operations are fully Indonesian owned and operated.

Pertamina's exploration and production rigs drill onshore locations throughout the archipelago. Pertamina's own production is approximately 100,000 barrels per day and is expected to triple in the next two years. Pertamina owns and operates all the refineries in Indonesia with a capacity of 400,000 barrels per day. The company is making plans for expanding its activities in petrochemicals and is currently concentrating on LPG, fibers, and fertilizers. Pertamina's shipping fleet is one of the largest based in Southeast Asia.

The company is required to provide the petroleum needs of the domestic market on a cost basis and it has solved the shortages and eliminated the black marketing that plagued the industry just a few years ago. In foreign marketing,

Pertamina's joint venture company in Japan has increased its sales by almost a hundredfold since 1966. Its telecommunications system is the largest and most sophisticated in Indonesia, and in many areas constitutes the only regional communications system. The company employs more than 37,000 people. The Oil and Gas Institute (Lemigas) in conjunction with Pertamina, runs a training academy which graduates 150 students each year from its one-year and three-year curriculums. It also conducts training programs for its employees throughout Indonesia and, in addition, it finances scholarships for study abroad.

Indonesia's production has risen steadily from 1966—467,000 barrels per day to 1,200,000 barrels per day estimated by the end of 1972. Over the same period, the market price per barrel for Indonesia's crude has almost doubled. As a percentage of total state revenues, oil's contribution has risen from 5% in 1966 to 31% in 1971 and is being counted on for over 40% in the years to come. Oil already accounts for almost 50% of Indonesia's total export earnings.

For the past few years, Caltex has produced about 82% of Indonesia's total production; Pertamina 12%, and Stanvac 6%. In 1972 the new producers, under Production Sharing Contracts, will start making substantial contributions.

Most of Indonesia's crude oil is of medium gravity, averaging about 35° API, and high in wax. All of it has a very low sulfur content, averaging about 0.2% sulfur by weight, compared with 2% to 4% for Middle East crudes. This low-sulfur quality makes Indonesia's crude especially desirable as a fuel in pollution-plagued Japan, and Japan is Indonesia's largest customer. Of Indonesia's total 1971 production, 27% was used domestically and the remainder was exported. Japan took 54%, the Philippines and Australia, 5%, and the United States and other Western Hemisphere countries, 14%.

Indonesia has produced a little less than 2% of all the world's oil since the modern oil industry began in 1859. In 1971, Indonesia's production of 892,000 barrels per day was also about 2% of the total world production of 45 million barrels per day. Indonesia's estimated reserves are generally put at about 10,000 million barrels, out of a total world figure

of 500,000–550,000 million barrels. Here again, Indonesia
has about 2% of the world's estimated reserves. Indonesia's
reserves are about half those of the United States but less
than one-twentieth those of the Middle East.

Indonesia has set as its objective total production of two
million barrels per day by 1975 and three million barrels
per day by 1980. To a great extent Indonesia's development
plans are based on meeting these projections.

Although Indonesia is one of the oldest producing areas,
the search for oil by modern methods is just beginning.
Whereas in the United States, 10,000 wells may be drilled
in one year, in 1971 only 500 wells were drilled in Indonesia.
Prior to the past few years, less than a tenth of Indonesia
had been geophysically surveyed using technology developed
since World War II. Generally, two years or more pass
between the initial surveys and the commencement of
drilling.

In addition to supervising contractors, Pertamina is
conducting its own extensive exploration and development
program. Its Djatibarang project in west Java—Pertamina's
first major discovery—is expected to be producing 50,000
barrels per day by 1973. In the old fields of northern Sumatra
and Kalimantan—fields discovered before the turn of the
century—it has applied new technology and recently has
made two significant discoveries. The latest discovery in
north Sumatra in July 1972 is a major break-through in
finding an additional producing area previously unsuspected.
These projects are completely planned by Indonesian
geologists and engineers, and all wells are drilled by
Indonesian crews.

With limited capital and manpower, Pertamina must, of
course, rely heavily on foreign oil companies for the rapid
development of Indonesia's oil. This reliance is particularly
necessary in the exploration and development phase,
because of the high costs ($30,000 per day to drill offshore)
and high risks. The foreign companies are willing to accept
this risk with only the hope of finding production as means
of recouping their investments.

Most of the projects of the foreign oil companies are
still in the preliminary or exploration stages. Seven have,

however, announced commercial discoveries and by the end of 1972, four will be producing at a total rate of approximately 200,000 barrels per day which will move up to 300,000 barrels per day in 1973.

The driving force behind the new Indonesian oil industry and the originator of the Production Sharing Contract, is the president-director of Pertamina, Lt. General Dr. H. Ibnu Sutowo. In 1972 Dr. Ibnu marks his thirty-second year as a medical doctor, twenty-seventh year as a military officer, and fifteenth year in the oil business. Of these three careers, Dr. Ibnu chose only the first—events of Indonesian history brought him into the other two.

On October 23, 1970, Dr. Ibnu welcomed President Soeharto aboard an oil barge in the Java Sea north of Djakarta for the dedication of Indonesia's first offshore production platform. This dedication was symbolic for both men. For President Soeharto, this was a result of the new economic atmosphere he had worked to create over the previous five years. These policies had not only brought foreign investment into the oil business but also into many other sectors of the Indonesian economy.

For Dr. Ibnu, the dedication ceremony for this production platform in IIAPCO's Cinta field marked the achievement of the first offshore production from a drilling program conducted under the terms of a Production Sharing Contract. For Indonesian oil, this dedication marked a promising beginning of its second century.

*   *   *

The development of Pertamina and the concept of production sharing are best expressed in Dr. Ibnu's words:

"In the past, the oil and mineral assets of developing and newly independent nations were being exploited by foreign companies on the basis of concessions that gave them all rights to explore, develop, process, and market. In the case of oil, the foreign companies were generally paying the governments involved 50% of profits. The amount of profit, however, depended upon net income, and the companies had, and used, wide latitude in determining both the sales price of oil and their costs for exploration and development. The companies sold to their own affiliates and controlled the entire production process so that there was room for considerable flexibility in accounting. The practical result of the system was that the foreign oil companies paid the governments on the basis of their books. Indeed, these books may have been correct but the governments had no way of checking and this created considerable distrust.

"Since we proclaimed independence in Indonesia in 1945, we have known that we must have control over our natural resources, and this was written into our constitution. However, declaring control and having the ability to exercise it are far apart and we had little knowledge of the oil business. In 1951, Parliament passed a motion prohibiting the granting of more concession or exploration agreements until we had a new oil law which would fulfill the requirements of the constitution. If we could not, at that time, prevent the abuses of the existing system we could at least avoid extending that system.

"Our new law, Law No. 44, that was finally enacted in 1960, specified that 'oil and natural gas mining is conducted only by the State, and only a State Enterprise is authorized to engage in oil or gas mining on behalf of the State.'

"When Parliament passed this law it was not ignoring the fact that the oil business requires a large capital investment, vast facilities, and a very high level of technology. They were aware that our own resources were lacking in every one of these respects. So, for that reason, Law No. 44 provided that foreign oil companies were to be permitted to operate in Indonesia. But it provided that the foreign oil companies could operate only as contractors to the state oil companies, and that the oil was, and remained, the property of the state until sold.

"At the time Law No. 44 was passed, we had three foreign oil companies operating, Shell, Stanvac, and Caltex. By 1963 all of their concessions had been changed to Work Contracts in accordance with Law No. 44. However, the satisfactions of making the change were, on our part, mostly moral because we still had insufficient strength or knowledge of the business to exercise the control that we had obtained.

"My own contact with these events began in 1957, when I was named president-director of one of the state oil companies, Permina, which, in 1968, became one of the merger partners to form Pertamina. In 1957, there was a general belief, both on the part of the oil companies and Indonesians, that Indonesians could not possibly manage an oil business—this skill was somehow thought to be limited to foreigners.

"Therefore, at the beginning, the purpose of Permina, as I saw it, was not primarily to increase income for the state, much as that was needed, but to develop the necessary knowledge and skills of the oil industry. My own profession was that of physician and I had no knowledge of the oil business. The others who launched into this venture with me were not much better prepared. Among us there was not a single engineer. This apparently unfortunate selection of personnel was not, however, through bad planning. There was simply a lack of people who were better qualified.

"Our lack of knowledge was, if possible, exceeded by our lack of money and lack of everything else. On the credit side, we had a certain amount of common sense and there is no doubt we had determination. We also had plugged wells, rusted pipelines, bombed refineries, and scrap-metal stills. And further, the oil industry we took over was in an area of active guerilla fighting.

"Nevertheless, we began to learn the oil business. We had a few wells that were still seeping oil, one leaky pipeline we managed to patch, and we repaired some of the vintage 1928 Dutch pumps. In May, 1958, we shipped our first cargo of 1,700 tons of oil from north Sumatra to Japan. With the $30,000 it brought, we bought welding rod, steel plate, and pipe and began to build the business.

"By 1960 we were doing well enough so that a Japanese group lent us $53 million. Much of this we used to rebuild our aboveground facilities and when we were making regular shipments we turned our attention to improving production. We bought drilling rigs and we learned how to use them.

"Besides paying our loan and rebuilding facilities, the main thing we did with our time and the money we earned was to teach ourselves the oil business. We conducted

courses in everything from drilling techniques to deprecia-
tion accounting, and we sent people abroad to study what
could not be learned here. In 1961 I made several trips
abroad and talked to political leaders as well as oil people
in Saudi Arabia, Iran, Iraq, and Venezuela. It was no
surprise to learn that they had many of the same problems
we had. And it was also apparent that all of us had a great
deal to learn, both technically and in the political area, to
solve our problems. Or perhaps, for those years, it would
be better to say 'cope with' the problems rather than 'solve.'

"In 1962 our income was up to $6 million, probably
about what some other oil companies spend for road maps,
and we felt confident enough to open our Oil Academy at
Bandung. It was moved to Tjepu in 1965, and placed under
Lemigas. It is now providing us with most of the technicians
and administrators we need to oversee and operate a vastly
larger business. We knew that if we were to properly
administer the Work Contracts under Law No. 44, and
progress beyond them, we would need all the trained people
we could get.

"By the time we bought Shell in 1965, we had the
knowledge and the trained people to step in and run the
operations. In 1970 we added the Stanvac refinery to our
holdings and today all refining, transportation, and
distribution are part of Pertamina's operations.

"Though the Work Contracts under Law No. 44 were an
important departure from the old concession agreements,
they still left much to be desired. I, and many others, felt
they gave the companies too much latitude in management
and marketing. What I was interested in was a method
whereby we would make decisions and not merely review
them after they had been made.

"A Production Sharing Contract, which we first introduced
in a limited form in 1961, has proven to be the answer.
Under production sharing, the production—the oil itself—
is divided, not the profits. I have hundreds of men who can
sound a tank and tell me how many barrels our 65 % of the
oil amount to, but I have very few men who can follow that
oil through complicated transactions and tell me how much
of it should show up in the company's profits.

"Under production sharing we can let the foreign oil company market our oil for us, or we can pump it into our tankers and ship it and sell it ourselves.

"Since 1966, we have written over forty Production Sharing Contracts, and though, from an oil company's view, they contain some fairly new concepts they are terms they can live with. The key provision in the Production Sharing Contract is Indonesian management control. This doesn't mean that we insist on making every decision but we do insist on being able to make any decision we find necessary. If we find the policies or practices of any of our contractor companies contrary to the best interests of Indonesia, we can change them by making a management decision; it no longer requires an act of Parliament. We pride ourselves on having good relations with our contractors and the cooperation in management has been excellent.

"Under the Production Sharing Contract, any non-leased equipment a contractor brings to Indonesia becomes our property when it enters. Once in production, the contractor is entitled to offset its cost in retained oil. On the other hand, if the company leaves, there is no argument over our buying the equipment—it is already ours. In order to get the best results we expect our contractors to make a major commitment to finding and developing oil in Indonesia.

"Our Production Sharing Contracts also contain signature payments. By this, a company must make a substantial investment before it can obtain an area for exploration or exploitation. Also, portions of the area must be given up at various intervals. Indonesia's needs are immediate and we want the oil earnings as quickly as we can get them. Without signature payments and the mandatory relinquishments, a company could very well delay its programs and this would not be in our national interest.

"The terms of Production Sharing Contracts reduce potential conflicts to technological and engineering problems and we market our own oil so there is no disagreement over price. We approve the contractors' work programs in advance so that arguments, if any, center on what the program should be, rather than over the appropriateness of past expenditures. We need the assistance of the foreign companies to develop our oil but we also need to control our own development. In this regard we believe, based on our experience, that the Production Sharing Contract is the best basis for cooperation.

"The fact that these terms are reasonable can be argued in several ways, but the most convincing way to argue it is to demonstrate that a great number of companies have accepted them, including almost every leading company in the industry. There are presently over thirty companies exploring and/or producing under Production Sharing Contracts. For exploration activities in 1968 they spent $45.5 million; in 1969, $90.5 million; in 1970, $113 million; in 1971, $207 million; and in 1972 they will spend about $237 million. This amounts to a total of $693 million through 1972, and does not include what we have spent at Pertamina.

"We have pride in the ability and training of our oil people, and we do think that now, in almost every area, we have men who will rank with the best in the industry. When this is said, some are prone to ask: If you have this ability why share with foreign contractors, why not just do it all yourselves?

"The answer to this lies in the matter of quantity of resources rather than ability. Even if every other area of development—agricultural, educational, medical—were made secondary to oil, we still could not afford the expenditures that are presently being made. If we could be satisfied to develop the industry over a twenty or thirty year period we could do it ourselves. But if we want a greatly increased production in a few years it can only be done by making use of the resources and skills of the foreign oil companies.

"There is another factor to be considered too. The foreign oil companies, even fairly small ones, are economically and psychologically attuned to high risk operations and the people in the business are gamblers in the best sense of the word. If they come up with a succession of dry holes it is their own money lost, and further, they can often recover a portion of it by tax write-offs or government subsidies. But as a national oil company, it is the people's money we are spending. While a two million dollar dry hole may be just a bit of bad luck for a contractor, there are people in Indonesia who would, quite properly, equate that two million dollars with the cost of a road, or of housing, or of a number of schools. We in Pertamina do extensive drilling, and generally we have been successful, but we think it both politically and economically sound to let the oil companies take the higher risks of offshore work which is where most of our new oil is to be found.

"Finding more oil is a critical and immediate need for our nation. This year it is estimated that over 40% of the state's revenues will come from oil. This is the money that builds the schools, constructs the roads, buys vaccines and hospitals, trains doctors, builds irrigation works, and improves the harbors. During the revolution we had *lasjkar minjak* or oil fighters who took upon themselves the responsibility of keeping the trucks and airplanes of the revolutionary forces supplied with fuel. We could very well think of ourselves at Pertamina today in the roles of the *lasjkar minjak* with an equal duty to the nation.

"Besides the direct contribution, we are also concerned with the secondary effects of the oil industry in the Indonesian economy. In 1966, the amount of the money spent by the foreign contractors in Indonesia was very small. Most equipment and provisions were purchased abroad, most of the personnel lived abroad, and laboratory work and data processing were done abroad. So one of our goals at Pertamina was to try to increase the amount spent in Indonesia. To do this, we have entered certain fields ourselves, or with associates. We provide the contractors with bases, office space, communications, air services, and, very recently, medical facilities. We and Lemigas are building the laboratories and obtaining the equipment and computers to permit all data to be analyzed in Indonesia. We have recently bought twenty-four helicopters to provide both transport and equipment lift to our own operations and to our contractors working offshore or in areas where there are inadequate roads.

"Another area that has been of concern to us has been communications. One absolute essential of oil exploration is good communications between the field operations and

the head office. We might have set up our own limited
system and each of the contractors might also have set up
their own systems. Instead we set up a complete integrated
network of telecommunications that not only serves oil
needs but also serves civilian needs in many areas.

"By necessity, Pertamina has also had to provide many
services needed within Indonesia and, in some cases, we
have entered a field simply because no other agency was
prepared to do so. We build roads, schools, mosques,
bridges, and utility plants in areas near our refineries and
oil fields. We have just completed the Pertamina General
Hospital in Djakarta. We build houses for our employees
and are now building them for the employees of contractors.

"However, we have not neglected our business as strictly
an oil company. During the past five years we have built, or
completely modernized, over 200 service stations and we
have also undertaken a fairly ambitious drilling program
on our own.

"Our most promising discovery has been at Djatibarang,
west Java. Here Pertamina geologists and drillers are now
developing a new major field that will go into production in
March 1973, at 50,000 barrels per day. Already, as drilling
continues, pipelines and loading facilities are being built,
and this activity has already had an effect on the West Java
economy. We are blamed for the rise in the price of land,
eggs, and coconuts, and we willingly accept the blame.
Because where prices are rising in a place like this, so are
incomes and with rising incomes we will see better medical
care and schools, and higher salaries for government, as
well as private industry, workers. A man who has just gotten
a job at Rp. 30,000 a month can well afford to pay more
for goods he could not previously afford at all.

"All of these activities and services require equipment
and manpower. If you have money or can borrow it,
obtaining equipment is no problem. In our case we can now
easily get equipment, but every person we employ must be
trained by us. So now, as in 1957, the development of our
people is still the most important objective. Our young
engineers and managers face even greater challenges than

we did in 1957 for they will have the responsibility for all phases of development of our oil resources.

"Though few would deny that Pertamina is making a major contribution to the Indonesian economy, there are those who will criticize us for the way we go about making that contribution. They will say that in a nation where poverty is all too much of a reality, that we in Pertamina should also be poor and look poor. It is, according to these critics, unseemly for us to work in air-conditioned offices, drive new automobiles, and live in good houses, while there are citizens who still lack enough money to provide themselves with decent food and clothing.

"This attitude assumes that poverty is the normal way of life and that those who live in another way are abnormal. But if we are to build a modern nation we must discard this notion of poverty being normal, or in any case inevitable, and see that in the modern world this poverty is abnormal. If, by our example, we show people that there is another way, and that way can be followed by Indonesians, then we will have accomplished a great deal. But if we sink ourselves to a level of poverty, what can we tell the people or show them? How can we tell people of the benefits of modernizing the economy if we keep old attitudes and use old methods to run our business? How can we tell people about the benefits of education if we educate our people and then pay them only enough for rice and shelter?

"Aside from hoping to show other people what Indonesians can do, we have some very practical reasons for running a modern and obviously prosperous business. In the oil business we are dealing with some of the largest and richest companies in the world and every day we must meet with, and negotiate with, people from these companies. And if we are to negotiate as equals and obtain the best terms we can for Indonesia, we must maintain some level of affluence that will make our role creditable. It is simply not psychologically possible for men who wear threadbare clothing and who ride in old cars or betjaks to negotiate satisfactorily with men who earn fifty thousand dollars a year and fly by company jet aircraft. And a man who has the essentials of a dignified life is much less tempted to compromise with his principles than is a man who lacks these things. Where you find old cars, run-down buildings, broken furniture, and low-paid officials, it is there that you are likely to find corruption and lack of initiative.

"So, one goal we have set for the company in the years ahead is to set an example for other sectors of the economy; to demonstrate a good, disciplined, modern, and all-Indonesian company. We also have other goals that are more directly connected with the company as an oil business.

"One of these goals is to make our fuels and lubricants available every place in the nation. Because our products are absolutely essential for improved land and marine transportation and for modernizing industry, agriculture, and fishing, we must make every effort to supply them in the type required and in the quantity required everyplace from Sabang to Merauke. By policy we do not make any profit from this marketing; and in remote areas even costs are not covered. But we are a national company with national responsibilities and the costs are well-justified because they help to build the nation.

"Another thing we must do is to prepare financially, by education, and by outlook, for a very large growth in the company. As Indonesia becomes more modern the demand for petroleum and petrochemical products will increase dramatically and we must prepare now to meet those needs. This means that we must build new refineries, buy new ships, add to our rolling stock, and build the factories necessary to produce the synthetics, the fertilizers, and the plastics that the nation will require. If we fail here to keep our company modern and growing then we will act not to advance the modernization of the nation, but will act as a brake on the modernization.

"Also, in the years ahead, the flow of crude oil from our wells and the wells of our contractors will increase greatly and this will call for expanded handling, shipping, and marketing facilities. Though we realize that the taxes paid by Pertamina are of great importance to the government and other sectors of the economy, these demands will certainly not be less in the future. But if we fail to keep pace with the needs for the growth of the company we will reduce the base on which those future taxes can be paid.

"A goal that has always been of great importance to us, and will continue to be of importance in the future, is the advance of education. Our contribution here includes what our taxes buy in other areas plus that of more direct impact on the company. If we are to grow as we must grow and to meet the challenges of the years ahead, then we must produce more and more highly trained people in every aspect of the oil business. Without improved education and improved skills, the vision of an improved Indonesia must remain just that—a vision.

"Perhaps our goals could be summed up this way: In the years ahead we hope to use the oil God has given us—oil as a product and oil as an income—in the best possible way to build the Indonesian nation."

CHAPTER 2

Bhinneka Tunggal Ika

If one were to choose three words with which to evoke a picture of Indonesia, the first two would be volcanoes and rice, for these two create the landscape most typically Indonesian, and the rice alone tells of the work, and indeed the life, of most of the people. The third word would be green, for this color is everywhere and in a seemingly limitless spectrum from the pale chartreuse of seedling rice to the darkest tones of the rain forest. There are, to be sure, other colors: There are the blues of skies and of the waters of the lagoons, there are white coral sands, golden harvest rice, and silver flags of cloud trailing from crests of the volcanoes. But it is the green that one remembers most and that gives this land an almost ethereal image.

One writer, perhaps equally enraptured by color and cartography, describes Indonesia as a garland of emeralds for the earth. And quite a garland it is, lying pendant from the equator for nearly an eighth of the circumference of the earth. It is a garland that stretches from the longitude of Rangoon to nearly that of Melbourne—the distance from San Francisco to Bermuda.

In this 3,000-mile garland which Indonesians refer to as "Tanah Air Kita" (Our Land and Our Water) there are nearly 14,000 islands though only 1,000 are inhabited. Most of the others are quite small, often only an acre or less of coconut trees. Though the islands are spread over nearly three million square miles of ocean, the total land area is only 735,865 square miles. This is an area equal to that of Western Europe, or to three times the area of Texas. In land area, Indonesia ranks fourteenth among nations and in Asia is exceeded in size only by China and India. With a population of about 121 million people, Indonesian ranks fifth among nations following China, India, the Soviet Union, and the United States. Over 90% of the land area is in five large islands, and of the five, two contain over 80% of the population.

Sumatra, the world's sixth-largest island, has nearly 25% of the land area of Indonesia (182,860 sq. miles) and about 16% of the population. It is an island of virgin forests flanking a central spine of volcanic peaks, some of which have elevations of over 10,000 feet. Below the mountains, meandering rivers drain low plains and empty into mangrove swamps and estuaries. Most Sumatrans live along the coast and nowhere is the island densely populated. Population is particularly sparse to the east of the volcanic spine and it is in the hills and jungles of this area where most of Indonesia's elephants, tigers, and rhinocerous are found. Oil, and plantation tobacco and rubber, provide some of the employment and most of the income, but the main occupations are growing rice and fishing. Sumatra produces 97% of Indonesia's oil, though this percentage is expected to drop in the near future as offshore fields come into production.

Java is the smallest of the five main islands (48,763 sq. miles) but it, and its closest neighbor, Madura, are the home of two-thirds of the people of Indonesia. Java and Bali, the island immediately to the east, are the islands where most Indonesian rice is grown. The weathered lava and ash from their volcanoes have formed a rich soil which, in combination with ample rainfall and sunshine, make these islands abundantly productive. Java's ability to support a large population has, throughout its history, given it a dominant position in both the culture and politics of the archipelago.

Djakarta, the nation's capital, is on the northwest of the island. With over five million people, it is by far the largest city in Southeast Asia. Surabaya, the second largest city of Indonesia, with a population of over a million, is on the northeast of the island. Bandung, in west Java also has a population of more than one million people.

The first oil drilling operation in the last century was in Java, and today there are still small producing fields near Surabaya and at Tjepu in central Java. Java produces less than 1% of Indonesia's oil, though a new and promising field is now being opened in west Java.

Kalimantan occupies about three-fourths of the island of Borneo, sharing this third-largest island of the world (287,400 sq. miles total) with the Malaysian states of Sarawak and Sabah, and the Sultanate of Brunei. Though the area of Kalimantan is 30% of the total of Indonesia, it has only about 4% of the population. Most of the people live along the coast and even the cities are scarcely more than villages of a few provision stores, Chinese shop houses, and streets that are muddy or dusty depending on the season. The interior is the home of the Dayaks who live in longhouses by the rivers and plant rice in "ladang" (slash and burn) cultivation. Oil fields near Balikpapan on the east coast produce about 2% of Indonesia's oil.

The scorpion-shaped island of Sulawesi (formerly the Celebes) has about 10% of the land area (72,986 sq. miles) and also about 10% of the population. It is an island of rugged and broken terrain with a long and dangerously reef-strewn coastline. Fishing, trading, and making copra are the activities of the coast, and wet (sawah) rice is also grown. Ladang rice is the main crop of the interior. The provincial capital of Makasar has, for at least a thousand years, been a trading and transshipment point for the spices grown in the Moluccas to the east.

West Irian, Indonesia's newest and third-largest territory, contains over 20% of the total land area of Indonesia but has a population estimated at less than one million. West Irian shares the island of New Guinea (after Greenland the world's second largest island—317,000 sq. miles total) with the Australian territory of Papua New Guinea. Characterized by extremes, the island has vast lowland rain forests and also snow-capped mountain ranges. The highest mountain in Indonesia is Mount Djajawidjaja (16,503 feet) in the Maoke range in West Irian. About half of the people of West Irian live along the coast and the remainder live in primitive conditions in small isolated valleys of the interior.

Cassava and sweet potatoes raised by slash and burn methods, are the main crops both on the coast and in the interior. The interior forests of West Irian are the home of birds-of-paradise and marsupials found nowhere else in Indonesian territory.

Separated by straits and seas, and within islands by swamps and dense forests in many places, over the centuries the people of the archipelago developed considerable local and tribal variation in speech, customs, and belief. Though the Indonesian language has become a common and unifying force in modern times—and is now spoken in at least elementary form almost everywhere—there are still nearly 300 dialects spoken in about the same number of "suku" (local ethnic groups).

The name "bangsa Indonesia" (Indonesian race) is commonly used to refer to all of the people of Indonesia including not only those of typical characteristics but also to members of aboriginal groups and the Papuans of West Irian who would not usually be thought of as included within that race. If there may be no ethnic basis for such an inclusive "bangsa Indonesia" it at least denotes a national pride and feeling of unity among such different groups as Islamic Atjehnese, Hindu Balinese, Christian Menadonese, and Stone Age Irianese.

The Indonesian national motto, "Bhinneka Tunggal Ika" means "there are many—there is one" or "unity in diversity." It is an apt motto for a nation that encompasses not only ethnic and cultural diversity but also a number of religions including Islam, Hinduism, Buddhism, and Christianity.

There is considerable evidence that Java was the home of one of the earliest forms of man and fossil hominoids have been dated to the early and middle Pleistocene. Whether such early forms of man joined later streams of evolutionary development is not known but they were certainly long gone by the time of the arrival of the ancestors of the present inhabitants of the archipelago. The earliest immigrants were people of Veddoid or Negroid stock and, though nothing is known of their origins or the time of their arrival, they were in what is now Indonesia at least 30,000 years ago.

More recent Proto-Malay immigrants came from Cambodia and China, possibly only within the past 10,000 years. It is assumed that there have been many migrations and considerable mixing between groups and also between new immigrants and inhabitants from earlier migrations. Doubtless the mixing was greater on the coast than in the interiors and possibly some tribes and groups of aboriginal people that presently inhabit the interiors of most of the large islands were driven from the coasts by the proto-Malay immigrants.

The Proto-Malay arrivals domesticated, or brought, the water buffalo and introduced the cultivation of wet rice. To extend rice cultivation they built irrigation works and terraces that even today are considered highly advanced examples of efficient irrigation and the control of erosion. They developed a culture of the village as a basic social unit and the village is still the basic social unit of the rural areas. They worshipped ancestors and earth spirits at megalithic offering sites and later developed gamelan orchestras and shadow plays. In the villages important decisions are still reached by deliberations under customary "adat" law, developed many centuries ago.

Trade with the islands that are now Indonesia began before the Christian era but appears to have been only incidental to the trade in silk, porcelain, and spices between China and India and Europe. Java was known to Ptolemy in A.D. 150 and it is known that cloves—grown at that time only in the Moluccas—made their appearance in Han China at an even earlier date.

During the fifth century, trade between China and India began passing through the Strait of Malacca and from that time on contacts between Indonesia and the outer world became more frequent. There is a Chinese reference to a trading station, thought to be in Sumatra, in the third century A.D., and there are also references to Hinduized kingdoms in the area during the same period.

The first millenium after Christ saw the rise and fall of a number of powers in the archipelago. Some of these claimed spheres of influence extending far beyond the islands and into the land-mass of southeast Asia. On Java, intensive wet rice cultivation provided the base for advanced social and communal organizations that culminated, in the thirteenth century, in the kingdom of Madjapahit. A Madjapahit king, Hayam Wuruk, and a brilliant prime minister, Gadja Mada, brought into being an empire that held sway over the entire archipelago and probably some of Indochina. It was a period of great prosperity and cultural advancement and came to be known as the golden age of Indonesian history.

On Sumatra, near the site of present day Palembang, a great maritime trading empire, Sriwidjaja, was founded in the sixth century. Here developed a flourishing center of Buddhist culture, attracting both traders and scholars from as far away as China. Indonesian history from the seventh to the seventeenth century is largely the history of the rivalry between the kingdoms of Java and Sumatra. Now only the grandeur of Borobudur and a few other temples in central Java remain as reminders of these empires.

Early in the fifteenth century, a rebel prince from declining Madjapahit set up a base at Malacca, across from Sumatra on the Malay Peninsula. He gathered around him a band of pirates, traders, adventurers, and other dissidents from Java. China gave some protection to the new city-state and it quickly prospered from both piracy and trade. It was in Malacca at this time that the languages of the traders mixed with the dialect of the area to become the lingua franca that eventually became the Indonesian language. It was also from Malacca that the Islamic religion was carried to most of the archipelago.

The carriers of the Islamic religion were the Muslim merchants from Arabia, Persia, and India. Marco Polo, on a mission from the court of Kublai Khan, wrote of Islamic communities in northern Sumatra at the end of the thirteenth century. From the thirteenth to the fifteenth century, Islam spread slowly along the coasts. From the time of the founding of Malacca, Islam spread rapidly until, within a century, it reached its present-day limits of the southern Philippines and the eastern Moluccas. Monotheistic Islam, already somewhat modified by its passing through Persia and India, never fully displaced the Hindu religion and earlier cults in central and east Java. The Portuguese brought Christianity in the sixteenth century though they never made a major effort to convert the people. Today sizeable Christian communities exist only in north Sulawesi and in the Moluccas.

Towards the end of the fifteenth century, the royal court and religious leaders of the last Hindu kingdom on Java, fled the pressure of Islam by crossing the narrow straits to Bali. There, alone in Indonesia, Hinduism survives to this day. Bali remained almost totally isolated from the rest of Indonesia until the early part of this century and neither Islam nor Christianity have as yet had much influence on the island.

The Indonesianization of ideas and religions has been characteristic of the region's history. Thus the Hinduism as it evolved on Java, and later on Bali, became a Hinduism much different from that of India. An assimilation of lesser extent has occurred and may still be occurring with Islam and Christianity. The ideological newcomers, parliamentary democracy and economic socialism, have also evolved and are evolving, into forms uniquely Indonesian.

*   *   *

During the fifteenth and sixteenth centuries, the population of Europe grew rapidly and with it the demand for spices, silks, porcelain, and other products of the East. The Chinese, at the same period, became large purchasers of Indonesian spices and sandalwood. Over 1,500 tons of cloves alone were passing through the port of Malacca each year by the beginning of the sixteenth century.

The fifteenth century was one in which the Muslim traders were spreading their influence throughout the islands, slowly expanding their trade routes and improving their techniques. While the Muslim traders were so engaged in the Indies there was a remarkably similar movement on the other side of the world. This was also the century in which the Portuguese traders were working down the west coast of Africa. When the Portuguese rounded the Cape of Good Hope in 1488, a collision in the Indies became inevitable.

In the first part of the sixteenth century the Portuguese
exploded into the Muslim trading areas of the Indian Ocean
and slaughtered on land and sea. It was the age of religious
zealots and the interpretation of scripture demanded blood
while the traders demanded profit. When Malacca was
captured in 1511, the Portuguese were in a position to
control the entire lucrative spice trade from Ambon to
Europe and theoretically should have been able to cut off
sea and overland cargoes that had historically gone by
way of the Persian Gulf. Militarily, the Portuguese were
almost always successful but incessant conflict bled the
empire white and prevented any consolidation of their
gains.

But, though their position remained precarious, the
demand for spices increased in Europe and they did manage
to control by far the largest part of the trade. That which
could be purchased for one ducat in Ambon could be
sold for the equivalent of 2,000 in Europe.

With political changes in Europe during the latter part of
the sixteenth century, the Dutch became the enemies of
Portugal. The traders of Amsterdam then sent ships to try
to break into the Portuguese spice trade. When the first
Dutch ships put in an appearance at Bantam in west Java in
1596, the local sultan made them welcome and invited them
to trade. When the Portuguese learned of the unwelcome
presence of the Dutch in their waters, the viceroy at Goa
dispatched an expedition to intercept them. When the
expedition arrived at Bantam, the Dutch had gone but the
Portuguese commander determined to teach the sultan a
lesson. During the ensuing engagement the Portuguese
were ignominiously defeated by the Javanese, and two of
their four ships were captured.

In the first and several subsequent expeditions, the Dutch
were cordially received by the Indonesians, and they were
particularly welcomed in the Moluccas. However, like
the Portuguese, the Dutch had their lawless and cruel men.
Because of cheating and unnecessary violence, Atjeh and
Madura became hostile to the Dutch and so, within a few
years, did most of the other areas and kingdoms.

In 1602, the Dutch East India Company was formed and
for the next two hundred years most of the warfare and

trade of the Indies was in the hands of, and the responsibility of, the company. In 1614, Jan P. Coen, trade director at Bantam, proposed to the directors of the East India Company in Amsterdam that they could monopolize the spice trade with great profit if they were willing to use sufficient force. Not only was Coen's suggestion accepted, but he was appointed, in 1618, as governor general of the Indies to carry out that policy. The English had, however, also established a trade in spices and they fought bitterly against the attempt to close the trade to them. In 1619 Coen fortified the west Java town of Djajakerta and renamed it Batavia. (It was given the name Djakarta in World War II. As of August, 1972 the spelling is being changed to Jakarta). Dutch rule spanned the next three hundred and thirty years.

In spite of a treaty between the Dutch and English in 1619, Coen continued to harass the English and was successful in driving them from Indonesian waters. He then undertook a bloody pacification campaign in the Moluccas in which the people of a number of islands were virtually exterminated and vast clove-producing areas were laid waste. However, it was not until about 1670, forty years after Coen's death, that the trade in cloves and nutmeg was brought under something like monopoly control.

The company was mainly interested in establishing military strong points throughout the archipelago to assist them in enforcing a monopoly of trade. The company had neither sufficient power nor any financial reason to attempt to administer conquered areas except when absolutely necessary. Initially, only the people in the coastal and spice-producing regions felt the presence of the Dutch. As the demand for tropical produce grew in Europe during the eighteenth century, the company expanded its efforts in Java and extended its influence into the interior. To avoid both political and administrative involvement, wherever possible, the Dutch utilized the local feudal rulers to further their economic goals. The company sought only profitable and exportable crops.

This was also a period when the company began to extensively make use of the Chinese traders as middlemen. By the time the Dutch arrived, sizeable numbers of Chinese were already living in the port settlements of the

archipelago, where they had been since at least the thirteenth
century. The Dutch found the Chinese useful from the very
beginning. Coen said that the colony could not get enough
of the industrious Chinese to bring out the wealth for the
Dutch coffers. The Chinese were talented traders and they
had an intimate knowledge of the local conditions and
markets. Also of importance to the Dutch, the Chinese were
culturally self-contained and were thus unlikely to ally
themselves with other groups. The local Islamic merchant
class lost its traditional trade as the Dutch control became
ever tighter, and finally lapsed into atrophy as its economic
role was assigned to the Chinese.

By the eighteenth century, most of Java was under Dutch
control. This called for a more formal administrative
apparatus than that required simply to collect crops, so the
Dutch gave the Javanese feudal rulers the role of aristocratic
bureaucrats. Though company policy continued to be
opposed to direct rule, a detachment became ever more
difficult to maintain. A higher level of exploitation required,
inevitably, a greater degree of control. Where the aristocrats
proved inadequate in forcing increased production, Chinese
were given areas and villages to exploit on a percentage
basis.

During the eighteenth century, the power of the Dutch
East India Company was unchallenged, except by pirates
and a few minor princes. The company, however, could
seldom report a profitable year. Corruption and inefficiency
took an ever-increasing portion of the revenue. Coffee was
introduced into Java in 1720 and promised to improve the
finances of the company, but the directors had little interest
in such prosaic commodities. They preferred to try to
balance their huge budgets with small shipments of
monopolistically controlled spices.

The efficiency of the company was also reduced by the
living conditions in Batavia. The Dutch crammed themselves
into a small fort and seldom ventured outside its walls. The
area was swampy and no wind penetrated into the living and
working areas. Malaria and other diseases took a fearful
toll. It was thought that bad vapors caused most illnesses

so the people lived and worked behind closed doors and windows in stifling heat.

In 1795, the Dutch East India Company, deeply in debt, surrendered its rights to the Netherlands government.

The Napoleonic Wars temporarily put Holland under France and therefore at war with Britain. The Indies made some preparation to meet a British attack but when the attack came they put up only a weak defense. The Indies surrendered to the British fleet in August, 1811, and the Dutch governor general was replaced by Stamford Raffles.

Raffles was an imperialist who, from his earlier posts in Malaya, had learned something of the cultures and languages of the area. He was convinced that it was in Britain's interest to control all of the East Indies. Analyzing Dutch policies as ruinous to both the economy and the society of the Indies, he proceeded to implement certain reforms, some of which had, in fact, been initiated by his Dutch predecessor. Raffles modified the system of forced deliveries and labor conscription and in their place introduced an almost equally onerous taxation and land leasing system. Raffles' style of government also had a place for the sultans, regents, and village chiefs who were salaried by the Batavia government. A jury system was tried and some tentative moves were made to abolish slavery. Tirelessly Raffles investigated, researched, traveled, and made notes for his *History of Java*. His period in office was, however, a short one. In 1815, a treaty between England and France returned the Netherlands monarchy to power and gave them back their colonies.

Though the upheaval and temporary British rule had brought some changes it was, again, business as usual. If the East India Company was no longer in business, the Netherlands East Indies (N.E.I.) government in its place was faced with the need to earn at least enough to pay the costs of its administration.

By the nineteenth century, it would seem that every possible method of force, deceit, and coercion had been tried in the Indies, but there was one remaining, and it was to prove most successful of all for the colonialists. Under the Culture System, introduced in the 1830s, the villages were given the choice of either turning over a land rent to the government—normally two-fifths of the crop—or cultivating one-fifth of the land in crops as ordered by the government. It was, of course, a tax in the form of compulsory labor. Sugar, coffee, and indigo were the main products under the system and their volume increased rapidly. Very soon the Netherlands East Indies were not only self-sufficient but were supplying nearly a third of the total budget of the Netherlands.

All the Dutch colonialist policies seemed to become unproductive as corruption and inefficiency of administration made inexorable inroads, and the Culture System was no exception. By the 1860s, all crops under the system had become unprofitable except sugar and coffee and their forced cultivation was discontinued. Forced cultivation of coffee continued until 1917. The N.E.I. stopped earning a profit for the Netherlands in 1877 and showed consistent deficits thereafter, as government expenditures increased. Such expenditures did little for the people but provided the services required by an ever-increasing population of Dutch immigrants.

A period, sometimes called the liberal period, began in 1877 and ended in 1942 with the Second World War and Dutch loss of the Indies. This period saw a gradual relaxation of harsh colonial policy, the territorial consolidation of the Indies, and the rise of private investment. The rapid industrialization of Europe, the growth of steam navigation, and the opening of the Suez Canal in 1869, all served to bring the distant Indies much nearer to Holland. Free enterprise and laissez faire economic sentiments were in vogue in Europe, and these ideas were brought by the new settlers to Indonesia where they spelled the doom of government monopoly. The pressures from private capital became irresistible and, in 1870, a new agrarian law was passed allowing private investors to lease land. The development of vast plantations commenced.

In 1860, a book was written by an ex-colonial official, Eduard Doues Dekker, called *Max Havelaar, or the Coffee Auctions of the Dutch Trading Company*. This darkling exposé of the true conditions in the Indies caused a sensation in

Holland. Slowly, the concern of the people of the Netherlands began to be felt in reform movements, though the new humanitarian goals were vague and often ambivalent. Some groups advocated positive programs and policies designed to bring the Indonesians and their society more into contact with the modern world, knowing that this would entail great efforts in the field of economic development and education. Others wanted to insulate the Indonesians even further from the disruptive influences of the modern world. These latter groups would expand the practice of indirect rule and attempt to preserve and strengthen what remained of Indonesian institutions, customs, and laws. As a result of this basic conflict, no clearly defined policy was ever followed.

*   *   *

Indonesian resistance to the Dutch began shortly after the first Dutch landings and continued throughout the period of their administration in the Indies. With the return of the Dutch after the Raffles administration and the increased pressure for production, regional unrest reached a peak in the first half of the nineteenth century, when there were literally scores of sporadic uprisings. The most noted of these struggles was the Diponegoro War that lasted from 1825 to 1830.

Pangeran (Prince) Diponegoro was the reclusive and mystical eldest son of one of the sultan of Jogjakarta's second wives. He dedicated his life to organizing Javanese in the hatred of aliens, both Dutch and Chinese. Most of central Java united under the prince, and for a brief period it looked as if the Dutch would not be able to withstand the guerilla tactics to which they were subjected. In the end, however, Pangeran Diponegoro was persuaded to negotiate with the Dutch. They promptly captured him and exiled him to the Celebes. With Diponegoro gone, his peasant armies dissolved and the revolt ended.

With the infusion of private capital into the Indies and the growth of the plantation system into new and often insecure areas, an effort was made to extend and consolidate Dutch power. Bali and Atjeh were both particularly thorny problems for the Batavia administrators, and for some time were left largely independent as long as they acknowledged overall Dutch suzerainty. However, in 1873, the Dutch began a murderous war against the sultanate of Atjeh, which lasted for thirty-five years. Finally, Atjeh, which had made diplomatic overtures to the Italian and United States Consulates—even offering the latter the strategic island of Sabang off the northern tip of Sumatra in exchange for a joint friendship treaty between the two countries— capitulated in 1908, although guerilla warfare continued for decades. It had been a major military effort by the Dutch involving thousands of troops and absorbing all the profits of the colonial administration. The war in Bali was shorter, as the Balinese rulers chose suicide in preference to continuing a hopeless resistance. In 1908, the last independent prince of Bali marched to his death carrying his sacred kris to defy the guns of Holland. The subjugation of Atjeh and Bali ended the last serious challenge to the Dutch authority based upon pretentions of regional independence.

At that time, movements for independence on a scale larger than regional had not appeared because there was an almost complete absence of any feeling of common identity among the people. From the earliest days of their rule, the Dutch had sought to govern by playing Indonesians off against each other and they had thereby created and accentuated mistrust between people of different region, social class, race, and religious interpretation.

Not only were the people lacking in contacts among groups, but they were also insulated from the social and economic changes that were taking place elsewhere in the world. This insulation had been maintained, since the latter part of the nineteenth century, by Dutch paternalistic policies that sought to preserve what remained of the culture and customs of the people. In the name of protection, the Indonesians were effectively denied both education and the broadening experience of participation in business and government.

The aristocrats, by then little more than functionaries in the colonial apparatus, were almost the only literate people in their stratified and impoverished societies. Perhaps the only shared experience of the vast numbers of people was Islam, the religion of 90% of the people. But even Islam, irregularly adhered to and obscurantist in its world view, was limited in its ability to inspire any strong sentiments of Indonesian identity among the people, at least before the turn of the century.

The year 1908, when the organized resistance of Atjeh and Bali ended, was also the year that saw the quiet birth of the modern Indonesian nationalist movement. Beginning in 1906, a pensioned Javanese doctor, Wahidin Sudirohusodo, had been traveling around the island of Java speaking and seeking support for his Javanese Educational Fund that was designed to further the education of Indonesians and preserve their culture. Among other things, he advocated the education of an Indonesian elite in preparation for eventual self-rule. On May 20, 1908, he established the Budi Utomo (Highest Endeavor) organization in Batavia. The following October, their first congress was held in Jogjakarta where it was resolved that the movement's goals would be the harmonious promotion of teaching, agriculture, trade, industry, and the arts, all in the name of an enhanced Indonesian self-consciousness. Now, May 20 is celebrated as Indonesia's National Awakening Day.

The first stirrings of Indonesian nationalism, or more precisely, Indonesian national consciousness, were, like Budi Utomo, generally quiet ones. Budi Utomo was an effort to generate a new sense of cultural worth, specifically among Javanese of high birth. Other groups identifying along regional and ethnic lines began to form at this time. One movement inspired by Raden Adjeng Kartini was devoted to the social emancipation and education of women. In 1915, a student in Batavia started the Tri Koro Dharmo (Three Noble Aims) to promote wider appreciation among Javanese youth for education and to further interest in language and culture. It also aimed to create a bond among Indonesian students in general. Later, this group became Jong (Young) Java, with counterparts forming in the outer islands.

The first audible call for independence came from the small Eurasian Indische Partij (Indies Party) founded in 1912. Its motto was "The Indies for those who make their homes here." The three founders, however, were exiled in 1913. The party was ahead of its time, but its effect on the embryonic nationalist movement was a marked one.

At this time, Islam began experiencing significant changes, starting in Mecca and Cairo, and soon spreading across all the Muslim world. At the end of the nineteenth century, reform-minded Islamic leaders and thinkers had decided that the Muslim religion and practice must be reconciled with, and brought into, the modern world. In Indonesia, the Muhammadijah (Followers of Mohammad) was founded in 1912 in Jogjakarta by Achmad Dahlan. Although its modernist spirit clashed with more conservative forms, its force steadily spread through Java and then into Sumatra. It established schools, hospitals, and Islamic libraries and generally broadened the scope of religion in everyday life. This renewing of Islamic identity and sense of place in the modern world was a vital sign of an awakening Indonesia.

In 1912, the same year the Muhammadijah was founded, the Sarekat Islam (Islamic Association), was founded in Surakarta. This became the first of the Indonesian mass movements, and a marker stone for the various nationalist movements that were to come.

At this time the indigenous industry in Java was largely confined to kretek (clove-scented) cigarette manufacture in Kudus and batik making in the Jogjakarta and Surakarta areas. Both of these groups were under heavy competition from enterprising Chinese. Sarekat Islam was founded by a prominent batik entrepreneur in Surakarta, initially as a check on the inroads of Chinese commercialism. Under the dynamic leadership of Hadji Agus Salim and H.O.S. Tjokroaminoto, Sarekat Islam quickly became a massive populist force numbering at least two million people by 1919. Sarekat Islam became considerably more than a group reflecting Islamic commercial interests. Great numbers of frustrated Javanese of all social strata and occupations joined its ranks. The voice of nationalism was no longer confined to educators or tradition-minded sentimentalists but was now beginning to be heard from the masses. One

of the leaders of the Sarekat Islam, Raden Achmad
expounded the cause in this way:

> The people have joined Sarekat Islam en masse
> because they seek their rights. They have sought
> them in vain from their legal chiefs ... It is the
> people that sees its rights continually threatened;
> that is why there is the great cry for them to unite
> themselves in order to defend and resist with
> more power those who rob them of their rights.

This movement came as a surprise to the paternalist
Dutch administration. As several writers have pointed out,
doubtless this also came as a surprise to the Indonesians
themselves, who had no conception of the extent of their
own frustrations, nor of the potential of a mass movement
to bring them to the surface. The Dutch reacted cautiously.
In 1914, they conferred legal status on the various branches
of the Sarekat Islam, but refused such status for the organization as a whole. The result of this tactic was to separate
the moderate central leadership from the rest of the organization and the branches soon came under the leadership of
more radical elements.

In 1914, a Dutch Marxist, Henrik Sneevliet, founded
the Indies Social Democratic Association (*ISDV*). This
became the basis for the oldest communist party in Asia,
the Indonesian Communist Party (Partai Komunis Indonesia
–*PKI*) that was founded in 1920. Joining forces with two
Indonesian Marxists in Semarang, Sneevliet's *ISDV* rapidly
and energetically built up a considerable following. In
1917, the year of the October Revolution in Russia, the
ISDV began infiltrating the Sarekat Islam. This was a natural
move for the *ISDV* because their Marxist anti-capitalism
merged very easily with the anti-foreigner stance taken by
the leaders of the Sarekat Islam. However, a showdown
between the Marxists and Tjokroaminoto and Agus Salim
resulted in the Marxists being expelled from the Sarekat
Islam leadership. At the same time the Dutch government
began deporting all foreign Marxists.

By 1923, all the leading foreign Marxists had been expelled
from the Indies, and the *PKI* came to be totally run by
Indonesians. New and important figures were entering the

picture, including Tan Malakka, a tireless organizer from
Sumatra, who was chairman of the *PKI* in 1922, and Muso,
a radical trade unionist from Surabaya. However, a successful
sweep by the Dutch police intelligence in 1925 resulted in
the top leaders of the *PKI* being forced to go either into
exile or into hiding. The leadership under Muso advocated
a desperate large-scale revolt, but Tan Malakka disagreed,
considering that such a move would be suicidal at the time.
Miscalculating communist strength, Muso proceeded with
his plans and Tan Malakka disassociated himself from the
group. On the night of November 13, 1926, the ill-fated
venture was launched in Batavia and was, as predicted, a
total disaster. Thousands were arrested and many were
later put in detention camps. What was left of the *PKI* went
underground and many members fled from the country.
The leadership, such as remained, was completely divided
amidst acrimonious charges and counter-charges. This
internal split of the *PKI* precipitated a bitter feud between
the two factions and had far-reaching effects on the later
growth of communism in Indonesia.

The rise of more strident nationalism, in the form of
Sarekat Islam and the *PKI*, brought a major change in
Dutch policies. Paternalism and condescension were no
longer relevant in governing a people beginning to clamor
for independence. The government elected to make some
concessions, and in 1917 the Dutch set up a Volksraad
(People's Council) as a purely advisory body to the governor
general. Membership was set at 50 % Dutch and 50 % Asian
(including Chinese). With its first sessions in May, 1918,
it quickly became apparent that it would become a forum
of nationalist discontent. For the first time Indonesian
leaders from all over the Dutch Indies were brought together
and they made good use of the opportunity to discuss their
problems and mutual aspirations.

The Volksraad was intended only as a token to the vaguely
stated Indonesian desire to participate in policy making.
To many, however, its creation seemed like an act of
weakness on the part of the government and, accordingly,
the extremists increased their demands. Many prominent
nationalists either never joined the appointive Volksraad,

or, like Agus Salim, soon disassociated themselves from it. Although the Volksraad never succeeded in taking any definite steps toward autonomy, it did, in 1927, gain technical equality in legislative power with the governor general. His right of veto, nonetheless, neutralized the concession.

Then, in the 1920s, the government, relatively indulgent at first towards the stirrings of nationalism, began moving against the obstreperous Sarekat Islam and the extremist *PKI*. This had the effect not of discouraging nationalism but rather of creating voids that were soon filled by new groups even more extremist in orientation. Some of these were organized by the students, both those studying abroad in Holland and in the few local institutions of higher learning to which Indonesians were admitted.

One of the most significant of these student groups was the Netherlands-based Perhimpoenan Indonesia (Indonesia Association) formed in 1924. Some of those who were to become the leaders of the Indonesian Republic were participants in this student organization. These included Sutan Sjahrir, Mohammad Hatta, Ali Sastroamidjojo, and Sartono. The members were greatly influenced by the various streams of Marxism and socialism prevalent in Europe, and the effect of these returning graduates on the nationalist movement was a profound one. Informal study groups were started in the major cities, with a marked emphasis on political organization and economics. The wider dissemination of public education was also an important target, and "wild schools" outside the established system were set up, creating a nationalistic awareness among the young.

On June 4, 1927, one study club in Bandung, taking advantage of a newly granted right of association, formed a group which became the Indonesian Nationalist Party (Partai Nasional Indonesia–*PNI*), advocating complete independence as their goal, and noncooperation with the Dutch as a primary tactic. A young graduate of the college in Bandung, Ir. (Engineer) Sukarno, was elected as chairman.

Sukarno, who was destined to become the first president of independent Indonesia, was born on June 6, 1901, in east Java, the son of a Balinese mother of high caste and a Javanese Islamic father who was a school teacher. While in secondary school in Surabaya, he had lived in the home of Tjokroaminoto which was a meeting place of the important figures of the early Sarekat Islam as well as the Marxists who would later form the *PKI*. Thus at an early age he was exposed to nationalism and he never diverted from his efforts to further its goals. By 1920, when he entered the Technical Institute at Bandung to study civil engineering and architecture, he had already established a name for himself as a skillful orator and polemicist, and was affiliated with the Jong Java group.

With Sukarno as the head of the *PNI*, both it and the other student nationalist groups flourished. On October 28, 1928, at the second congress of a youth group, Indonesia Muda (Young Indonesia), the famous Sumpah Pemuda (Youth Oath) was taken resolving that the Indies comprised one nation and one country, and were to be joined by one language, Bahasa Indonesia. At this congress, a musical composition named *Indonesia Raya* (Greater Indonesia), was introduced and adopted as the national anthem of an independent Indonesia.

When the government found that the growing *PNI* was increasingly following an "extremist" course, it stepped in and, on December 29, 1929, arrested Sukarno along with other leaders. Standing trial, Sukarno made an eloquent defense in which he defined his association with Marhaen, the Indonesian Everyman, "depressed, desperately poor." He was sentenced to three years imprisonment and the *PNI* was banned. Though Sukarno was in jail, the nationalist movement actively continued.

The question of noncooperation was much debated, as was the problem of whether creating a large mass organization to reach as many people as possible was a better tactic than organizing small well-prepared cadres of elite leaders. This latter approach was advocated by Sjahrir and Hatta.

After two years of imprisonment, Sukarno was released and gave his support to the mass movement strategy. In 1933, he was again arrested and, without trial, he was exiled to the island of Flores. The following year Sjahrir and Hatta were also exiled to outer islands.

The three nationalists were kept in exile for the rest of the decade, isolated from the movements and organizations they had set in motion.

The 1930s brought efforts by the various nationalist groups to integrate themselves into a more united front and this was also a time when a considerable attempt was made to approach the Dutch more moderately. It was to no avail. The Dutch were unyielding on the subject of increased self-government for the Indonesians. With the nationalist movement greatly weakened and its leaders under strict surveillance, it was not likely the Indonesians could muster enough strength to cause serious trouble. A general atmosphere of despair and cynicism set in and the nationalists felt they were farther away than ever from achieving their goals.

In 1940, the Volksraad passed the Wiwoho Resolution, a moderate demand calling for self-government within the framework of the Netherlands Constitution. By the time the Dutch reply came in August of that year, Holland had been occupied by the Germans and its government was in exile. Under these circumstances, the Dutch did not want to judge the resolution on its merits and stated that they had no intention of considering any plans concerning a final constitutional development or of any other change in the status of the Netherlands East Indies.

This was the final straw for many Indonesians wavering in their attitude toward the Dutch and nationalism. The anti-West thrust of militant Japan seemed more and more attractive to the Indonesians as their resentment and frustrations reached a peak.

*   *   *

The Japanese forces, striking out all over East Asia and the Pacific in late 1941 and early 1942, launched their attack on the Netherlands East Indies on February 14, 1942. On March 9, the Dutch surrendered. The subsequent period of Japanese occupation was the turning point in the Indonesian drive towards nationhood. It changed, virtually overnight, what a score of uprisings and rebellions of the nineteenth century, and all the impassioned politicizing of the twentieth century, had failed to do; it broke the spell of Dutch domination.

The Japanese not only removed the Dutch from power, but irrevocably discredited them in the eyes of the Indonesians. It was sobering for the Indonesians to observe the humiliation and maltreatment of the Dutch who, mere weeks before, had appeared to be invincible rulers. For Indonesian nationalists, this was the final act in a chain of events that began with the arrival of the Dutch at Bantam in 1596. It was an affirmation of Asia, a physical and psychological extirpation of the myth of Western supremacy.

The knowledge that the deathblow was being struck to Dutch imperialism in the Indies resulted in an exuberant welcome for the conquering Japanese. All the trappings of nationalism were brought out into the open: the flag of red and white, the anthem *Indonesia Raya*, the national language of Bahasa Indonesia. The Indonesians thought the Japanese had come to liberate them and give them self rule. The Japanese, however, were at war and they needed to exploit, in the shortest possible time, the resources of the archipelago, especially petroleum and rubber. They had neither the time nor the strategies for anything less essential. In fact, the initial outpouring of goodwill by the Indonesians towards their "Greater East Asia Co-Prosperity Sphere" partners led the Japanese to believe that they could achieve their ends with little more than a nod at Indonesian nationalism. Before the year was out, growing hostility on the part of the populace showed the overbearing Japanese their mistake.

The three principal leaders of Indonesia, Sukarno, Hatta, and Sjahrir, hastily formulated a plan to deal with the Japanese. Agreement was reached among the three for overt cooperation with the Japanese led by Sukarno and Hatta with strengthening the nationalist movement as the ultimate goal. It was also decided to create an underground group, led by Sjahrir, with Hatta as the link, in order to keep abreast of outside events and to avoid a too-vulnerable concentration of nationalist forces. The Japanese were probably aware of these developments, and the real intentions of the Indonesian leaders toward them, but as the war progressed, and a Japanese victory became increasingly elusive, the need to retain the cooperation of the Indonesians became all the more important. The period of Japanese occupation was a race against time for both sides with each feverishly implementing its own program while mouthing assurances of common purpose to the other. For the occupiers, it was a drive to harness the raw materials and manpower of the Indies to their war effort. For the nationalists, it was the first opportunity for them to extend their cause to the hitherto uninvolved mass of rural Indonesians.

Although the three and a half years of Japanese occupation were brutal ones for the Indonesians, especially when the war began turning against the Japanese, it was also a period that provided great psychological benefits. They learned much about their own capabilities. They were increasingly given positions in civil administration that were denied to them under the Dutch. In many cases, they were more competent in their jobs than their Dutch predecessors or their Japanese counterparts. The wartime petroleum industry was an outstanding example of a situation in which the Indonesians proved themselves capable of assuming positions of considerable responsibility.

Sukarno and his associates were allowed full use of the Japanese propaganda apparatus and the privilege to travel all over spreading nationalism. In return, they were expected to exhort the Indonesians to cooperate with Japanese recruitment of labor battalions and the mobilization of strategic raw materials, such as rice, rubber, and oil, for the war effort.

In September, 1943, the Japanese began recruiting Indonesians into a home-guard type of organization called *PETA* (Sukarela Tentara Pembela Tanah Air–Volunteer Army of Defenders of the Homeland). This was the forerunner of the Indonesian Army, and, like other Japanese-sponsored bodies, soon became more pro-nationalist than pro-Greater East Asia Co-Prosperity Sphere. Although growing reaction to Japanese occupation policies manifested themselves in three *PETA* revolts in early 1944, by the time the war ended in August, 1945, almost 120,000 Indonesians were under arms in *PETA* units.

In late 1944, the Japanese Army Command on Java began appointing Indonesians as residents and subresidents on Java and Madura. These positions represented concessions of real significance, especially since the new Japanese premier had promised independence "in the very near future." In March, 1945, an Investigating Committee for the Preparation of Indonesian Independence was set up by the Japanese and it included most of the prominent nationalist figures. On June 1, 1945, during the course of a meeting, Ir. Sukarno presented his Pantjasila (Five-Fold Way), as a philosophical guideline for an independent Indonesia. The Pantjasila was not only a synthesis of the major streams of Indonesian social and political thought, but it also offered the promise of reconciliation among the diverse nationalist groups. Sukarno eloquently took the meeting through his concepts of nationalism, humanitarianism, representative government, social justice, and belief in God, as embodying the direction of the new Indonesia.

The Japanese continued making concessions and promises without ever granting outright independence to the Indonesians. On August 7, 1945, in another effort to retain Indonesian goodwill in the growing debacle, the Japanese Southeast Asia Command announced the formation of the Indonesian Independence Preparatory Committee as the prelude to a transfer of governmental authority. Sixty-two members, with one Indonesian secretary and one Japanese observer, proceeded with cooperation and speed to draw up a constitution for an independent Indonesia. This was the Constitution of 1945.

During the following week, Sukarno and Hatta were flown to Japanese headquarters at Saigon where they were promised that independence would be granted on the twenty-fourth of that month. However, the war ended on the fifteenth thus placing the nationalist leaders in a difficult position. They realized that now the Japanese could neither give nor acknowledge independence for Indonesia. Rising against the Japanese and proclaiming unconditional independence might free the Republic from a possible made-in-Japan stigma, but the risk was also great of this action bringing on a conflict with the still overwhelmingly powerful Japanese forces.

Sjahrir and some of the radicals in the underground groups pressed for an immediate proclamation of independence. Sukarno disagreed, unsure of sufficient popular support. This was a confusing time for everyone. The Japanese themselves had yet to announce their surrender (they would on the twenty-first). None of the Indonesian leaders knew what might or could happen. Sukarno and Hatta continued to delay, but in the early morning hours of August 16, they were abducted from Djakarta to the *PETA* garrison of Rangasdengklok, about fifty kilometers from the city, by a group of student activists. Freed later that day, Sukarno was finally persuaded that the time was indeed ripe. That evening started an all-night session among nationalist leaders, meeting in the Japanese Admiral Maeda's residence, to work out a plan and draft a declaration.

At 10.00 A.M. on August 17, 1945, in the front garden of Sukarno's home, with Hatta beside him and a few patriots and guards as witnesses, Sukarno read some lines typed on a piece of paper torn from a school notebook, thus quietly and simply stating the independence of Indonesia:

> We Indonesians hereby declare Indonesian independence. Matters pertaining to the transfer of authority and other affairs, are to be arranged properly, and in the shortest time possible.
> In the name of the people of Indonesia:
>
> SUKARNO–HATTA

Thus began the fight to be free, and MERDEKA became the rallying cry of the people.

CHAPTER 3

Oil of the Indies

Long before the modern uses of oil were discovered in the Western World, the people of Indonesia had found several practical uses for the dark liquid they found seeping from the earth in various places in their islands. Possibly the first contact Westerners had with the oil of Indonesia came during a battle at sea in the sixteenth century, when Sumatrans burned two Portuguese galleons by hurling oil-soaked fire balls at them. This battle in the Strait of Malacca was the first, but far from the last, disagreement between Westerners and Indonesians involving oil.

Earth oil, as it was called prior to the last century, was also valued for medicinal purposes. The Dutch, when they came to the archipelago, were not long in adopting its use and frequently the officers of the Dutch East India Company were instructed to send this earth oil back to the Netherlands where it was used in attempts to obtain relief from stiffness of the limbs.

When whale oil could no longer meet the rapidly increasing need for oil for lamps, the search turned from the sea to the land. Though the use of petroleum for illumination had been known since the time of Herodotus, in 500 B.C., it only became important in the modern world after the discoveries at Titusville, Pennsylvania, in 1859. During the next two decades the search for oil spread throughout the world.

Jan Reerink, a government storekeeper, was the first man to make a commercial search for oil in the Netherlands East Indies. After traveling to Holland and finding financial

42

backing there, Reerink returned and set up camp near Tjibodas, west Java, in December 1871. He used an ox-driven Pennsylvania drilling rig in his search but he had trouble with the soft soil which kept caving in, and after drilling four wells, none of them commercially promising, he ran out of money.

Reerink's reason for drilling in the Tjibodas region was the abundance of surface seepages in the area. Prior to the development of modern geological analysis and geophysical techniques, exploration wells were almost always drilled in areas surrounding surface seepages. These oil seepages proved to be relatively good guides to producible oil and the shallow wells necessary in such areas could be drilled by the simple equipment and techniques available.

In 1883, Aeilko Jans Zijlker, while inspecting tobacco fields he managed near Langkat, north Sumatra was overtaken by a monsoon rain and took shelter in one of his tobacco sheds. As it grew dark, his foreman, who was from the district, lit a torch for him which burned very steadily with a peculiarly bright flame. The foreman told Zijlker that he had dipped the torch in the dark liquid that covered the surface of a nearby pond. The next morning they went to the pond and Zijlker recognized the smell of what was then called illuminating oil. Zijlker set up a company in order to exploit this promising discovery and he obtained capital from Holland to finance his operations. The first well that he drilled was at Telaga Tiga, but it produced hardly more than the surface seepages. His second well, drilled at Telaga Tunggal on June 15, 1885, proved the area's commercial potential and started a wide search for oil in the Netherlands East Indies. Surabaya, Djambi, Perlak, the Palembang region, and eastern Borneo all showed promising oil seepages that led to exploratory drilling.

With a firm discovery as a basis, Zijlker returned to Holland to establish a company for the production, refining and marketing of illuminating oil. Through his efforts, and those of some influential friends in The Hague, his company received the title of "Royal" and thus Royal Dutch was established on June 16, 1890.

The first managing director of Royal Dutch was J.A. De Gelder. With past engineering experience in the Indies, De Gelder tackled the job of finding new wells and developing the company. The company's administrative base was established at Pangkalan Brandan in north Sumatra, and there they built a refinery that was completed in February, 1892. They also began building facilities at nearby Pangkalan Susu to handle ocean shipments. By 1898, Royal Dutch had completed construction of the storage and harbor facilities that were to make Pangkalan Susu Indonesia's first oil shipping port. By the final years of the century Royal Dutch was shipping oil and kerosene, then used for lighting, to all the markets of the Far East.

Another oil company had been established at Surabaya in eastern Java in 1887 by Adrian Stoop, a former employee of Zijlker. Surabaya was well-known for its seepage oil and this oil had for many years been used in tanning leather and sold for medicinal use. Stoop obtained reasonable success from his drilling efforts near Surabaya and in 1890 he erected his first refinery at Wonokromo, just outside the city. He soon extended his operations into central Java and in 1894 he set up a second refinery at Tjepu.

Another early arrival on the oil scene of the Netherlands East Indies, was the Shell Transport and Trading Co. They found oil in eastern Borneo and, in 1894, set up a small refinery in Balikpapan.

By the turn of the century, oil had been discovered in north Sumatra, south Sumatra, central and eastern Java, and east Borneo, and refineries had been established in each area. There were, at that time, eighteen companies exploring for oil or producing oil in the N.E.I.

In the first years of the century, two of these companies emerged as leaders—Royal Dutch in production and refining and Shell in transportation and marketing. The Shell company had been founded by Marcus Samuel, an Englishman who also traded in shells—hence the name of his company—and spices. He moved into the lucrative oil shipping business in the developing years of the industry and his company achieved an important position in this field.

Discussions were conducted in 1901 between Shell and Royal Dutch and they resulted, in 1902, in the formation of a joint company to handle shipping and marketing for both firms—the Shell Transport and Royal Dutch Petroleum Company, Ltd.

While Royal Dutch prospered and continued to advance its position by acquisition and expansion, the Shell company fell into financial difficulties due to adverse developments in its American operations. The company had, further, failed to improve upon its small base in the discovery and production of oil in the N.E.I. Shell's potential was further reduced by a 1904 amendment to the Mining Law of 1899 that stopped the granting of further oil concessions in the N.E.I.

With consideration for these adverse circumstances, Marcus Samuel contacted Henri Detering, the successor to De Gelder, with a view of arranging a merger between Shell and Royal Dutch. Samuel proposed a merger with each company receiving 50 % of the assets of the new company. Detering, also aware of the circumstances, offered Samuel 40 % which he accepted. Thus, on February 24, 1907, was formed the Royal Dutch/Shell group of companies that was soon known worldwide simply as "Shell."

Under the parent holding company, three operating companies were created. These were Asiatic Petroleum for marketing, De Bataafsche Petroleum Maatschappij (*BPM*) for production and refining, and the Anglo-Saxon Petroleum Co. for transportation.

Three years later, in 1910, the Shell group absorbed another producing company in the N.E.I. and in the following year they bought out the last independent producer— Shell's domination of the oil industry in the Netherlands East Indies was then complete.

Although by 1900, Royal Dutch had achieved clear leadership in production and refining in the N.E.I., it was engaged in fierce competition with Standard Oil in Far East marketing. Standard had been marketing kerosene in the Far East long before Royal Dutch entered the field.

As oil production in north Sumatra grew during the last decade of the century, Standard sent representatives to the area to attempt to purchase some producing wells and facilities. The company received many offers from small companies that wanted to sell concessions for unexplored or minimally developed areas but they found nothing that suited their program. At that time Standard hoped to avoid entering into exploration and development in the N.E.I.

In response to these feelers by Standard, Royal Dutch mounted a campaign to keep the company out of the N.E.I. and they sought, not without success, to arouse protectionist sentiments and to influence the government both in Batavia and in the Netherlands.

Immediately before and shortly after the turn of the century, the Far East oil market was growing rapidly and in view of this growth, Standard felt an increasing need to develop production in the area. By 1910 Royal Dutch/Shell controlled all production and refining in the N.E.I. and there was then no hope for Standard to buy anything there as a going operation. They recognized that if they were to obtain any part of the oil of the N.E.I. they would have to enter into an active exploration and development program.

To initiate operations in the N.E.I., Standard of New Jersey (as this company had become after the old Standard was broken up by antitrust action) formed a subsidiary, the American Petroleum Co. The company intended to buy up unexpired exploration permits in the N.E.I. and, to circumvent Dutch laws that restricted the activities of foreign firms, the subsidiary formed another subsidiary, the Nederlandsche Koloniale Petroleum Maatschappij (*NKPM*).

NKPM commenced operations in 1912 and bought such concessions as it could obtain from minor and defunct firms. It is not surprising that these areas proved to be very poor—they had certainly been looked over and rejected by Shell. From 1912 to 1921, *NKPM* drilled a total of sixty holes of which fifty-seven were dry. Of the remaining three, one proved noncommercial and the other two were of only marginal value. In 1920, *NKPM* had a total production of 100 barrels per day as compared with Shell's 48,000 barrels per day.

At this time, oil activities in the N.E.I. were still governed by the Mining Law of 1899 that had been amended in 1900 and again in 1904. The 1904 amendment freezing the granting of new oil concessions was clearly passed in an attempt to keep out firms that were not already operating in the N.E.I. The law was further amended in 1918, with apparent intent of resuming the granting of oil concessions.

Earlier concessions, before 1904, had been granted for periods of up to seventy-five years and under them the government received a fixed price per acre conceded plus a percentage of the value of any oil produced. Section 5-A of the 1918 amendment assured there would be a considerably higher return to the government from any new concessions granted. A company entering into a 5-A Contract, as they came to be called, would pay the N.E.I. 4% excise on the value of crude shipped, a 20% tax on oil profits, plus a general tax on corporate profits of 20%. The return to the government amounted to slightly less than 50% of profits and this was generally higher than the oil producing nations of the Middle East were receiving prior to World War II.

After the passing of the 1918 amendment, many oil companies, including a number of American firms, expected to purchase concession areas in the N.E.I. As time passed without any new areas being declared open for development, the companies began to protest to the N.E.I. government. They were suspicious that a way was being sought to give preference to Dutch firms and their suspicions were somewhat confirmed when Shell was given a number of prewar German concessions.

The American firms made their position known to the United States State Department, and the State Department then tried to apply pressure at The Hague to get the Netherlands government to order a change in the apparently discriminatory action of the Batavia administration. Real pressure began to be exerted when Congress passed the General Leasing Act of 1920. This act required the denial of leases of public lands in the United States to the companies of any nation that discriminated against American companies.

The Dutch government assured the American oil companies that new concession areas in the N.E.I. would soon be released. The first area that was expected to be released was the Djambi area of south Sumatra.

The Djambi area contained many oil seepages and it looked extremely promising to all geologists who had made investigations. Prior to 1918, the government had approached Shell with the proposal that they form a joint venture company to exploit the area. Shell declined and there was at that time, of course, no danger that the area would fall into outside hands.

The American oil community and State Department were then shocked to learn, in 1921, that this valuable area was to be granted to a joint company that was to be a partnership between Shell and the N.E.I. government. The new company was named Nederlandsche Indische Aardolie Maatschappij (*NIAM*).

International repercussions quickly followed the announcement of the Djambi allocation. Shell subsidiaries in the United States were denied leases on public lands in Utah, Wyoming, and Oklahoma. The Dutch government was informed that such leases would only be granted if they could demonstrate nondiscrimination on the part of the N.E.I. administration. Though the Djambi allocation was not changed, the pressure did result in a relaxation of restrictions on all American companies involved in the N.E.I. and in the opening up of oil concessions to American firms.

NIAM was given a charter in July, 1921, that was valid until December 31, 1960. The profits of *NIAM* were to be split fifty-fifty with the government. Shell was given total responsibility for management, development, and field operations. In addition to the Djambi area, the company received concessions near Palembang, on the east coast of Sumatra, along the Gulf of Aru, and in parts of Borneo including Bunju Island. Of the three main regions in which *NIAM* was given exploration rights, only the Gulf of Aru failed to reach the production stage prior to World War II.

Although Standard of New Jersey was particularly disappointed about the Djambi allocation, their prospects in the N.E.I. were greatly improved in that same year by *NKPM's* discovery of the Talang Akar field on a purchased concession in central Sumatra. Talang Akar developed into the largest field that was to be discovered in the N.E.I. prior to World War II.

The story of the discovery of Talang Akar is one of those fascinating tales that occur so often in the annals of the petroleum industry.

The drilling chief had been ordered to notify the head office when the lower Palembang sands were pierced and the Telissa layer had been reached. This was the normal level at which drilling was stopped. The drilling chief notified the office, as instructed, in mid-December but he kept his crew drilling because they were being paid by the footage drilled. Because of the Christmas holidays, an order to halt the drilling was delayed, and on December 26, 1921, a layer of prolific oil bearing sands was discovered just a few hundred feet below any previously known producing horizon in Indonesia.

To process the oil from Talang Akar, *NKPM* decided to erect a refinery in Sumatra. They chose a site at Sungei Gerong on the Musi River near Palembang just across the river from the Shell refinery at Pladju. By early 1926, *NKPM* had completed a pipeline from the field to Sungei Gerong and in May the refinery went on stream with a capacity of 3,500 barrels per day.

Standard of New Jersey finally succeeded in receiving its first direct oil concessions in the Indies in June 1925. They were granted areas in Java and Madura, plus additional acreage surrounding their Talang Akar concession. The actual allocation of the concession rights was held up until July 17, 1928, because of the Dutch government's demand for assurances by the United States government that sanctions against Shell in the U.S. would also be lifted. Diplomacy clearly played a great role in persuading the Dutch to allow the American companies to participate in the N.E.I. American diplomats and drillers were beginning to work together as their counterparts in Europe had been doing for decades.

In September, 1933, Standard merged its *NKPM* holdings into a new joint venture corporation, the Standard-Vacuum Petroleum Maatschappij (*SVPM*), later changed to P.T. Standard Vacuum Petroleum (Stanvac) in 1947.

The new corporation resulted from the merger of Standard of New Jersey's production and refineries with Socony Vacuum's (Standard of New York, now Mobil) extensive marketing outlets throughout Asia, Australia, and East Africa. With the formation of this new company, and the discovery of two new fields, an expansion of the Sungei Gerong refinery was necessary. A new pipeline was laid and the refinery capacity was increased to 40,000 barrels per day in 1936, and to 45,000 barrels per day in 1940. The company discovered one last field, Lirik, before the Japanese invasion. By the time World War II broke out in Asia, Stanvac's Sungei Gerong refinery was the largest in the Far East.

The success of Stanvac in obtaining concessions did not necessarily mark the beginning of any rapport between the Netherlands East Indies government and the American oil companies—their presence was always resented. Gulf Oil entered the N.E.I. in 1928, and took up options on an area that had formerly been issued to a Dutch concern. They applied for a concession area in north Sumatra in 1930 but, after long delays, their request was denied.

Standard of California first sent geologists to the Netherlands East Indies in 1924, and they encountered the same difficulties as Standard of New Jersey. The company was refused concessions in north Sumatra in 1929, and in Borneo and New Guinea in 1932. Upon the advice of the State Department, Standard of California formed a Dutch subsidiary, Nederlandsche Pacific Petroleum Maatschappij (*NPPM*) in 1930. The company's persistence was finally rewarded when the *NPPM* was given a concession for a wild and little-known area in central Sumatra that Standard of New Jersey had earlier refused. A contract was signed in June 1936, for the area known as the Rokan Block. In the same year, Standard of California entered into a major overseas partnership with the Texas Company (Texaco). The two companies pooled their interests in most of Asia, thus marrying the Texas Company's marketing strength in the Far East with the production strength of Standard of California in the Middle East. As part of this alignment,

NPPM became owned in equal parts by the two American giants and became a member of the group known as California Texas Oil Company (Caltex).

Caltex spudded its first exploration well in the Rokan Block in mid-1939 at Sebanga, 65 km. (40 mi.) north of Pakanbaru. The results of the drilling showed there was oil within the block. Caltex also made a discovery at Duri, but this area was soon overshadowed in exploration priority by a highly promising structure between Pakanbaru and Sebanga. Preparations for the first test drilling proceeded and on the eve of the outbreak of war a drilling rig was moved onto location. The Japanese invaded Sumatra before the Caltex crew could begin drilling and the Japanese used the rig to drill the first well in the Minas structure. Drilling was commenced in December 1943, and a year later oil was struck at 2,107 feet. The initial flow was 800 barrels per day. After the war the Minas developed into one of the twenty-five largest fields in the world.

The international oil industry, as it evolved up to World War II, was dominated by seven companies, usually referred to as "the Majors." Of these seven companies, five were American–Standard of New Jersey, Standard of New York, Standard of California, Gulf, and Texaco. One was essentially British–British Petroleum (BP)–and the seventh, Shell, was a sixty-forty split between Dutch and British interests. Of the seven major world oil companies, five were present in the N.E.I., forming the Big Three—Shell, Stanvac (Standard of New Jersey and Standard of New York), and Caltex (Standard of California and Texaco).

For the exploration of Netherlands New Guinea, the N.E.I. government induced the Big Three to pool their resources to form the N.V. Nederlandsche Nieuw Guinea Petroleum Maatschappij (*NNGPM*). Shell and Stanvac each held a 40% interest in the company and the remaining 20% was held by the Far Pacific Investment Company, a subsidiary of Caltex. The company was operated by Shell, since they had been doing survey work in New Guinea since 1928. On May 23, 1935, *NNGPM* reached an agreement with the N.E.I. government granting them exclusive rights for a fifty-year period to an area known as the New Guinea Block near Sorong in the far west of the island. In undertaking its exploration program, *NNGPM* faced many difficulties. Most of the difficulties were due to the area's isolation. The climate with its almost daily rainfall and the difficult terrain added to the problems. *NNGPM* was forced to import laborers into New Guinea, primarily Dayaks from Borneo, because the local people proved to be uninterested in the difficult work. The company made a number of finds prior to 1942, but although *NNGPM* had received promising results from its initial drilling, the company was forced to abandon the area in February of 1942 without receiving any return for the millions of dollars invested.

*   *   *

The top management of Shell prior to World War II consisted entirely of foreigners. Most of these were Dutch, but there were a few British, Rumanians, and Americans. This group, classified as European Personnel, lived as a society by itself. Their living quarters were separate, as were their clubs and recreational facilities. On the next level were the Eurasians. Depending upon the circumstances, a Eurasian might be considered European Personnel, but more often the classification was that of Higher Asian Personnel. On the third level were the Chinese, many of whom came from Singapore and Hong Kong. They enjoyed a slightly higher level of pay and privilege than the Indonesians, but still remained below the Europeans and Eurasians.

At the bottom of the social and economic structure were the Indonesians. Though, with few exceptions, Indonesians were classified in one grouping by the company, they divided themselves by sukus and occupational groups and recognised different levels of status.

All Shell personnel received free medical aid, housing, and usually access to some recreational facilities. One group of elderly gentlemen in Djambi still remembers quite well the Saturday nights they spent before the war, gambling at the company's recreational lounge for Indonesians. In most areas, Shell maintained stores where the employees could purchase goods at very reasonable prices. According to N.E.I. law, 75% of the employees of a company had to be either Dutch citizens or citizens of the Netherlands East Indies. However, there were only a few Indonesians employed in administrative, supervisory, or technical positions in the oil companies. In most cases the workers learned such skills as they had by on-the-job training rather than by formal instruction. The companies had not yet instituted extensive training programs to help develop the skills of the Indonesians in the industry. Thus, there were only a few with the higher level skills that would be necessary to operate the petroleum industry in the absence of the Dutch.

Usually the best field position that an Indonesian could reach was foreman, and there were huge differences between European and Indonesian salaries. Generally, the Indonesian employee's salary was adequate only for food and clothing and other necessities. In spite of the great contrast between the conditions for the expatriates and the Indonesians, the oil towns did not develop into spawning grounds for labor conflict or strong nationalism. There were some nationalist groups within Shell prior to World War II, but the company took a very intolerant view of workers who joined them. Labor disputes, whether of political or other motivation, were dealt with severely. As a result, Shell had little trouble maintaining discipline in their labor force before World War II. The same restrictive practices and policies were generally followed by Stanvac and Caltex.

The Netherlands East Indies oil industry on the eve of World War II was principally Shell and Stanvac; Caltex not yet having gotten into production. Shell was by far the largest. The company's operations extended from north Sumatra to New Guinea and included concessions in every known producing region with the exception of central Sumatra. The operations of Stanvac were limited to south and central Sumatra. Between them the companies dominated the colony's domestic marketing as well as production, with Shell again having much the larger share. In the field of joint ventures, Shell also dominated the others, holding a 50% interest in *NIAM* and 40% in *NNGPM* with Shell being the operator of both joint venture companies. In production, the Netherlands East Indies was the fifth-largest producer in the world although its total output accounted for only 3% of the world's production. Oil, however, accounted for 25% of the N.E.I.'s total exports and was exceeded in value only by rubber.

With the outbreak of hostilities in Europe in 1939, and the German invasion of the Netherlands in the late spring of 1940, the future of the Netherlands East Indies became very uncertain. Not only was the N.E.I. the largest producer of oil in the Far East (averaging about 62 million barrels per year in 1939 and 1940) but it was also a substantial rubber producer. Clearly, both oil and rubber were of value to the Japanese, and with the attack on Pearl Harbor and Malaya, it was certain that the N.E.I. would be the next target for invasion.

The Dutch realized that they would not be able to hold out against a Japanese attack and they had earlier developed a plan to destroy all of the oil facilities before they could be captured. The destruction program was carried out by the N.E.I. Army in cooperation with the companies. Primary facilities in Borneo and Java were at least partially destroyed, as were most facilities in Sumatra. This destruction consisted of burning the refineries, plugging the wells with cement, and dynamiting the pipelines. However, because of the hurried nature of the operations, the job was not always completed. In south Sumatra, Stanvac's Sungei Gerong refinery was almost completely destroyed, but Shell's Pladju refinery, located just across the river, was virtually untouched.

The Japanese launched their swiftest attacks towards the oil fields and were in complete control by the end of March. They divided Indonesia into three commands. Sumatra, the primary oil producer, was under the control of the Japanese Seventh Army headquartered in Singapore. Java and Madura were under the control of the Japanese Sixteenth Army with headquarters in Djakarta. The remainder of Indonesia was placed under the control of the navy which

maintained its headquarters in Makasar. The oil operations
fell under the jurisdiction of the regional military commands.
In Sumatra, the entire oil operation was under the command
of a major general in Palembang. This responsibility was
further divided into areas with a colonel in charge of each
area.

The Japanese wasted no time in commencing to rehabilitate
the fields and refineries. Their first move was to gather
all of the former oil company employees, many of whom
had scattered at the time of the invasion, and set them to
work making repairs. Initially, many of the workers looked
upon the Japanese as liberators and they worked for them
willingly. In a short time, most of them learned to change
this view of the Japanese. The Japanese used a forced labor
system in the oil fields and refineries and most of the laborers,
called Romushas by the Japanese, were brought from Java.
Tens of thousands of Romushas were utilized by the Japanese
both inside and outside Indonesia. They were forced to
live under the most difficult conditions and thousands
died of illness and malnutrition.

The Japanese were not particularly competent in the oil
business; many of the men assigned to oil projects in Indonesia were drafted directly from school and had no practical
experience. Recognizing this fact, the Japanese utilized
the few well-trained Indonesians to the maximum extent
possible. Most Indonesians in the oil industry continued
to be manual workers, as they had been for the Dutch. The
Japanese, however, established two schools to instruct
Indonesian workers. Many present employees of Pertamina
are graduates of these schools. Though the quality of instruction left something to be desired, the fact remains
that this was the first major effort to train Indonesians
for the oil industry.

The task of rehabilitation of the fields and refineries
was by necessity makeshift and innovative. Most of the
facilities had to be rebuilt by cannibalizing and using scrap.
Such new equipment as was received was mostly from
Germany and was not always adapted to the needs. The
Japanese decentralized the refining operations by building
small stills near the producing areas in order to decrease

vulnerability from bombing attack. They also made maximum use of abandoned wells and wells that had not been plugged. With the use of a great deal of labor they were able to repair refineries and pipelines. Production figures for the war period are rather questionable, but according to De Golyer and MacNaughton's *Twentieth Century Petroleum Statistics,* 1943 was the peak year in the occupation period. In that year production reached 48 million barrels, which was approximately twice the amount produced in either 1942 or 1944. Only 7.6 million barrels were produced in 1945. The great reduction can be attributed to heavy Allied bombing attacks. By the end of the war, most Indonesian oil facilities had suffered extensive bomb damage.

The war years, in spite of hardships, in many ways proved a very valuable experience to the Indonesians. The Dutch were gone and the Japanese did not know a great deal about the oil industry. For almost four years the Indoesians, in effect, ran the industry under the most adverse conditions. By necessity, they learned a most crucial lesson— they were capable of doing the job. This lesson brought a new confidence that aided the push for political independence.

CHAPTER 4

Merdeka

In August, 1945, Japan totally collapsed following the devastation of two cities by atomic bombs. With their sudden capitulation, an immense power vacuum was created throughout Southeast Asia, catching the Japanese area commanders, Allied leaders, and local nationalists, all uncertain of their positions.

The victorious Allies suddenly had responsibility for vast ex-colonial areas. There had been almost no contacts with these areas during the wartime years and the Allies had little appreciation that a whole new generation of nationalists had sprung up in many places during the half-decade of Japanese occupation.

The Allies and local nationalists were of differing opinions as to the future of French Indochina, the Dutch East Indies, and British India, Burma, Malaya, and north Borneo. The colonial powers intended to regain control as quickly as possible and to re-establish their prewar positions. President Roosevelt held traditional American sentiments of anti-colonialism and might have used his position to force clear-cut promises of self-determination for these areas. Instead, he accepted the need for maintaining the wartime alliance as free from internal dissensions as possible and did not strongly press the issue.

Japan surrendered on August 15, 1945, and on that same day all of the Netherlands East Indies was included in Lord Mountbatten's Southeast Asia Command (SEAC). The British were, of course, the major prewar colonial power in south and east Asia and it is not surprising that their commanders saw it as their duty to return all Japanese occupied territory to rightful owners as quickly as possible.

In October, British troops and British-officered contingents of Indian and Gurkha units landed in Sumatra and Java, augmenting a small task force that had already been sent to Djakarta. Their orders were to maintain order, release military and civilian internees, and to assemble Japanese troops for repatriation. Mountbatten's deputy, Rear Admiral Patterson, announced that the British troops were to maintain order until such time as the government of the Netherlands East Indies was able to resume functioning. Somewhat later, Patterson received orders that he was not to use British military units to intervene in Indonesian internal politics, and that he should attempt to bring about negotiations between Indonesian leaders and the Dutch. The Dutch, who had begun arriving via Australia, were naturally strongly displeased by the new orders.

The Indonesians were, at that time, rapidly uniting in the struggle to achieve Merdeka. During September and October, clashes were increasingly common between radical youth groups on one side and Japanese troops on the other. The British were caught in the middle.

In November, full-scale conflict broke out in Surabaya between Indonesians and British, Gurkha, and Indian troops. Fighting was savage and casualties were heavy, particularly among Indonesians, many of whom fought with only bare hands and bamboo spears. Ultimately the Indonesians were forced to withdraw, but the Battle of Surabaya, a true baptism of fire for the Republic, soon became a rallying point and symbol of self-sacrifice to inspire the Republican forces in the even more difficult days to follow. The anniversary of the battle, November 10, is now nationally celebrated as Heroes' Day.

For the Dutch, the battle was a sign that their return to power in the Indies would be both costly and difficult. For the British, weary of fighting in an area that did not directly concern them, the events at Surabaya gave all-too-clear evidence that the situation in Indonesia was far more complicated than they had supposed. Bringing the Dutch

and Indonesians together in negotiations became a goal
of urgent priority for the British.

The Dutch were, however, not interested in negotiations
and were determined to regain the area as a colony. World
War II had left the Netherlands in a state of devastation
and the riches of the Indies were considered essential to
the rebuilding of the mother country. Historically, this
role for the N.E.I. seemed a valid one. After the Belgian
revolution in 1830, the N.E.I. had provided badly needed
funds to rebuild Netherlands industry and return the mother
country to influence and prosperity. It was, however, more
than just economics—there were also strong emotional
attachments between the Dutch people and their former
colony.

Lieutenant Governor General designate, Dr. Hubertus
van Mook, calculated that 15,000 troops would have to
be deployed in order to re-establish complete Dutch control
in the N.E.I. But to equip and transport such a force was
completely beyond the means of the economically prostrate
Netherlands government in 1945. The problem for van
Mook was then clear: He must quickly establish Dutch
control over all strategic and economic strong points
under the cover of the British forces. The main towns and
seaports were quickly returned to Dutch control, and so
were many plantation, mining, and petroleum refining areas.

All possible efforts were made by the Dutch to brand
the leaders of the newly proclaimed Republic as terrorists
and to discredit the whole nationalist movement as Japanese
puppetry. The Dutch, then, were adamant in their refusal
to even meet with Sukarno and the other Republican leaders
and it was only after considerable British pressure that
this stance was modified. Besides the use of direct and
borrowed force, the Dutch tried to consolidate their position
by utilizing their traditional tactic of divide and rule. Wherever
possible they set up local and regional governments, ostensibly
under Indonesian leaders, but always under men clearly
amenable to serving Dutch interests.

On January 4, 1946, the Republican government transferred
its capital from Djakarta to Jogjakarta in central Java.
After this departure, there were two Indonesias, one Dutch

and one Republican. In 1947, further pressure was applied by a blockade of Republican areas. It was hoped the Republic, thus weakened and isolated, would be forced to capitulate.

If the Dutch strategy and tactics reflected their urgent economic and psychological need to regain their colony, the Indonesian leaders had an even more intense desire to maintain their independence. In this they were sustained by the belief that other nations would aid their cause once the circumstances of the Indonesian struggle were known. There were, however, factors making outside support and sympathy difficult to obtain, especially in the newly established United Nations. There was a certain stigma, one carefully nurtured by the Dutch, of the Republic being an eleventh-hour creation of the Japanese. And, clearly, if the Republic was a Japanese creation, then its leaders were not only rebels but collaborators. Indonesian leaders were also concerned with this image of the nation, and of the interpretation that might be placed upon their own roles during the occupation. In wartime all groups tend to be viewed as either friend or enemy so in the immediate postwar period few leaders of the victorious nations had either the time or the inclination to try to determine the merits of different degrees of collaboration.

Sutan Sjahrir twice became prime minister during the revolution and was also a leader of the Indonesian Socialist Party (*PSI*). His position was always that Indonesia must exist within the Anglo-American power sphere. He believed that all vestiges of Japanese indoctrination, organization, and education had to be quickly eliminated if ties with, and support of, the West were to be obtained. He recognized that the West, and particularly the United States, was the only source of urgently needed technological help and development capital. He also believed that the most important goal of the Indonesian revolution must be the development of a strong democratic government.

The leaders of the Republican government—President Sukarno, Vice-President Hatta and Prime Minister Sjahrir— were all agreed on the necessity for negotiating a settlement with the Dutch. The leaders needed to show the people tangible results and they were also aware that if a military and diplomatic stalemate between the Republic and the Netherlands was prolonged, the leadership of the revolution would be in danger of falling into the hands of extremists. The extremists, religious, political, and military, would be much more likely to divide the people and to turn the world community against an independent Indonesia.

As the revolution progressed, an emphasis upon negotiation rather than combat became increasingly difficult for the leaders to maintain. With each military withdrawal and political concession, the credibility of the leadership suffered and the chances improved for extremists. The very name of parliamentary democracy began to be popularly associated with weakness, inaction, and a compromise of the revolutionary spirit. This prejudice became deep-rooted in the years following the revolution. The ability of extremists to arouse popular support on the basis of this prejudice would prove to be the bane of later efforts to maintain or strengthen parliamentary democracy in Indonesia.

By mid-1946 the British succeeded in bringing Republican leaders and the Dutch together. Sjahrir rejected a Dutch proposal that a democratic partnership be formed to govern the Indies until such time as the people were capable of deciding their future status. Sjahrir made a counter proposal: In return for Netherlands' recognition of the Republic in Sumatra, Java, and Madura, the Republic would join a commonwealth-type Netherlands Union. Further talks in Holland on this proposal failed because of the strong opposition of the conservatives in the Dutch government.

With this failure to reach settlement of the conflict by negotiation, feelings hardened on both sides. From March 1946 onwards, the Dutch had begun landing and deploying troops to replace the departing British. The situation worsened drastically for the Republic as Dutch "mopping up" actions increased their hold over territory.

On March 25, 1947, the first major agreement—the Linggadjati Agreement—was signed between the Netherlands and the Republic. It provided, among other things, for de facto recognition of the Republic in Java, Sumatra, and Madura; a United States of Indonesia to be set up cooperatively by 1949; the creation of a Netherlands-

Indonesia Union with the Dutch monarch as its head; and the return of Dutch properties to their owners. By the Linggadjati Agreement the Dutch exchanged very limited political concessions for large economic concessions. Though the agreement was initialled on November 15, 1946, the signing was delayed by considerable opposition in the Netherlands. After its signing a groundswell of Indonesian dissatisfaction with the agreement brought down Sjahrir as prime minister. It was clear to many of the nationalists that although by de facto recognition the Republic was stated to exist, the Dutch had conceded nothing about its right to exist, and had implicitly retained the right to try to destroy it.

On July 21, 1947, the Dutch invaded the Republic in what came to be called the "first police action." Their reasons for the invasion were alleged violations of minor provisions of the Linggadjati Agreement. Two weeks of combat—mostly rear guard action by the Indonesian National Army (Tentera Nasional Indonesia—*TNI*)—ended after the U.N. Security Council, acting on a resolution by Australia, called for a cease-fire. The Council invited Indonesia's delegate, Sjahrir, to present the Indonesian case before it and this he did most persuasively. A three-nation Good Offices Committee was created. Holland chose Belgium, Indonesia chose Australia, and the representatives of the two nominees chose the United States as the third country. Considerable time passed as the parties argued over where the talks would be held. Finally, the unarmed U.S. Navy transport *Renville,* was sent to Djakarta to serve as a neutral site for negotiations. "Under perceptible American pressure," as one of the Indonesian leaders put it, the Indonesians reluctantly accepted the terms offered and the Renville Agreement was signed on January 17, 1948. The Dutch retained their advanced military position while the Republic was assured of a future plebiscite to determine the popular will on the status of Indonesia. Although the Republican leaders suspected that at any time the Dutch would try to complete their offensive, they felt that in a popular vote they could recoup any military losses they would sustain. In any case, the Republic really had no choice but to accept the Renville terms. The Indonesian leaders were aware that if the provisions were not accepted it was probable that they would lose such mediating services as they had and that the issue would be returned to a stalemate in the U.N. Security Council. The revolution would then either be taken over by extremists or deteriorate into an extended and mutually exhausting war of attrition.

Signing Renville was one thing, implementing it quite another. Neither side really liked the terms. Prime Minister Amir Sjarifuddin's cabinet fell because of the popular discontent with the Renville terms. The Indonesian leaders put a major effort into presenting to the world their own picture of the situation while the Dutch continued consolidating their position and cultivating their federalist states. The year 1948 saw little progress toward a permanent settlement of the dispute.

In August, 1948, a new element entered the uneasy situation. The former *PKI* leader, Muso, the chief engineer of the abortive 1926 communist uprising, unexpectedly returned to Indonesia after an absence of twelve years in the Soviet Union. His sudden reappearance was naturally viewed with misgivings by the Republican leaders since their control over extremist factions was shaky at best. Their suspicions of Muso's intentions were not long in being confirmed. He immediately set out to gather all the leftist groups into the classic communist "front strategy." His efforts were purportedly to buttress the defense and inject new revolutionary spirit into the resistance to the Dutch.

Hatta, as the new prime minister, had begun a program to increase government control over the unruly private armies that had formed throughout the Republic. These groups, both Islamic and left-wing, were to be either disbanded outright or integrated into regular *TNI* units. To Muso, it appeared that the *PKI* must take over leadership of the revolution immediately or it would lose the opportunity as Hatta's program reduced the number of potential *PKI* supporters. The *PKI's* opportunity was improved by widespread anger at an overly conciliatory government and by the privations caused by the continuing Dutch blockade.

In September, 1948, leftist political, labor, and armed youth groups (already loosely merged in a People's Democratic Front–*FDR*) began coalescing around Muso's *PKI* leadership and rumors of a communist revolt began circulating. Miscalculating his strength and the extent of popular support, as he had in 1926, Muso began active resistance to Hatta's policies. The *FDR–PKI* obtained further support from dissident army units in east Java and in central Java around Surakarta and Madiun. Within a month they were in open revolt against the Republican government situated in nearby Jogjakarta. This was the Madiun Affair (Peristiwa Madiun), the infamous "stab in the back" to the Republic that was already desperately pressed by blockade and the threat of growing Dutch power.

Fighting broke out in Surakarta on September 16, 1948 and during the next ten days, the *FDR–PKI* units set up a "liberated area," with headquarters at Madiun. Sukarno and Hatta were appalled at the outbreak of this civil war, and they feared that this would give the Dutch the excuse they wanted to intervene and destroy the Republic. President Sukarno, in a radio broadcast, branded the uprising as a design to overthrow the government of the Republic, and called upon the people to choose between the communist, Muso, and the legitimate Sukarno-Hatta government. Madium was quickly retaken by the *TNI* and by the beginning of December the revolt was crushed. Most of the *FDR–PKI* leaders were either killed or put into prison.

Prior to the Madiun revolt, the communists in Indonesia had been considered to be a dedicated, patriotic group, as indeed they had been during the Japanese occupation and the early stage of the revolution. Merdeka, not Marxist-Leninism, had been the rallying cry for them as for other groups in the days before Muso's return. After the revolt, however, the communists were seen as the proverbial "musang berbulu ajam" (wildcat in chicken's feathers). Assassinations and scorched-earth tactics of the communists in their last stands gained for them the undying hatred of the Indonesian Army. By 1949, communism as a movement seemed permanently discredited in Indonesia.

Though, internally, the Madiun revolt placed the very

revolution in jeopardy, it became the turning point in Republican attempts to enlist the sympathy of the West to their cause. The revolt had been originated by the communists and the Republicans had firmly crushed it. This fact was not lost on the United States, embroiled as it was in efforts to contain communism elsewhere in Asia. Up until this time, the United States had officially maintained a neutral position, with its European commitments with Holland tempering anticolonial sentiments. After Madiun this position changed and the United States then began to apply pressure on the Dutch.

Ironically, the Dutch themselves helped create further pro-Republican sympathy. Claiming that the Republic's operations against the *FDR–PKI* had infringed the borders established by the Renville Agreement, the Dutch, on December 17, 1948, presented an ultimatum to the representatives of the Republic in Djakarta. It demanded that the high commissioner be granted the authority to send Dutch Army units to any point in the Republic he thought necessary to maintain order. Acceptance of the ultimatum was demanded within eighteen hours.

Not only was the time allowed too short for the representatives in Djakarta to obtain an answer under any circumstances, but the Dutch had also ensured the outcome by cutting all wire communications to Jogjakarta.

After the Djakarta delegation refused to accept the ultimatum, the Dutch commenced the bombing of Jogjakarta at 5:30 A.M., on December 19. With this the Dutch began their "second police action." In one day they captured most of the Republican leaders and seized their capital, and then quickly occupied almost all the territory of the Republic.

World opinion was outraged by the Dutch move, and this time the reaction was swift. On December 22, 1948, the United States terminated Marshall Plan assistance earmarked for the Netherlands East Indies and threatened to cut off all aid to Holland—aid amounting to approximately $400 million annually which equalled what Holland was spending on its Indonesian campaign.

Then, on January 28, 1949, the Security Council passed an unprecedentedly strong motion demanding that the

Dutch restore the Republican government to Jogjakarta. The resolution further called for the resumption of negotiations, and for the transfer of sovereignty to Indonesia, to be effected no later than July 1, 1950.

The Dutch were then in serious trouble internationally and, moreover, the Republican territory was by no means pacified. An attack on Dutch forces in Jogjakarta was undertaken in March, 1949, by Republican units under the command of Lt. Colonel Soeharto. His troops occupied key points within the city and subsequently made an orderly withdrawal when Dutch reinforcements arrived. By this action the Republic demonstrated to other Indonesians and to the world that they continued to be a power to be reckoned with.

Negotiations were resumed on April 14, 1949, in Djakarta between Dr. Mohammad Roem and Dr. van Royen. An accord was reached on May 28, which provided for a ceasefire with negotiations to follow in The Hague. The end of three hundred and twenty-three years of colonial administration, over three years of Japanese occupation, and four years of revolution, was near at hand.

By now, however, the Indonesian freedom fighters were so suspicious of the Dutch that there was considerable doubt whether the Republican forces in the field would accept any negotiated compromise that could be obtained by their leaders. Many leaders, moderate as well as radical, urged a continuation of the war until a clear victory was attained.

It was the task of Lt. Colonel Soeharto to locate the "panglima besar" (supreme commander), General Sudirman, and persuade him to support the Roem–van Royen Accord by withdrawing from his guerilla headquarters and transferring with his staff to Jogjakarta, now again under Republican control. On July 10, General Sudirman, who had commanded the Republican forces since 1946 and was near death from tuberculosis, was carried on a palanquin into Jogjakarta in solemn procession. He died shortly thereafter.

On November 2, 1949, final agreement was reached at the Round Table Conference in The Hague. With the exception of West Irian—settlement of its much-debated status was postponed for a year—the entire former Netherlands

East Indies was transferred to the Federal Republic of Indonesia (Republik Indonesia Sarekat–R.I.S.). The agreement included an interim federal-style constitution and provided for sixteen member states—the Republic and fifteen created by the Dutch. Simultaneous with a transfer of sovereignty ceremony in The Hague, on December 27, 1949, the Dutch flag was lowered at Gambir Palace in Djakarta and the Indonesian red and white raised in its place. Merdeka had finally been achieved.

*　　*　　*

To the Indonesians, Merdeka meant not only new political rights but also new rights to their own natural resources. Article 33 of the Constitution of 1945 embodied these rights and stated that all resources of the land and water of Indonesia belong uniquivocably to the people.

Although the leaders of the revolutionary government were willing to concede some economic rights in exchange for political recognition by the Dutch, there was strong popular resistance to any such concessions. Three centuries of colonial domination had left its imprint on the minds of the people and, intoxicated with the spirit of Merdeka, it was by no means their intention to return anything to foreign control.

In the power vacuum created by the defeat of Japan and before the arrival of the victorious Allied forces, plantations, factories, oil fields, and refineries were taken over and informally made into the people's property. With the return of the Dutch and other former concessionaires under the aegis of the British, a little-documented struggle for these properties occurred within the revolution.

In the oil fields and refineries there sprung up indigenous companies organized and operated by groups of armed workers calling themselves *lasjkar minjak* (oil freedom fighters). These men, oil field and refinery veterans of the colonial days and the Japanese occupation, had the skills and equipment to place a limited amount of production at the disposal of the Republic. The revolutionary forces were, from the beginning, desperately in need of kerosene and aviation and motor vehicle fuel. The supply of these needs was the *lasjkar minjak's* self-appointed task in the revolution and they were determined to resist by force any attempts by the Dutch or others to reimpose outside control on what they considered to be their own industry. The revolution saw the development of three worker oil companies; one each in central Java, south Sumatra, and north Sumatra.

In north Sumatra, when news of Japan's surrender and Indonesia's declaration of independence was received, a tense situation developed as the newly formed *lasjkar minjak* units began openly challenging the Japanese managers and garrisons for control of the fields. The Japanese were in the process of withdrawing from the oil field areas to Medan to await the SEAC teams that were to administer their repatriation.

At Pangkalan Brandan, Djohan was the *lasjkar minjak* leader. Djohan, a large, forceful man, was one of the few Indonesians to achieve a position of some responsibility in the prewar oil industry. Born in western Sumatra, he attended a vocational school before joining Shell's northern Sumatra operations in 1926. He rapidly rose from apprentice laborer and in only eight months he became an assistant foreman. Later he was promoted to supervisor of refinery repair and maintenance operations and he also superivsed a number of construction projects. By the mid-1930s, he was Shell's head of maintenance and repair. In 1938, Shell sent him to Holland for six months of technical training. When war preparations began, all Shell employees were given military rank or rating and Djohan was designated a sergeant. His assignment was to destroy the fields and refineries when the Japanese invasion became imminent. To destroy what he and his men had so laboriously built over the years was more than Djohan could bear—he refused to carry out the assignment. Shortly thereafter, and while in the hospital, he was arrested for insubordination. Shipped to Java and imprisoned there, Djohan was eventually freed by the Japanese, and, in due course, returned to north Sumatra. There the Japanese enlisted his services to rebuild the Dutch-destroyed oil facilities. Upon inspection, Djohan promised to rebuild the works not in the hoped-for one year, but in eight months, which he did.

In late August, 1945, Djohan headed a delegation of six workers that went to the Japanese garrison commander and demanded a transfer of control. The commander, Colonel Sato, aware that he was held responsible for maintaining the fields, refused the workers' demands. "I then pointed to his head," Djohan relates. "And seeing our anger and determination, he knew what I meant." But Sato still refused to give them complete control and the workers began harassing the Japanese and calling for their ouster. At this point the Japanese head of personnel, Mr. Nagaharu Nakamura, intervened. Nakamura had developed a friendship with Djohan and he agreed to help Djohan get the fields.

By this time, the British and Gurkha troops had occupied Medan and were on the point of taking over the oil facilities to hold them pending Shell's return. The British commander had indicated his intention of moving his troops into the area. Nakamura, however, advised him to hold off lest the workers fire the wells. An understanding was reached between Nakamura and the British commander whereby, in the interest of maintaining order in the region, the fields would, as an interim measure, be transferred from the Allies through Nakamura to the Indonesians.

The transfer took place in September, 1945. Nakamura represented the Japanese and the representatives of the Republican government were Resident Abdul Karim and Laut Siregar, a lawyer. Djohan represented the workers. Addressing Djohan, Nakamura said, "The English Army has given me, Nakamura, the fields, so now I turn them over to you." This simple transfer was later followed by a formal signing ceremony.

As a historical side note, Mr. Nakamura entered the Japanese oil business after the war. He returned to Pangkalan Brandan in 1961 when a Japanese consortium undertook to assist in the rehabilitation of the area. He is currently managing director of Far East Oil Trading Company Ltd., a fifty-fifty Pertamina–Japanese joint venture which sells

Pertamina's production in Japan. Nakamura is sometimes jokingly told he should have kept what he had, since he seems to have spent the rest of his life buying it back.

Both the British officer in command and the Japanese agreed that the oil fields ultimately belonged to the Dutch and considered the transfer only a temporary expedient. There was, however, no question of ownership in the minds of Djohan and his workers—the fields were theirs, and they never meant to give them back to the Dutch.

The workers formed an organization with R. H. Sapardan, another ex-Shell employee, as general manager and with Djohan as his second-in-command. At this time, Teuku Mohammad Hassan, governor of North Sumatra, authorized a division of the North Sumatran and Atjehnese fields, the latter he assigned to Abdul Rachman and his deputy, M. Hassan Abbas.

The fields, pipelines, refinery, and port facilities were all in ruins from neglect, intentional destruction, and Allied bombing, and nothing could be done to restore production other than what the workers could do themselves. A small amount of crude was, however, produced and refined and marketed locally. The income from this source maintained the company on a barely self-supporting basis.

In the early morning hours of August 13, 1947, some three weeks after the Dutch began their "first police action," the workers, complying with instructions from Republican leaders, applied scorched-earth tactics to the oil refineries and depots, and organized a general evacuation north to Atjeh. The Dutch in nearby positions, upon hearing news of the destruction, decided not to occupy the area. They had no desire to subject themselves to guerilla attack over burned-out properties.

When Djohan saw that the Dutch were apparently not planning to enter the area, he and thirty of his workers re-occupied the deserted Pangkalan Brandan refinery. While establishing an advance party presence they began to make rudimentary repairs to the equipment. However, in December 1948, the "second police action" was launched, this time to finish off the Republic. Once again the workers destroyed Pangkalan Brandan's operating equipment which, at this time, consisted of little more than one small still. Again, the Dutch made no move to occupy the area and it remained virtually empty except for roving guerilla bands.

In the final stages of the revolutionary struggle, a number of workers and their families trickled back into the Pangkalan Brandan area. These were difficult times and food was very scarce. The main activity was growing crops for subsistence with the help of tools made from scrap metal. As time went on, some repairs were made and a small local trade in kerosene and gasoline was built up around Pangkalan Brandan. The destruction of the facilities remained nearly complete.

After the transfer of sovereignty in December, 1949, the north Sumatra workers and their families continued to scratch out a subsistence and continued making repairs. They built up a marginal, self-supporting oil business that continued for another eight years.

The south Sumatra *lasjkar minjak* group formed the Republic of Indonesia Oil Company (Perusahaan Minjak Republik Indonesia–Permiri) before the departure of the Japanese. Permiri was largely the creation of Dr. Mohammed Isa, the Republican government representative in south Sumatra. He felt that some measures had to be taken to prevent the *lasjkar minjak* from provoking open warfare with the Japanese. Also, Dr. Isa recognized the urgent need for oil both as fuel for the revolutionary forces and as a source of revenue for the Republic. In south Sumatra, the Japanese were only too willing to transfer the oil properties to the Indonesians, but such willingness offered no particular guarantee of their personal safety in the confused and emotion-charged environment. Dr. Isa recalls one tense incident:

> There was a lot of trouble between our people and the Japanese troops in Pendopo. I went there with the chief of police to investigate. When we arrived, the workers were in a highly excited state, running around with their 'bambu runtjing' [sharp-pointed bamboo lances] and guns they had just taken from the Japanese. The fields were confiscated and twelve of the Japanese were placed in the worker's custody.

Confrontations such as these between the Japanese and the Indonesians were becoming widespread throughout south Sumatra as resentment against the Japanese grew with an also growing anxiety over the future of the Republic. With the founding of Permiri, the situation became somewhat calmer as the restive *lasjkar* were given some direction and mobilized for specific tasks.

The driving force behind Permiri, was J.M. Pattiasina. He had entered the oil industry by going to work for Shell in 1935. He worked on the technical staff, specializing in refinery maintenance and operations at the Pladju refinery. He also devoted time to developing a refinery technicians' school in Pladju. By the outbreak of the war he was one of the three senior Indonesian technicians in the Shell south Sumatran organization. When the Japanese parachuted into the refinery area in February, 1941, Pattiasina fled to Java, where he evaded capture for almost a year.

The Japanese made a careful search for oil technicians whom they desperately needed to begin work on supplying their war needs for petroleum. Even Dutch prisoners from Shell were widely employed since few Japanese had any actual experience in the industry. Eventually Pattiasina was found by the Japanese and returned to Pladju where he was placed in charge of refining. After operations were running smoothly, he was put in jail. He was soon released, however, and sent to Sungei Gerong to help rebuild the Stanvac refinery that had been almost completely destroyed during the Dutch retreat. He also worked on a number of small field refineries in Prabumulih, Kentan, and Pendopo which had been set up in order to disperse the refining efforts to reduce vulnerability from Allied air attacks.

In south Sumatra the situation was somewhat complicated because, although taking over the Shell properties could be construed as aiding the revolutionary struggle against the Netherlands, Stanvac's presence in the area was also America's presence. While such distinctions would not occur to the men who made up the *lasjkar* units, the revolutionary government had to be more circumspect in their dealings with the Americans than with the Dutch. Accordingly, Stanvac was allowed to proceed ahead of the

SCRAP IRON STILLS FROM THE OLD REFINERY AT PANGKALAN BRANDAN—KEPT AS A MEMORIAL OF THE INDUSTRY DURING THE WAR AND REVOLUTION.

Dutch in surveying its damaged refinery. Work on the Stanvac refinery at Sungei Gerong began in 1946. Although Shell was able to get a few technicians into their Pladju refinery across the river, they found it necessary to wait until Dutch forces had obtained some control over the area before they could start any work.

On New Year's Day, 1947, the Dutch began a heavy air and naval bombardment of Palembang and a bitter fight lasted for five days. A negotiated settlement was reached whereby the Republican forces (out of ammunition) withdrew to a perimeter of the city some twenty kilometers out. With this withdrawal, Permiri was forced to set up headquarters at Prabumulih. Here Pattiasina again supervised the reconstruction of a partially destroyed field refinery from the occupation period. Other small refineries were jerry-rigged out of scrap metal at Pendopo and Mangundjaja.

Following the Battle of Palembang, the Dutch immediately began work to place their Pladju refinery back in operation. By mid-1947, both Stanvac's Sungei Gerong refinery and Shell's Pladju refinery were ready to receive oil—but there was no oil.

Permiri had taken over the two refineries when the Japanese left. They only grudgingly accepted the Republican government's decision to allow Stanvac to make repairs. To them the presence of any of the foreign oil companies brought back memories of a period they thought had gone forever. After the Battle of Palembang, Permiri evacuated the area of the refineries but they still maintained control of the oil fields and the pipelines. Instead of permitting any oil to go to the refineries, they built a number of small stills in the fields and these continued to supply fuel for the hard-pressed Republican forces. They also sold gasoline and kerosene in the local markets in the same manner as their compatriots in north Sumatra.

When the Dutch advanced in south Sumatra during the "first police action" Permiri units lost control of most of their field positions. Pendopo and Prabumulih were given up in August, 1947, and from that time the Republicans controlled only the Djambi field farther north, and a small field and refinery at Mangundjaja.

Djambi then became the major area of Permiri operations. Oil from Djambi was refined locally and also shipped through the blockade to Singapore where it was sold for much-needed foreign exchange. Also refined here at the Kenali Asem field was much of the aviation fuel used to fly Republican leaders on foreign missions. Djambi became an important supply base and the airfield was used by Republican as well as American and Australian pilots who overflew the Dutch blockade. Oil operations continued until the "second police action" in December, 1948, when Permiri had to evacuate the area and ceased to exist. Although Permiri was dissolved, and all the oil fields theoretically returned to the concessionaires, fighting continued sporadically in the area until the cease-fire in 1949.

During the period when the fields in north and south Sumatra were in the hands of the Republic, the local groups remained in control of their areas though they loosely coordinated their efforts with the regional representatives of the Republican government. Due to the Dutch blockade and generally poor communications, there was very little contact between the groups in Sumatra and the Republican government in Jogjakarta.

In Java, the Republican government set up a body which took control of all oil operations in central Java. This was the National Oil Mining Company (Perusahaan Tambang Minjak Nasional–*PTMN*). A regulatory body was also set up under Ir. Anondo as coordinator of mining and industry within the Ministry of Welfare.

PTMN's activities were mainly concerned with the old Shell holdings around Kawengan, including the refinery at Tjepu, and the smaller field of Bongas to the west. This part of north-central Java is a barren and poverty-stricken region and had been a traditional *PKI* recruiting ground. From 1946, with the formation of the first government-authorized labor unions, the political temperament of the area was always clearly to the left. Most of the roughly 1,200 workers in pre-Madiun Tjepu belonged to the Union of Oil Workers (Sarikat Buruh Minjak–*SBM*). When the Indonesian Communist Party established its headquarters in Jogjakarta in 1947, the new political direction of the *SBM* became quickly apparent. By the middle of 1948, almost half of the Tjepu workers belonging to *SBM* were vociferously in support of the *FDR*.

The recently returned Muso apparently kept the *SBM* leaders at Tjepu informed concerning his plans for rebellion. With hundreds of sympathetic workers, and access to the Kawengan fields and refining facilities, Tjepu was strategic to the interests of the *FDR–PKI*, as it was to the Republic. A few days after fighting broke out in Madiun itself, local rebels and about a fifth of the leftist *SBM* workers entered and occupied positions within the refinery area. There they awaited the arrival of pro-rebellion military units that were expected to join at Tjepu to bolster the worker defense there. As it turned out, however, government troops arrived first. For two days there was fighting throughout the Tjepu area and casualties were heavy among inhabitants who were caught in the crossfire. The rebels' stubborn defense was finally broken by the arrival of Siliwangi units from Madiun. Before they surrendered, the rebels destroyed much refinery equipment badly needed by the Republic.

With the "second police action" the remnants of the *PTMN* operations were moved back into the isolated fields of Nglobo, Semmangi, Ledok, and Wonotjolo. Evidently the Dutch did not consider these worth fighting for and even after the transfer of sovereignty, Shell made no serious effort to recover them.

Despite the uncertainties created by the revolutionary struggle, all three major companies returned to Indonesia just as rapidly as it was possible for them to do so. Although Stanvac had received some cooperation from the Republican government, for the most part the Big Three returned to Sumatra in the wake of Dutch military advances. Shell had technicians serving in military capacities, thus ensuring their presence even while recently captured areas were being secured. Due to its remote location in central Sumatra, and the presence of strong Republican forces, Caltex was the last to recover its properties. As they were recovered, most of the oil facilities lay in ruins. To facilitate the oil companies' reconstruction programs, the N.E.I. government approved "let-alone" policies which exempted reconstruction funds from exchange controls. These agreements were continued by the Indonesian government after independence. By the time of the transfer of sovereignty in 1949, all three foreign oil companies were busily engaged in rehabilitation, with both Stanvac and Shell soon approaching their prewar production.

CHAPTER 5

New Nation Politics

With the transfer of sovereignty on December 27, 1949, Indonesia completed its struggle to secure the independence that had been proclaimed by Sukarno and Hatta on August 17, 1945. Now the leaders could turn from revolution and negotiation to the manifold tasks of forming a government and rehabilitating the devastated economy.

Though there is little doubt that the agreements reached at the Hague were the best the Indonesian negotiators could obtain, the structure of the government they created had many obvious flaws. The new Republik Indonesia Sarekat (R.I.S.) consisted of sixteen states including the old Republic plus six other "negara" and nine small "daerah" of Dutch creation. By the new constitution, the legislative branch of government was to consist of a senate with two members from each of the sixteen states and a House with one hundred and fifty members to be elected on the basis of population. Though the old Republic contained over half of the population it was limited to one-third of the seats in the House and its voice was only equal to that of the smallest daerah (100,000 people) in the Senate.

As soon as this new government was created, demands began to made on all levels and in almost all areas for it to be changed from a federal to a unitary government. Demonstrations began and they were openly encouraged by Sukarno, Hatta, and leading cabinet members. They hoped to be forced by the people to create a governmental structure that they had sought but had been unable to obtain at the Round Table negotiations.

Though as an independent nation, Indonesia was presumably free to change to any government desired, the federal constitution had been negotiated and was a condition of their obtaining independence. The existence of a strong popular mandate was therefore considered necessary if the contemplated change of government was to be regarded as necessary, or in any case inevitable, by other nations and domestic opponents. Such a mandate, or at least visible evidence of it, was not difficult to obtain. Even most of those who believed a federal system was best-suited to Indonesia's needs recognized the one they had was clumsy and would be unworkable. The structure of the federal government was also regarded as the work of the colonialists and for that reason alone many people supported its change.

Opposition to the Unitary Movement was strong, however, in the new state of East Indonesia and among former members of the Royal Dutch East Indies Army (*KNIL*). The Moluccas and other islands of East Indonesia contained large Christian communities that closely identified with the Dutch. They also had a considerable trade with the Netherlands, and there was a certain amount of concern that this would be jeopardized.

By the terms of the Round Table the *KNIL* was disbanded. Some of the members were demobilized and others were to be merged into the Indonesian Army. The Dutch and Eurasian officers were particularly unhappy about these arrangements and at all levels there was dissatisfaction over salary, pension rights, and chances for promotion of ex-*KNIL* men in the *TNI*.

The Unitary Movement was greatly advanced in January, 1950, when Captain "Turk" Westerling, leading a force of demobilized *KNIL* troops, briefly captured Bandung and attempted to promote a coup. This overt military action, led by Dutch officers, added strength to the general feeling that the federal structure was a Dutch-imposed Trojan horse.

Beginning in February, eleven of the new states dissolved and merged with the Republic. Two more *KNIL*-supported revolts broke out in April in the state of East Indonesia and large-scale fighting took place before organized resistance ceased.

Negotiations during the month of May produced an agreement calling for the drafting of a new constitution which would create a unitary system of government. The result was the Constitution of 1950, duly ratified by both the Federal Government and the Republic and signed by President Sukarno on August 15, 1950. It was announced two days later on the fifth anniversary of the proclamation of independence.

The new constitution created a single-chambered Parliament made up of one representative for every 300,000 citizens. Pending elections, it was provisionally made up of the members of the House and Senate of the Federal Government plus fifty-nine additional members from the Republic, which had the effect of increasing the proportionate representation of the Republic. Apart from the elimination of the federal structure, the general pattern of the new constitution rather closely resembled that of its 1949 predecessor. As before, the president had the power to appoint the cabinet formateurs and to dissolve Parliament. The Cabinet, not the president, was responsible for the entire policy of the government. The president, by the terms of the new constitution, was thus technically removed from responsibility for the day-to-day affairs of state. Provision was also made for a vice-president, but his only stated role was to succeed the president in the event of death, disability, or absence. Like its predecessor, the Constitution of 1950 was only provisional. The permanent constitution would be adopted by the Constituent Assembly whose members were to be elected.

*   *   *

Indonesia, in a mere eight months, had transformed its government from federal to unitary with reasonably little discord. However, resolution of other matters would prove more difficult for the young republic. Of the many issues competing for attention, four were particularly important: (1) religion and the issue of a Muslim state; (2) regional discontent; (3) the place of foreign capital in the economy; and (4) the future of West Irian.

Differences over the relation of the Muslim religion to the Indonesian state were felt strongly enough to pose a threat to national unity. Indonesia is nominally 90 % Muslim, but many Muslims, including Sukarno, believed that the Indonesian state should be secular. The latter prevailed, and the ideological basis of Indonesia was, and still is, the Pantjasila (Five Principles), one principle being the belief in God—but with the affairs of state and religion separate. In direct opposition to this secular approach is a major concept of Muslim tradition—the Islamic State or "Darul Islam." The advocates of a Muslim state were sufficiently influential to create a threat to unity even during the struggle against the Dutch. In fact, by 1950, a Darul Islam had already existed for two years, complete with its own army, in the border country between West Java and Central Java. Its original anti-Dutch stance had by then degenerated into terrorism against the Republic. The federalist and non-religious government of the R.I.S. was considered by the many zealous Muslims to be a betrayal of the tenets of Islam. Some Muslim leaders still believe that, had general elections been held immediately following the transfer of sovereignty, an Islamic victory and an Islamic state would have resulted. By the time elections were held in 1955, the nationalist and communist parties had consolidated at the expense of the Islamic ones, denying them their victory.

Differences between the various regions also posed a major threat to national unity. A large amount of regional identification is to be expected where a nation is divided into a number of islands, but such identification is particularly deep-rooted in Indonesia. The histories and cultural traditions of the early kingdoms, the inconsistent impact of Islam, the divide-and-rule tactics of the Dutch, and the very fact that most of the physical revolution had been limited to Java and Sumatra, all contributed to the differentiation. Not a month passed after the transfer of sovereignty before revolts erupted in the outlying regions. Though they had different causes, they were all based in part on fears of Javanese domination.

Although the Indonesian leaders had overwhelmingly opted against federalism, they were by no means as one on the idea of a centralized government running the country from Djakarta. The Constitution of 1950, taking this sentiment into account, bowed in the direction of decentralization of governmental authority, but left the matter open for future decision.

Pursuant to the Constitution, the central government established provinces. However it also pre-empted most taxing authority, with the provinces receiving subsidies from the central government. In his 1954–1955 annual report, the governor of the Bank of Indonesia, Sjafruddin Prawiranegara, argued persuasively for more provincial autonomy. Addressing himself to the problem of balancing the budget, Sjafruddin noted that only about 12 % of regional government budgets were raised from their own sources with the balance coming from the central government. He maintained that those percentages could and should be reversed and that greater financial independence of the regions was necessary.

There were increasing feelings in the outer provinces that foreign exchange earnings were being applied disproportionately to benefit Java. Java, to be sure, had most of the people, but the outer islands had most of the exportable mineral resources and crops. As the feeling of unfairness grew, regionalists were increasingly inclined to take economic matters into their own hands by smuggling to Singapore from Sumatra and to the Philippines from Sulawesi and other eastern islands.

Compounding the religious and economic problems causing discontent in the regions, there was also tension in the army along regional lines between the territorial commanders (panglimas) and the Central Command in Djakarta. Not surprisingly, in light of the largely independent campaigns they had carried out against the Dutch, many army officers emerged from the revolution with the attitudes of autonomous rulers. As panglimas in the provinces, they often considered that they owed only nominal allegiance to Central Command in Djakarta.

Economic policy and, in particular, the role of foreign capital was also a divisive issue. In 1950, the Indonesian economy was predominantly foreign owned and managed in its industrial, export agriculture, transportation, and banking sectors. A survey commissioned by the government and published in 1952 stated the value of foreign investments in Indonesia in that year as U.S. $2,240 million of which $1,470 million was Dutch. Large Western firms dominated estate agriculture, shipping, aviation, banking, exporting, and oil, and were also important in internal distribution, manufacturing, and insurance. The Chinese controlled moneylending, land transport, rice milling, and many varieties of small-scale manufacturing. By contrast, Indonesian enterprise was limited, as it had traditionally been, to growing crops, largely on a subsistence basis, and to a few small manufacturing operations, particularly batik dyeing and making of kretek (clove-scented) cigarettes. Indonesians also raised some export cash crops including copra, tea, and coffee.

Earnings of foreign exchange through exports were small in terms of population. In 1950, stimulated by the rise in rubber prices caused by the Korean War, export earnings exceeded U.S. $1,000 million. It was to be twenty years before that mark would again be reached. In common with all developing nations, Indonesia experienced a gradual decline in the terms of trade in the two decades following 1950.

A source of special bitterness to many Indonesians was the assumption, at The Hague, of an external and internal debt amounting to over U.S. $1,000 million. About two-thirds of the debt was owed to Holland and it was widely maintained that the bulk of the debt arose from Dutch military operations against the independence movement.

Against this background, there was a crucial question that would recur well into the 1960s concerning the role that private foreign capital should play in the development of the economy. The new nation did not come to the question uncommitted, since the policy of the Republic had been to solicit international diplomatic support for its cause by offering assurances of an open and cooperative post-revolution investment climate. The Political Manifesto of November 1, 1945, stated, among other things, a willingness to share Indonesia's great latent wealth, and promised to return as much property as strategically possible to former foreign owners. This commitment was confirmed later in the Round Table Agreements whereby the Republic undertook to recognize and restore all legitimate and qualifying concessions and licenses granted under the former government, as well as to permit full exercise of the claimants' rights. However, the Round Table Agreements also recognized Indonesia's right to expropriate property for the public benefit with just compensation.

It would be wrong to infer that the Republic's economic assurances were given totally as a matter of expedience. They truly reflected the conviction of the moderate coalition in control during the revolutionary period and the early years of the nation. Although leaders like Hatta and Sjahrir were naturally attracted to Marxism by reason of capitalism's association with colonialism, they were also strongly anticommunist social democrats. Moreover, they pragmatically recognized Indonesia's continuing, and indeed urgent, need to employ foreign capital and technology. Allied with them, philosophically and often politically, were the modernist leaders of the Islamic community.

Opposed to the views of these men stood a coalition which, for want of a better term, might be named "radical nationalists." This group opposed the compromises made at The Hague and resented the Dutch foreign investments which the Round Table Agreements permitted to dominate the developed sector of the economy. They also resented the presence of the Dutch who continued to control much of the economy and the working lives of large numbers of Indonesians.

Sjafruddin, in his 1952–1953 Report of the Bank of Indonesia, noted the groundswell of popular sentiment:

> I would mention the feelings of hatred and aversion evinced by the Indonesian community in regard to foreign enterprise in general... as regards foreign industries, the economic problem in Indonesia must therefore be regarded as primarily psychological. Their feelings of hatred date back to colonial days and the subsequent revolution and are based on a false notion of the function of foreign capital in the present-day economy.

Even in financially sophisticated circles there was widespread feeling that the sooner foreign capital and foreigners left Indonesian territory, the better conditions would be for Indonesians. Unfortunately, much of the debate throughout this period on the role of private foreign capital tended to assume an "either-or" polarization. Either foreign capital must be accepted on the old colonial basis, or rejected in toto. Only later would Indonesia's leaders begin to look more closely at Indonesia's objections to the way foreign capital had operated in the country and begin redefining Indonesia's relations with foreign capital in terms of specific Indonesian objectives.

Unlike the differences of opinion on religion, regionalism, economic policy, and many other matters, the great majority of Indonesians stood together in their desire to liberate West Irian from the Dutch. In this unity of purpose lay the attractiveness of the issue for Sukarno. He not only passionately desired to exorcise that last vestige of colonialism from Indonesian soil, but he also saw in this issue a way to generate a heightened sense of national consciousness.

West Irian was the major unresolved issue at the Round Table. A fear that its continued discussion would hinder achievement of a basic settlement resulted in the issue being shelved for a period of one year. The status quo of West Irian would be maintained for one year, at the end of which the question of the area's future political status would be determined. To Indonesians, the only question to be debated was when the transfer would occur. To the Dutch, the question was whether or not it would occur.

The Indonesian claim was based on: (1) West Irian had been administered as a unit of the former Netherlands East Indies; and (2) there were historical, cultural, and economic ties between West Irian and the islands of Indonesia and at least 200,000 of the 800,000 residents of the territory were ethnically Indonesian. If the basis of the Indonesian claim was somewhat tenuous, the Dutch had no valid reason for retaining the area, though they belatedly sought to act as the defenders of Irianese rights to self-determination. In view of the historical precedent, it was not a convincing position.

In 1951, bilateral talks failed amid growing acrimony, and in November, 1951, the Netherlands Parliament officially incorporated West Irian into the Kingdom of the Netherlands.

Indonesia then placed the issue before the United Nations General Assembly where it was debated inconclusively three times between 1954 and 1957. In February, 1957, a resolution was introduced requesting the president of the General Assembly to appoint a Good Offices Commission to assist in negotiations between the Netherlands and Indonesia. Again, nothing conclusive resulted as the required two-thirds majority failed to be reached. From here the problem of West Irian passed from the field of diplomacy to the field of crisis politics.

*   *   *

Shortly after the American Revolution, George Washington, concerned about the havoc that political factionalism could bring to a fragile new nation, had expressed hopes that national affairs be conducted without the creation of political parties. Nearly one hundred and seventy years later, Sukarno and other Indonesians held similar hopes for their new nation. But such was not to be. Even before independence, the Indonesian nationalist movement had been highly splintered, and by 1950, there were well over two-dozen political parties and organizations and their numbers and divisiveness grew with the passing years.

The five most important of these political parties were the Masjumi, the Muslim Scholars, the Indonesian Nationalist Party, the Indonesian Socialist Party, and the Indonesian Communist Party.

The Masjumi party evolved from the giant Muslim corporation of the same name created under the Japanese in 1943. It encompassed all the varied Islamic communities throughout Indonesia, both modernist and conservative, syncretist and orthodox. It remained the dominant Islamic party but in the first few years after the transfer of sovereignty it experienced some drastic schisms. One of the groups which broke away was the conservative Muslim Scholars Party. The division had ideological overtones since the Masjumi leaders were reform-minded and generally pro-Western in their approach to politics and economic development. With the Muslim Scholars Party almost exclusively Javanese based, the split also had geographic characteristics which tended to become more pronounced as time went on. In effect, the Masjumi became the party of the outer islands, though it also had a following in west Java. On many political issues the Masjumi had close ties with the Socialist Party as both were strongly in favor of private foreign investment and took a pragmatic approach to economic development.

The Muslim Scholars Party (Nahdatul Ulama–*NU*) was conservative Muslim and strongly Javanese in complexion. It was founded in 1928, in opposition to the reform movement spreading through world Islam. Its leadership contained few men trained in economics or with modern administrative skills and its members generally held cultural and religious ministries in the cabinets in which the party participated. Politically, it has been described as opportunistic by reason of its willingness to join coalitions with strange bedfellows, most notably the communists. In principle, however, it probably shared with these groups an anti-Western orientation by virtue of its determination to defend national values against the inroads of Western cultural and political concepts.

The Indonesian Nationalist Party (Partai Nasional Indonesia–*PNI*) was Sukarno's original party as revived in 1945. With the attainment of sovereignty its original goals were realized and it became a leading party. There ensued a major struggle between its moderate and radical-nationalist wings, with the former dominating during the early fifties, and the latter increasingly thereafter. Sukarno became disenchanted with the *PNI* because he believed it had become ineffectual and had lost its old vitality and revolutionary fervor. The *PNI* leaders largely saw the party as the defender of the secular state against those forces that would impose an Islamic state. The *PNI* was also strongly Java-based. *PNI* members were in all levels of the bureaucracy but the party was relatively weak among members of the business community.

The Indonesian Socialist Party (Partai Socialis Indonesia–*PSI*) was the party of Sjahrir, who, with Sukarno and Hatta, formed the original triumverate of political leadership.

The party's origins and approach date back to the first ideological split in the nationalist movement in the late 1920s when Sjahrir and Hatta, freshly returned from Holland, argued their concept of a small party of cadres as opposed to Sukarno's mass-based approach. The *PSI* remained elitist and dominated by intellectuals who had received Western educations. It enjoyed great influence, notwithstanding its small size, by reason of the acknowledged abilities of so many of its members. Advocates of moderate democratic socialism, the *PSI* leaders were strong supporters of Indonesia's use of foreign capital and technology in the task of economic development.

The Indonesian Communist Party (Partai Komunis Indonesia–*PKI*) had also experienced divisions in its history. One part, the Murba (Proletariat) party broke its affiliation with the Communist International and became a genuinely nationalist party. The *PKI*, by far the larger faction, retained its international ties and accordingly, tried to follow Comintern worldwide strategy, even when this was not suited to the particular needs or opportunities in Indonesia. When it pursued the "right" strategy it sought to cooperate with nationalist leaders and parties, including those that in a historical context had been regarded as the enemy. When following the "left" strategy, the party adopted a truculent, noncooperative, and sometimes violent course with respect to bourgeois nationalists and any other groups that opposed their policies.

The party's success in following either a "left" or "right" strategy had not been great—they were usually out of step with events in Indonesia. Thus they were disastrously defeated in 1926 and they were again defeated, and created many and powerful enemies, at Madiun in 1948. In 1950, in trying to follow the current "left" strategy, they organized mass trade union movements and created industrial disruptions that most leaders found intolerable in the weak and struggling economy. Under a strongly pro-Western prime minister, Sukiman, the government took action against them and thousands of *PKI* members were arrested in a roundup called the Sukiman Razzia.

As had been the case following the previous debacles, the party leadership was reorganized. A younger faction

led by the Sumatran, Dipa Nusantara Aidit, came to control
the party replacing survivors of Madiun and Sukiman
Razzia.

The emergence of Aidit to party leadership corresponded
with a switch to the "right" strategy throughout the
communist world, as the cold war settled down to a nuclear
stalemate. The new line was formally enunciated by Aidit
on May 23, 1952, on the occasion of the 32nd Anniversary
of the party. The *PKI*, which had previously vilified Sukarno,
now acclaimed him as the great leader of the nation. Support
for the Cabinet—an unprecedented move—was pledged.
Even the more obvious of the party's leftist cliches and
slogans were dropped.

The change to the "right" strategy permitted Aidit to
enter tactical coalitions with various moderate parties,
including the *PNI*, in order to try to isolate and cripple more
formidable adversaries, including the Muslim Scholars,
Masjumi, and the *PSI*. Furthermore, by seeming to make
the *PKI* more responsive to Indonesian needs and espousing
nationalist aspirations, Aidit could proceed to build a
much larger movement than would have been possible
while following a "left" strategy.

Moving for increased power and control of the entire
political structure was President Sukarno. His all-consuming
interest had been, and would continue to be, the building
of a sense of national consciousness to bind together the
diverse cultures and peoples of the vast archipelago into
one Indonesian nation. At the time of the transfer of
sovereignty this job was hardly begun.

Flamboyant and a brilliant orator, Sukarno's favorite
description of himself, according to former U.S. ambassador
Howard P. Jones, was that of journalist Louis Fischer:

> The best key to Sukarno is love. He is the great
> lover. He loves his country, he loves women, he
> loves to talk about women, he loves himself.
> (Jones, p. 50 quoting Fischer p. 155)

Sukarno commanded the affections of the masses in Indonesia
in a way no other man could and even his political rivals
found it difficult to imagine governing without him.

Vice-President Hatta, by contrast, was a scholarly, reflective man with little flamboyance. Sukarno's description of Hatta says much about both men:

> Hatta [is] a man totally opposite to me in nature. Hatta is an economist by trade and disposition. Careful, unemotional, pedantic. A graduate of Rotterdam Faculty of Economics, he was still walking around mentally with those books under his arms, trying to apply inflexible scientific formulas to a revolution.
> (Adams, p. 117-Quote occurs in context of dispute over mass-based versus cadre tactics in the late 1920s.)

Hatta also supported the campaign to regain West Irian, but he advocated moderation with first priority being given to domestic economic development.

Hatta's political influence, then, was of a quite different sort than Sukarno's. If he had neither the inclination nor the charisma to single-handedly lead the country, his participation in government was an assurance to Sumatrans, other regional groups, and the people of various small party affiliation, that their interests were being considered.

The Sultan of Jogjakarta had power akin to that of Hatta and he symbolized the merger of the old and the new. Though he was the traditional feudal leader of millions of Javanese, he was also one of the strongest supporters of the independence movement. The sultan studied economics in Holland and was respected as a modernist and a man of high integrity. His participation in any cabinet lent it a special luster and added a warranty of fitness and integrity. In times of crisis, his name would always appear at the forefront of those proposed to form new cabinet.

The Indonesian National Army (Tentara Nasional Indonesia—*TNI*) also constituted a significant potential force. Many of its officers emerged from the revolutionary struggle with a deep mistrust of politicians and representative government. Throughout the revolution there was strong military resistance to civilian efforts to exercise control over army units and the political and military leaders often differed on how to achieve the common goal of obtaining independence. The military considered the politicians to be far too eager to negotiate concessions with the Dutch and both the Linggadjati and Renville Agreements had weakened the army's tactical position as a result of territorial concessions. When Jogjakarta fell in 1948, the military lost further trust for the politicians when Sukarno and Hatta and their staffs allowed themselves to be captured rather than going to the hills with the army. With most of the civilian leaders captured, only the army was left to maintain the Republic and thus the army leaders saw themselves as the major force behind the attainment of sovereignty.

Despite misgivings about civilian parliamentary democracy, the army was at first content to assume a nonpolitical role while devoting its energies to internal problems of organizing and consolidating forces. It was a major task of the Central Command to select, discipline, and integrate the ragged bands of irregulars that had emerged from the rice fields and jungles as the *TNI*. The leadership in this task fell to the young chief of staff, General A.H. Nasution.

General Nasution comes from Tapanouli, in the rugged interior of north Sumatra. It is an area which other Indonesians describe as producing good soldiers and crafty chess players. Nasution was one of the few army leaders to receive his initial military training in the Royal Netherlands Indies Army. Joining *KNIL* in 1940, after a brief period as a school teacher, he attended the Military Academy at Bandung until 1942, when he received his commission as subaltern. When the half-hearted *KNIL* resistance collapsed, he briefly went into hiding. After the Japanese released captured Indonesian military personnel, he returned and continued his training under the Japanese. During the revolution he became the commanding officer of the Siliwangi Division of west Java. The officer staff of this unit came closest to a professional elite in the Republican forces. Elements of this division were instrumental in crushing the communist revolt at Madiun in 1948.

After Madiun, Nasution was appointed the all-Java commander. In 1950, at the age of thirty-two, he was appointed army chief of staff and began his campaign of reorganizing the army. He was quickly faced with problems of both a political and a military nature. The army had to be greatly reduced in size and thousands of unruly partisan irregulars had to be dismissed. The structure of command had to be organized and consolidated. The Army Central Command had to be organized to permit autonomy in fiscal affairs and personnel assignment. In these undertakings, Nasution was often obstructed by the panglimas of the outer regions and by civilian politicians, both of whose interests lay in the creation of a more decentralized army.

The army found it could not attain its goals without political help and an informal alliance grew between army leaders and some of the *PSI* and Masjumi leaders with whom they had bonds of ideology, friendship, and sometimes kinship. It was with these groups that Nasution found support for his concepts of a centralist and modern *TNI*. However, the other elements in Parliament strongly opposed such consolidation, fearing it would ensure for their rivals, the *PSI* and Masjumi, a permanent hegemony over the real power of government. It was not difficult for these other groups to obtain support for their views from soldiers resentful of demobilization, and those panglimas seeking greater autonomy over their own areas of command. As a result, in 1952, considerable parliamentary pressure was placed on the Central Command to submit to nominal civilian government control. The army reaction took the form of a rather half-hearted coup known as the "October 17 Affair." Although not possessing any one strongly articulated view, the intention of those leaders participating was to press Sukarno to dissolve the "coffee house" Parliament, hold elections, and, in general to exercise more personal power.

Sukarno, however, although also disillusioned with Parliament, was not to be dictated to. Moreover, he was apprehensive about the chances of an Islamic sweep at the polls if elections were held at that time. Sukarno made his disapproval of the coup known over the radio and also did some behind-the-scenes maneuvering. The October 17 Movement collapsed and General Nasution resigned.

In retrospect, General Nasution feels that the semi-forced

retirement was what he needed to reappraise the Indonesian Army and its place in society. He concluded that not only had he been too naïve politically but that he had been mistaken in taking a too technocratic and managerial approach to army modernization. During the revolution, the army and the people had been one. By reforming along Western lines he was, in effect, moving away from that close association. In Indonesia, as he saw it, the army must constitute a social force following a "middle way" between that of the Western concept of the army as an apolitical servant of the state, and that of a total military takeover of government, as the military dictatorships of some Latin American countries. The army, to be most effective, must become involved in all sectors of the society. It would have both a civil and military function. Moreover it would stand as a corrective unifier and as the ultimate guardian of the revolution. Such were his conclusions, the concepts of the "middle way" and also of the "dwi-funksi" (the dual role). Nasution's chance to structure the army in accordance with his new views came three years later when continuing demonstrations of army loyalty persuaded Sukarno to reinstate him as chief of staff.

*   *   *

These, then were the major parties and forces that were quarrelling and competing in the political and economic arena of the developing nation. From the signing of the unitary constitution in 1950 until elections were held five years later, no less than five cabinets held power. The first three cabinets, generally coalitions of the moderates from the Masjumi, *PNI* and the *PSI*, maintained a considerable continuity of policy in spite of their almost-annual personnel reshuffles. Among other things, these cabinets attempted to hold down expenses and to make realistic projections of revenue. They also embarked on a series of moves to consolidate banking and credit systems, they introduced a system of cooperatives, they tried to reserve future manufacturing growth for Indonesians, and they launched a program to bring more Indonesians into trade and import businesses. The cabinets, however, resisted pressure to employ the extreme measure of nationalizing foreign business, arguing that such moves would be only destructive considering the lack of qualified Indonesians, and that such actions would jeopardize foreign exchange earnings and preclude future foreign investment.

In foreign affairs, they determinedly followed a nonalignment policy, one which they characterized from the beginning as "independent and active." This involved neutralism in the Cold War and a degree of moderation in the effort to obtain West Irian. Domestically, these cabinets took a firm line against labor agitation and other internal disorders. Prudent as these policies may have been on a long-term basis, they failed to produce results that could be seen by the people who had expected that a greatly improved standard of living would accompany the attainment of sovereignty. Because there was little concrete evidence of improvement in the lives of the people, extremist groups— and particularly the communists—were able to grow in power and they further exacerbated the feelings of frustration and discontent of the people.

This discontent manifested itself, in 1953, in the formation of the first cabinet dominated by the radical-nationalist wing of the *PNI* under Prime Minister Ali Sastroamidjojo. The first Ali Cabinet was in power for almost two years. In foreign affairs, its stance was more openly active as Sukarno began his drive to make Indonesia the leader of Third World nations. In April, 1955, the Ali government hosted the first Afro-Asian Conference in Bandung, West Java. At Bandung, Chou En-Lai, Nehru, and other leaders endorsed the principles of anticolonialism and nonalignment.

Domestically, Ali attempted to implement a much bolder program of Indonesianization than had his predecessors. The most drastic attempt in this direction was announced in August, 1954. From that time, 85% of all import licenses would be allocated to Indonesian nationals. It quickly became evident that the move was unwise, or at least premature. "Ali Baba" firms emerged with an Indonesian front man "Ali" given an office but no duties by "Baba" the silent-but-dominant Chinese or foreign partner. This system of allocating licenses became a natural breeding ground for corruption. This period also saw the beginning of serious inflation and a rather flagrant *PNI* party favoritism in staffing the bureaucracy. This staffing policy led to the appointment of a large number of Javanese to high positions in the outer islands, thereby increasing regional tensions. A conflict over the choice of the army chief of staff finally toppled the Ali Cabinet.

It was followed by a caretaker government of moderates under Prime Minister Burhanuddin Harahap who briefly held office during the long-awaited national elections. The task of organizing the elections and registering voters had been massive and expensive and took over two years to complete. The elections were held in September, 1955, and outside observers were impressed with the manner in which they were conducted. As had been hoped, the elections resulted in the elimination of a great number of the minor splinter parties (over forty had contested), and some interpreted this as a sign of the gradual maturation of Indonesian politics. The two surprises were the results of the voting for the *PSI* and the *PKI* parties. The socialists were almost eliminated, after drawing less than a million votes, while the *PKI*, a mere seven years after Madiun and five years after Sukiman Razzia, emerged with 16.4% of the vote which clearly placed the party—with Masjumi, *NU*, and *PNI*—as one of the four major parties.

All concerned had hoped that the elections would result in some mandate from the people, or at least an indication of their desires, upon which an effective government could be structured. This, however, did not result, and with the exception of the *PSI* losses and the *PKI* gains, the disputatious parties and factions were returned in about the same positions they had held before the elections.

When, inevitably "government as usual" returned after the elections there was heightened criticism by the press, first against the parties and then against the very legitimacy of the parliamentary system itself. The realization that the elections had not brought about a change in the quality of government acted as a catalyst for all the bitterness and frustrations that had built up in the years since sovereignty

was obtained. It became a period of futile search for scape-
goats while effectiveness of government continued to
decline. There were accusations of widespread corruption
and a governmental paralysis halted programs of economic
development and administrative reform. It seemed to many
that the political leaders had become impossibly remote
from the people and were serving only their own ends.
Feeble response by the parties' spokesmen to the multifarious
charges, suggested that even they had come to believe them.
In the eighteen months after the elections, the moderate
political parties and the political system itself fell into
disrepute.

Three powerful forces remained outside the workings of
the government and were thus untainted by its failures.
These forces were President Sukarno, the *PKI* (which
had been denied participation in any cabinet), and the army.

As president under the Constitution of 1950, Sukarno held
a position with relatively few formally delegated powers.
However, his actual power far exceeded that stemming from
his constitutional role as head of state. His prestige on the
popular level was unparalleled by that of any other figure
and this reality had to be taken into account by any cabinet
considering the formulation of policy that might run counter
to his views.

Three major factors enabled Sukarno to maintain and
increase his personal authority though lacking an organization
of his own: (1) the mutual mistrust of leaders both civilian
and military; (2) the lack of confidence of many leaders in
their own ability to govern; and (3) the lack of realization
by the tradition-oriented people concerning their own vital
role in the workings of democracy. "They [the masses]
looked to the government for paternal leadership, and
expected the leader to have the behavior and appearance of
a largely traditional nature." (Hindley, p. 240)

It was a role made to order for Sukarno. He exuded
self-confidence; he exploited the divisions in the power
structure of the day; and he eminently fitted the image of a
classical Javanese god-king. With few exceptions, in the
years 1950–1955, Sukarno seemed content in his role as
symbolic leader of the nation. However, as the political

situation deteriorated following the elections, Sukarno realized that major changes had to be made. Doubtless he also realized that he alone had the power and influence that would be necessary to make them. In short, Western imported democracy did not suit Indonesia at the current state of development and it could not cope with either its philosophy or its institutions.

Sukarno could reasonably count on General Nasution's backing in a drive to replace the parliamentary government with one headed by himself as executive. This, after all, had been the purpose of the October 17 Affair. Moreover, Sukarno knew he could offer Nasution the support he needed to extend Central Command control over the regional commanders. Nasution's situation in 1955, in this regard, was worse than it had been in 1952.

Following the October 17 Affair, one of Parliament's first moves had been to drastically cut the military budget. This forced the panglimas to form, or increase, their alliances with regional business groups, often as the only means of raising money to continue their functional responsibilities, including the payment of their troops' wages. Likewise, identification with, and support of, local political interests became increasingly necessary as they found themselves cut off from central government support. Thus regionalism was, in 1955, rapidly getting a military arm—an intolerable situation from the point of view of both Nasution and Sukarno.

Sukarno, a consummate political strategist, was, however, wary of the army. Possessing the guns, and potentially a strong centralized command, it might find the occasion to use more power than was fitting. If Sukarno was to expand the role of the army he needed some counterpoise and this he found in the *PKI*.

As a party, the *PKI* was the most competently led, the most tightly disciplined, and the most confident. Its large organizations for labor, farmers, and plantation workers were dominant in their respective fields. Its labor federation, *SOBSI*, included the very aggressive and fast-growing Union of Oil Workers (Persatuan Buruh Minjak—Perbum).

The *PKI* was also vastly ambitious and its seemingly

inevitable growth would have to be channeled toward the most constructive ends. Sukarno realized that both the army and the *PKI* were dangerously detached from accountability within the established political framework. Their increase in visibility might balance them against each other and this would also provide some degree of accountability, at least that of public opinion.

For all his fears of the army, *PKI* Chairman Aidit knew that an alignment with nationalism, and in particular with Sukarno, was not without its dangers. The mercurial Sukarno was still an unknown quantity and identifying with his brand of nationalism was definitely a gamble. A symbiosis of communist dogma and Sukarnoism might cause irreparable confusion in the party ranks. Numbers might be gained, but at the cost of commitment, and hence, reliability. At worst, Sukarno might, like Chiang Kai-Shek in 1927, savagely turn on the communists when they had served his purpose. However, Aidit had little choice, and he was fortunate that Sukarno needed the *PKI* as much as they needed him. But the price the *PKI* was to pay for new support was to be a significant loss of mobility and freedom of action.

Sukarno extended his patronage to yet another group, the "Generation of '45." Not strictly a party, this movement represented the regrouping of various forces from the revolution which would be expected to provide Sukarno with new symbols and new political lieutenants in the coming period. Prominent in the "Generation of '45" were the pemuda (youth) groups whose members had been of student age during the revolutionary struggle. As their name indicates, these men represented a theme of returning to the spirit of the revolution when petty sectarian differences were, with the mellowing of retrospect, seen to have been sublimated for the common cause. This was an ideal theme for the arch-nationalist, and self-proclaimed perpetual revolutionary, Sukarno.

When Sukarno began supporting one of the *PKI*'s long-professed goals, that of a national coalition government, with the *PKI* represented in the Cabinet, a political reaction set in among the conventional parties and even the radical nationalists. Fear of the communists, "political cannibals,"

as one Indonesian politician called them, now brought some
last-minute efforts at reducing the interparty strife. But it
was too late for that; ideological differences had become
too ossified and mutual scapegoating too bitter. By 1956,
the Islamic and nationalist parties had little in common
except their fear of the *PKI*. And Sukarno's speeches,
beginning in this period, hinted at his intentions to bypass
both the parties and the system.

Thus, on March 26, 1956, at the opening of the newly
elected Parliament, Sukarno emphasized the inappropriate-
ness of Western-style democracy for Indonesia, which he
said must develop forms reflecting its own heritage. In a
speech on October 28, 1956, in which he called attention to
the mistake in 1945 of establishing the parties, he told of a
recent "dream" of his that all political leaders, perceiving
the errors of the system, would unanimously agree to "bury
the parties." Two days later, he amplified this theme,
praising the single-mindedness of society in the People's
Republic of China which he had recently visited. Liberal
democracy had not been the answer to Indonesia's needs
and he said, "What I would like to see in this Indonesia of
ours is guided democracy, democracy with leadership, but
still democracy." Public reaction to these speeches was
varied and uncertain; nobody knew quite what Sukarno had
in mind with this implied "Konsepsi" (plan) for government
other than that he was opposed to the political parties.

Perhaps the most significant result of Sukarno's new
political alignment and his steady progress towards
authoritarianism came when Vice-President Hatta resigned
on November 30, 1956. In his last speech, Hatta deplored
the regression of Indonesian democracy, and he indicated
that he could no longer assume responsibility for the government's actions. Hatta's resignation had grave repercussions,
particularly outside Java. In December, 1956, the military
commanders of north, central, and south Sumatra seized
control of civil administration in their respective areas. This
was not a secessionist movement for they pledged loyalty to
the government. However, at the same time they called for
Hatta's return to government and increased autonomy for
the regions.

In February, 1957, after a silence of four months, Sukarno finally announced his "Konsepsi" at a mass meeting. He proposed, first, a new cabinet—a *gotong-rojong* Cabinet. He sought to evoke, by the choice of title, the traditional Indonesian spirit of community cooperation. All parties with a certain minimum number of seats in Parliament would be represented, including the *PKI*. Second, a National Council would be established, comprising all facets of Indonesian society, the parties, the military, youth, and religious groups, labor, etc. These functional groups were to speak for society as a whole in the same way as the new *gotong-rojong* Cabinet was to reflect a consensus in Parliament. And, of course, Sukarno himself would provide overall guidance towards consensus in both of these new bodies. The *PKI* and *PNI* accepted the new plan while the Masjumi rejected it out of hand.

In the meantime, a new autonomous command came into being in east Indonesia calling itself Permesta. The situation grew tense and newspaper editorials ominously speculated on the possibility of civil war.

With the second cabinet under Ali Sastroamidjojo on the verge of collapse, General Nasution, and his deputy, Gatot Subroto, decisively entered the scene. After first unsuccessfully attempting to reconcile Sukarno and Hatta, now not even on speaking terms, the two generals suggested to Sukarno that they impose martial law under the State of War and Siege Law. This law, first enacted in 1939, had, like most civil and criminal laws of the N.E.I., been incorporated by Indonesia. Invocation of the law would be a face-saving device legalizing the military control over civilian affairs and, thus, avoiding a direct confrontation between his forces and the regional commanders in Sumatra and east Indonesia. Under martial law, the Central Command would also have a wide range of powers and options with which to tackle the regional crisis. The President accepted this strategy, and on March 14, 1957, he proclaimed martial law. The death knell of parliamentary democracy was tolling.

While Sukarno began to implement his new-style democracy, the regional issue entered a sort of limbo.

Meanwhile, national frustrations over West Irian increased, aggravated by constant *PKI* agitation. The West Irian issue increasingly manifested itself in harassment of the Dutch community. Although by 1957, Dutch investment had dwindled drastically the popular wisdom continued to blame the nation's economic difficulties on the presence of the Dutch, and to a lesser extent the Chinese.

In 1956, after an unsuccessful attempt to negotiate further modifications on the Round Table Agreements, Indonesia repudiated most of its debt to Holland. On December 1, 1957, a few days after the United Nations' failure to create a Good Offices Committee for the West Irian dispute, and one day after President Sukarno miraculously escaped an assassination attempt (later linked to Islamic extremists), the government declared a twenty-four hour general strike against Dutch firms, a ban on Dutch language publications, and a cancellation of Royal Dutch Airlines (KLM) landing rights. Passions, at this point, quickly carried the movement beyond the government's control. On December 4, the Dutch-owned Royal Packet Shipping Company (KPM) was seized without Cabinet knowledge, by a *PNI*-affiliated seamen's union. Even in the supercharged atmosphere, this precipitate move surprised everyone, including the *PKI*. However, the latter's labor front, *SOBSI*, quickly took the initiative. Two days later, Prime Minister Djuanda, heading an emergency extra-parliamentary cabinet, announced the closing of all Dutch consulates and the expulsion of all Dutch nationals except a few experts and technicians who were required to stay. Formally taking control of the confiscated properties, he turned them over to General Nasution under the War and Siege Law. This military assumption resulted in some confrontations with the communists who had taken initial control over many seized properties. The *PKI* relinquished the properties to the military.

There is no doubt that the nation needed strong leadership, and Sukarno was ready to provide it with his Guided Democracy. However, before Sukarno could bring his plans to full fruition, he had to confront a challenge to his power that would threaten the very future of the nation.

As December reached a close, many respected leaders who had consistently opposed Sukarno's increasing alignment with the *PKI* and who had been subjected to a constant stream of abuse and threats, proceeded to central Sumatra where, two months later, they declared an alternative government, the Revolutionary Government of the Republic of Indonesia (*PRRI*) under Sjafruddin Prawiranegara.

CHAPTER 6

Search for an Oil Policy

At the time Indonesia obtained independence, all three foreign oil companies had returned and were busily engaged in rehabilitating their facilities. Faced with the active presence of the companies, and with the foreign investment guarantees of the Round Table Agreements just concluded, it was logical that the new government would elect to confirm the "let-alone" agreements concluded by the N.E.I. government with the Big Three. Apparently, this was done with little discussion; presumably the issue was lost in the press of more urgent matters that followed the transfer of sovereignty.

The question soon arose as to the status of the former Shell concessions in northern Sumatra and central Java that had remained in Republican hands for the duration of the struggle for independence. Since both northern Sumatra and central Java were within the boundaries of the Republic, as the boundaries of that member state were defined under the federal constitution, it was the Republic, as a member state of the R.I.S., that first devised a plan for them after the transfer of sovereignty. This Unification Plan, largely drafted by Ir. Anondo, called for the creation of a Central Petroleum Board to administer oil facilities in both northern Sumatra and central Java. The purpose of the plan was to,

> restore production, to provide work for the workers, and to end the near chaotic conditions in the management resulting from obscure authority

104

... thereby improving the central government's control. The petroleum administration was to facilitate the restoration to the Dutch proprietors if the conditions for return were met. However, it reportedly would be ready to continue operations itself if [Shell] was not in a position to return. (Sutter, p. 816)

Before the Unification Plan could be implemented, the federal government was changed to a unitary government in August, 1950. By an act of the first cabinet under the unitary government, oil affairs were placed under the jurisdiction of the minister of trade and industry, Dr. Sumitro Djojohadikusomo. Dr. Sumitro was one of the Western-educated, elitist, and pragmatic members of the *PSI* party who played very important roles in the early Republic. Although only thirty-two years old, Dr. Sumitro had already established a reputation as an economist. During the revolutionary period he had served the Republic, first as minister plenipotentiary for economic affairs in Washington, D.C., and later as chairman of the Republican delegation's Economic and Financial Sub-committee at the Round Table negotiations. There he devised and presented the Indonesian argument on the question of the debt owed the Netherlands. Starting with the figure presented by the Netherlands delegation, Sumitro demonstrated that once the war-related figures were subtracted, the Netherlands actually owed Indonesia money—a conclusion which reportedly astonished and shook the Netherlands delegation.

Dr. Sumitro believed that in the immediate future Indonesia must maintain existing, and attract new, foreign investment. This required a favorable investment climate, and to establish such a climate Indonesia must, among other things, fulfill the commitments made at the Round Table, including the return of the Shell concessions. Thus Dr. Sumitro opposed the plan to unify the fields under government control. His position was that the Round Table Agreements were explicit on the matter of ownership—the fields belonged to Shell—and accordingly there was no basis for government intervention.

Although the return of the fields to Shell was not inconsistent with the Unification Plan, the plan did expressly recognize the possibility of retention by the government. Moreover, it was known that some groups wanted to use the plan to forestall a return, while they gained time to prove to Parliament that Indonesians possessed the capabilities needed to repair and operate the fields.

Whatever the legal and economic merits of Dr. Sumitro's stand, it failed to take into account the changing political climate and the increased opposition to return. Already voices from leftist political parties, labor groups, and radical nationalists, were arguing that Indonesia should retain the fields and that Indonesia could develop them as well as Shell. Nirwonojudo, the manager of the central Java operations, decided to take action based upon these nationalist feelings. Nirwonojudo was a lawyer who had been involved in oil since the early days of the revolution. To some who knew him he was a visionary—idealistic, socialistic, and a bit impractical. Others are more harsh; in their view he was simply a political opportunist. Although not a communist, he shared the view of many in Indonesia that he could work with the communists.

In the face of Dr. Sumitro's disapproval, Nirwonojudo made a play to take control of the northern Sumatra fields. In January, 1951, with backing of the leftist oil union, *SBM*, he announced the establishment of the Republic of Indonesia Oil Mining Enterprise (Perusahaan Tambang Minjak Republik Indonesia–*PTMRI*). Under supposed authorization of the Unification Plan, Nirwonojudo left the central Javanese fields under the administration of his assistant, and proceeded to north Sumatra. Taking advantage of a vacancy in the office of governor of North Sumatra, Nirwonojudo announced the suspension of Djohan as the local manager of Langkat. Quickly, Nirwonojudo began negotiations for the export of crude oil to Singapore. If Nirwonojudo had been able to complete a sale, his plans might have succeeded. The Cabinet fell in March, 1951, and with a successful sale behind him, Nirwonojudo might have been difficult to dislodge. However, Dr. Sumitro, working in conjunction with the newly appointed governor of north

Sumatra, quashed the plan. Upon learning of the export plan, Dr. Sumitro sent a cable to the new governor instructing him to stop the exports. Nirwonojudo's office in Medan was raided for "smuggling" and, thus stymied, he returned to Java.

On March 1, 1951, the terms of a temporary truce were worked out. Management in central Java was left with Nirwonojudo's *PTMRI*. In north Sumatra, Sumitro instructed the governor to divide the management between Atjeh, were Teuku Amir Husin al Mudjahid would continue as general manager, and Langkat, where Djohan would be in charge. Both managers were instructed to work towards facilitating the return of the oil fields and the other properties to Shell.

This early skirmish foreshadowed much of what was to come in the 1950s. There was conflict over the basic question of retention of the fields, rivalry for their control, and a consequent failure to develop either the central Java or north Sumatra fields.

*   *   *

In August, 1951, Parliament focused its attention on oil for the first time. Teuku Mohammed Hassan, chairman of the Committee on Trade and Industry, had a natural interest in oil. An Atjehnese, he had been appointed as the first governor of North Sumatra, the birthplace of Shell and the site of the now-disputed Shell concession. Moreover, as governor he had played a role in the transfer ceremony in 1945. In 1951, Hassan spent several months studying the many aspects of Indonesian oil and mining. He came to two conclusions: (1) there was good reason to believe that, if nationalized, the north Sumatra oil fields could be made into a paying proposition; (2) Indonesia was not getting an adequate return from the foreign companies under the "let-alone" agreements and existing taxes.

Hassan did not advocate legislation based merely on his own study. Instead he drafted, and obtained support for, a motion to create a commission to inquire into oil and mining problems. The motion was supported by the Cabinet and passed unanimously on August 2, 1951. By the motion Parliament:

I. Urges the Government to form within one month a State Commission of Mining Affairs, with the task of:

  (a) investigating as soon as possible, problems of oil extraction, and of tin, coal, gold, silver, and other mining in Indonesia;

  (b) drafting an Indonesian mining law in harmony with present conditions;

  (c) providing the Government with its considered opinion on the attitude to be taken by the Government concerning the status of the oil extraction in north Sumatra in particular, and other oil production in general;

  (d) providing the Government with its considered opinion on the status of mining in Indonesia;

  (e) providing the Government with its considered opinion on taxes on petroleum products and the fixing of oil prices;

  (f) making other proposals concerning mining matters to the enrichment of the State; completing its report within three months, and submitting it to the Government and Parliament.

II. Urges the Government to postpone all granting of concession and exploitation permits, pending the results of the work of the State Commission on Mining Affairs.

The commission authorized by the motion was given three main tasks: (1) to advise on tax arrangements with the Big Three; (2) to draft a new mining law; and (3) to advise on whether the former Shell concessions in north Sumatra and central Java should be returned to Shell.

Of these, the first was the most pressing. Stanvac's "let-alone" agreement was to expire at the end of 1951, while the agreements with Caltex and Shell would expire at the end of 1953 and 1955 respectively. Thus negotiations with Stanvac were approaching as the commission began its work.

Two events in world oil provided an important backdrop to the deliberations of the commission. In Venezuela, in

1948, a new government had won major concessions from the foreign companies based on a fifty-fifty split of profits between the company and the Venezuelan government. After initially resisting this formula, all the Majors adopted it as a new line of defense in their worldwide negotiations with host countries, perceiving that fifty-fifty had a natural sound of equity to it.

The other event occurred in Iran in 1951. Led by an aged revolutionary, Mossadegh, Iran nationalized the holdings of the Anglo-Iranian Oil Company (now British Petroleum— BP) which held all of the concessions there, and turned them over to a newly created national company. The Iranian adventure ended three years later with a settlement whereby Anglo-Iranian received compensation. A new eight-company consortium was formed including BP, Shell, Jersey Standard, Socony Mobil, California Standard, Gulf, Texaco (all the parents of the Indonesian companies were thus involved), and the French, Compagnie Française des Pétroles.

The venture was a costly one for Iran. Mossadegh's basic premise was that the British needed Iran's oil more than Iran needed oil customers. Accordingly, Iran rejected several proposals which would have reorganized the National Iranian Oil Company and created a new Anglo-Iranian subsidiary (with Iranian participation on the board of directors). In the face of Iran's refusal to compromise, Britain's Foreign Office announced it would enforce an embargo against any country attempting to purchase Iran's oil. It then supported this declaration by bringing lawsuits against several Italian and Japanese purchasers and this deterred all other buyers. Iran lost three years of oil export earnings before a settlement was reached.

So far as is known, no responsible Indonesian leaders urged adoption of the course taken by Iran, but great attention was focused upon the Venezuelan settlement.

Hassan, in his speech in support of his motion of August 2, stated that the Big Three were actually earning five times as much as they reported. He contended that they kept prices of crude much lower than they should be, and as evidence he cited an offer by a Japanese group to pay 950 rupiahs per ton of crude, compared to the 100 rupiahs per ton the companies were reporting for tax purposes. Secondly, Hassan contended that the companies were improperly inflating their operating costs.

Interestingly, in discussions between Hassan and foreign oil company officials shortly after the Hassan motion was published, the companies proposed a fifty-fifty profit split. Hassan replied that he feared operational costs would then rise. He countered with a proposal that the proceeds from production be shared on a fifty-fifty basis, which reportedly left the foreign officials nonplussed.

After two years of negotiations, complicated by two cabinet changes, Stanvac and the government reached a new "let-alone" agreement in March, 1954. Stanvac undertook a four-year investment program of $70 million to $80 million from funds earned abroad. To facilitate this investment, Stanvac was given an exemption from import duties on all imported capital equipment. The tax arrangements of the agreement approximated the fifty-fifty formula obtained by other producing countries. Stanvac also undertook to continue efforts to Indonesianize its staff and to extend Indonesianization to the top levels of local management. The term of the agreement was four years, although the exemption on import duties was for ten years.

The Stanvac agreement set the pattern for the later agreements with Caltex and Shell. The agreements of Caltex and Stanvac were later extended so that they would terminate concurrently with Shell's at the end of 1960.

The second task given to the commission was to draft a new mining law to replace the N.E.I. Mining Law of 1899. Not until the end of 1956 did the State Commission on Mining Affairs submit a draft to Parliament, and even after this was done, Parliament failed to act. In drafting the law the commission was plagued by the fundamental split which existed over the role foreign capital should play in Indonesian development.

Meanwhile, the government elected to strictly implement Part II of the Hassan Motion whereby Parliament urged, "the Government to postpone all granting of concession and exploitation permits, pending the results of the work of the State Commission on Mining Affairs." Ironically,

virtually no discussion had been devoted to the postpone-
ment provision when the motion was considered. It was,
of course, a sensible provision in terms of the three months
which the commission was originally given to complete its
task. In fact, the provision continued in effect for ten years
and proved most costly to both the companies and the
government.

Various reasons are cited for the long delay in enacting
a new mining law. A common explanation is that the time
was needed simply to do a proper investigation. Others
suggest that influence of the Big Three was responsible.
However, Shell and Stanvac were not well-served by delay
since they very much needed new areas to develop. Another
possible cause of delay that is sometimes cited is the struggle between regionalists and Djakarta over the allocation of
government revenue originating in the provinces. Whatever
the causes, the decade closed without the enactment of a
new oil or mining law and without the granting of any new
oil concessions.

Even so, Indonesian oil production increased steadily
throughout the 1950s. In 1951, production was 151,900
barrels per day and by 1959 this had increased to 373,100
barrels per day. These figures, however, conceal the fact
that Indonesia was losing its position among world oil
producers, dropping from fifth to twelfth from 1940 to 1960.

Caltex was the least affected by the freeze on new
concessions. It had been the last of the Big Three to return
to Indonesia, assuming operations in its swampy, jungle-
covered concession area in January, 1949. Before the war it
had been a company joke that the initials of the Indonesian
subsidiary, *NPPM*, stood for the "Non-Producing Petroleum
Men." But the company had every expectation that its
costly groundwork in Indonesia would soon pay off.
During World War II, the Japanese, using drilling equipment
already in position at a site selected by Caltex geologists,
had struck oil in the Minas field. In 1950, Caltex set about
the task of exploiting Minas while continuing exploration
efforts elsewhere in its concession. In May, 1952, the first
exports of crude from Minas were shipped in shallow-draft
tankers via the Siak River.

With Minas, and to a lesser extent, Duri, promising bountiful returns, Caltex undertook a $50 million expansion program as agreed in the extension of its "let-alone" agreement with the government. The key project in the expansion was the development of a harbor for ocean-going vessels at Dumai, then a small coastal village of perhaps 400 people. By constructing a new wharf and tank storage facilities at Dumai, Caltex could avoid the tanker draft limitations of the Siak River. A thirty-inch pipeline was constructed from Duri to Dumai and two additional pipelines were built from Duri to the Minas field. Caltex also constructed a road which cut through the thick jungle between Pakanbaru in the south to Dumai in the north, a distance of 180 km. (112 mi.). On July 15, 1958, Duri crude was for the first time pumped through the new pipeline to a 38,000 dwt. tanker alongside the new wharf at Dumai. A year later all the facilities were completed, and Caltex ceased using their river tankers.

By 1954, Caltex crude oil production had reached 43,000 barrels per day. By 1956 this had doubled. From zero production at the beginning of the decade, Caltex production climbed to over 200,000 barrels per day by the end of the decade. Minas would become one of the twenty-two fields in the world to produce over one billion barrels of oil (a mark reached in 1969), and the only field in Indonesia to do so. Meanwhile, besides its Duri and Minas fields, Caltex discovered five additional fields and many other promising sites awaited further exploration.

Caltex was perfectly content to leave the price-controlled local marketing to Stanvac and Shell. Although the construction of a refinery was periodically discussed with Indonesian authorities, Caltex preferred to limit its Indonesian activities to exploration and exploitation with all of its crude going to foreign markets.

Caltex initially proposed building its field headquarters in the town of Pakanbaru on the Siak River, however, Muslim leaders in the town opposed such a Western intrusion. Consequently, Caltex constructed its town on the other side of the river at Rumbai, 6 km. (3.7 mi.) to the north. The contrast between the model American-style community which eventually took shape in Rumbai, and in the town of Pakanbaru became the source of some political difficulty, but, on the whole, Caltex was in the least politically exposed position of the three foreign companies. Unlike Caltex, both Shell and Stanvac had developed fully integrated Indonesian operations prior to World War II and both sought to return to such operations after the war. Stanvac's concessions were all located in south and central Sumatra and its sole refinery was at Sungei Gerong near Palembang in south Sumatra. The fields near the refinery were, in general, fully explored and developed. In central Sumatra, however, Stanvac had discovered the promising Lirik field in 1939, and it remained to be exploited. With the production leveling off in the south, and few other prospects there, Stanvac needed to develop Lirik; the extension of the "let-alone" agreement in 1954 paved the way to do so.

The Lirik field lay in the same kind of swampy, jungle land that Caltex was working 100 km. (62 mi.) to the north. To get the oil out, Stanvac built a 94 km. (58 mi.) road and a pipeline to the Siak River. The oil was carried to the Sungei Gerong refinery by small tankers. The Lirik field came on stream in 1958, at 12,000 barrels per day.

While Lirik was being developed, Stanvac introduced modern secondary recovery techniques in its south Sumatran fields in an effort to arrest the declining production there. Although they enjoyed some success, this solution was at best a stopgap; Stanvac desperately needed new concession areas. Because of the Lirik field, Stanvac's production continued to rise in the 1950s to a peak reached in 1960. But by 1960, in the fields the engineers knew what the statistics failed to reveal: there was not enough to do.

While Stanvac strained to maintain production, it proceeded with a $40 million modernization of its refinery at Sungei Gerong. At the end of the war, Stanvac had found the refinery devastated, but by 1949 they had rebuilt it to something over prewar capacity. In 1954, they undertook to bring the refinery up to completely modern standards and capacity was raised from 64,000 to 71,000 barrels per day. The first catalytic cracking unit in Southeast Asia was also installed along with a polymerization unit, a sulfuric acid plant, and additional water, steam, and electrical power facilities. By the end of the decade, Stanvac was, like Shell, importing crude oil from abroad to supply its refinery.

Shell's activities were the most geographically diverse of the three companies. Large refineries were located at Pladju near Palembang, at Balikpapan in east Kalimantan, and in addition there were two small refineries on Java at Wonokromo south of Surabaya and at Tjepu in central Java. Shell was faced with a shortage of local production throughout the 1950s which was met by the import of crude, first from Sarawak and later from the Middle East.

Indonesian marketing of oil products was approximately 60% controlled by Shell and 40% by Stanvac, with the Indonesian companies contributing a trickle. Both companies retained ownership of their service stations, leasing them to independent dealers who paid a nominal rental of one rupiah a month. The companies performed major maintenance and repairs on the stations. Gasoline ("bensin" in Indonesian) was supplied on a pay-on-delivery basis with the company also acting as collector of the government sales tax. Kerosene, the other principal domestic petroleum product, was distributed through a relatively small number of independent dealers, most of whom maintained networks of subdealers who made delivery throughout the archipelago.

During the 1950s, the demand for both kerosene and gasoline greatly increased. In the case of gasoline, this was attributable to the great increase in the number of motor vehicles. In the case of kerosene, the increased usage reflected a changeover from wood and charcoal, stimulated, in part, by a desire to be modern, but probably more stimulated by the unrealistically low price at which kerosene was sold.

Both kerosene and gasoline were selling at bargain prices and the bargains increased as the decade progressed. Indonesia had inherited an extensively controlled economy from the Dutch and both gasoline and kerosene were among the commodities that were price controlled. As the 1950s progressed, the government failed to raise gasoline prices sufficiently to keep up with increases in cost. This was due in part to inertia, in part to the desire to avoid the public outcry which always attended such increases, and in part to the desire to squeeze the foreign-owned oil companies. As a consequence of the financial squeeze, the companies failed to construct additional service stations, and, in addition, reduced maintenance of all facilities. By the end of the 1950s a number of undesirable practices had arisen. In the topsy-turvy deficit operations, Shell rewarded its salesmen on their ability to limit sales rather than increase them. Orders of price-controlled fuel products were conditioned upon accepting orders of non–price-controlled lubricating oils. Requests for repairs to service stations were largely ignored. These were merely the first warning signs of a major crisis to come in domestic marketing.

*   *   *

Indonesia had inherited from the Dutch a fairly complete set of labor protective laws and practices reflecting a humanistic thrust of Dutch policy against laissez faire capitalism. Minimum wages were prescribed, albeit at a very low level. The working week was limited to forty hours and the status of unions was recognized. There was, however, no provision for the designation of a single union as the exclusive collective bargaining agent of an industry or plant and this gave rise to perpetual competition between unions. A multiplicity of unions existed in the oil industry and most were affiliated, at least loosely, with political parties.

The most militant of the unions in the oil industry in 1951 was the Perbum, a *PKI* affiliate. The links between the Perbum and the *PKI* ran through the All-Indonesian Central Organization of Labor (*SOBSI*). *SOBSI* was organized in 1946 to be a coalition of the entire Indonesian labor movement, however, from the beginning, it was dominated by communists. The other non-communist unions had dissociated themselves from it by the time of the transfer of sovereignty. This left *SOBSI* as the organization of *PKI*-affiliated unions and there was considerable overlap between its leadership and the leadership of the *PKI*. In

1950, *SOBSI* had a membership of 200,000, but a year later the membership had increased to 1,000,000 due to its militant stance and the workers' disappointment over lack of improvement in living standards. Other *PKI* affiliates existed in estate agriculture and a number of other fields including women's and veteran's groups.

In February, 1951, in an attempt to cut off Indonesian exports that were aiding the U.N. action in Korea, the *PKI* succeeded in organizing a strike of 500,000 estate workers and members of shipping-related unions. Violence became commonplace, and some European planters were killed. Against this backdrop, the government issued Military Decree No. 1 on February 13, 1951 which prohibited strikes in "vital" industries. Virtually all industries were classified vital, including oil. In June, despite the ban, the *SOBSI* launched new strikes, ostensibly over the issue of annual bonuses. By the end of June most of foreign-owned enterprises were shut down, including the oil industry. Amid increasing violence and disorder, the government, under Premier Sukiman, moved against the *PKI* and by the end of the month 15,000 people were in custody. A series of emergency laws designed to stabilize labor relations followed. On September 17, the government rescinded the law on strikes and promulgated instead Emergency Law No. 16/1951 which established a system of compulsory mediation and arbitration.

During the first Ali cabinet three years later, a number of reforms were introduced. A collective labor agreement law specified a two-year time period for all labor agreements with a one-year extension permitted. The minister of labor was also empowered, after consultation, to extend settlements to other areas of the same industry.

As anti-Dutch feelings arose in the later half of the 1950s, the unions took a new stand against Dutch firms. It was the unions, and not only the communist affiliated ones, that initiated the takeovers of Dutch properties at the end of 1957. As the decade closed, the Perbum had emerged as the dominant union in the oil sector. It was always at the forefront of labor-management conflicts and was second to none in striving for higher wages as well as promoting non–bread-and-butter issues such as more worker and Indonesian participation in management.

Before the War, when only a handful of Indonesians received any secondary or college education, the oil companies had little incentive or opportunity to Indonesianize at the staff and management levels. After the transfer of sovereignty, the companies were not slow to realize that Indonesianization of management would be at the forefront of the demands which they would face from the Indonesian government. Lest there be any doubt that this would be the case, the Round Table Agreements themselves expressly provided for regulation to the end that at the "earliest possible period, eligible Indonesians" might be brought into the "direction [management] and staff" of all business enterprises in Indonesia; and further, for the provision of training courses "with the objective that after a reasonable period, the predominant part of the leading staff personnel of the enterprises will consist of Indonesian nationals." (Financial and Economic Agreement, The Hague Agreements, Article 3).

Throughout the 1950s, there were differences between the companies and the Indonesian government respecting the pace of Indonesianization. Thus the mid-1950s agreements between the government and the respective companies included specific commitments on Indonesianization. The companies' new point of view was indicated by Stanvac in 1953:

> The management considers that one of its important objectives is to train the greatest possible number of its Indonesian employees in the technical and administrative skills that are required in the oil industry. Emphasis on such training is important to the future progress of the nation. It is also important that opportunity should exist for each employee to advance according to his ability and efforts.
>
> The highly technical nature of the oil industry requires the employment of a number of trained

specialists from overseas because an adequate supply of such personnel is still not available locally. The aim, however, is to train Indonesians for these technical and supervisory positions, as rapidly as possible. (*S.V.P.M.*, *Forty Years of Progress 1912–1952*)

The companies' Indonesianization efforts tended to follow a common pattern. The jobs most readily given to Indonesians were in domestic sales, public relations, and personnel. The technical jobs presented the greatest difficulty because of the lack of Indonesian engineers. Also, the companies were slow to Indonesianize financial positions, perhaps more for security considerations than training reasons.

To increase the supply of geologists and petroleum and chemical engineers, all three companies inaugurated scholarship programs. In 1953, Stanvac reported it had established ten scholarships at the University of Indonesia; nine at the Technical Institute at Bandung in civil, mechanical, electrical and chemical engineering, geology and mining; and one at the Law Faculty at Djakarta. Other programs ranged from general classes in language and arithmetic, through six-month staff courses, to part-time programs at both technical high school and college levels.

Each of the companies also duly appointed Indonesians to the boards of directors of the local companies. Caltex hired Julius Tahija as one of its three directors and it is generally agreed that he was instrumental in keeping Caltex out of many possible political difficulties. In 1956 Tahija formulated a community program under which Caltex donated funds for the construction of various community facilities with particular emphasis on its immediate neighbors, Pakanbaru and Dumai, and sponsored merit scholarships both in Indonesia and the United States. The Caltex scholarships did not limit study to a particular field or tie the recipient to an employment contract.

By the end of the decade, each of the Big Three had charts and statistics to show that substantial progress had been made towards bringing Indonesians into all phases and levels of their operations. To many Indonesians, however, including a number of young men in the programs, there was an illusory quality to the figures. All too often they felt that they had been given no meaningful role in their company's planning or operations. What was missing, in most cases, was the opportunity to decide under the pressure of responsibility. Moreover, many decisions were not even made in Indonesia but at company headquarters in New York, London, or The Hague. Indonesians at all levels wanted, and demanded, more responsibility and greater Indonesian control of the industry.

*   *   *

The rising tide of anti-Dutch feeling over West Irian indirectly boosted the opportunities for Indonesians in Shell's activities. Shell, because of its large international ownership, escaped the takeovers which befell wholly Dutch-owned enterprises in Indonesia at the end of 1957. However, the expulsion of Dutch nationals which accompanied the 1957 takeovers made necessary a considerable shakeup in the Shell staff. Most Dutch managers and staff members were replaced, over a six-month period, by British and American personnel, and also many Indonesian employees were promoted to positions of greater responsibility.

Of even more importance, were the changes that occurred at this time in the operations of the joint government-Shell company, *NIAM*. With the transfer of sovereignty, the Indonesian government had acquired the Netherlands East Indies' 50% ownership of *NIAM*, just as it acquired other assets of that predecessor government.

In colonial times *NIAM* had operated as an integral part of Shell's Indonesian operations. The N.E.I. government was a passive partner limiting activity to board of directors representation in Holland and the appointment of one general representative in Indonesia. Despite the leverage provided by its 50% ownership, in the early 1950s the Indonesian government limited its involvement to the appointment of Indonesian representatives. The seat of

NIAM remained in The Hague where three Indonesian directors sat with their Shell counterparts. In Indonesia, the company continued to be run as an integral part of Shell with a general representative, also Indonesian, making periodic reports to the board at The Hague. However, in 1958, Indonesianization of *NIAM* was begun in earnest. In negotiations, which were held in the context of the takeover of Dutch-owned firms and the expulsion of Dutch nationals, it was agreed that the name of *NIAM* would be changed to P.T. Permindo (Pertambangan Minjak Indonesia–Indonesia Oil Mining, Inc.) and its headquarters would be shifted from The Hague to Djakarta. It was also agreed that the entire company would be Indonesianized with Shell providing the necessary training and technical assistance during the transition period. The *NIAM* holdings included two of Shell's important Indonesian fields, Djambi in south Sumatra, and Bunju, the island off the northeast coast of Kalimantan. Shell retained its 50% ownership of the newly named Permindo. At the time of the change, the concession had only two more years to run to its expiration date of December 31, 1960. Shell may well have hoped to increase its chances of being allowed to retain its interest in Permindo by cooperating fully with the Indonesianization program.

P.T. Permindo established corporate headquarters in Djakarta on January 1, 1959, and the management of the company began to take on a new complexion. For the first time, executives of the company were appointed— previously they had been supplied on loan from Shell.

Management of the new company rested to a large degree with Indonesian nationals. The two managing directors, who were to represent the respective interests of the joint owners were, for Indonesia, R.A.A. Moh. Sediono, as administrative director, and, for Shell, Mr. Vredenberg, as technical director. Sediono, a career civil servant, had previously served as *NIAM's* general representative in Indonesia. He retired in 1960. His successor was Ir. L.G. Tampubolon, the first Indonesian to graduate with a degree in mining engineering from a university in Holland, where he began his studies before World War II. After the war he completed his studies, and returned to Indonesia where he worked on various mining projects before joining Permindo.

The concept of Indonesianization, as applied in Permindo, was to develop an Indonesian management team trained in Shell management methods. To head the program, Kamil Usman, an official from the Ministry of Labor, joined Permindo as the first Indonesian personnel manager. Permindo's operations involved more than 2,200 employees with approximately 1,600 in Djambi, 400 in Bunju, and 200 at headquarters in Djakarta. Shell provided technical assistance in all phases of operations as well as management training. Initially, there were perhaps as many as sixty expatriates in Djambi, the major area of activity, and five in Bunju. This number steadily declined as the program progressed.

In Djambi, the most important field area, the personnel department was under Mr. R. Suhardi Prawironto, an army officer on a civic mission assignment. He elected to remain in oil and presently serves as head of Pertamina's personnel division. Suhardi trained for the assignment with Shell before taking up his post at Djambi. He greatly accelerated the pace of Indonesianization once he took over. He also tried to harness national pride to the end of improving work performance and labor relations. Addressing the employees at Djambi, Suhardi said that more would be expected of them now that Permindo was an Indonesian-run company operated for the benefit of the nation. This struck a responsive chord and labor relations at Djambi immediately improved.

The beginning of the Indonesianization of Permindo was in many ways a natural development corresponding with the return of many young men to government service after completion of studies under government scholarships. One of these returning students was Drs. Ismet Akil, presently the chief of Pertamina's geological branch. Ismet attended Holland's Leiden University on a government scholarship and graduated with a degree in geology in 1956. Upon return, he was assigned to the Department of Mines under Ir. Anondo. Ismet then became *NIAM's* first Indonesianization trainee, spending three years at Djambi followed by a brief stint at Bunju. He requested and received further training with Shell and worked in the United States, first in New York and later in Shell fields at Billings, Montana. Returning to Indonesia in 1960, Ismet formed Permindo's exploration department where he was aided by a Shell expatriate for about six months before taking over the department.

Other present-day figures in Pertamina also came from the Permindo team. Pertamina's treasurer, John Abdi, responded to an advertisement in a Djakarta newspaper, and was hired in September, 1959. A holder of a bachelor's degree in business administration, Mr. Abdi had worked as an accountant for a Dutch-owned agricultural estate which was taken over by the government in 1958. He was hired expressly to replace an expatriate finance man. He took over the position after training for six months at Shell's Djakarta headquarters.

Some of those who joined already had a good deal of oil experience. Ir. Trisulo, now Pertamina's director of Exploration and Production, became disillusioned with Stanvac's Indonesianization program after four years with that company. He resigned and joined Permindo in 1960, as head of exploration and production in Djambi.

In production operations, the technical assistance contract negotiated with Shell provided that Shell would aid Permindo by supplying technical advisors, operational assistance, and materials that the company would need while establishing its own purchasing department and technical capability. As need dictated, and it frequently did, Permindo could request supplies from Shell which would then transfer the materials from one of its Indonesian or other Far East supply depots.

Combined production from Bunju and Djambi held steady during the two years of Permindo's operations. As the original concession neared its end, there was a conflict of interest over production rates with Shell seeking to increase production and Indonesia to hold it down.

Permindo possessed no refining facilities so, as before, Djambi crude was sent by pipeline to Shell's Pladju refinery for processing, while Bunju crude was shipped to Balikpapan as provided for in the technical assistance contract with Shell.

Permindo also began to enter domestic marketing. Previously, *NIAM* had contributed to the domestic supply through Shell's facilities. But, in accordance with its objective regarding management, Permindo established its own domestic marketing facilities, obtaining service stations from Shell which were re-marked to show the Permindo trade name.

When the original *NIAM* concession ended on December 31, 1960, all assets reverted to the Indonesian government. Shell had hoped that its cooperation in the Indonesianization of Permindo would result in favorable consideration being given to renewal of its interest in the concession. But by this time the Indonesian government had different ideas. Although there was reportedly some bitterness on the Shell side over the termination of its interest in Permindo, Indonesian sources state that Shell was never given any assurances that its interest would be renewed. And, to Shell's credit, it continued to cooperate, providing technical assistance and training to the wholly Indonesian-owned successor of Permindo in the early 1960s.

*   *   *

An opportunity for a different approach to Indonesian participation in the oil industry was presented by the disputed Shell concessions in north Sumatra and central Java. After Nirwonojudo's abortive attempt to unify northern Sumatra and central Java production and fields under his *PTMRI,* the two areas continued to run largely upon their own devices. *PTMRI* operated on a marginal basis in central Java, essentially an impoverished, makeshift organization working worn-out fields. It was eventually taken under military control in 1957 forming Nglobo Oil Mining (Tambang Minjak Nglobo c.a.–*TMNca.*)

In Langkat, Djohan operated as general manager under the charter issued by the governor of North Sumatra using the name Langkat Area Oil Mining (Tambang Minjak Kabupaten Langkat–*TMKL*). The charter specified that *TMKL* should be self-supporting. Employing about 425 workers, Djohan embarked on a modest rehabilitation program involving the construction of two small stills and he had plans to build four more.

In Atjeh, however, there were financial problems. Many workers, including the Javanese who were brought to the area by the Japanese, fled to the security of Atjeh when the "police actions" had threatened the Langkat area. The Atjehnese directors apparently refused to pay the workers who came from other regions. The workers then returned to Djohan's operation at Pangkalan Brandan. Djohan recalls that he put them to work making agricultural equipment for sale to the local farmers.

Those who favored retaining the northern Sumatra and central Java properties cited the willingness of several foreign companies to lend technical assistance to rehabilitate the fields. They disputed the contention that Shell would modernize the local facilities, maintaining that Shell would simply ship the crude to their larger refineries. Finally, they argued that if the properties were retained by the government, no compensation would be due to Shell since the Dutch themselves had destroyed virtually all the facilities during their retreat in World War II.

In Djakarta, during January, 1952, the State Commission on Mining affairs submitted its advice to the government after visiting the north Sumatran fields. On August 12, 1952, Prime Minister Wilopo announced that, based on the commission's report, the Financial and Economic Council had recommended return to Shell and the Cabinet intended to follow the recommendation.

However, resistance to the return was growing. Antara News Agency had reported on July 25, 1952, that trading circles in north Sumatra felt that return to Shell would be injurious to local enterprises since foreign-controlled enterprises tended to buy little from local traders and producers. The Economic Committee of Parliament was also against return. They demanded, and got, a commitment from the Cabinet that consultation with Parliament, or at least the Economic Committee, would precede any final decision. The committee then dispatched its own investigating teams to the oil sites—four men to north Sumatra and two men to central Java. The minister of civil service affairs in the

Cabinet also publicly took issue with the return proposal. Next, Nirowonojudo re-entered the fray. In an open letter to several political party leaders, he maintained that output could be greatly increased in northern Sumatra with only minor repairs. Most important of all, was the movement building in the *PNI* against return. This movement corresponded with the rise of the radical nationalist element of the party to control over the moderate wing of Prime Minister Wilopo. On August 21, 1952, the North Sumatra branch of the *PNI*, under the chairmanship of the newspaperman Mohammad Said, resolved:

> To demand from the Government and the House of Representatives to nationalize the North Sumatra Oil Fields within a period of not exceeding six months, as from the date of this statement, as an irrevocable condition to build up the State Oil Mines in accordance with the STATE and NATIONAL interests. (Said, p. 58)

The resolution went on to urge adoption of the position by the *PNI* Central Committee. Two weeks later they were successful. The *PNI* Central Committee decided:

> (1) Not to restore the North Sumatra Oil Fields to the owners of the concession.
> (2) To demand that the Government take over this property for the benefit of the people.
> (3) That the Government should nominate an Executive Committee with the task of implementing Paragraph 2 within the shortest possible time. (Said, p. 59)

In September, 1952, the four-man north Sumatran team advised Parliament that government operation of the fields was possible and that temporary emphasis should be placed on crude export while improvements were made. They also urged unification of management under a team of experts. The two-man central Java investigating team submitted a legal conclusion rather than a technical one: The Constitution of 1950, they maintained, required nationalization.

Undeterred by the Central Committee's position, the minister of economic affairs, Mr. Sumanang (*PNI*-moderate wing) held fast to his position that return was better for Indonesia than nationalization.

At the *PNI* National Congress in December, the *PNI* adopted its Executive Committee's position. This placed the party officially against the position of the *PNI* ministers in the coalition Wilopo Cabinet. Now officially at odds with his own party, the minister of economic affairs stopped pressuring for the return of the oil fields to Shell, and the matter was temporarily shelved. After the fall of the Wilopo Cabinet, there was a crisis borne of inability of the Masjumi and the *PNI,* now controlled by its radical-nationalist wing, to form a cabinet. In an effort to bridge the ideological gulf, the two parties agreed, among other things, to postpone indefinitely a decision as to the status of the fields.

The attempt to bury differences failed, and the next Cabinet was headed by Ali Sastroamidjojo of the *PNI* in coalition with the *NU* and with parliamentary support from the *PKI.* Masjumi was in opposition and the exclusion of the Masjumi was one factor precipitating the rebellion in Atjeh under the leadership of Teuku Daud Beureh, the former revolutionary governor of the region. He proclaimed a State of Darul Islam on September 20, 1953, against the "pro-communist and anti-Islam" government. This movement soon established control of considerable territory.

With the Ali Cabinet preoccupied by the rebellion, it postponed solving the problem of the status of the fields. The north Sumatran oil fields then became the center of a new conflict concerning the administration of the fields. What followed was a battle-royal involving accusations, counteraccusations, investigatory committees, and as a consequence, an inability to accomplish any rehabilitation or development.

The first sign Djohan had that his local control was in jeopardy came when he was summoned to Djakarta in 1953 by the minister of economic affairs in the first Ali Cabinet, Mr. Iskaq. He informed Djohan that even though his was a government enterprise, he still had to pay taxes. Djohan responded that the only way he could pay taxes was to fire half of his workers. Djohan returned to Langkat; the taxes were not paid.

As 1953 closed, northern Sumatra operations were still under divided control. The general manager of the Atjehnese operations, Husin al Mudjahid, had left to join the Daud Beureh forces. Abdul Rachman, his deputy, succeeded him. His unenviable job was to keep the enterprise going in the face of rebel sabotage, strikes, harassment by the Perbum, and the loss of local marketing outlets. With markets made inaccessible by reason of guerilla activities, workers' pay soon fell in arrears. In early 1954, the government gave the Atjehnese operations a small subsidy.

Djohan was at least amenable to return of the fields to Shell while Abdul Rachman was strongly opposed, as were Perbum leaders. A band of other unions, tired of the inaction, urged return to Shell at the end of 1953. Instead, the Ali Cabinet dispatched a commission to report on conditions and recommend a plan of development. Included on the commission was Nirwonojudo.

Although a Japanese group had expressed interest in a joint venture for development, the *PNI* opposed cooperation with them. After the commission reported back, Minister of Economic Affairs Iskaq decreed that all northern Sumatra oil affairs would henceforth come directly under his ministry (April 12, 1954). Concurrently, he appointed Nirwonojudo the ministry's coordinator for oil affairs.

To assist in rehabilitation, the government granted a subsidy of ten million rupiah (about $200,000). Proponents of nationalization such as Mohammad Said had argued that, "only Rp. 5 million would be required for the rehabilitation and reconstruction of projects [to meet a production objective of] 1 million tons per year." (Said, p. 51)

These last projections, and the plan to be implemented, called for concentration on rehabilitation of production as opposed to that of the refining facilities. Export of crude oil would be the short-run target to put the enterprise on a paying basis.

On April 13, 1954, Nirwonojudo once again set out for north Sumatra to set up headquarters. This time, unlike the period three years before, he was armed with the title of "Coordinator" and the mandate of the government. His mission was to combine the Langkat and Atjehnese operations under his administration, ensure adherence to central government instructions, and improve accountability, organization, and operations. Finally, he was to implement a rehabilitation program to the end that the enterprise might become self-sufficient and capable of returning a profit to the government.

Upon arrival in Medan, Nirwonojudo met with Djohan and Abdul Rachman to discuss means of combining their respective areas into a single enterprise, North Sumatra Oil Mining (Tambang Minjak Sumatera Utara–*TMSU*). The fiscal affairs of Abdul Rachman's Atjehnese operations were in such a deplorable state that Nirwonojudo decided to relieve him. His choice as successor was the local Perbum branch chief for Atjeh, Bachtiar Asli. The position was retitled "Chief of Langsa (Atjeh) Operations." Djohan's position was correspondingly retitled, "Chief of Langkat (North Sumatra) Operations." Nirwonojudo next merged the Langkat and Atjeh enterprises into *TMSU*.

Djohan was popular with most of his assistants and men, Perbum excepted, and the Langkat operations, in contrast to Atjeh, were well-run. Accordingly, most of the Langkat section chiefs joined in a letter to Nirwonojudo protesting his interference. A few days later, Abdul Rachman announced the formation of his own competing North Sumatra Oil Company with Djohan as his deputy. Nirwonojudo's entity was the legally constituted one although Djohan and Rachman claimed the contrary. The governor of North Sumatra later agreed that Nirwonojudo's authority took precedence over the earlier provincial mandates.

On May 21, Nirwonojudo suspended Djohan and the section chiefs and workers who supported him. For support Nirwonojudo looked to Perbum, and therefore, his new deputies were largely Perbum affiliated. New workers were brought in under Perbum aegis as well. Nirwonojudo eventually succeeded in gaining operational control of both areas.

Nirwonojudo had the upper hand, but his opponents were by no means defeated. Not only personal but sectional and union opposition now existed. The invader from Java had supplanted the local leadership by allying with the Javanese-dominated Perbum (Perbum's strongest following was among Javanese workers who had been originally brought to the fields as forced laborers by the Japanese). As a well-known and respected figure locally, Djohan also had some political muscle. Consequently, the *PNI* regional leadership was soon informed that Nirwonojudo must go. The other unions, resenting Perbum's aggrandizement at their expense, also made their voices heard. Over the summer months of 1954, no less than three parliamentary committees (Finance, Economic, and Labor) dispatched investigators to assess the situation.

The variations in the committee reports showed the political split over the question of who should manage the area. The Economic Committee's report was most critical of Nirwonojudo, charging him with excessive haste, inflexibility, and poor judgment; all to the detriment of the implementation of the plan. It also noted that the governor of North Sumatra and the police there felt that prior consultation with them might have averted the trouble. The Finance Committee investigators, on the other hand, generally approved of Nirwonojudo's efforts, while the Labor Committee noted a poor psychological atmosphere and discrimination against workers who opposed the coordinator.

When the air cleared, Nirwonojudo was still coordinator. But compromise was attempted at the end of 1955 through the appointment of Djohan as superintendent, a position that was to be equal in authority to that of coordinator. Not surprisingly, the creation of this unhappy association led only to more disputes. With the more conservative Harahap Cabinet in power, this time it was Nirwonojudo who was dismissed. However, despite Nirwonojudo's dismissal, Djohan was unable to wrest control from the, by then, entrenched Perbum.

Meanwhile, political opinion was moving in a direction favoring Indonesian retention of the oil fields. All three committees dispatched to investigate the Nirwonojudo-Djohan dispute had urged resolution of the oil fields' status. The *PNI* had been dominated by its radical-nationalist wing for over two years, and even the Masjumi party no longer objected in principle to retaining the fields.

In March, 1956, after Indonesia unilaterally abrogated the Round Table Agreements, a state Advisory Commission on Implementing the Abrogation of the Round Table Conference Agreements studied the north Sumatran oil situation. Pursuant to its proposals, the second Ali Cabinet announced on October 24, 1956, that the oil properties would not be returned to Shell. Government Regulation No. 34 of 1956 was promulgated asserting central government control over the fields in Atjeh and North Sumatra to be known as the North Sumatran Oil fields. It authorized a corporation to be formed to manage the operations with the notation that a corporate body would provide the best management in technical and commercial matters. The minister of economic affairs was empowered to establish this corporation.

In the fields of North Sumatra and Atjeh, after eight years of squabbling, the facilities still lay practically in ruins and operations were at a virtual standstill. Equally important, the Indonesian government had little practical control over field activities. Although Indonesian export figures reveal no shipments, Japanese import figures record imports of north Sumatran crudes during the years 1953–1956. Presumably oil was lightered from Atjeh to Penang or Singapore and transshipped to Japan.

On June 16, 1957, a citizens group at Pangkalan Brandan held a public meeting attended by an estimated 15,000 people. After many speeches decrying the stagnated situation, the meeting resolved that the central government should take over the administration of *TMSU* for the people's well-being and to stop the sale of scrap iron by the coordinator of *TMSU,* which, they maintained, should be used for rehabilitation.

On July 22, 1957, one month after the meeting, the ministers of industry and trade assigned jurisdiction over the north Sumatran oil fields to the army chief of staff. In a letter to Prime Minister Djuanda, the minister of industry, Inkiriwang, outlined the terms of the transfer as agreed in a meeting between his ministry, the Ministry of Trade, and the army staff. *TMSU* would be incorporated with all shares to be owned by the government. The regional areas would be given a chance to participate in the enterprise. Management would be vested in the army chief of staff in his capacity as war administrator. Priority would be given to rehabilitating the fields in order to export crude to earn funds for further development. Capital would be supplied as needed and the Ministry of Industry would continue to give guidance and assistance. Hopefully, assignment to the army would end the political haggling.

CHAPTER 7

Assignment to Dr. Ibnu

In 1957, Indonesia stood on the brink of its most severe crisis since securing independence. For the past eight years it had struggled to resolve basic economic and social questions. Economically, its currency was melting from heated inflation, its natural resources generally lay untapped for lack of a basic policy concerning the role of foreign development capital. Politically, the past eight years had seen eight cabinets.

The exodus of foreign capital and technical personnel, the growth of regional unrest into rebellions, the declining influence of moderate leadership, and the growth of the *PKI*, marked this decade. It was in this atmosphere that Colonel Dr. H. Ibnu Sutowo received his assignment to form a national oil company.

After eight years of civilian control had produced nothing in the oil fields of north Sumatra but local anarchy, dispute, and a succession of failures, it is not surprising that the formation of this oil company was assigned to the army. This was in part a matter of default. Parliament and the political parties were in disarray and disrepute and there was no government agency other than the army that would be capable of giving the direction that would be necessary to get operations underway. It was in part a matter of the conditions in north Sumatra. Under the chaotic and rebellious political situation prevailing there at the time, operations involved military force and security almost to the same degree that they involved matters more usual to an oil company. Further, such an expanded role fitted well with the philosophy of Chief of Staff Nasution who saw the army as a dynamic force in nation building.

In its role to assist the economic development of the regions, General Nasution and his central staff had close contact with Ir. Djuanda Kartawidjaja, who served several times as minister for planning and also as prime minister. In coordination with Ir. Djuanda, the army's financial and economic affairs staff had studied the problems of north Sumatran oil. It was on the basis of this study that the agreement was signed between Nasution and the ministers of industry and commerce in July, 1957. It was followed by a decree of the minister of industry dated October 15, 1957, which completed the transfer of authority to the army and authorized the incorporation of a limited liability company, North Sumatra Oil Mining Exploitation, Inc. (P.T. Eksploitasi Tambang Minjak Sumatra Utara–*P.T. ETMSU*).

The incorporators, on behalf of the government of the Republic of Indonesia, were Dr. Ibnu and his assistant, Major Harijono. The board of directors set forth in the articles consisted of the nominees of: (1) the minister of industry; (2) the minister of finance; (3) the minister of trade; (4) the Atjeh military commander and governor of Atjeh; and (5) the North Sumatra military commander and governor of North Sumatra. The last two directors' positions represented General Nasution's attempt to appease the quarreling leaders of the two districts involved. They were also given the promise that the oil company would help develop roads, ports, and schools. The first three directors' positions represented the natural choice of government officials interested in oil development—finance, industry, and trade.

Shortly after *P.T. ETMSU* was established, General Nasution ordered its name changed to reflect that oil was a national asset and that the company was not merely a provincial operation. A new name was suggested by Anondo to Ibnu and Harijono, and thus, the articles were amended effective December 10, 1957, to change the name to National Oil Company, Inc. (P.T. Perusahaan Minjak Nasional–P.T. Permina).

There is a story, probably apocryphal, concerning the selection of the first president-director for the new national oil company. The story goes that General Nasution was considering three officers for the post and that their backgrounds from civilian life were law, engineering, and medicine. After careful deliberation, he decided that the lawyer would argue too much, the engineer would plan too much, but that perhaps a doctor could cure this ailing industry.

In fact, as operations deputy to Nasution, Dr. Ibnu was in charge of overseeing the execution of army activities, including the takeover of the oil fields. However, oil was only one of many assignments, and initially Dr. Ibnu can only mark the receipt of his new assignment in terms of "another folder being placed on my desk, although this one was of particular interest."

*   *   *

Thus at the age of forty-three, Dr. Ibnu was commencing his third career, following professions as a medical doctor and a military officer. Becoming a doctor had been Ibnu's goal since he was a student in primary school. His father was a civil servant for the Netherlands East Indies government, a district head in central Java. By virtue of his father's position, Ibnu was among the few Indonesians permitted to attend Dutch schools, which were far superior to the schools ordinarily available to Indonesians. Education was important in the family and the eleven children—seven boys and four girls—all finished secondary education. Ibnu, at the age of sixteen, entered the Netherlands Indies Medical School in Surabaya for the ten-year course combining university and medical studies. He finished this course in nine years and, in the process, mastered German and Dutch—the texts were in German and the instruction was in Dutch. Like many Indonesian leaders, he has by necessity become something of a linguist, maintaining a reasonable fluency in five languages.

After graduation in May, 1940, Dr. Ibnu was assigned to work for the government health services for seven years. He was posted to south Sumatra as the public health officer attached to the transmigration program designed to settle people from the crowded island of Java to the sparsely populated outer islands. In south Sumatra, this program was being jeopardized by the high incidence of malaria and secondary diseases stemming from inadequate nutrition. Ibnu instituted a three-phase attack: He obtained better food, enforced the taking of medicine (including house-to-house roll calls where quinine pills were swallowed in his presence), and started jungle clinics.

Since secondary school, Ibnu had been aware of the independence movements and had joined various youth groups as a sympathetic, if not very active, participant. When his university studies were finished he became more active. Although nationalist activities were restricted and sometimes prohibited by his employers, the N.E.I. government, Ibnu organized a youth political party in South Sumatra in 1941. He realized that politics, economics, and medicine were strongly interconnected. People's health depended on their economic conditions and the economic conditions depended on the political system. Towards improving the political system, Dr. Ibnu began lecturing about the need for independence while making his medical rounds. On the practical side, he formed economic cooperatives for the purchase and distribution of commodities among the 12,000 resettled Javanese in his medical district.

In February, 1942, the Japanese occupied south Sumatra. Less than a month before, Dr. Ibnu had received his entire requisition of medical supplies and, not being too sure what would happen under the Japanese, he decided to hide these supplies in small caches throughout the area. They lasted him for the duration of the war, saving many lives.

Following the Dutch defeat there came a wave of looting and disorder, so Ibnu organized a vigilante corps. In order to provide minimum necessary food, he instituted rationing and a controlled distribution system. He soon became, in effect, the civil head of the area as well as its physician. Although the Japanese considered Ibnu a troublemaker (he struck one Japanese officer who threatened him), they needed his leadership in administering the area, so he was given a reasonably free hand. His activities soon included teaching and discussing the concept of a "Greater Indonesia." Ibnu explained to the Japanese that the people must learn about "Greater Indonesia" before they would be able to understand "Greater East Asia."

In August, 1945, with World War II over and the revolution begun, Dr. Ibnu was requested by one of the independence leaders in south Sumatra, Dr. Gani, to gather arms and to take charge of Palembang, south Sumatra's largest city. At this point, Ibnu, thirty years old, was chairman of the local Pemuda (Youth) Congress, head of the South Sumatra Medical Service, chief officer of the Palembang branch of the People's Security Guards (one of the forerunners of the Indonesian Army), plus the leader of a battalion of Pemuda irregulars.

Towards the end of 1945, there were frequent skirmishes with the Allied forces which had been sent to occupy Palembang on behalf of the Dutch. By late 1946, these forces had been replaced by Dutch troops and on January 1, 1947, the five-day battle began for possession of the city. The Dutch finally delivered an ultimatum to evacuate the city or it would be bombed. Ibnu took the last train out, with his wife, Sali, then expecting their second child, and their two-year-old daughter.

After the first Dutch offensive, Dr. Ibnu was appointed army chief of staff for South Sumatra, with the rank of major. He continued as chief medical officer. For the remainder of the revolution he quite literally carried one bag of medical supplies and one bag of dynamite.

After the transfer of sovereignty in 1949, Dr. Ibnu wanted to concentrate on building a medical practice and his own hospital, so he refused an opportunity to go abroad for advanced military training. By 1953, he was very much involved in his medical activities, though still maintaining his active military status. Within two years, however, internal problems in the army, and growing problems on the national scene, forced him to again devote more time to his military career. He was appointed panglima for south Sumatra in 1955 and, in addition to this post, Nasution asked him to come to Djakarta in 1956 to organize army logistics. As problems increased—territorial revolts were brewing, and West Irian was taking on a military as well as diplomatic aspect—Nasution gave Ibnu the double assignment as deputy-operations and chief administrative officer for the War Administration which was created in 1957 to administer the new martial law.

When the additional assignment came for him to form and direct the new oil company, Dr. Ibnu was already one of the busiest men in the government and was holding two major military posts simultaneously. "It is good training to operate under very demanding conditions," Dr. Ibnu recalls of these times. "You must deal with the essentials, the fundamentals. What do you want to do? Who do you have to help do it? What resources do you have? The resources and people you have must then be used to accomplish what you have to do. It does no good to spend time wishing you had more or worrying whether what you have is enough. Good planning is necessary, but once you have determined what the objective is, who the people are, and what resources are available, then is the time for action.

"There was no overall plan at first for north Sumatra, we simply needed to organize the fields so we could ship oil to earn foreign exchange. The most important thing we had to do was to learn the oil business ourselves. We already knew we had the oil which could be sold so that we could buy necessary equipment. We needed the people, those who would work hard, who could develop themselves and then in turn, develop the oil business."

Dr. Ibnu was faced with the task of forming a staff to operate the company headquarters in Djakarta. As his operational assistant, Dr. Ibnu chose Major Harijono who had worked for a German company before the Japanese occupation and also had experience in the purchasing branch of the army under Ibnu. Another assistant selected was Major Geudong, who was put in charge of the financial and administrative side of the organization. Major Geudong was an infantry officer who had served in an administrative capacity in Army Central Command from 1951 to 1957. The third man to join the team was Captain Affan, who also had administrative experience, and thus became Major

Geudong's assistant. None of these men had any prior oil experience.

Initially, the company did not even have an office of its own. Dr. Ibnu and Major Harijono shared an office at Army Central Command, while Major Geudong and Captain Affan set up their office in a small sitting room of Major Geudong's house. With no cars for transport, Captain Affan had to hire a betjak (pedi-cycle cab) to pick up the mail, being careful to remove his rank insignia since, at that time, officers were not expected to use betjaks. Affan relates, "I was also the typist and clerk for the first few months, since I had no lieutenants." Later they received some clerical help from Army Central Command. Without an official office, the company had no address until Affan set up a P. O. Box 2659. A cable address came next when they found out that an important telegram from the U.S.A. had been returned "Addressee Unknown."

Not until May, 1958, did the company obtain its first petroleum engineer, Ir. Soediono. He received his degree with the first petroleum engineering class to be graduated from the Technical Institute at Bandung and came on loan from the State Planning Bureau. Mr. Sunarjo, of the merchant marine, was hired in an advisory capacity for shipping. When the first two tankers were purchased in 1959, he was put in charge of the shipping operation.

It was this small group of men in Djakarta that commenced the operations. By necessity, they followed a slogan that was a favorite of their boss, "Beladjar sambil bekerdja" which translates, "Study while working."

The oil fields which Permina took over in 1957 were the same ones in which Shell had started almost seven decades earlier. Most of these northern Sumatra oil fields and facilities were located in border country between North Sumatra and Atjeh. Atjeh had a long history as an autonomous area and had always resisted the influence of the Dutch. Although the Dutch were finally able to bring Atjeh under their control, they were forced to give the Atjehnese certain freedoms that were not extended to the other areas. The Atjehnese are devout Muslims, and as their history attests, fiercely independent. North Sumatra, on the other hand, had been more cooperative with the colonial regime. Its capital, Medan, had long been the leading commercial center of the area. The Dutch had made Medan their base of north Sumatran operations, and it was the major city in the region. Although there were divisive elements in North Sumatra, the region was considered to be much more politically stable than its neighbor to the north.

The major oil refining facilities of north Sumatra were located at Pangkalan Brandan, some 83 km. (52 mi.) to the northwest of Medan. This refinery, the first built in Indonesia by Royal Dutch in 1892, was destroyed by the evacuating Dutch, bombed by Allied planes in World War II, and again destroyed by the Republican forces retreating during the "police actions." The refinery had never been rebuilt, but by 1957, minor repairs had been made and the refinery was operating on a very small scale. The shipping facilities for the fields and refinery were located at Pangkalan Susu, 25 km. (16 mi.) to the north of Pangkalan Brandan. The facilities at Pangkalan Susu had been hard-hit by Allied bombing, and had never been repaired. Only a few of the storage tanks were usable, the jetty was badly damaged, and the pumps that had been used to move the crude from the tanks to the ships were inoperative. It was also questionable if the channel was still navigable as no ships were known to have gone out of Pangkalan Susu since the war.

The primary prewar oil field was located at Rantau, which is in Atjeh. The Rantau field is approximately 55 km. (34 mi.) from Pangkalan Brandan. It first went into production in 1929, and became Shell's main field in their northern Sumatra operation. During the war this area had escaped major bomb damage. Primitive stills had been built in the Rantau area during the war, and were still in use, although their capacity was very low. Two other small fields were located some 70 km. (43 mi.) and 100 km. (62 mi.) to the northwest of Rantau. At the time of the transfer to the army these fields were inactive.

Four eight-inch pipelines provided the vital links between the fields in Atjeh and the refinery at Pangkalan Brandan and the shipping facilities at Pangkalan Susu. Only one of these four lines was usable, and just barely at that. Virtually no repairs had been made since the war and in many places the lines were rusted through and totally covered with jungle undergrowth. Repairing the pipelines was no small task because of the terrain and also because of the guerilla activity in the area.

This is an area of hills and dense forest and the land is crisscrossed by rivers and streams. In 1957, the roads were very poor, generally just muddy trails, and bridges were nonexistent. It could take as long as eight hours to drive from Medan to Pangkalan Brandan. The farther north one traveled the more difficult the conditions became, and it would often take twenty-four hours to get from Pangkalan Brandan to Rantau. The roads were often impassable, and this was their usual condition in the rainy season.

The politics were as inhospitable as the terrain. The strains of regionalism were strong in both North Sumatra and Atjeh. In 1953, the Darul Islam (*DI*) rebellion broke out in Atjeh, and remnants of this movement were still active. Fighting between government forces and the *DI* rebels was still common in 1957. Within the government forces there was a quarrel between the commander in North Sumatra and the commander of the Atjeh region. And below them, each of the unit officers commanded the respect of his own troops, but it was never certain whether or not they would support the regional panglima. Thus the military situation was dangerous and almost completely unpredictable.

The political situation in North Sumatra and Atjeh was thrown from confusion to chaos with the outbreak of the *PRRI* rebellion in February of 1958. This rebellion received support both in North Sumatra and Atjeh. In Atjeh, the establishment of the *PRRI* brought about a resurgence of fighting in the areas around the oil fields. Fighting was also frequent in the areas around Pangkalan Brandan and Pangkalan Susu.

The money that had been given to the *TMSU* by the central government in 1954 had been expended by 1957 with much of it allegedly going for political purposes. There was a small amount of production—primarily refined in the stills that had been repaired with scrap prior to the formation of the *TMSU*. As a result of the incessant

political infighting, rehabilitation had come to a dead halt
by July of 1957.

After taking responsibility for the north Sumatra oil
facilities, Dr. Ibnu's first priority was to sell crude oil as
soon as possible in order to earn foreign exchange needed
for further development work. It was in this connection that
Dr. Ibnu began a business association and personal friendship with Mr. and Mrs. Harold Hutton of Orange,
California. Hutton was an independent oil man with
considerable experience in Asia. He had made his first trip
to Djakarta in 1956, where he met and formed an association
with Mr. Joe Gohier who had several years' business
experience in Indonesia. Together they began to survey
the oil business.

Early in their investigation, they were approached by
Nirwonojudo who claimed he was the only man to do business with for north Sumatra crude. According to Hutton,
"Nirwonojudo just didn't ring any bells so we started
looking for a more solid approach. This led us to Ir.
Djuanda, then minister of planning, to get a reading on
future prospects." In August, 1956, Hutton, Gohier,
Djuanda, and Djuanda's assistant, Ali Boedijardjo, held
several discussions and exchanged ideas on how Indonesia
might go about developing its oil resources. These meetings
continued periodically into 1957 and were joined by Ir.
Anondo, who was head of the Directorate of Mining. In
June 1957, Ir. Djuanda, then prime minister, told Gohier
that Dr. Ibnu would be taking over responsibility for the
north Sumatran oil fields and a meeting was arranged between Hutton and Ibnu for the following month. Hutton
and Gohier were also given permission to visit the facilities
in north Sumatra. They were the first Western oil men to
inspect the fields since the Dutch left in 1942.

When Dr. Ibnu and Hutton were introduced by Prime
Minister Djuanda, they established an immediate rapport
and this has continued through the fifteen years in which
Hutton's company, Refining Associates (Canada), Ltd.
(Refican) has been associated with Pertamina. The timing
was right for this association. Dr. Ibnu was entering an
entirely new field and Harold Hutton and his wife, Betty,

had thirty years' experience in the oil business, encompassing production, refining, marketing, and finance. Hutton's proposal to Ibnu was that they could help Indonesia set up a viable national oil company without becoming involved in concessions or promotion deals.

In retrospect, Hutton believes that his willingness to further the idea of Indonesian management and control was the key to his striking a responsive chord, first with Djuanda and then with Ibnu. "In 1957, Indonesia was suspicious of foreigners and big foreign companies. They wanted to try it on their own and I encouraged them. Evidently, I was the first foreign oil man to believe an all-Indonesian oil company could succeed. I told Dr. Ibnu, 'All it takes to build an oil company is oil!'"

Hutton had previously negotiated contract terms with Djuanda and Anondo. This draft contract was passed on to Ibnu and Harijono. After a brief reading, Ibnu, Harijono, Hutton, and Gohier sat down, typed out a new draft, and signed it on December 10, 1957. Harijono wanted to take a few days to review the contract with attorneys and advisors but he was reassured by Ibnu. "Surely you can trust the work of Mr. Hutton and Minister Djuanda" he said. "Let's get started." Since nobody on the Indonesian side had much knowledge of marketing contracts, it probably would not have mattered how many days they read over the clauses.

The contract they signed is probably the shortest oil sales contract on record; single spaced it would be less than two typewritten pages. Contained in this brief document there was, however, one clause that could cause serious concern—the guarantee clause, reading:

> The Seller represents that the oil to be produced from the above property and the right of the Seller to deliver the same as free and clear of encumbrances or other obligations, and the *Seller hereby guarantees* the title to all crude oil delivered thereunder. (Emphasis added)

This clause would soon get a thorough review.

Concurrently with the discussions and negotiations with Hutton for the marketing of crude, legal steps were taken to establish ownership over the crude. The first step was to examine and test Government Regulation No. 34 of 1956, which asserted the authority of the central government over the oil fields in the provinces of Atjeh and North Sumatra but was not specific on the question of ownership.

Hutton consulted with Washington, D.C. attorneys regarding the status of the title to the crude oil and the authority to market it. The attorneys considered that Regulation No. 34 of 1956 was insufficient to establish title since it dealt only with management and did not at all purport to establish ownership over the fields which were thus legally part of the Shell concessions. On this basis, shipments of crude would be subject to seizure by Shell. Hutton had to inform Permina that the guarantee clause might become more than a formality and that Permina would have to pay if Shell successfully pressed a claim. Since Permina had no money and was already making plans based on anticipated crude sales, Dr. Ibnu was extremely upset. He, in effect, told Hutton and Gohier, "You are the ones with experience, you solve this problem. The oil is yours once you load it in your tanker." At the same time, he instructed Harijono to help solve the problem on the Indonesian side. How to do so was up to them, he told them, but the problem must be solved quickly.

Harijono and Gohier took their problem to Basarudin Nasution, S.H., who had been a leading attorney in the army, serving as judge advocate general, and assisting in the establishment of the military justice system and military law school. To Basarudin, the solution was very simple. Since March, the State of War and Siege Law had been in effect. Among other things, it gave the army chief of staff the power to promulgate ordinances in lieu of parliamentary law.

Basarudin, as a private advisor to the chief of staff, suggested that Nasution use this power to revoke the concessions. General Nasution agreed with Basarudin. The order was drafted, discussed with Prime Minister Djuanda, who initialled his approval, and then signed by General Nasution for promulgation on February 1, 1958. The Ordinance of the Military Authority No. Prt/PM/017/1957 cancelled the Shell concession and took back the designated areas, together with all the installations to be found in these areas, and directed that a national oil mining company would take charge of managing and working these oil fields. A copy of this order was sent to Shell.

There was no immediate reaction, but within a month, there evolved a tale of three cities that were involved in various ramifications of the order.

In Djakarta, word came from the Indonesian Foreign Office that the British embassy was claiming compensation on behalf of Shell. The Indonesian Foreign Office itself did not understand what had happened or why. The diplomats called a meeting for an explanation at the Foreign Office. When Harijono and Basarudin showed up, they faced a battery of a dozen lawyers and officials from the Foreign Office. Basarudin argued successfully that the emergency War and Siege Law prevailed over the ordinary status of the concession contract, which was also law. It turned out that the Foreign Office was not so concerned with the legal argument, which, once explained, they readily accepted as being correct, as they were with its justification. What could they tell attorneys at the British embassy to establish a justification for taking these Shell properties when all the other Shell properties had remained with the concessionaire? Basarudin's answer was that the Dutch had abandoned these areas in 1942 with a scorched-earth policy. Thereafter they never reoccupied these areas, even when they could have done so during the "police actions." Further, even after the transfer of sovereignty no Shell presence was ever established and the local workers had been in occupation of the fields for the past fifteen years. It was time for more decisive development efforts.

In the end, the Foreign Office seemed satisfied with this explanation, as well as with the legality of the ordinance, and discussions were started regarding compensation. The value of these areas to Shell was a guess at best, considering the condition under which they had been abandoned fifteen years earlier. Furthermore, the concessions themselves were due to expire within a few years, which made it unlikely that Shell would devote much attention to this area in comparison with their other field locations.

Shell was in a somewhat delicate negotiating position with regard to the northern Sumatra fields and had to consider its other interests throughout Indonesia. Shell was also interested in the new mining legislation being discussed in Parliament and did not want to start any litigation that might later prejudice its position in obtaining new exploration permits. Shell's production was on a downward trend, and the company was much in need of new areas to exploit. Although the north Sumatra fields might have solved their production problem in the short run, the workers there were hostile to the company, the area was politically unstable and a large investment would be required in order to resume production. The issue was allowed to drift without decision though both parties agreed that Shell would be given favorable consideration when and if new oil concessions were granted.

In Los Angeles, the Huttons received two representatives of Shell who flew in from The Hague. At a dinner meeting, the Shell representatives asked Hutton if he was serious in his intention to purchase oil from the new Indonesian company. Hutton assured them that he was. The conversation then changed to general subjects not related to oil and after dinner the Shell representatives and Hutton shook hands and went their separate ways. Again, Shell did not press the issue.

In Tokyo, a legal brief was prepared to establish before the courts that Permina had the right to market the oil. Hutton had agreed to give up the guarantee clause, figuring the Nasution order clarified title. However, he wanted this tested prior to making the first shipment to Japan, so he engaged the services of a Japanese attorney who had won a major case involving revocation action in the Middle East. Copies of the Indonesian Constitution, relevant decrees, and the revocation ordinance, were translated from Indonesian to English to Japanese. The case was tried in the province of Kainan at the remote port where the first shipment was expected to unload. A favorable decision was granted in the lower court and this was enough for Hutton. He immediately dispatched the small coastal tanker, *Shozui Maru*, for Pangkalan Susu to load the first crude shipment from the port in fifteen years.

At this point, Hutton had a substantial investment in equipment and in legal and operational expenses. He and his employees had worked on the project for nearly eighteen months. He had no guarantee clause, he could get no insurance on either ship or cargo since North Sumatra was an active civil war zone, and no safe anchorage was assured since rebel troops occupied the island just two miles away from the dock at Pangkalan Susu. He and Betty flew in from Japan and joined the ship at Medan to see for themselves how their gamble would pay off.

During all the time the negotiations had been going on, and while the legal matters were being worked out, work was going ahead in the fields and at Pangkalan Susu.

General Nasution's first action in July 1957 had been to send Colonel Samidjo, a senior *TNI* officer, to northern Sumatra to investigate, and recommend solutions to the complicated military and operational problems there. He set up offices at Medan and his first act was to appoint Nirwonojudo as his chief assistant. This selection was not a promising one. Nirwonojudo was far too involved with the local factions to be truly effective and his association with Perbum made him suspect to all the other groups.

Shortly after the incorporation of Permina, Colonel Samidjo was relieved of his other military duties and appointed as managing director of the north Sumatran operations. Nirwonojudo was dismissed and Lt. Colonel Arif was appointed as chief deputy, along with three other deputy officers; Major Nukum Sanany, Captain J. Karinda and Captain Singarimbum. These men set out to organize the operations, but still got off to a slow start because they were unable to reconcile the different labor factions in the field. The situation was complicated by the outbreak of the *PRRI* rebellion in February, 1958. Lt. Colonel Arif, the man who was scheduled to replace Colonel Samidjo, joined the rebels, while Colonel Samidjo returned to Djakarta to take up a new position. Major Geudong, who had recently taken charge of finance and administration in Djakarta, was sent to fill the gap in north Sumatra.

The choice of Major Geudong was made partly because of his Atjehnese descent. With the situation precarious in North Sumatra and Atjeh, it was felt that an Atjehnese,

昭瑞丸
東京
SHOZUI MARU
TOKYO

with friends and acquaintances on both sides of the rebellion, would be able to ease Permina's security problems.

There was active fighting in the area, and every movement required a military escort. As no troops were sent to north Sumatra with Major Geudong, he had to rely on borrowed troops when he could get them. The trip to Pangkalan Brandan or Rantau from Medan was grueling and dangerous. Because of a general shortage of troops, and doubts about which troops were loyal to whom, reasonable security could seldom be obtained for the Permina men who wanted to venture out to the field locations. Even when they were able to get out to the fields they were often met with hostility by the local laborers, particularly the Perbum men who had held the top positions in the *TMSU*. The state of anarchy was indicated by a Perbum section chief who refused to allow Soediono to see some reports that had been made during the Shell days unless Soediono paid for them—he claimed that the documents were his own personal property.

Besides maintaining security, Geudong was also faced with the problem of paying the employees. A large portion of the initial capital given to the company went for this purpose, and more went to pay old *TMSU* bills. Under these circumstances very little rehabilitation could be accomplished in the fields in the first months.

Work was, however, going ahead in Pangkalan Susu in preparation for the first shipment. The man primarily responsible for this work was Major J.M. Pattiasina, who arrived in April with a battalion of troops from the Sriwidjaja Division of south Sumatra. He had been sent to north Sumatra at the request of Dr. Ibnu to provide security for the areas around Pangkalan Brandan and Pangkalan Susu. Ibnu had known Pattiasina since the days of the revolution, and was familiar with Pattiasina's reputation as a competent and tough officer. His troops provided security for repair operations of the facilities at Pangkalan Susu, and he also assigned his troops as an additional work force for these efforts.

With assistance from Refican's field supervisor, Walter Redman, workers welded, patched, clamped, hammered, soldered—"fixed it with chewing gum and baling wire"—

HAROLD AND BETTY HUTTON AND THE SHOZUI MARU AT PANGKALAN SUSU LOADING PERMINA'S FIRST CRUDE OIL SHIPMENT—MAY 24, 1958.

and put together a workable connection between the wells
and storage tanks. They used the highest storage tanks at
Pangkalan Susu so that the oil could flow by gravity to the
jetty. On May 24, 1958, loading commenced to the *Shozui
Maru*. It was a small 3,000 dwt vessel, and took only about
1,700 tons of crude, which had a market value of about
$30,000. The main reason for using such a small ship was
that no one was sure of the depth of the channel. Continual
depth soundings and dead slow ahead was the rule all the
way to avoid shoals and submerged wreckage from the war.
There were six men and one woman on the vessel besides
the crew. Major Harijono, Major Pattiasina, and Basarudin
Nasution represented Permina, while Jimmy Perkins, Joe
Gohier, and Harold and Betty Hutton were from Refican.
The oil was loaded with no difficulty and was soon on the
way to Japan. Their joint efforts had paid off.

*   *   *

A few weeks after the first shipment of crude oil to Japan,
Major Pattiasina was appointed as Permina's technical and
exploitation director. He established his headquarters in
Pangkalan Brandan and, in his very direct manner, set out
to organize the operations. The choice of Major Pattiasina
was a natural one considering his experience in the oil
business. His wartime experience in rebuilding refineries in
south Sumatra ideally suited him to undertake the rehabilitation that had to be done and, as in south Sumatra, he had not
much more to work with than old scrap iron. In September,
when Major Geudong returned to Djakarta to resume his
duties as director of finance and administration, Major
Pattiasina was appointed managing director. Although Dr.
Ibnu made monthly inspection trips, Pattiasina was given
overall control of all operations in northern Sumatra.

It was apparent to Pattiasina that he would have to solve
several problems before he could rehabilitate the facilities
and expand the operations. One of his most immediate
problems involved the tense military situation. Both Darul
Islam and *PRRI* rebels were active and had supporters
among the oil workers. When he arrived in April, he had

set out to reduce the rebels by cutting their supply lines. He also adopted a strategy of directly approaching the rebels to elicit their support for his efforts. Pattiasina knew that the primary thing people in the area wanted was an opportunity to make a decent living, and he convinced a good number of the rebels to work for him as laborers and pipeline guards. These workers also provided him with a good intelligence system.

The second problem involved the animosity that had developed during the *TMSU* years among the various groups of workers. Upon being named managing director, Pattiasina banned the Perbum and took over their head-quarters in the compound at Pangkalan Brandan, which was the best facility that had been built in the *TMSU* days. Combined with the banning of the union, he made several moves to eliminate Perbum members from managerial positions and to generally reduce their influence throughout the organization. He bluntly fired people he believed were working against him and he also transferred some of the more troublesome ex-Perbum members to remote field locations in Atjeh.

Another tactic Pattiasina used to establish control was the creation of a management board. This board consisted of the top people from all factions that were represented in the local labor groups. A good many of the old Perbum men, who had held top management positions in the *TMSU*, were removed from their positions and promoted to the Management Board. The stated function of the board was to formulate policy for the new company. In fact, because of the political bickering and personal hatreds that had developed through the years, it was almost impossible for the members to reach a decision. Even if they did manage to agree on something, Pattiasina would ignore their recommendations if they conflicted with plans that he had already made. The final move in this area was the establishment of a new union, which Pattiasina totally controlled, to replace the banned Perbum.

A "no work, no pay" policy was also implemented. This rewarded those people who were actually working, and forced out those who were not. It also served to identify

people who had been placed on the payroll in the *TMSU* days but had never really worked for their salaries.

Pattiasina's initial moves against the communists and his generally strict and no-nonsense attitude gained him the respect of the former Shell hands, particularly those who were led by Djohan. They had gone through many difficult years together from the discriminatory years with Shell, the hardships of the Japanese occupation, to the disappointing years following the war and independence. Djohan and his workers had seen several efforts to get the fields in production before Pattiasina arrived. All of them had failed and this experience naturally made them somewhat skeptical of this new attempt. Gradually, however, they began to join the team and work for the new company. Problems did arise between Pattiasina and Djohan, both being forceful personalities, but they were quickly settled when it became apparent to Djohan that Pattiasina would do things only one way—his own way.

With virtually no equipment or materials, work was begun to make further repairs to the storage and port facilities at Pangkalan Susu. The condition of the storage tanks and pumps severely limited the amount of crude that could be handled so the first priority was to get them back in full working order. In addition to repairing the pumps, jetty, and the storage tanks, work was begun on repairing the pipelines that ran from Rantau to Pangkalan Susu. It was here that Pattiasina's efforts to win over the rebels paid off and many former rebels were hired to work on repairing the pipelines. Almost all of the former rebels were strongly anti-communist and thus anti-Perbum.

Work was also begun at Pangkalan Brandan to repair the refinery in order to produce more gasoline and kerosene for the local market, which, in turn would generate funds to pay the employees and make local equipment purchases. Permina suffered from an acute shortage of funds and selling to the local market was almost the only means of meeting the payroll for the field operations. Again, old scrap was used to repair the facilities.

Pattiasina found a scrap dealer's yard near Medan which

was full of old plate, pipe, and machinery. In this apparent junk Pattiasina saw such things as piston rods, pipe, couplings, and other "oil field iron," much of which was in perfectly good condition. Pattiasina sent his troops to the yard and recovered over fifteen boxcar loads of material that had been sold as scrap over the years. Pattiasina's position was that the materials still belonged to the state as its sale had never been authorized, so its title passed over to Permina with the rest of the facilities in north Sumatra. Even if the legality of the seizure might have been questioned, few people in north Sumatra were inclined to challenge Pattiasina on any point. Scrap iron was gold to Pattiasina and he mined it wherever it could be found.

During the first three years of Permina's history, a core of experienced men was formed in north Sumatra and many of its members now hold key positions in the Indonesian oil industry. Brig. General Pattiasina is now head of the Projects Division of Pertamina. Among his assistants during this period, J. Karinda is now Pertamina's representative in Amsterdam, Husni is head of Unit I (North Sumatra), and Rani Junus is head of the Telecommunications Division. Ir. Soediono is the deputy director of Exploration and Production. Ir. Sumbarjono is in charge of the Planning and Development Section of Migas. Ir. Astoto heads Unit VII (Singapore). Attorney Tirto Utomo is the deputy head of the Legal, Foreign Affairs, and Foreign Marketing Division. From the Djakarta office, Ir. Soedarno is now director of Refining and Petrochemicals, Geudong is deputy director of Finance and Administration, Affan is president-director of P.T. Pertamina Tongkang, and Harijono is president-director of P.T. Pelita.

*   *   *

In Djakarta, Dr. Ibnu realized that his small operation could never be more than that without additional capital. The business needed much more cash than could possibly be generated by small exports of crude and refinery sales to the local market. Contrary to the viewpoint of the times, which regarded foreign capital as a form of colonialism,

Ibnu recognized the need for foreign investment. The need was crucial since Permina could expect no further funds from the Indonesian government. Before beginning a search for capital, Ibnu laid down one basic principle: Permina, as a national company developing a national resource, must maintain control and management. This requirement cooled an initial interest by Stanvac, which had proposed a development program for Permina under their control and direction. There were, in fact, good reasons why Stanvac and others doubted Permina's ability to manage a development and rehabilitation program. Permina was controlled, and to a great extent staffed, by army officers who had little or no experience in the oil business. The area of the company's operations was an area of active guerilla fighting. Also, by 1959, the Indonesian government was swinging strongly towards the left and showing an almost total disregard for sound economic principles. It would, perhaps, be difficult to imagine a worse investment prospect or climate. Whoever entered this political and financial wonderland would need some exceptional faith in Indonesia's long-term future and a great need for Indonesia's oil. Fortunately, there were some Japanese who qualified under both considerations.

Mr. S. Nishijima arranged the first introduction between Japanese capital and Indonesian oil, which has now formed an important partnership for the two countries. Before the war, Nishijima had lived in Indonesia for several years as a staff member of a trading company and he spoke the language fluently. During the war, he was assigned to Rear Admiral Maeda's Naval Liaison Office in Djakarta. Nishijima and Maeda were very closely associated with the inner circle of Indonesian independence leaders and were present when the Declaration of Independence was signed during the predawn hours of August 17, 1945. No doubt because of this involvement, Nishijima was jailed by the Dutch as a suspected war criminal. He was not released until late 1947; he returned to Tokyo in 1948. Five years later he was again making trips to Indonesia on various government and business missions. In 1957, Nishijima served on the Japanese War Reparations Commission to Indonesia under the direction of the senior Japanese industrialist, Mr. A. Kobayashi.

Nishijima returned to Djakarta in June, 1958, on behalf of a Japanese group looking for a liquified petroleum gas project. Through old friends from the occupation days, he quickly arranged for a meeting with Dr. Ibnu. At about the same time a second Japanese group also approached Ibnu. As soon as the Japanese realized they were competing against each other, they reorganized into a consortium for dealing in Indonesia, known as the Kobayashi Group, an investment group coordinated by Mr. A. Kobayashi. A field survey team of eleven engineers was sent to Indonesia in September, 1958, and on the basis of their report a proposal was drafted in early 1959.

In March, 1959, Ibnu visited Japan to commence negotiations. Although he was the president-director of Permina, senior Japanese businessmen were taken aback that they were dealing with only a colonel, who was only in his forties and looked even younger. Ibnu, on the other hand, could only grit his teeth over the slow pace of negotiations. He later told an aide that if yesterday accomplished three steps forwards, today would surely begin two steps back. Negotiations and government approvals required a full year before signing on April 7, 1960.

These negotiations were severely criticized on both sides. In Indonesia, the idea of doing business with the former enemy was certainly not popularly accepted. Additionally, there was general hostility to any foreign business involvement in Indonesia. In Japan, the leftward-leaning policies of Sukarno and the economic chaos of his regime were viewed with apprehension. Also, there was considerable doubt as to whether this mere colonel could survive politically. Here began one of the early rounds of the rumor that Ibnu would soon be replaced.

The agreement that was being formulated credited equipment purchases in exchange for crude oil. At that time, such a barter agreement was contrary to Japanese governmental policy, which allowed only open-account agreements. Mr. Kobayashi had to enlist the support of the prime minister, Mr. N. Kishi, in order to win final approval. In a 1972 interview with Mr. Kishi in Tokyo, the former prime minister recalled his reasons for supporting the proposed agreement: "As prime minister, I had visited Indonesia to conclude the war reparations discussions in 1957. I was well acquainted with Indonesia's potential with its large population and rich natural resources. I believed that once Indonesia was organized it would be a great nation and under these circumstances Japan should help its development. Development and stability in Indonesia were essential to peace and stability in the Far Eastern region. Therefore, it was important for Japan to develop trade with Indonesia, and the young Colonel Ibnu had impressed me and my advisors as a good leader worth supporting. It has turned out to be an excellent association."

The Japanese had originally offered a thirty-year joint venture, but this was not accepted because of the Indonesian government policy which prohibited all further foreign participation in joint ventures in Indonesia. The parties eventually settled on a credit agreement with a "production sharing" arrangement. The agreement called for the Japanese to extend a $53 million credit in the form of equipment, machinery, materials, and technical assistance to Permina over a ten-year period and Permina would repay the loan in crude oil. Originally, this was to be based on 40% of increased production over a basic amount. The amount was eventually fixed at 35 million barrels with the Japanese having the chance to share excess production. In effect, this was a ten-year loan to be repaid by a specific quantity of crude, with a bonus if production was substantially increased.

In order to implement this contract, the Kobayashi Group formed a new company which was named North Sumatra Oil Development Cooperation Co., Ltd. (Nosodeco). As required by the agreement, Permina opened offices in Tokyo to oversee equipment evaluation and purchase, while Nosodeco opened offices in Djakarta, and also sent a technical advisory group to Pangkalan Brandan. The association between Japanese capital and Indonesian oil was underway. This first contract has been extended and the final payment will now be made in late 1972. The current managing director of Nosodeco as this contract is brought to a successful conclusion is the man who started it, Mr. S. Nishijima.

While the negotiations were going on with the Japanese, Ibnu was also bringing the company into the first stages of the shipping business. He purchased two small river tankers from Caltex, renamed *Permina I* and *Permina II*, to be used to shuttle the crude from the shallow harbor at Pangkalan Susu to the Strait of Malacca. These 1959 purchases were the start of a fleet now over 1,000,000 dwt.

In only three years time, Permina had formed the nucleus of an organization, reopened the north Sumatra fields, started marketing crude oil, and raised over $50 million for future development.

As Dr. Ibnu said, recalling this period in north Sumatra: "Oil is a very normal business, everybody who has the chance to learn and work, can do it. We realized that in north Sumatra when we had the opportunity to run the business ourselves. Acquiring the technical knowhow was not easy, but it was absolutely necessary and indeed it proved possible—we proved to be capable."

CHAPTER 8

Oil and Guided Democracy

Although it has been said that the invocation of martial law under the State of War and Siege Law on March 14, 1957, closed the curtain on the period of parliamentary democracy in Indonesia, it was actually only the first step in a transition that lasted over three years. Certainly the invocation of martial law greatly facilitated the transition to Guided Democracy, as did the dual crises of West Irian and regionalism. Yet in 1957, the country was still under the Constitution of 1950, and accordingly Sukarno, on March 15, 1957, appointed a new cabinet formateur who twice attempted to bring into being Sukarno's long-sought "four-legged" cabinet—one including the *PKI*. He was unsuccessful because both the Islamic parties and the *PNI* adamantly refused to participate in a cabinet containing the communists.

Sukarno then took another tack. He appointed himself as formateur and announced a cabinet headed by Ir. Djuanda. This "working cabinet" included no communists. Two months later, on June 15, 1957, Sukarno created a National Council (Dewan Nasional) with a purely advisory role. The council embodied Sukarno's ideas of representation for functional groups in the society and thus both *PKI* Chairman Aidit and General Nasution were included. There was no provision for the council under the 1950 Constitution, but it closely resembled the Supreme Advisory Council of the Constitution of 1945. The Cabinet rarely took action opposed to its advice.

159

The frustrations of the year 1957 culminated with the failure of the U.N. General Assembly to adopt a pro-Indonesian motion on West Irian on November 29. The Cabinet gave orders for the twenty-four-hour strike. The takeover of Dutch enterprises and expulsion of Dutch citizens began.

As 1958 opened, the regional issue moved back to the center of the stage. The takeover of the Dutch shipping line had exacerbated regional tensions. The KPM line captains had been ordered to sail their ships to non-Indonesian ports when word of the takeover came, and shortly thereafter Indonesia, under pressure from insurance companies, was obliged to release those vessels seized in Indonesian ports as well. The result was that 78 % of inter-island shipping capacity was lost. The breakdown of inter-island shipping further stimulated regionalism and increased smuggling with Singapore and the Philippines.

Shortly after the assassination attempt against Sukarno, a number of prominent Masjumi leaders fled Djakarta for Sumatra under a stream of abuse, intimidation, and accusations that they had participated in the assassination attempt. Included in their number were two ex-prime ministers, Natsir and Burhanuddin Harahap, and probably the two best financial minds in the country, Sjafruddin Prawiranegara, head of the Bank of Indonesia, and Dr. Sumitro (who had left Djakarta somewhat earlier). In January, these men met with the military regionalists including the Sumatran military commanders in an attempt to form a strategy.

General Nasution, although a Sumatran, saw the regionalist movement as a clear challenge to central authority and a threat to national unity. In its military aspects, it undermined his long efforts to assert Central Command control over the panglimas. His deputy for operations, Colonel Dr. Ibnu, saw another aspect of the proplem. He was instrumental in Central Army Command efforts to persuade Colonel Simbolon and others not to proceed. He told them their move was wrong because it would simply play into the hands of the *PKI*. However, Ibnu and others who sought to forestall the rebellion were unsuccessful.

In January, Sukarno, still shaken by the assassination attempt, went abroad for a rest. While he was gone, Lt. Colonel Hussein, military commander in central Sumatra, sent a strongly worded "Charter of Struggle" to Djakarta on February 10, 1958. The charter denounced Sukarno, his Guided Democracy, and the *PKI*. It demanded that Prime Minister Djuanda resign within five days and that Hatta and/or the sultan of Jogjakarta be appointed as formateurs of a national working cabinet pending elections. It also demanded that Sukarno resume his constitutional status. Djuanda categorically rejected the ultimatum on the following day.

Against the advice of sympathetic moderates including Hatta, who urged continued negotiation, the disaffected regionalists then took a step which precluded a compromise. On February 15, 1958, they proclaimed the Revolutionary Government of the Republic of Indonesia *(PRRI)*, headquartered in Bukit Tinggi, west Sumatra. A few days later another regionalist group, Permesta, on Sulawesi declared its support for the Bukit Tinggi government and broke off relations with Djakarta.

Central government and Army Command action was swift and well-executed. General Nasution dropped paratroopers at Pakanbaru, central Sumatra, quickly secured the city and the nearby Caltex facilities. In south Sumatra the panglima was wavering. Here, Colonel Ibnu was especially qualified to appraise the situation. Drawing on his seventeen years of experience in the area, Colonel Ibnu advised Nasution that to send Javanese troops there would surely cause the area to align with the rebels. He told Nasution that he would handle south Sumatra and that he needed only some weapons which he would place in the proper hands. Ibnu flew to south Sumatra and made the necessary liaisons. Ibnu also took the opportunity to move against *PKI* elements in the area. South Sumatra remained loyal to the government.

In May, the rebel strongholds of Padang and Bukit Tinggi fell without any great struggle and by the end of July the Permesta group had lost its capital of Menado after some stiff resistance. Although guerilla warfare continued for several years, this essentially marked the end of the ill-conceived and poorly coordinated attempt to contest the new power of Sukarno.

The *PRRI* rebellion posed delicate problems for Caltex, located as it was in the heart of rebel territory. Julius Tahija handled negotiations with the *PRRI* personally, maintaining close contact with the rebel commander, Colonel Hussein. Tahija recalls meeting with Hussein just before the outbreak of the rebellion. "I told Hussein very clearly that Caltex's contract was with the central government." When the *PRRI* later demanded that Caltex make tax payments to it, Caltex refused.

Caltex's relations with the central government were no less delicate. At this time, U.S. Secretary of State Dulles was making statements expressing sympathy for the *PRRI*, and suspicions of covert United States aid to the rebels were strong. In his book, U.S. Ambassador Jones recalls how he and two Caltex officials met with Prime Minister Djuanda. Notwithstanding the strained relations between the two governments, Djuanda entrusted Ambassador Jones with a general outline of the government's strategy in the Caltex area:

> 'I am going to trust you,' Djuanda said finally, his manner heavily serious. 'I shall require your word of honor that what passes between us will not reach outside sources. If it should, many of our soldiers' lives might be sacrificed. This is a grave responsibility for me and for you.' He then outlined in very general terms the plan of campaign, not in sufficient detail to give away any military secrets, but enough to reassure me that the Indonesian government was taking every precaution in its plans to ensure that the Caltex oil-producing installations would be protected. At the end, however, he advised us to evacuate all women and children to cover any unforeseeable eventualities. (Jones, p. 69–70)

On March 9, the government formally requested Caltex to suspend operations and evacuate dependents. The next day the government captured Pakanbaru and a week later Caltex was informed it could safely resume operations. With the rebellion for the most part crushed by the end of 1958, Sukarno returned to elaborating his new-style democracy. Prime Minister Djuanda was one of the many development-oriented Indonesians who favored a change to a more action-oriented form of government. As he told U.S. Ambassador Jones: "We need a government that can make decisions and get things done...and we somehow need to recapture the spirit of 1945, when we were all working together to win our independence." (Jones, p. 238) On November 7, 1958, Djuanda announced Cabinet approval of Sukarno's still undefined notion of Guided Democracy, following a meeting at the Presidential Palace. Armed with the Cabinet's endorsement, Sukarno addressed the Constituent Assembly on April 22, 1959. This body, elected in December, 1955, had been in session for three years, attempting to formulate a permanent constitution (the Constitution of 1950 was still only provisional). In his speech Sukarno formally presented the government's—his and the Cabinet's—recommendation that the assembly readopt the Constitution of 1945 in unamended form.

Rooted in the revolution, the Constitution of 1945 was well-suited to the widespread desire, voiced by Djuanda, to recover the spirit of national unity which had prevailed during the revolutionary period. It also provided the kind of strong executive which many, including Djuanda, felt was needed.

Under the Constitution of 1945, members of the Cabinet were appointed by the president, not Parliament, and served at his pleasure. Parliament (Dewan Perwakilan Rakjat–DPR) shared lawmaking power with the president as well as budgetary authority, but the president was not responsible to it in that it had no power to remove him from office. The president was responsible to the People's Consultative Assembly (Madjelis Permusjawaratan Rakjat–MPR), the highest repository of the people's sovereignty. It elected both the president and the vice president for a five-year term, and was charged with drafting the constitution and determining broad lines of national policy. Composed of all members of Parliament, plus territorial and functional group representatives, the Consultative Assembly was required to meet at least once every five years in order to elect the president. It could also meet upon petition of a required percentage of the membership. A third body, the Supreme Advisory Council (Dewan Pertimbangan Agung– *DPA*), was to serve as an advisor to the president and could make proposals to him on its own initiative as well.

Despite the national mood favoring change, the Constituent Assembly soon deadlocked over Sukarno's proposal to adopt the Constitution of 1945. The deadlock centered on the religious issue that had plagued the country since independence. The Muslim parties were willing to return to the Constitution of 1945 but demanded an amendment directly incorporating the "Djakarta Charter" into the constitution. The Djakarta Charter, drawn in June, 1945, obliged Muslims to observe Islamic law. Non-Islamic groups in the Constituent Assembly opposed this modification and a two-thirds majority could not be obtained.

The deadlock persisted, and as positions hardened, a governmental crisis developed. On June 2, 1959, the proposal to return to the Constitution of 1945 failed for the third time to obtain the necessary two-thirds vote. Sukarno, as so often was the case in times of political crisis, was abroad. General Nasution, in his capacity as central war administrator, banned political activity until further notice. However, contrary to widespread predictions that it would seize power, the army remained loyal to Sukarno.

When Sukarno returned, the need for action was urgent. Under pressure, the Cabinet resigned and purported to give Sukarno executive powers to run the country. By decree Sukarno then dissolved the Constituent Assembly and, on July 5, 1959, reinstated the Constitution of 1945 without the amendment desired by the Muslims. Four days later he appointed a new working cabinet with himself as prime minister and Djuanda as his first minister. On July 23, Parliament buttressed the shaky legal basis of Sukarno's new order by approving the return to the Constitution of 1945.

Sukarno's next step was to bring the parties under his control. By decree, the President took broad powers to ban, or dissolve parties deemed not to be serving the national interest. In March, 1960, after Parliament had refused to accept his new budget and had infuriated him by its frosty reception of the visiting Premier Khrushchev, Sukarno dissolved it. In its place, he announced the establishment of a new 261-member *gotong-rojong* (mutual help) Parliament. Sukarno allocated 130 seats to nine of the parties, including the *PKI*, but excluding the Masjumi and *PSI*. The functional groups, as selected by Sukarno, were allotted 131 seats. A few days later, Sukarno announced the membership of his new *gotong-rojong* Parliament and departed on a four-week world tour.

Opposition to Sukarno's highhanded changes finally coalesced around the Anti-Communist Democratic League, an organization which included the Masjumi, the *NU*, the *PSI*, the Catholic, and the Protestant parties. Belatedly, they sought to forestall Sukarno's drive towards authoritarianism. They and their newspapers vehemently attacked the Sukarno-appointed Parliament, the increased role of the *PKI* in national affairs, and Sukarno himself.

In the midst of the furor, the Dutch indirectly aided Sukarno's cause by announcing a plan for military reinforcement of West Irian. This event completely displaced the domestic issue as all parties and the press rushed to condemn the Dutch. Sukarno, returning from another overseas trip, rode this wave of nationalistic and anti-Dutch feeling using it to equate opposition to him with disloyalty. Thus characterized, the opposition soon withered away.

On June 24, 1960, the new *gotong-rojong* Parliament was installed. By a series of moves, Sukarno ensured its subservience. Standing rules were drawn up under Sukarno's direction by the Cabinet instead of by Parliament itself; the President appointed the Speaker, traditionally the prerogative of Parliament; a presidential decree announced that the members of Parliament served no fixed terms, but rather at the pleasure of the president. Finally, Sukarno advised the new Parliament, in an inauguration speech, that if unable to reach unanimity, they should leave decisions to the president on all issues of state business.

On August 15, Sukarno completed his new structure when he installed a provisional People's Consultative Assembly. As previously noted, this was the highest body of the national government, a kind of super-parliament, empowered to elect the president who was responsible to it, and to set the broad lines of state policy. Although theoretically the mandatory of the Consultative Assembly, Sukarno, by appointing the functional group representatives, and with the remainder coming from his newly installed *gotong-rojong* Parliament, was legally responsible solely to a political body which he had chosen himself, using his powers under the Constitution of 1945.

On the fifteenth anniversary of Indonesia's independence, August 17, 1960, Sukarno was able to report "the conditions for the journey are complete." By reinstating the Constitution of 1945, Sukarno had effected a radical change in his position from that of a head of state, with a largely symbolic role, to that of president with full executive powers. More important than the structure was the climate of subservience which Sukarno had established. From this time, Parliament and the Consultative Assembly played secondary roles in the formation of governmental policy. The defeat of the *PRRI* rebellion had also enhanced Sukarno's position by discrediting the Masjumi and *PSI* parties, two major centers of opposition to him, while the *PNI*, Sukarno's traditional party, was safely in the hands of the pro-Sukarno group.

The two principal power centers beyond Sukarno's control were the mutually antagonistic *PKI* and the army. The Army Central Command under General Nasution had favored, indeed some say had been behind, both return to the Constitution of 1945 by decree and the measures taken to discipline the parties. General Nasution and his group also stood staunchly behind the campaign to quash the rebellion and to regain West Irian, by force if necessary. However, on other aspects of Guided Democracy, the army leadership was strongly at odds with Sukarno, particularly Sukarno's belief that he could work with, and control, the

PKI. Army efforts to suppress the *PKI* using martial law powers were a frequent source of conflict and compromise between the Nasution group and Sukarno. Army support for the final phases of Sukarno's Guided Democracy was apparently gained only by a tacit agreement that no communists would be named to cabinet posts.

The army's own position and prestige were greatly enhanced during the 1957–1960 period. The Central Command's military campaign against the rebels was impressive. Moreover, under Nasution's doctrine of the "middle way", many army officers were selected to head the newly taken-over Dutch enterprises. Finally, the functional group government gave the army positions in the Cabinet and representation in the Consultative Assembly and Parliament.

The *PKI* also held mixed feelings about Sukarno and his movement to Guided Democracy. The *PKI* was second to none in support of the West Irian campaign, the takeover of Dutch properties, and the central government movement against the *PRRI*. It also supported the campaign to destroy the Masjumi and the *PSI*. But they watched uncomfortably as Sukarno and Nasution dismantled the parliamentary structure. However bad bourgeois democracy was, it was preferable to fascism, Aidit had warned at the Sixth Plenary Session of the Central Committee in the spring of 1958. In fact, however, the *PKI* had little choice but to follow Sukarno in hopes that he would provide them with a shield against the army. Thus, on October 27, 1959, the *PKI* called for a full implementation of the Sukarno concepts, including formation of a *gotong-rojong* cabinet with *PKI* participation. Sukarno, although he did not give the *PKI* any cabinet posts, provided the necessary protection.

An example of the relationship is provided by the army-*PKI* conflict over the holding of the *PKI's* Sixth Congress. The army first ordered the congress banned. Aidit announced that the *PKI* would go ahead despite the ban. Sukarno then stepped in as mediator: the congress was postponed, not banned, and conducted under close army supervision. The *PKI* was well-treated by Sukarno in other respects as well. Although excluded from the Cabinet, the *PKI* received 69 seats in the *gotong-rojong* Parliament, and were well

represented on other bodies as well: Aidit was named one of the deputy chairmen of the Provisional Consultative Assembly.

* * *

For the next five years, Indonesia would pursue the vague goal of *socialism à la Indonesia* under the Sukarno-created and Sukarno-dominated system of Guided Democracy. Perhaps the most striking characteristic of the period is the dominance of one man—Sukarno. His views and his doctrines, embodied in an endless stream of slogans, homilies, and acronyms became the official, and indeed the only, policy of the nation. That which characterized Sukarno also characterized Indonesian policy—rhetorical, dramatic, extravagant, exhortatory, undisciplined, and nationalistic to the point of xenophobia.

Great as Sukarno's power was over the formal organs of government, he was still faced with the task of balancing the power of the army and the *PKI*. But the army, the *PKI*— indeed whoever sought to influence policy or increase his political power—did so at the public and verbal level in a Sukarno-imposed framework. Because so many of his slogans and doctrines were vague, opposing groups could often invoke Sukarno's words with equal authority, particularly on domestic issues. Final resolution usually depended on whether or not the President himself chose to address the issue.

In late 1964, a prominent group of moderate leaders, concerned about Indonesia's and Sukarno's increasing involvement with the communists, formed a body to oppose this trend. Significantly, they called themselves the "Body to Support Sukarnoism." Sukarno eventually intervened against the group, dissolving it by decree.

An examination of three of Sukarno's basic doctrines will help convey the atmosphere of the times:

Manipol–USDEK. Sukarno's Independence Day Speech to the nation of August 17, 1959, was entitled *The Rediscovery of Our Revolution.* After Sukarno consolidated his power, this speech was officially adopted as Indonesia's Political

AT THE 45TH ANNIVERSARY OF THE INDONESIAN COMMUNIST PARTY—1965.

Manifesto—abbreviated *Manipol*. *Manipol's* thesis was that Indonesia had wandered from its proper revolutionary course by erroneously adopting Western institutions ill-suited to Indonesian culture, such as "free-fight liberalism" and Western democracy in which "fifty percent plus one dictates" to the rest of the community. Sukarno proposed a return to the "true revolutionary spirit" by the implementation of five concepts—the first letters of which in Bahasa Indonesia make up the acronym *USDEK*. These are: (1) return to the Constitution of 1945; (2) adoption of *socialism à la Indonesia*; (3) Guided Democracy; (4) Guided Economy; and (5) Indonesian identity (the objective here was to stress Indonesian culture and combat "cultural imperialism," e.g. Western music and motion pictures).

NASAKOM. This is an acronym for what Sukarno identified as the three major elements in Indonesian society: nationalism, religion, and communism. All three, he maintained, must be included in Indonesian government.

NEFO–OLDEFO. *OLDEFO* (Old Established Forces) are the West and colonial powers. They are confronted by the Third World–the new nations–and also by the Communist bloc which together make up *NEFO* (New Emerging Forces). Under this view, Sukarno increasingly aligned Indonesia with the Communist bloc, abandoning Indonesia's neutralist foreign policy.

Indonesia's foreign policy during 1960–1965 was active and flamboyant. The period from 1960 to 1962 was dominated by the campaign to regain West Irian. On August 15, 1962, after thirteen years of sporadic negotiations which culminated in some clashes between Dutch and Indonesian forces, the West Irian question was finally resolved in a way highly favorable to Indonesia. Under the terms of the settlement, West Irian became a U.N. trusteeship, but Indonesia would, and did, take administrative control of the area on May 1, 1963. Not later than 1969, a plebiscite of the territory would be conducted under U.N. supervision whereby West Irian's 800,000 people would decide between incorporation in Indonesia and independence. (In 1969, the United Nations accepted the report that the people of West Irian had, by an act of free choice, elected to join Indonesia.)

The United States played a major role in the resolution of

the West Irian question, with Ellsworth Bunker successfully acting as mediator. United States' policy towards Indonesia had shifted rapidly after its earlier expressed support for the *PRRI*. During the Kennedy presidency, further improvement took place. Indonesia's highly personalized diplomacy often reflected Sukarno's feelings of personal warmth towards the American ambassador to Indonesia, Howard P. Jones, President Kennedy, and Robert F. Kennedy.

With the West Irian issue settled, the United States and other Western nations hoped that Indonesia would finally turn her attention to economic development. This did not suit Sukarno, however, who envisioned Indonesia as the leader of the Afro-Asian nations. In this self-appointed role, not a year later, he was embroiled in *Konfrontasi* with what he viewed as the neo-colonialist puppet state of Malaysia —the puppeteer being Great Britain. Although professing no territorial ambitions for Indonesia, Sukarno took up the cause of self-determination on behalf of the two British areas of Borneo that had been assimilated into the new Malaysian Federation. The campaign against Malaysia involved a new and expensive mobilization of Indonesian troops and society while conveniently serving Sukarno's domestic objective of maintaining a high degree of revolutionary fervor.

Sukarno's campaign against Malaysia was, to many in the West, the last straw. In the United States there was growing popular, congressional, and government criticism of Sukarno's adventurous foreign policy, his personal life, domestic dictatorship, and increasing alignment internationally with the Communist bloc and domestically with the *PKI*. A watershed of sorts was reached on March 25, 1964 when Sukarno proclaimed to the United States, in a widely circulated speech, "To hell with your aid!"

In 1964–1965, Sukarno increasingly aligned Indonesia first with the Communist bloc and then, as the Sino-Soviet split deepened, with China. In January, 1965, he led Indonesia out of the United Nations, proposing a new world body made up exclusively of the new emerging forces with China and Indonesia as its leaders.

Although he espoused the national objectives of a Guided Economy and *socialism à la Indonesia*, Sukarno himself took little interest in economics. This was dramatized in an exchange between Khrushchev and Sukarno during the former's visit in 1960. As recounted by Ambassador Jones:

> The two men [Sukarno and Khrushchev] were discussing the economic development program of [Indonesia] and Khrushchev asked Sukarno for budget and production figures—apparently stressing the necessity for cutting back on consumer expenditures. When Sukarno waved the question airily aside, Khrushchev, shocked by Sukarno's lack of concern for such details, almost shouted to him, 'You're no socialist! Socialism is figures, figures, figures! You've got to know where you are every minute of the day or night.' (p. 337)

This disinclination on Sukarno's part became fatal when coupled with his failure to entrust economic affairs to someone with the ability and the authority to make the hard decisions required by Indonesia's straitened economic circumstances.

With the takeover of Dutch properties, the government assumed a much larger role in the economy, and one that overburdened its existing supply of managerial talent. Consideration was given to allocating some of the former Dutch properties to private Indonesian businessmen, but this was rejected, and all of them became state enterprises.

The economy, already burdened by the very high costs of Sukarno's aggressive foreign policy, was further strained by the cost of implementing Sukarno's own pet projects: costly monuments built on lavish scale, trips abroad with large traveling parties, and expensive centers to host international conferences.

The basic economic blueprint, if such it could be called, reflected the unique Sukarno approach. In August 1956, the National Planning Bureau had formulated a modest five-year plan with the purpose of integrating various regional development schemes into a single national one. However, the *PRRI* rebellion had intervened to preclude any meaningful implementation. Three years later, the National Development Council (Depernas), under the chairmanship of the lawyer, historian, and revolutionary leader, Mohammad Yamin, met to draft an eight-year plan in the spirit of *socialism à la Indonesia* and the Indonesian consciousness. A year later they presented their product— instead of a useful working document, it was a monumental, 5,000 page glorification of the revolution. It was divided, symbolically, into seventeen volumes, eight divisions, and 1,945 paragraphs, thus memorializing the date of independence (17-8-1945). The plan consisted of a "shopping list" of "B" projects which were to be financed by funds from "A" projects—those sectors of the economy which could be expected to produce revenues, among which was the oil industry. The plan contained virtually no indication of priorities nor of the interdependence of the various projects. The projected revenue from the "A" projects at best would supply less than half of the funds needed to implement the plan—the plan was silent on the sources to be tapped to make up the difference.

Private foreign capital was one possible source to bridge the gap. In 1958 Indonesia had enacted a foreign investment law, but this legislation, which had been sought by the moderate cabinets since the transfer of sovereignty, did not result in any inflow of foreign capital. The investment climate was clouded, to put it mildly, by the takeover of Dutch properties, the *PRRI* rebellion, and later by Indonesia's mobilizations to secure West Irian, and to confront Malaysia. Moreover, in spite of the law, Indonesia still seemed undecided on the question of foreign capital's role. Sukarno, in a series of policy statements, declared that Indonesia opposed any new foreign ownership in the Indonesian economy and that foreign capital would be accepted only on a loan basis. In 1962 and 1963 this policy was married with the concept of repayment of foreign credits through production sharing in the area of national resources development.

The plan contemplated a foreign exchange cost of $2.5 billion over and above the amount used to finance the payment of imports at the then current level. Over three-fourths of this increase ($1.95 billion) was to come from the oil sector—$750 million in new investment—and a

$1.2 billion ($150 million per year) increase in government earnings from oil exports.

The consequences of this disregard of the laws of economics were as disastrous as they were predictable. Although Indonesia had been plagued by severe inflation since 1953, what had gone before paled to insignificance with the 1960–1965 figures. The year 1965 saw a truly runaway inflation in which government printing presses were literally unable to keep up with the need for new paper money. The cost of living index rose astronomically:

Cost of Living Index (Djakarta)
(March, 1957–February, 1958 = 100)

1963	1,612
1964	3,300
1965	13,382
1966	153,180

In real terms, the economy stagnated, export earnings dropped, and external debt rose. With the money system in shambles, hoarding and corruption were rampant. The transportation and communication infrastructure was neglected. Probably only the fact that 70% of the Indonesian people lived at a subsistence level essentially outside the money economy saved Indonesia from a major catastrophe. In the face of its multitudinous problems, the Indonesian government often opted for an ostrich-like approach as exemplified by the government ban on the release of Bank of Indonesia's annual reports during the period 1961–1965.

Domestically, Sukarno's authoritarianism increased over the 1960–1965 period and with it the suppression of dissent. The Masjumi and *PSI* were forced to disband as were other "anti-Indonesian" organizations, including the Anti-Communist Democratic League, the Rotarians, and the Boy Scouts. Many political opponents were either imprisoned or forced to flee the country. Newspapers daring to criticize were either suspended or completely shut down.

First Minister Djuanda died in November, 1963. With his death, Indonesia lost one of her most dedicated public servants and one of her most influential moderates. The week after his death, President Sukarno formed a new cabinet naming himself again as prime minister.

The *PKI* grew steadily throughout the period and increasingly the government's programs were *PKI* initiated. The *PKI* also enjoyed considerable success in its most important task—the insinuation of its doctrines into the armed services. By 1965, it had virtual control of Indonesia's air force and had obtained considerable influence in the navy and national police. The army leadership, however, remained staunchly anti-communist, but even the army suffered from *PKI* influence, and by 1965, pro-*PKI* officers were not uncommon in the lower and middle echelons.

If the *PKI* and the army represented two relatively independent and mutually antagonistic forces which Sukarno sought to balance, there was still a third group whose power was in general derivative from Sukarno himself. In this group were the men and organizations that had served Sukarno, either out of loyalty, ambition, or both, and rose to power as a consequence of his favor. Included in this group were his three deputy prime ministers, two of whom, Subandrio and Chairul Saleh, were viewed by many, including themselves, as rivals for Sukarno's power.

Among the many positions held by Chairul Saleh was that of minister of Basic Industries and Mining. In this capacity he directed Indonesian oil affairs. As minister, Chairul Saleh was the single most powerful figure in Indonesian oil during the 1960–1965 period. Chairul was born in central Sumatra in 1917 and attended secondary and law school in Djakarta. During the Japanese occupation, he was both a leader in a Japanese-sponsored youth organization and a participant in the underground. In 1945 he was with the group of youths who kidnapped Sukarno in an effort to persuade him to hasten the proclamation of independence. A fiery economic nationalist, he violently opposed the Round Table settlement and after the transfer of sovereignty he led a group of guerillas who fought against the Indonesian government in west Java. Eventually captured, he spent two years in jail before being released by Attorney General Mohammad Yamin and sent to Holland on a government scholarship. Chairul spent five years in Europe studying politics, first in Switzerland, then at Leiden University. He was expelled from Holland for political activity, and then he proceeded to Germany after the minister of education (the same Mohammad Yamin) arranged for another scholarship. Ambassador Jones reports, "Saleh told his professors he wanted to learn all that the Germans knew about the accomplishment of revolution by legal means." (p. 434) Others report that Chairul learned at least as much about poker, a game at which he excelled to his profit.

In 1956, Sukarno met Chairul while touring Western Europe. Chairul later claimed that he then submitted a student association memorandum to Sukarno that outlined the ideas which eventually formed the basis for Guided Democracy. Back in Sukarno's good graces, Chairul returned to Indonesia in 1956 and was instrumental in the founding of the Generation of '45, of which he was named chairman. Shortly thereafter, he also made his peace with General Nasution. Requesting a meeting with the general, Chairul told him that he had noted Nasution's changes in doctrine and that he, Chairul, had consequently changed his position vis-á-vis the army and Nasution himself. His group (the Generation of '45) was grateful to Nasution, he said, for his efforts to integrate the irregular forces into the *TNI*. He told Nasution of his impending appointment as minister of veteran affairs, and to further the burying of past conflicts, he requested as his secretary general the *TNI* commander who had led the army forces against him in west Java. Chairul's appointment as minister followed.

When Sukarno formed his Working Cabinet on July 9, 1959, Chairul was one of the nine men named as core ministers, being nominated as minister of Reconstruction and Development and concurrently as junior minister of Basic Industries and Mining. There were nine core ministries in the Working Cabinet—besides Chairul's position there were Defense, Foreign Affairs, Internal Affairs and Regional Autonomy, Finance, Production, Distribution, People's Welfare, and Special Affairs. Each core minister had under him four to eight other ministers, whose efforts he was supposed to coordinate. The number of ministers greatly increased during the 1960–1965 period as Sukarno used the assignment for patronage purposes.

Chairul had left Indonesia as a rough-hewn rebel; he returned as a polished man of the world. Handsome, intelligent, and socially popular, Chairul's star was clearly on the rise; his prospects were perhaps exceeded only by his own ambitions. On March 6, 1962, he was named chairman of the provisional Consultative Assembly, and eighteen months later he became third deputy prime minister.

As minister of Basic Industries and Mining, Chairul had jurisdiction over the oil sector which he no doubt saw as important to his political aspirations. He was assisted by three deputy ministers—one for mining, one for basic industry, and one for personnel and administration. The deputy for mining was Ir. Anondo. A 1938 graduate in civil engineering from the Technical Institute at Bandung, Ir. Anondo was already a veteran civil servant in the mining sector. He had served in equivalent positions since the amalgamation of the federal state into a unitary government in 1950, and before that with the Republican government at Jogjakarta where he headed the ministry section which oversaw the revolutionary oil companies.

Ir. Anondo's mining department had worked closely with the Commission on Mining Affairs after that body was created by the Hassan Motion in the 1950s, providing it with technical data, and working on drafts of the proposed new oil law.

In anticipation of the increasing role of nationally controlled oil companies, Ir. Anondo was instrumental in the establishment, in 1959, of a program under which young men attached to the ministry were assigned to the oil companies for practical training in oil operations.

Ir. Anondo had also contributed to preparation of Law No. 10 which was enacted on April 25, 1959, two months before Chairul Saleh's tenure began. This law revoked a number of concessions not only in oil, but in other mining areas as well, on the grounds that the concessionaires had failed to carry out development efforts in the years since 1950, or had done so only on a minimal basis.

Indicative of the increased activity of the Indonesian government in mining and oil affairs, was the decision taken in the early days of Chairul Saleh's ministry to divide Ir. Anondo's mining jurisdiction into three bureaus—Geology, Oil and Natural Gas, and General Mining. The Bureau of Oil and Gas (Biro Minjak dan Gas Bumi—Migas) was created on January 1, 1960. Today Migas continues to regulate the oil sector. Over the years it has undergone a number of changes in status—bureau, directorate, department, directorate general. As head of the newly created bureau, Chairul selected Basarudin Nasution, Permina's former legal advisor. Chairul's selection of Basarudin was, according to Basarudin himself, a good example of the balancing of political forces so characteristic of Indonesian politics.

Basarudin had a long history of association with the army, and he was related to General Nasution. Though he had refused an army commission, he had acted as army legal advisor in a civilian capacity. However, the army had a strongly qualified candidate for this responsible position who was then studying oil marketing in the United States. To Chairul, Basarudin was preferable to a man directly affiliated with the army. And Basarudin was also related by marriage to Chairul Saleh. By the time the army's candidate returned to take up his expected position, Chairul had already established Basarudin in the post.

Though his selection may have been based upon other factors, Basarudin was prepared for his new job. His legal credentials and experience were particularly relevant to his duties because Chairul was determined to place his oil program on a sound legal basis. Basarudin had also briefly studied oil matters in the United States in 1959, under arrangements made by Dr. Ibnu at the request of General Nasution.

When Basarudin took over, Migas was nothing but a name and one man—himself. In need of qualified assistants, Basarudin was assigned a staff selected from throughout the ministry. Many of these men continue to serve in Migas today. Ir. Oetojo Boenjamin heads the Safety and Calibration Office, Ir. Hantoro is now head of Exploration and Production and Drs. Nurdin is the head of Personnel and Labor Relations.

Basarudin recalls that one of his first assignments from Chairul Saleh was to secure the position of his new bureau as the sole regulator of oil and gas. At the time there was a competitor in the Oil Office (Kantor Minjak) which was attached to the office of Prime Minister Djuanda. The Oil Office was created in 1958 as an advisor to the Price Stabilization Board, also created in that year, to combat domestic inflation. Its official function was to advise the board on domestic distribution of petroleum products and their pricing. Headed by an army colonel, M.T. Harjono, the Oil Office sought a voice in general oil policy as well. If the Oil Office succeeded, Prime Minister Djuanda would have a larger say in oil affairs, and Chairul Saleh a somewhat lesser one. Although both agencies continued in existence through 1960 and 1961, Chairul Saleh's bureau eventually won the bureaucratic battle, and the Oil Office was dissolved in 1962.

By far the most important task facing Basarudin was the drafting of an oil law. For nine years this had been on the Indonesian agenda. The commission created by the Hassan Motion had by this time disbanded, and a committee in the ministry had taken over the task. In the early drafts of a new law, oil had been included as part of the general law on mining. Chairul Saleh eventually decided, however, that oil and natural gas should be governed by a separate law. Thus Basarudin personally took over the task, assisted by his Migas legal staff.

Chairul Saleh approved their draft and sent it to the Cabinet. President Sukarno signed the draft law on October 26, 1960. The President used his emergency powers and the law became effective upon promulgation the same day. The Parliament ratified it in February, 1961. Nine years after the Hassan Motion, Indonesia finally had a new oil law.

The enactment of Law No. 44 provides a good example of the political trade-offs Indonesia had made in opting for Guided Democracy. An action-oriented government was what most Indonesians wanted; one free of the time-consuming, faction-ridden legislative process which they

had found so characteristic of their parliamentary democracy. No longer could regional spokesmen, or oil company influence, or simply the inability to form a majority, prevent action.

Article 3 is the basic operational provision of Law No. 44. In contrast to the previous mining law, it states: "the mining of oil and gas shall only be undertaken by the State," and "mining undertakings of mineral oil and gas are exclusively carried out by State Enterprises." The scope of "mining undertaking" is broad indeed. As defined under Article 4, it encompasses all of the activities of an integrated oil company, including exploration, exploitation, refining, processing, transportation, and marketing.

Law No. 44 does not specify which state enterprises would be given an "authority to mine." This was left for determination by the government. Similarly, the geographic extent of each such enterprise's mining authority was left to the discretion of the minister having jurisdiction over oil and gas mining (Article 5). However, Law No. 44 does define what a "State Enterprise" is, "an Enterprise as meant in Government Regulation in the place of a Law No. 19, 1960 regarding State Enterprises." Law No. 19 had been enacted on April 19, 1960, to provide a common regulatory framework for government-owned companies, the number of which had mushroomed with the takeovers of Dutch-owned properties.

The role of foreign companies, and for that matter, any other companies not qualifying as state enterprises, and hence ineligible to receive an "authority to mine," was dealt with in Article 6. It states: "The Minister may appoint other parties as contractors for the State Enterprises, if required for the execution of operations which *can not or can not yet be executed by the State Enterprises* involved as holders of the authority to mine themselves." (Emphasis added) Relations between any such contractors and the state enterprises were to be governed by a Contract of Work which would be effective only when ratified by law. Basarudin states that the "ratified by law" provision was included in the interest of providing assurances to the oil companies. The explanatory memorandum to the provision makes the point less directly:

> Since the Contract of Work ...is of utmost importance for the development of the [oil industry] to ensure sufficient skill [and] to obtain and attract sufficient capital at the present stage of the mineral oil and gas industry, [the contract] must be ratified by a Law before it can become effective.

It was strongly opposed by Dr. Ibnu who maintained that relations should be governed by contract and nothing more. Neither Law No. 44 nor the official commentary thereto provided any definition or specification as to the nature of a Contract of Work. Because the situation would vary, the comment notes, content was intentionally left "entirely to the discretion of the Government."

Dr. E. Sanger, today the head of Pertamina's Legal, Foreign Relations, and Foreign Marketing Division, provides an insight into the behind-the-scenes debate on this provision. Dr. Sanger, then a young lawyer in Migas and the recent recipient of a Ph.D. from a German university where he had studied with Chairul Saleh, was one of the men who worked on Law No. 44. Among the groups to be consulted as to the proposed law's content was the *PKI*. Since Sukarno's appointment of *PKI* representatives to the National Council in 1957, the *PKI* had been consulted in all policy matters. The *PKI* was very strong in 1960—not as strong in numbers as it would become later, but highly influential. In the midst of Dr. Sanger's work, Chairul Saleh informed him that he would meet with Sakirman, one of *PKI's* leading theoreticians, to discuss the law's content. The talks between Sanger and Sakirman lasted five days. Sakirman argued that no foreign participation should be allowed in the Indonesian oil industry. Sanger took the opposite position: "From P.T. Permina's experiences in needing capital and technology, we already knew that if we relied solely on the national companies to develop our oil industry, it would take too long. Oil already played an important role as a source of foreign exchange and would be counted on for more. To develop a national industry, we would need foreign knowhow and capital. Perhaps most important of all was foreign marketing and Permina's successful experience with Refican. The experiences of Permina were the inspiration for Law No. 44's Article 6, the article allowing for foreign participation when needed."

After five days of talks ended without agreement, Dr. Sanger recalls, "I reported back to Chairul Saleh. Chairul simply said, 'We'll do it our way,' and that's the way the provision on foreign companies went to the cabinet."

Law No. 44 clearly signified the beginning of a new era in Indonesian oil. It is sometimes stated to be a natural corollary to Article 33, Paragraphs (2) and (3) of the Constitution of 1945, which are cited in the Law's preface. The pertinent Constitutional provisions are:

Sect. 2. Branches of production which are important to the State and which affect the life of most people, shall be controlled by the State.

Sect. 3. Land and water and the natural riches therein shall be controlled by the State and shall be exploited for the greatest welfare of the people.

The phrase "controlled by the State" seems to leave ample room either for state regulation of private companies or for the exclusive conduct of mining by state enterprises. However, the decision manifested by Law No. 44 to opt for the latter form of control reflects oil's classification as one of the stratigic minerals by the General Mining Law, Law No. 37 (promulgated on October 14, 1960). Also the decision probably does conform more closely to the intent of the draftsmen of Article 33 in 1945, than mere regulation of a foreign-dominated industry.

After a decade of independence, Indonesia still did not control its oil industry to the degree most leaders felt proper. As Dr. Ibnu noted: "As panglima of South Sumatra in 1956, I was not even permitted to enter the Shell facilities at Pladju." The continuation of these foreign enclaves was simply not acceptable to the majority of Indonesians, recalling, as it did, the extraterritorial basis on which foreign enterprises operated in colonial times.

The enactment of Law No. 44 raised two fundamental and basically distinct questions. The first was strictly a domestic matter: How many state enterprises would be invested with an "authority to mine"? The second concerned the foreign companies and their respective governments: Would they negotiate pursuant to Law No. 44, and if so what would be the terms of the undefined Contract of Work?

The answer to the first question—the number and identity of the state enterprises under Law No. 44—was readily found. Even in 1960, there were proponents of the creation of one national oil company. History and the politics of the moment, however, dictated another answer—there would be three national oil companies, each having a historical base in the 1950s and each reflecting, more or less, one of the three major political groupings of the time.

P.T. Permina was the army's company. With three years of operations behind it, Chairul Saleh could not have changed this even if he wanted to. By Government Regulation No. 198, 1961, enacted and promulgated on June 5, 1961, P.T. Permina was amalgamated into P.N. Permina (Perusahaan Negara Pertambangan Minjak Nasional—State National Oil Mining Company).

As a counter to the army, and a concession to the *PKI*, Chairul established P.N. Permigan (Perusahaan Negara Pertambangan Minjak dan Gas Nasional—State National Oil and Gas Mining Company) by Government Regulation No. 199 also enacted and promulgated on June 5, 1961. It was the most poorly endowed of the three companies, initially being assigned nothing but the few played-out fields of Nglobo Mining Co. (*TMNca*) in central Java—fields Shell had not bothered to reclaim. Located in one of Indonesia's most poverty-stricken and communist-inclined areas, P.N. Permigan would naturally have a leftist orientation.

The third company, P.N. Pertamin (Perusahaan Negara Pertambangan Minjak Indonesia—State Indonesian Oil Mining Company) was formed by Government Regulation

No. 3, enacted and promulgated February 13, 1961. This was the government's company, formed from the assets and organization of Permindo, the one generally regarded as having the best-trained personnel, and the odds-on favorite to emerge as the dominant company of the three.

Law No. 19, the law which provided a common regulatory framework for state enterprises in all sectors of the economy, provided for the establishment of General Management Boards—the *BPU's* (Badan Pimpinan Umum), whose function was to coordinate the policies of the state enterprises in the same sector. On June 7, 1961, the *BPU* Minjak was established. Dr. Ibnu was named chairman, and the president-directors of P.N. Permigan and P.N. Pertamin were named as members. Basarudin Nasution sat on the board representing the new Bureau Migas. The other two members were from the Oil Office—Colonel M.T. Harjono and his assistant, a young economist, Drs. Sakidjan Atmosudigdo, now head of Pertamina's Central Statistics and Information Division. The status of the *BPU* was somewhat peculiar. Officially it formed one division of the ministry, but, as Dr. Ibnu pointedly noted, it really had no policy making power nor legal teeth. By virtue of its diverse composition, and the fact that Dr. Ibnu considered its meetings generally more political than productive, the *BPU* was for the most part inactive.

At the first meeting of the *BPU*, Dr. Ibnu struck a characteristic theme. Addressing his fellow *BPU* members, he said, "Just because we are the leaders of Indonesian oil does not mean we know anything. Our most important job is to learn as much as we can in the shortest possible time."

There was indeed still much to be learned. But optimism was the keynote for the national companies. They were to have a chance to help create the "just and prosperous society," to fulfill the aspirations of Merdeka.

Though, with the passage of Law No. 44, the future looked promising for the Indonesian national oil companies, this could certainly not be said of the Indonesian prospects for Shell, Stanvac, and Caltex.

CHAPTER 9

Negotiations with the Big Three

With the promulgation of Law No. 44, the major companies suddenly found their positions in jeopardy. The companies were not only concerned about the impact of the new law upon their Indonesian operations, but also what precedent it might set for other areas of the petroleum world. The important question raised by Law No. 44 was Indonesia's intent concerning future relations with the foreign companies and the law was by no means specific. By the companies' standards, they had, at least since the war, been good citizens in Indonesia—dutifully training Indonesians, paying good wages, building schools and roads, helping the nation and their local communities. Now they were confronted with what they regarded as a unilateral abrogation of their concession rights.

Although those who drafted Law No. 44 did not consult with the Big Three on the content of law, they carefully considered their possible reactions. On the one hand, the law was clearly to specify a change in the status of the oil companies from concessionaires to contractors but, on the other hand, it was hoped that this change could be made by negotiation rather than litigation or nationalization. Indonesia did not have the funds to compensate the companies if it had to nationalize the properties, nor could it afford to take the expropriation route Iran had unsuccessfully tried in 1951.

Article 22 shows the Indonesian effort to strike an acceptable balance. Its first paragraph clearly provided for the termination of the Big Three's previous mining rights.

But an effort was made to coat the bitter pill in Paragraph 1 with some sugar in Paragraph 2. It provided that the Big Three would receive priority over other applicants as contractors in their present mining areas. The article also provided for a flexible negotiation period during which the companies could continue to exercise their concession rights. Only after the expiration of this period "which shall be as short as possible and determined by government regulation" would their concessions expire.

The Big Three could not realistically consider terminating their oil activities in Indonesia, and seeking compensation on the grounds that Law No. 44 constituted an expropriation of their property, although, according to Dr. Sanger, this was their initial reaction. In the first place, even under the prior Dutch law it was far from clear that the concessionaires held title to oil in the ground; and, in any case, Article 33 of the Indonesian Constitution explicitly stated that "land and water and the natural riches therein shall be controlled by the State and shall be exploited for the greatest welfare of the people." Secondly, Indonesia was not alone in its new assertiveness against the oil companies. World oil prices had dropped drastically in 1960, and governments of producing countries throughout the world were rebelling against the Majors' efforts to reduce the posted prices upon which their fifty-fifty agreements were based. All the countries were contending that the Majors themselves and not market forces controlled the prices of oil. In September, 1960, the Organization of Petroleum Exporting Countries (OPEC) was formed by Iraq, Iran, Kuwait, Saudi Arabia, and Venezuela to combat the reductions. Indonesia joined in 1962.

Also, if the companies could accept the provisions of Law No. 44, the law did contain some promise of benefit. The way was finally cleared for the granting of new exploration areas, and this was a matter of particular importance to Shell and Stanvac, both of which were experiencing declines in production in their existing areas.

On balance, then, the Big Three's course was clear—they would negotiate with the government on the terms of Law No. 44, and seek to make the new status of "contractor" as nearly equivalent as possible to the previous one of "concessionaire." If they did not own the oil in the ground, they could still seek to retain final say over the management of its extraction and its disposition, and make a fair share of the earnings. So, all three companies decided to continue their operations despite the legal uncertainty.

The first round of negotiations commenced in late 1960. The government was anxious to obtain full implementation of the law, but the companies were content to proceed at a leisurely pace. Early in the negotiations, it was decided that any agreement reached would apply retroactively to January 1, 1961, the date on which the existing "let-alone" agreements expired.

Major differences quickly emerged in the negotiating positions. The first concerned the split of net operating profits. The government asked for 60% of the profits; the companies agreed to this allocation, but asked for a "production allowance" which would effectively reduce the Indonesian share.

Also in question was the extent to which Indonesia would have the right to participate in pricing. Heretofore the government had no say in the establishment of export prices. Indonesia, in common with other oil exporting countries, maintained that the drop in world oil prices in 1960 was largely due to the oil companies' manipulation. The Big Three contended that market forces controlled prices and that the recent price drop was due to a great surplus of oil on the world market caused by recent discoveries in the Middle East. The companies strongly desired to preserve their exclusive right to set prices.

The third issue was the duration of the contract. The companies wanted at least forty years (the period under the 5-A Contracts). The government offered a much shorter period.

Indonesia needed foreign exchange to finance its newly promulgated Eight-Year Plan. To meet this need, Basarudin Nasution proposed that the companies advance a total of $1,200 million against future production. The companies showed an interest in this proposal, but their interest evidently never went beyond politeness and the proposal was dropped.

After ten months of negotiations there was still no settlement in prospect. The first phase of negotiations ended in August of 1961, when Basarudin Nasution, who had led Indonesian negotiators, was ousted from his position as head of Migas. This was a consequence of the continuing duel for control over oil affairs between Prime Minister Djuanda and his cabinet's Oil Office on the one hand, and Chairul Saleh on the other. Reportedly, Djuanda was indirectly testing the idea of a separate department for oil, and the prospective minister being recommended was not Chairul, but Basarudin. It is said that when Chairul heard of this he was so enraged he smashed his fountain pen against the desk, breaking it in two, and had to call for another one to write out Basarudin's dismissal.

Basarudin's replacement as head of Migas, Iskandar Notobroto was also a lawyer and had, like Basarudin, previously served as a legal adviser to the army. Although Iskandar handled the day-to-day affairs of Migas, the negotiations with the Big Three were taken over increasingly by Lukman Hanafiah, S.H., a young lawyer in private practice. Hanafiah was appointed special legal adviser for oil and played a large role in policy matters during the remainder of Chairul Saleh's tenure.

With negotiations stalemated, Presidential Decree No. 476 was promulgated on August 28. The decree stated that "the division of the earnings between the Government and the companies concerned is effected on the basis of 60% for the Government and 40% for the foreign companies." Further, the decree stated that the government would participate in all future determinations of the selling price of crude oil and refined products. Thus the decree resolved two of the points at issue in the negotiations in Indonesia's favor. Nevertheless, negotiations with the Big Three continued to lag.

While Shell, Stanvac, and Caltex were reluctant to negotiate new positions under Law No. 44, several other companies showed interest in entering Indonesia under the new terms. Pan American, the exploration subsidiary of Standard Oil of Indiana, was one such company. At the time Lukman Hanafiah entered the negotiations, a draft agreement had already been completed between Pan Am and the government and the contract was signed on June 15, 1962. For the first time since before World War II a new area was thus opened for exploration and exploitation.

The Pan American contract established important precedents for further negotiations with the Big Three. Now it could be demonstrated that a large foreign oil company was willing to operate in Indonesia as a contractor on Indonesia's terms. Pertamin was given the "authority to mine" as provided for by Law No. 44 and Pan Am became a contractor to Pertamin. Pan Am received a large block west of the Caltex field in central Sumatra, an area that Stanvac had hoped to receive.

The contract contained a number of provisions designed to ensure that Pan Am diligently explored and developed its contract area. A maximum of thirty years was allowed with ten years in which to "discover petroleum, which in its judgement can be produced commercially." Pan Am agreed to commence exploratory operations within six months. A schedule of exploration investment commitments during the first eight years of the contract required a minimum of $1.25 million for the first year and increased progressively to over $6 million in the eighth year. The total commitment was $28.5 million. Pan Am was also required to relinquish 25% of its contract area after five years and an additional 25% after ten years. Pan Am was entitled to select the portion to be relinquished. By this provision, Pan Am was given an incentive to explore expeditiously so that it might exercise its choice wisely. After three years of exploration operations, Pan Am was given the option to relinquish all or part of its area without penalty, subject to payment to the government of any unexpended portion of the first three years' investment commitment. If Pan Am surrendered less than the total contract area, however, it remained liable for the balance of its eight-year commitment.

Indonesia also improved its financial position over that negotiated under previous contracts. For the first time, the government received a cash bonus, $5 million paid by Pan Am, upon the signing of the contract. A second bonus of $5 million was contingent on reaching production of 15,000 barrels per day. Beyond the bonuses, which were not recoverable, Pan Am agreed to pay Pertamin 60% of operating profits (the revenue from petroleum produced after payment of specific operating costs) or 20% of the value of Pan Am's gross production, whichever was higher. This payment would relieve Pan Am of all Indonesian income taxes.

The contract between Pertamin and Pan Am was primarily a profit sharing arrangement rather than a production sharing arrangement. Essentially, Pertamin was to receive dollars, not oil. However, the value of the oil was defined in terms of the "realized price." The Indonesian negotiators believed that Indonesia was better served by keeping its oil revenues based on the realities of the market place. In this respect Indonesia diverged from the course of Middle Eastern countries. In the Middle East, the governments reacted to price decreases proposed by the international companies by simply refusing to consent to the change. For some time, then, the "posted price" of Middle Eastern oil had been a fictitious one, used for tax purposes only.

However, to keep the "realized price" concept from being abused, Indonesia demanded, and got, two kinds of protection. First, a price committee was established consisting of one person from each side, and if needed, a neutral third party. More important than this legal machinery was the provision whereby Pertamin secured "the right to elect to receive, at the point of export, up to twenty percent (20%) of the petroleum produced by Pan Am." The 20% in-kind election was a hard-won victory for Indonesia. Pan Am wanted to sell the entire Indonesian share, but finally agreed to a 20% portion, which Indonesia could elect to sell itself, and an exclusive sales agency for Pan Am to sell the balance of the Indonesian share.

Under the contract, Pertamin was explicitly a tax-collector and implicitly a government auditor of Pan Am's activities. The opportunity to receive payment in oil was the one important exception to Pertamin's general role in the contract as a passive partner to Pan Am. The contract provided that Pan Am would have complete responsibility for management. Pan Am also undertook to Indonesianize its work force, but the commitment was only at the usual 75%, a level already exceeded by the Big Three.

The Pan Am contract was of major significance in negotiations with the Big Three. Clearly, they would now have to negotiate similar contracts. However, the Big Three's position was quite different from Pan Am's and they could logically expect somewhat better terms. Pan Am had not relinquished existing concessions as the Big Three were being required to do. There were also broader dimensions to the Big Three's negotiations, particularly in the case of Stanvac and Shell. Agreement was required not only as to production, but also as to refining, domestic distribution, and marketing. Thus, although the execution of the Pan Am contract set a valuable precedent, there remained many unresolved issues. The negotiations soon bogged down again. Through the rest of 1962 and the early months of 1963, talks continued without significant progress.

In March, 1963, with no agreement yet in sight, Chairul Saleh asked Lukman Hanafiah what he thought should be done. Hanafiah suggested that an ultimatum should be given to the oil companies to make them get down to hard negotiating. Based on this recommendation, Government Regulation No. 18 was issued on April 26, 1963. It set an expiration date for the negotiation period of June 15, 1963, at 2400 hours—a mere seven weeks away. If a new agreement was not reached by that time it provided that the three companies would have to liquidate their operations.

The impact of this so-called ultimatum resounded throughout the world oil community. The companies responded to what they viewed as brinksmanship on the part of Indonesia with some brinksmanship of their own and threatened to walk out. The breakdown was naturally viewed with alarm by the United States government. The Hickenlooper Amendment, which had been recently enacted, required an automatic cut-off of foreign aid to any country that nationalized U.S. foreign investment without adequate compensation. This action had a precedent in Ceylon, where aid was terminated after the nationalization of refining and marketing facilities. In addition to its protective interest, the United States was concerned because of the importance of the oil sector to the Indonesian economy. If an agreement was not reached, Indonesia could be expected to turn to the Soviet bloc for aid, further pushing Indonesia into the Communist camp. With talks threatening to break down, the United States then intervened directly. The U.S. government's decision to intervene in the negotiations was reportedly welcomed by President Sukarno, who appreciated this indication of high government concern. No doubt the companies also welcomed it.

Arrangements were made for a top-level discussion in Tokyo, involving not only the Indonesia negotiators and the parent company representatives, but a special team of advisors from the U.S. government as well. Tokyo was selected because it was the site of proposed talks between President Sukarno and Tunku Abdul Rahman, prime minister of Malaya, on the subject of the proposed formation of the Federation of Malaysia. Many of Sukarno's top advisors, including Chairul Saleh, were to accompany the President to Tokyo. Although the political talks at Tokyo were not successful in averting Indonesia's later *Konfrontasi* with Malaysia, the oil talks were successful.

The oil negotiations began on the second day, May 31, of the three-day Tokyo conference. Chairul Saleh and Lukman Hanafiah represented Indonesia. Attorneys of the international parent companies were there with the representatives of Caltex and Stanvac. Although Shell sent representatives to Tokyo, it did not participate in the meeting. The special United States government team was headed by Wilson Wyatt, and included Abram Chayes, legal adviser to the Department of State, Walter Levy, an internationally-known oil consultant, and Ambassador Jones. In the talks the team served as conciliators listening to both sides and offered such assistance as they could. Starting at 8:00 in the evening, talks lasted all night and finished at 5:30 in the morning.

After the all-night session, the end result was the Heads of Agreement dated June 1, 1963 (also signed by Shell). They established the basic grounds of understanding regarding the new contracts. Back in Djakarta, details of the final contracts were worked out by a joint ministry team headed by Ir. Anondo, including, from the private sector, Hanafiah as legal advisor and Utomo Yosodirjo as economic adviser. On September 25, final agreements were signed. They are generally referred to as Contracts of Work (Perjandjian Karya).

The companies relinquished their existing concessions to the government and in return, became contractors to the state companies. Each of the Big Three was assigned as contractor to a different state company. The alignments were: Shell–Permigan, Stanvac–Permina, and Caltex–Pertamin. The companies were given twenty-year exploitation contracts for their former concession areas and were given thirty-year contracts in designated new areas (ten years for exploration and twenty for exploitation). All three companies chose areas in close proximity to their existing operations. Stanvac received an area in central Sumatra surrounding its Lirik field. Shell chose two new areas in south Sumatra and an area adjacent to its newly developed Tandjung area in Kalimantan. Caltex obtained two areas near its Duri field in central Sumatra.

Substantively, the provisions of the Contracts of Work, as to exploration and exploitation of crude oil, closely followed the Pan Am model. They included an undertaking by the contractor to explore and develop diligently, backed by minimum exploration investment commitments, and mandatory relinquishment of 25% of the area after five years of exploration and another 25% after ten years. A sixty–forty profit split in favor of Indonesia was also provided with both a signature bonus and production bonus of $5 million each for the new areas. The "realized price" concept was retained and there was provision for a value committee in the event of dispute as to price. The foreign contractor was appointed as the exclusive sales agent to market the state enterprise's oil, but the state enterprise reserved the right to elect to take 20% of aggregate production in kind. Management control was retained by the foreign contractor.

The contracts also provided for the sale of all Shell's and Stanvac's refineries and the domestic marketing and distribution assets of all three companies. Refining facilities would be sold over a period to begin in ten years and end in fifteen years. At the time, Shell and Stanvac were not particularly happy about this clause of the contract, for the refining end of their business in Indonesia had been fairly profitable, primarily because they had been able to export over 50 % of their refined products to other Far East markets. However, the companies accepted the fact that the refining operations would also have to be turned over to the Indonesians. On the Indonesian side, it was felt it would probably take ten to fifteen years to develop the knowledge and skills to run the entire operation on their own. Although over 75 % of the employees of the refineries were Indonesians, there was still a serious shortage of Indonesian engineers and administrators. The price for sale of the refineries was based on the original cost with reductions depending on the year of transfer.

Sale of marketing facilities was provided for within a five-year period. These included all retail outlets and distribution organizations, although it excluded international aviation, marine bunkering, and the blending and packing of lubricants. The payment to be made for the marketing assets, was based upon 60 % of their original cost. For each year that passed before the actual sale was made, this would be reduced by the amount of 5 % and the price to be paid on the date of sale would then be set at 60 % of this reduced amount.

The companies also agreed to supply the Indonesian domestic market with crude oil and refined products at cost plus fixed fees. Shell and Stanvac had complained since the end of the 1950s that they were losing money in selling price-controlled gasoline and kerosene in the domestic market. Indonesian investigators disputed this, contending that Shell and Stanvac were not losing money but simply making less. In any event, Shell and Stanvac continued a noninvestment policy with respect to service stations; no new stations were built and existing stations were generally allowed to deteriorate.

Caltex, meanwhile, had also entered the distribution area on a small scale. Regional agitators in central Sumatra, spearheaded by the *PKI*, noted that despite Caltex's large oil production, there were no gasoline service stations in Pakanbaru or Dumai. Caltex began building stations on a modest scale, first in Pakanbaru and Dumai and later in west Java as well.

In 1962, the Indonesian government had promulgated a pro rata decree under which each of the Big Three was obligated to supply the domestic petroleum requirements in the percentage of its Indonesian crude production to total Indonesian production. Caltex, which had theretofore exported all of its Indonesian production, thus was required to contribute to Indonesia's needs for the first time.

No increase in the price of gasoline or kerosene was permitted and costs continued to rise with inflation. In the years 1962 and 1963, most who were familiar with the situation would agree that the Big Three were subsidizing the Indonesian consumer.

The Contract of Work changed this. It provided a guaranteed return to the Big Three for crude at $0.20 a barrel plus cost, refining at $0.10 a barrel plus cost, and distribution at $0.10 a barrel plus cost. This provision, unlike the others of the Contract of Work, was not retro-active. Thereafter the Big Three presented periodic accounts of their rupiah and dollar costs for each operation to the government.

The act of signing the Contracts of Work did not complete the negotiations; ratification still had to be obtained by Parliament. In Parliament, the contracts were fiercely attacked by the *PKI*, and other leftist groups, as a "giveaway to foreign capitalist imperialism." The attack, although vigorous, was relatively brief and the contracts were ratified on November 28, 1963.

Within oil circles there were also opponents of the Work Contracts. One was Dr. Ibnu; he maintained that management should be retained by Indonesia, and that Indonesia should have the right to take its entire share in-kind rather than just 20%. He believed that the role of the state companies was too passive. They merely reviewed, but did not make decisions.

On the other side, government proponents of the Work Contracts felt that this agreement was the best that Indonesia could obtain at the time. Although they acknowledged that management still remained in the hands of the companies they felt that the companies were much more accountable to the government than they had been under the old concession agreement. The basic point of contention here was a matter of degree. Just how far the government could have pushed in 1963, and whether or not more attractive terms could have been obtained, is a matter of conjecture. It might suffice to say the Work Contracts were an interim solution, and one that was necessarily brought about through compromise. It was, in any event, an important step forward.

*   *   *

The enactment of Law No. 44 and the compromise contracts negotiated, offered some hope for progress to both the Indonesians and the Big Three. However, these hopes soon withered. On September 18, 1963, representatives of the Big Three received a portent of things to come during the final negotiations on the Contracts of Work in the new Hotel Indonesia in Djakarta. In the midst of their labors, from the conference room windows they viewed the sacking and burning of the British embassy that was located directly across the street. An impassioned crowd had been aroused to violence by the *PKI* over the new policy of *Konfrontasi* against the proposed Malaysian Federation. Lukman Hanafiah did his best to put a good face of the situation. Addressing his counterparts, he said, "Gentlemen, that is today, you must think of tomorrow." Unfortunately for the Big Three, the "tomorrows" increasingly threatened more of the same. The realities were a financial squeeze developed by inflation and unrealistic exchange rates; labor problems characterized by wildcat strikes and takeover attempts; and an extremely adverse political climate as Indonesia began its rush to the left. The companies merely coped with situations that arose in the best way they could. They developed responses of sell out, fade out, or hide out. As for selling out, Shell decided to sell all their Indonesian assets while Stanvac wanted to sell their refining facilities and less productive fields while retaining their best fields. All three companies attempted to fade out by not asserting themselves and avoiding political confrontation. Caltex, with its remote location and lack of refining and marketing facilities, was literally able to hide out in its jungle location.

Being able to operate at all became a problem as the communist-dominated labor movements began to show their strength. Perbum continued to call for the nationalization of the oil industry. Perbum was instrumental in various walkouts, strikes, and other challenges to the companies. Incidents and tension mounted throughout the years 1963, 1964, and 1965.

Shell's labor difficulties in Kalimantan are illustrative of conditions, although perhaps they were more severe than elsewhere. Balikpapan received the major thrust of the leftists' bid for dominance because it was the focal point of all eastern Kalimantan. The region's military commander, General Soeharjo, was sympathetic to the *PKI*, and under his protective wing, Perbum and other leftist groups began to disrupt operations to the point of forcing a shutdown. The problems reached a climax in the last months of 1963.

It was customary for Shell to send ice out to the work parties in the fields to keep foodstuffs cool. On one particular ice run, the Shell workers were continuously stopped by local military and police personnel and each group took portions of the ice. When the Kalimantan general manager heard about this, he went to General Soeharjo to make a complaint. In an angry confrontation the general manager lost out, and he was placed briefly under house arrest.

About the same time, it was declared that no foreign languages could be spoken in Balikpapan. Indonesian employees risked jail sentences if they were caught speaking to their expatriate colleagues in other than Indonesian. Shortly thereafter, General Soeharjo and Perbum established a "komissar system". The "komissars" were outsiders who were unfamilair with the company's routine and they were responsible directly to General Soeharjo. They monitored and relayed all communications and instructions between the management and the laborers.

From Shell's point of view, the Kalimantan situation was unbearable. In its efforts to avoid shutting down the refinery, Shell's main office management had these possible alternatives: They could approach the Indonesian government and request an inquiry into the situation, but this approach was blocked because of Soeharjo's strategic importance in the current *Konfrontasi* with Malaysia. And Soeharjo had the support of the President behind him. This set of circumstances effectively cancelled out Shell's second option—to ask for help from the Indonesian Army. Representatives of Shell had approached the commander in chief of the army, General Yani, regarding the situation in Balikpapan. They requested the transfer of General Soeharjo to another post. It was reported that General Yani issued the transfer order, only to have his order countermanded by the President. The third alternative for Shell was to solicit aid from the foreign embassies in Djakarta. Although the embassies could not assist Shell directly, they could help by showing deep concern for the safety of their respective citizens in the Balikpapan area.

In December, 1963, Shell and the foreign embassies arranged an official visit to Balikpapan. Representatives from the American and French embassies, among others, joined Shell management personnel for the trip to get a first-hand view of the situation there. By doing this, the embassies involved expressed their anxiety over the Kalimantan situation to both the central government and to General Soeharjo. Reports from Shell personnel in Balikpapan at that time stated that the visit did help lessen the tension somewhat, but operational difficulties continued.

In January, 1964, Iskandar Notobroto vacated his position as director of Migas. His replacement was Ir. Wijarso. Wijarso, a veteran of eight years in the ministry, was entering the oil side for the first time. Unlike his two predecessors, Ir. Wijarso is an engineer by training, turned, as he prefers to describe it, "oil-bureaucrat."

Wijarso recalls 1964 as a relatively quiet year, so far as government relations with the Big Three were concerned. Officially there were only two events of significance. In

August, 1964, Indonesia decreed that the transfer of marketing assets contemplated by the Contracts of Work would proceed on an accelerated one-year basis. Although this did not precisely square with the Contract of Work proviso that the transfer would proceed according to schedules provided by Shell, Stanvac, and Caltex respectively, it apparently encountered no resistance. Pertamin was nominated as the company to receive these assets and run the marketing operations.

The Contracts of Work had guaranteed a return to the Big Three on marketing operations at a rate of cost plus $0.10 a barrel, but operations were increasingly difficult. Notwithstanding the severe inflation, the Indonesian government was unable to increase prices because of leftist political pressure. As a result, demand soared and the beginnings of gasoline and kerosene shortages and an accompanying black market made the distribution task not only difficult operationally, but politically hazardous. Chairul Saleh's problems were somewhat reduced by the decision to accelerate the transfer. By purchasing these facilities, the government could ease leftist pressures by presenting the nation with visible proof of their moving in on the oil industry—every gas station in the country.

The total amounts to be paid to the companies for the stations, depots, terminals, and road and rail tankers were approximately; Shell $8 million, Stanvac $4.5 million, and Caltex $300,000. These figures give a good indication of the extent to which each company was involved in domestic marketing. By July, 1965, Pertamin had completed the transfer of all marketing facilities. Indonesia was for the first time in complete control of domestic marketing.

The second event was a dispute over the rate of exchange applicable to the Big Three companies. The exchange rate had been set at a base rate of 250 rupiah per dollar. However, export industries, including oil, had regularly received bonus exchange under Indonesia's complex multiple exchange rate system whose purpose was to keep Indonesia's export products competetive in world markets. Thus, at the time of the signing of the Contracts of Work, all oil companies received not only the 250 rupiah rate but a 65 rupiah bonus as well, for each dollar earned or converted. Under the Work Contracts, each company covered its rupiah expenses first from rupiah generated by local sales, and, to the extent this was insufficient, they had to convert foreign currency earnings at a rate of exchange which was defined as:

> the official general rate of exchange in effect at the time of conversion plus any bonus or incentive payments *available to similar industries*, provided that if any more favorable rate of exchange is available to any other *oil enterprise* operating in Indonesia, such more favorable rate of exchange shall also be available [to the Big Three] ... for example as of May 27, 1963, the rate in effect would be 315 rupiahs to one United States dollar.
> (Article 17; Emphasis added)

In June, 1964, the meaning of the provision came into dispute. Indonesia raised its export bonus payment from 65 rupiah to 270 rupiah, making the rate 520 for most export industries, but in the oil sector the rate was held at 315. This would hurt the national companies, but it would hurt the Big Three far more. The Big Three objected, arguing that the "similar industries" provision required a raise in the oil rate as well. Not so, said Wijarso, "similar industries" meant only other oil industries, and unless consent were given by September 30 to a continuation of the 315 rate, export permits for the next quarter would not be issued. Shell and Stanvac capitulated at the end of September. Caltex held out until October 1, and then followed suit. Having established the legal point, the government then granted the new 520 rate to the companies. Even so, inflation soon outran this exchange rate also.

As 1964 closed, the pressures increased against foreign capital in general and foreign oil companies in particular. By March, 1965, Perbum pressure for a takeover of the foreign oil companies had reached such intensity that Chairul Saleh concluded something must be done if disruption of operations was to be averted.

Chairul went to President Sukarno, who, despite his own public movement to the left, still shared Chairul's view that Indonesia could not afford to nationalize the oil industry. From the President, Chairul secured an open mandate to implement any plan he might be able to devise to take the initiative out of the mounting *PKI*-led nationalization drive. In secret talks between Chairul and the agitators, Chairul feigned agreement with the latter's nationalization objective. To that end it was agreed that demonstrations would be conducted against the foreign companies at an unspecified date in the near future. Chairul made sure that the non-communist unions would also participate. However, Perbum apparently got suspicious of Chairul's intentions, and accelerated the date of the demonstrations. In the late afternoon of March 18, Nurdin, the Migas official in labor relations, learned that the *PKI* intended to conduct demonstrations the next day. Thus forewarned, Chairul, Dr. Ibnu, Lukman Hanafiah, Anondo, Wijarso, and their top staff worked through the night drafting the decrees necessary to put Chairul's plan into effect. Wijarso, having spent a sleepless night, decided that in fairness, the heads of the various companies should not sleep undisturbed. In the early hours of the morning he placed calls to each and inquired whether company operations had been disrupted.

The next day, the *PKI* proceeded with the demonstration, but Chairul Saleh was prepared. He made the following carefully worded announcement:

> For the purpose of securing the oil companies as well as for continuing to recognize the property rights of the foreign oil companies, upon guidance of the President, the Government immediately places all foreign oil companies under the control/supervision of the Republic of Indonesia Government.

This announcement specified that this action was temporary in nature and being taken without prejudice to the companies' property rights.

Committees were set up to supervise each of the four companies—Caltex, Shell, Stanvac, and Pan Am. Each committee consisted of members from the appropriate state companies, Migas, senior Indonesian oil company staff, and members of the labor unions. The duty of these committees was to look into all the day-to-day affairs of the companies, in which they theoretically had a say. Privately, key members were instructed to concentrate on Indonesianization and not to disrupt the companies' operations.

PKI Chairman Aidit knew that Chairul had stolen initiative but there was little he could do. In late June, 1965, he addressed a Perbum conference, calling on the government to drop the facade of government supervision and to proceed with nationalization of the foreign oil companies. Aidit, along with many other left-wing leaders, continued to agitate for this action. He called on the workers to "give more blows to American imperialists so that Indonesia can be free of their hands."

Although the sale of the marketing assets lowered their exposure politically, economically only Caltex was in a good position with its large and profitable production from the Minas field. Geographically, Caltex was also in the best position. Its operations were in central Sumatra, away from the principal areas of Perbum agitation. Essentially, Caltex, in its remote location, kept a low profile and continued to pump its oil out.

Shell and Stanvac, on the other hand, were facing a bleak financial future. Their new exploration efforts were just getting started and existing production was still declining. Financially, their parent companies were the biggest petroleum companies in the world and could weather even this storm. But the political climate by 1965 indicated that there would probably be no end to this storm other than that which might come with a communist takeover. They decided to salvage what they could by selling out.

* * *

On April 1, 1965, Chairul Saleh divided the Department of Basic Industries and Mining into three departments—Oil and Natural Gas (Migas), Mining, and Basic Industries. Each department was headed by a minister with Chairul Saleh retaining the position of minister of Migas, the most important of the three. Chairul also retained ultimate jurisdic-

tion over Mining and Basic Industries as well as certain
other sectors of the economy as the senior "core" minister
of development. Within Migas, Ir. Anondo continued to
direct finance and administration, while Ir. Wijarso directed
the technical side.

Concurrently with this reorganization, Dr. Ibnu was
appointed as minister of state, attached to Third Deputy
Prime Minister Chairul Saleh, with a special assignment in
oil and gas. Dr. Ibnu's position as minister of state did not
carry functional responsibilities in the Department of
Migas, but in effect was a recognition of his position in
Indonesian oil.

In April 1965, Stanvac approached Dr. Ibnu, in his
position as minister of state, offering to sell their Sungei
Gerong refinery and several of their older south Sumatran
fields for $50 million. A few months later Shell went even
further; they proposed negotiations concerning sale of their
entire Indonesian operations. By September 1965, closing
negotiations were being separately conducted with both
companies. Dr. Ibnu carried out the negotiations assisted
by a few members of his staff from Permina, Ir. Soedarno,
Dr. Sanger, Drs. Sakidjan, P. Siregar, and Tirto Utomo.
Throughout the months of July, August, and September,
this team visited the various areas to evaluate the companies'
assets and check inventories. The question of price was
approached in the framework of the Contracts of Work
provisions that had established a formula for buying the
refineries in ten to fifteen years and the eventual acquisition
of all assets at the end of the twenty-year old-area rights
and thirty-year new-area rights.

The companies' bargaining position was not strong
considering the decline of their operations in Indonesia,
decreasing production, increasing rupiah expenses, runaway
inflation, and the ever -mounting polarization of the nation's
political forces between the army and *PKI*. Nobody could
ascertain what would happen when the building pressure
burst the dam of Sukarno's embrace. Before negotiations
could be concluded, on the night of September 30, 1965,
the dam broke. Further negotiations would have to await
the subsiding of the flood.

CHAPTER 10

Permina, Pertamin, Permigan

The decision to create three national oil companies—
Permina, Pertamin and Permigan—after the enactment
of Law No. 44, simply recognized the status quo. All three
companies were operating at the time and two of them,
Permina and Pertamin, were well-established and growing
in size and competence.

Permina, under the leadership of Dr. Ibnu and Pattiasina,
was starting to rehabilitate the north Sumatra fields with
the aid of the Nosodeco loan. Pertamin, with the assistance
of Shell, was operating the former *NIAM*/Permindo fields
at Djambi and Bunju.

The third company, Permigan, still lacked a viable
economic base and it had under its control only a few tiny
fields in central Java and some scrap-iron refinery equipment
put together during the war. The total Permigan production
was only 800 barrels per day as compared with Permina's
15,600 and Pertamin's 30,000. The total of the national
oil companies was only 10% of national production.

Still, despite the modest scale of their operations, no
one doubted the potential importance of the national oil
companies. Their change in status under Law No. 44
presented an occasion to reconsider the leadership of the
respective companies.

Dr. Ibnu recalls that he was not at all sure he would
continue to lead Permina. He was widely known for his
anti-*PKI* feelings, and with the President following his
NASAKOM policy of rapprochement with the *PKI*, it
seemed to Dr. Ibnu that an officer more in tune with the

politics of the times might well be selected to replace him. He was called for a discussion with Chairul Saleh: "Chairul told me, 'you are too bullheaded and too army.' by which he meant too pro-Nasution. I replied, 'That's the way I am, I'm not likely to change.' Chairul shrugged and laughed. Then he made me chairman of the *BPU*."

On June 17, 1961, Dr. Ibnu was appointed president-director of P.N. Permina, with Major Pattiasina as technical director and Major Geudong as administrative director. Although Dr. Ibnu's appointment was not formally announced until nine months after the enactment of Law No. 44, he continued to lead Permina in the interim period.

As in the case of Permina, where consultation with the army on any change would be required, so, too, with Permigan, Chairul Saleh's power to change was narrowly circumscribed. The company was not only leftist but also strongly regionalist and the central government could not readily impose a board of outside directors on the company. The Diponegoro Division of central Java was also jealous of its prerogatives respecting the company, and since 1957 its interest had been recognized by the presence of Major Prodjosumitro as the administrative director. He remained in office as did the previous technical director, Hadi Gondo-wardjojo, who had served in similar capacities since the days of the revolution. The only change Chairul made was to appoint Nirwonojudo as president-director. Nirwonojudo had been out of oil affairs since his adventures in north Sumatra ended in 1957, but was still highly regarded in central Java where he had started his oil career.

Unlike Permina and Permigan, Pertamin gave Chairul the opportunity to pick his own team. He took his time, appointing a board staffed by Migas officials in the interim. As finally appointed, the president-director of Pertamin was Ir. Effendi Saleh. A mechanical engineer, Effendi was an experienced manager having previously served as head of the Indonesian state railways. However, he had no previous experience in oil save for a short training stint in Djambi. Joining him as administrative director was Saleh Siregar, an economist by training, who had experience both in banking and with a state paint enterprise, but like Effendi

Saleh, had no previous oil experience. As technical director Chairul named a young chemical engineer in the ministry, Ir. Omar Hassan Asaari, the only one of the three who also served on the interim board. He had been educated in Japan, and had worked in the Department of Mines since returning to Indonesia in 1956.

By the middle of the year 1961, the leaders of each of the new state oil enterprises had been officially appointed and were embarked on their efforts to give substance to the idea of a national oil industry. In practice, each company's leadership had very different ideas about what that meant.

*   *   *

The directors of Permigan took over an enterprise which was still in the scrap-iron stage of operations and was years behind the other two national oil companies. Despite its small size, Nirwonojudo may well have viewed his appointment as president-director with some satisfaction. As events turned out, it was the peak of his long up and down career in national oil.

Permigan's field holdings were thirty and forty-year-old fields with scrap-iron distilleries, and a small marketing organization that sold the production in the surrounding towns of central Java. The management's short-term plan was to rehabilitate their fields while seeking to acquire more valuable assets. Production in 1961 held at about 800 barrels a day. Through the *BPU,* a government loan was received and applied to payment of employees' back wages. Some was left over for maintenance and rehabilitation.

In April, 1962, Permigan received an important input to its holdings. Shell had experienced labor problems in their central Java operations from the time the Dutch forces had reclaimed the Kawengan and Wonosari fields and the refinery at Tjepu from *PTMN* during the revolution. In early 1962, matters got worse and the workers threatened to forcibly take over the facilities. Shell therefore wanted to sell, and acquiring these assets would greatly broaden Permigan's base of operations. On March 6, 1962, the head of Migas, Iskandar Notobroto, was authorized to negotiate the purchase for Permigan. Agreement was quickly reached and, by a contract executed on April 6, 1962, the Indonesian government purchased Shell's production and refining facilities in central Java including offices, residences, the pipeline from Tjepu to Surabaya, and the Surabaya storage facilities and terminal. The purchase price was £1.5 million sterling payable in five annual installments, with the first due one year from the date of sale. The sales contract provided that if a Contract of Work under Law No. 44 was signed with Shell within one year, the purchase price would be set off against up to 45 % of any bonus payments Shell was required to make to the government. Although the Contract of Work was in fact signed somewhat beyond the one-year limit, this provision was honored and, to Indonesia's further benefit, the payment was offset not against the signature bonus but the contingent production bonus. Despite this link to the Contract of Work, the Tjepu sale occurred independently of the Contract of Work negotiations and reportedly had no effect on them.

From Shell's standpoint, the sale improved its Indonesian position. It disposed of an aged refinery and two fields of small and declining output located in an area of considerable labor trouble while, at the same time, creating goodwill with the Indonesian government. While marginal to Shell, the combined output of Kawengan and Wonosari was more than three times the production of Permigan's other fields. The refinery at Tjepu had a capacity of 3,000 barrels per day and was a major addition to the scrap-built refineries. The pipeline to Surabaya was leaky but could be repaired to provide a direct outlet for exporting crude. It had formerly been used to send crude in excess of refinery capacity to Surabaya and thence by tanker to Balikpapan for refining.

Permigan's hopes for additional growth lay in attracting foreign capital to further develop its areas in central Java and to develop other areas. Though it was never formalized, it was generally understood that Permigan had jurisdiction over all of Java and the islands in eastern Indonesia. The most important of these were the West Java Block and the Bula field on the island of Ceram in the Moluccas. Both the West Java Block and Ceram had originally been Shell concessions, and both were among those cancelled for non-development by Law No. 10 in 1959. Of the two, the West Java Block was the most promising. Before World War II, Shell drilled a number of wells in the area and found oil and gas at shallow depths. During the revolutionary period, *PTMN* had plans to build a lubricating oil plant at Bongas, but Dutch advances made this impossible, and the retreating Indonesians used scorched-earth tactics to destroy all facilities. As Law No. 10 worked its way through Parliament, Shell made a belated effort to save its concession by mobilizing a drilling team and sending out invitations to the drilling inauguration ceremony. The government saw the purpose of this hasty activity and, shortly before the announced ceremony, Shell was informed that its concession was cancelled.

A number of foreign companies had expressed interest in the development of west Java. In mid-1961, the Ministry of Basic Industries and Mining put out feelers to the Roumanian trade mission in Djakarta. Negotiations began in earnest at the beginning of 1962. The talks went beyond development of the west Java fields. Nirwonojudo was especially interested in constructing a large refinery on Java. It would be not only the first large refinery on the island but also the first large one controlled by an Indonesian state enterprise. The proposed project, as embodied in a mutually agreed but non-binding project specification on January 26, 1962, and in an agreement in principle, also non-binding, completed at the end of 1962, contemplated a three-phase development. First, a refinery would be constructed at Gresik in east Java, north of Surabaya, with a throughput of approximately 41,000 barrels per day. Its projected cost was $40 million and of this Roumania would supply a $25 million credit. Roumania was, however, unwilling to supply the $15 million estimated to be required for pipe, gauges, and certain other specialized equipment that it needed for its own petroleum industry. Thus it was agreed that Indonesia would obtain the remaining $15 million loan from some other country.

Under the second phase of the proposed agreement, Roumania would supply drilling equipment worth $15 million for the development of the west Java field. As in the case of the refinery, a credit with another country would also be required for certain items. The third phase covered miscellaneous requirements including 300 railroad tank cars, which would be assembled in Indonesia, a lubricating oil and sulphuric acid plant, and a drum factory. Repayment of the credits would not be from oil, but rather from other raw materials including rubber.

Although both sides were initially enthusiastic about the proposed deal, this changed with the arrival of the Roumanian advance party. The group was critical of local conditions and, moreover, Roumania was skeptical about the likely implementation of the third country credit. At the time, Indonesia was exploring possibilities with French, American, and Swiss groups. It soon became apparent that Roumania was dragging its feet on the project.

Meanwhile, Permigan received a number of professionally trained people from Migas. Migas had to move carefully in this respect for "interventions" by Djakarta were still suspect. Migas began by assigning five men as a part-time staff to the Board of Directors. Two of these, Sutrisno (Ben) Samsoe, a U.S. trained geologist, and Ir. Sumbarjono, who had been with Permina in north Sumatra, eventually spent full time on Permigan's operations. They were joined in 1962 by Ir. Rumboko, a graduate of Penn State with three years' experience with Stanvac, and Dr. Wahjudi Wisaksono, who returned to Indonesia after completing his studies in Holland. Dr. Wahjudi became Permigan's head of refining.

While the deal with the Roumanians lagged, Ir. Sumbarjono and Dr. Wahjudi did some rehabilitation work in west Java on their own. Sumbarjono took forty men to the Bongas area, where Shell had drilled three wells. His purpose was to demonstrate a flow of oil to stimulate investor interest, and two of the Bongas wells were regarded as highly promising. In 1963, they went into production, selling the crude to a limestone smelter for direct burning. Dr. Wahjudi, to keep himself busy, built a small refinery using materials from Tjepu.

The Bula field in Ceram was, like west Java, the subject of much talk and little action. Prior to World War II, Shell drilled 43 wells in the area and discovered some oil. During the war, the Japanese continued exploration, and drilled three more wells. Allied bombing destroyed the facilities and Shell never rebuilt them. In 1960, Chairul Saleh sent a team to Ceram to evaluate its potential. The Japanese were quite interested in the Ceram field. In 1962, Mitsui approached Permigan with a proposal to send a joint expedition to the island. Arrangements were made, and in that same year the two-nation team set out. Ir. Sumbarjono headed the Indonesian group and Admiral Maeda (ret.) was in charge of the Japanese group. (This was the same Admiral Maeda who had played such a helpful role in the days prior to Indonesia's declaration of independence.)

In 1963, a second joint expedition went out to explore the Ceram area. In August of that year, it was reported that a contract was concluded with Mitsui to work Ceram under a production sharing plan, with 40% of the crude to be delivered by Permigan as payment for Japanese loans. This announcement was premature. When the Indonesian delegation headed by Sumbarjono went to Tokyo in December, 1963, they were informed that Japex, a partly government-owned concern, would handle the exploration. Japex was primarily interested not in Ceram but in two areas offshore, one off Bunju island and the other off Sangga-Sangga field in Kalimantan. Chairul Saleh tried to put together a package deal linking the offshore areas with the development of the Bula field on Ceram and rehabilitation work at Tjepu. Nirwonojudo handled the negotiations. This Japanese group, who had not been interested in Ceram to begin with, believed that the data derived from the two joint teams and the old Shell work in the area was insufficient to justify a major commitment. They wanted either new drilling, financed by Permigan, or, alternatively, they would make a nominal commitment in the first stage of perhaps $2 million, while they further investigated the area. Permigan lacked the funds to finance any new drilling, and Nirwonojudo was determined to get a better commitment. He held out for $40 million. Chairul Saleh assigned a group of Indonesian engineers to study the problem. They agreed that, based on the information available, the Japanese position was not unreasonable. Still, Nirwonojudo held to his position and negotiations died without agreement.

The year 1963 saw major changes in Permigan's board of directors. Effective August 1, 1963, Hadi Gondowardjojo retired as technical director. Two men were named to succeed him: Ir. Sumbarjono became project director and Ir. Sutan Assin, a graduate in mining from Holland's Delft University and a five-year veteran with Shell, was named production director. Drs. Soekotjo, an economist with five years' experience in the ministry, replaced Major Prodjosumitro as administrative director.

Sutan Assin recalls that he was not particularly welcomed by Nirwonojudo who seemed to resent young newcomers. Sutan Assin found there was a convenient way to avoid any conflict—he was assigned responsibility for overseeing Shell's implementation of the Contract of Work. In this capacity he spent most of his time at Migas, and in 1965, was named as head of Shell's supervisory team. Two Migas officials were also assigned to the supervisory team, Drs. S.B. Pulungan, who today is Pertamina's comptroller, and Ir. Hantoro.

In the case of Soekotjo, there was no outlet such as Sutan Assin found. Soekotjo spent his one year at Permigan in acrid debate with Nirwonojudo. Soekotjo particularly resented the reference of all management questions to a council of company labor leaders. In fact, this practice was the mark of things to come. In January, 1964, company councils of labor leaders (Dewan Perusahaan) were created for all state enterprises. The councils were to be consulted on all policies whether labor-related or not.

Another Permigan project began in mid-1963 under the direction of Mr. Soemantri, a veteran engineer with considerable field experience who had also assisted Permina in its early years. This project was the reconstruction of the wax plant at Tjepu that had been idle since before the war. Permigan wanted to use the wax plant to process the residue from its Tjepu refinery. In postwar years, Shell had piped this to Surabaya and then to Balikpapan for further processing. Permigan's board, however, wanted their own plant, preferring to "stand alone" rather than rely on Shell. Until the wax plant was completed in 1964, Permigan simply burned the residue.

In 1964, Nirwonojudo's long and stormy career in oil came to an end. To Perbum, Nirwonojudo had proven a useful ally in the early years, but his usefulness decreased as the *PKI's* power and influence increased. By 1964, the *PKI* was clamoring for a larger voice in the oil industry. The creation of the company councils in January was one answer to this demand; appointment of a Perbum-affiliated president-director of Permigan would be an even better one. Nirwonojudo was not in Chairul Saleh's good graces in any event; his stubbornness on the Japex deal and reports of some "palace politicing" by Nirwonojudo may well have clinched the decision to remove him.

On August 24, 1964, Chairul Saleh announced a series of changes in the boards of both Permigan and Pertamin. Drs. Soekotjo left Permigan for Pertamin, replacing Saleh Siregar who moved up to president-director. Nirwonojudo was reassigned to the ministry, where shortly thereafter he retired and ended his active career in Indonesian oil.

Replacing Nirwonojudo as president-director of Permigan was Sumarjo Legowo, a good-natured member of Perbum and a man who has been described as a "cocktail party communist." Sumarjo was a lifelong trade union man, and at the time of his appointment was the second deputy chairman of Perbum. In March, 1964, he had been appointed as head of Permigan's company council.

Drs. Soekotjo's replacement at Permigan also was Perbum affiliated. He was Kusumo Utojo, a one-time Stanvac marketing employee. More important politically than either Sumarjo or Kusumo Utojo, was Maladi Jussuf, who became secretary to the board. A tough *PKI* member of long standing, Jussuf had won fame during the revolution for his daring leadership of a battalion that bore his name.

In 1964, the long-lagging negotiations with the Roumanians picked up with the delivery of the 300 railroad tank cars as agreed in the miscellaneous phase of the original proposal. In February, 1965, a separate deal was made for one shipment of Roumanian lube oil. However, no further progress was made toward closing the agreement as to the refinery or the drilling equipment. In early 1965, the Russian trade mission stepped in to at least partially fill the breach. They offered a package deal for development in west Java, including drilling equipment, bulldozers, mobil workshops, and spare parts. The contract signed on July 5, 1965, between V.O. Machinoexport and Permigan valued the equipment at approximately $1.15 million. An eight-year credit at 4% interest was provided against a letter of credit.

The common ideological bent between Permigan and the Russians and Roumanians proved no guarantee of good commercial relations. The trial lube oil shipment from Roumania apparently suffered sedimentation en route and arrived in unsatisfactory condition in September. There were soon complaints from both sides concerning the Russian equipment deal. The Russians complained of slowness on procurement of the letter of credit. Permigan sent five men to Moscow and Kharkov for training on the Russian equipment. Instead of receiving training on the type of equipment that was to be sent to Indonesia, several were sent to "on the job" training on taxicabs.

Because of the continued depletion of nearly exhausted fields, the failure to apply modern secondary recovery techniques, and the inability to bring any new areas into production, the production of Permigan dropped steadily. From a high of 2,700 barrels per day in 1963, it had dropped to about 1,800 barrels per day by the third quarter of 1965. So things stood on October 1, 1965, a day which, among other things, precipitated Permigan's demise.

*   *   *

Pertamin's new directors assumed the reins of a truly professional company. Effendi Saleh and Saleh Siregar were both experienced administrators and backing them in personnel were Kamil Usman and Suhardi, both Shell-trained during the Permindo period. Assisting Saleh Siregar in finance was Mr. Soemantri, an accountant who had been *NIAM's* general representative in the early 1950s, and John Abdi, who also had trained in the Shell system. As technical director, Omar Hassan, himself a chemical engineer, had two well-trained and experienced division heads. Drs. Ismet Akil, a geologist—recently returned from the United States after two years of seasoning with Shell—continued as head of the Exploration Division. Ir. Trisulo, the four-year Stanvac veteran, stepped up from his position as Permindo's head of exploitation and production at Djambi, to head the division in Djakarta.

Competent administration was one thing, growth and development was another. Growth and development requires taking certain risks. To find oil, a company must place money at risk—either its own or someone else's. By previous experience neither Effendi Saleh (railroads) nor Saleh Siregar (banking) was attuned to running a high risk enterprise and it was their conservative approach that prevailed. Perhaps the desire to maintain the Shell standard of professionalism also had an inhibiting effect. Ir. Omar Hassan recalls that, "We thought that we could do everything ourselves onshore without foreign assistance while maintaining the Shell standard. We were not willing to risk making mistakes so, in fact, our exploration effort was quite limited."

In Djambi, the company re-explored a number of old areas first explored by *NIAM*. Shell continued to offer technical assistance in the years 1961 and 1962. A service contract was also concluded with a French company for seismic work. Planning for the development of a new area, the Kuang field, also proceeded in the predrilling stages. On the exploitation side, rehabilitation work was done on several wells in Djambi. By 1963, there were two seismic crews and two drilling rigs working in the Djambi fields. In two years, Pertamin drilled only four exploration wells, none of which yielded petroleum in commercial quantities.

Even the small program in Djambi looked large as compared with Bunju where virtually no new development took place. As a consequence of Pertamin's policies, production declined steadily throughout the 1960–1965 period, dropping from 30,000 barrels per day in 1960 to less than half of that by 1965.

However, what was done on the technical side was done well. Pertamin's geologists and engineers knew what to do and how to do it. They simply were not allocated sufficient funds to carry out necessary programs on a reasonable scale. Moreover, alone among the three state oil companies, Pertamin made no significant efforts to bring in foreign capital to assist in exploration and development, though several companies showed interest in such programs. Nor did Pertamin seek to extend the limits of its mining authority. Some indication of Pertamin's conservative management policies is given in a kind of end run which the technical department made during 1964 with Migas. In that year a new exploration program outside of Pertamin's existing boundaries in south Kalimantan was approved informally by Migas without the assignment of an "authority to mine" lest it be vetoed by Pertamin's management.

With Pertamin's own exploration programs lagging, Dr. Ibnu, in his capacity as chairman of the coordinating body, *BPU*, attempted to put the talents of Ismet Akil and Trisulo to work on other matters. In 1963, he offered them the positions as heads of the Exploration and Exploitation Department of the *BPU*, in which capacity they would coordinate the policies of all the state oil enterprises, co-ordinate monitoring of the foreign contractors, and develop plans for mining areas not yet assigned to any state enterprise. Saleh Siregar, perhaps sensing a "talent raid" opposed the proposal. But Ismet and Trisulo did work on a part-time basis for the *BPU*, drawing up a program for the development of the Bongas area in west Java before that area was assigned to Permigan.

In 1963, Pertamin made a considerable improvement in the disposition of its crude production from Bunju Island. During the *NIAM* days and since, all Bunju crude had been shipped by tanker to Balikpapan for refining and sale through the Shell organization. In July, 1961, John Abdi made cal-culations that showed that the tanker and refinery fee charged by Shell left Pertamin with only $1.25 per barrel at the well head. An affiliate of Mitsubishi offered $1.62 a barrel. After eighteen months of negotiations by Saleh Siregar, in March, 1963, a contract was finally signed between Pertamin and Mitsubishi whereby the Japanese company would take all Bunju production over a five-year period at a price of $1.62 f.o.b. Bunju. Unlike Permina's Nosodeco agreement, the Pertamin agreement was a straight purchase with no technical or material assistance. Characteristically, Pertamin improved its financial return but not its capability or scope of operations. Once the contract was concluded its position was purely administrative.

Though Pertamin's own production was declining, it was establishing a reputation for professional administration and the safeguarding of state funds. Unlike Permina, which fought to plow back every dollar it earned into increased capacity and education, Pertamin punctiliously accumulated reserves and paid its taxes. Pertamin was therefore selected to superintend monitoring of the Pan Am Work Contract, and when the Big Three signed their Work Contracts, Pertamin received the most important company, Caltex, which by this time was producing over 50% of Indonesia's crude oil. With both contractors, Pertamin concientiously performed its role, according to the contract. By contrast, Permina and Permigan, for the most part, left their job of contract administration to Migas. Pertamin received no immediate monetary return for performing this task; for it never was decided whether or not the state enterprise would receive a fee for performance of its regulatory and tax collection services under the Contracts of Work.

Pertamin's biggest success was in the development of domestic marketing. During the Permindo transition period, Shell had begun to turn over service stations to Permindo. The purpose, according to a former Shell executive, was to allow Permindo to "show its flag." Operationally, however, the stations continued to be run as an integral part of the Shell marketing organization.

Despite some hard feelings on Shell's part when its interest in the Permindo concession was not renewed, the cooperative program in domestic marketing was retained, and Pertamin continued to increase its marketing capacity. Shell continued to assign service stations to Pertamin, apparently with the general understanding that compensation would be made in accordance with the formula to be agreed upon in the Contracts of Work.

In 1961, Pertamin hired a recent college graduate, Drs. Abda'oe, as its first trainee in marketing. After a period at Shell marketing headquarters in Djakarta, Drs. Abda'oe was given the task of creating an active marketing policy for Pertamin. As was characteristic of the entire Permindo-Shell cooperative Indonesianization program, Pertamin's entry into marketing operations was carried out on a gradual step-by-step basis. Shell assigned five people from its marketing department to join Drs. Abda'oe in forming a marketing organization.

Pertamin began direct marketing by setting up a small administrative center in each of the four principal marketing centers—Djakarta, Surabaya, Semarang, and Medan. Money collection was the first task assumed and customers were asked to make payments to Pertamin's bank account while delivery orders and product distribution continued to be handled by Shell. Next, Pertamin began preparing delivery orders on their own and expanded their offices into five to ten man administrative and financial units. Shell still managed product delivery.

Thus by the time the Contracts of Work with the Big Three were ratified in November, 1963, Pertamin had established a smoothly functioning marketing organization. With Pertamin's marketing expertise established, Saleh Siregar set out to convince Chairul Saleh that Pertamin was the logical company to take over domestic marketing when it was transferred from the Big Three. Pertamin's reputation for punctilious administration and financial conservatism bolstered his case. He succeeded, and, by an order dated December 11, 1963, Pertamin was designated to receive all of the Big Three's domestic distribution assets. Three months previously, Permina had been authorized to build a tanker fleet for the transfer of fuel products domestically and for export. On January 27, 1964, the situation was clarified. Pertamin would have responsibility for all domestic distribution except sea transportation. The logical corollary was that Permigan would specialize in refineries, but this was never officially decided or promulgated.

The assignment of domestic marketing responsibility was a major coup for Pertamin and Saleh Siregar. Pertamin's partner under the Contracts of Work was Caltex which had only minor domestic marketing facilities as compared with Stanvac and Shell. Thus if the theory of the Contracts of Work were carried forward, Permina and Permigan would have become the dominant companies in domestic marketing.

Next, Saleh Siregar presented a proposal to Chairul Saleh, to accelerate the transfer of marketing assets. It would be cheaper for Indonesia to proceed with the purchase in the first year, he maintained, rather than to continue to pay for distribution at $0.10 a barrel. Chairul Saleh agreed, although probably more to ease the political pressure for nationalization than because of Saleh Siregar's economic argument. The Big Three also readily consented. In August, 1964, it was announced that the transfers would be effected over a one-year period instead of the five years contemplated by the Contracts of Work.

On September 4, 1964, Saleh Siregar officially relieved Effendi Saleh as president-director of Pertamin. The latter departed shortly thereafter to Bangkok to join the staff of Economic Commission for Asia and the Far East (Ecafe). In a farewell speech, Ir. Anondo, on behalf of the ministry of basic industries, paid tribute to Pertamin's excellent organization and its close cooperation with the ministry as developed by Effendi Saleh.

Ir. Omar Hassan stayed in his post as technical director of the company. Drs. Soekotjo joined as administrative director. The reshuffle did not create any major changes in Pertamin; Saleh Siregar had already established himself as the dominant voice at Pertamin, and his elevation to president-director merely confirmed this development.

The transfer of marketing assets and personnel was done on an area-by-area basis, and was completed in July, 1965. The transfer greatly increased the size of Pertamin. To its own organization of approximately 2,200 employees, it added double that number. Because most of the newcomers would take substantial cuts in salary, Shell and Stanvac agreed to pay each of their former employees a lump sum equal to the difference in salary over a two-year period. The new Pertamin employees were, for the most part, enthusiastic about joining the national company. Not only did their responsibilities increase but working within a state company was felt to be a contribution to the national cause.

While Pertamin greatly increased its size of operations by taking over domestic marketing, it also entered into the most problem-plagued area of Indonesian oil operations. Price controls had become totally unrealistic. In the year 1961, the price paid at retail for one liter of gasoline in Manila, Singapore, Bangkok and Bombay would buy in Djakarta 4.2, 3.1, 2.0, and 3.2 liters respectively. In the following years, the *PKI* blocked all attempts to raise prices despite the soaring inflation. By 1965, the government controlled price of a liter of gasoline was less than the un-controlled, inflated price of a glass of tea.

The consumer was, however, not receiving the benefit that might appear from the artificially low prices. Some of the oil products were smuggled to more profitable markets in Singapore and Malaysia. At home, a virulent black market developed. The illicit operators would purchase petroleum products from suppliers or tanker agents, and resell them at higher prices when the service stations ran out of stock. Another tactic was to purchase large quantities from retailers at the fixed price plus a kickback, and then sell on the black market when the shortage occurred. Because of the high demand and the extent of the black market involvement, shortages of supply were commonplace. It was not uncommon for the black marketeers to sell gasoline for ten to fifteen times the fixed price, and kerosene prices were even higher. The black market problem became a national scandal and Sukarno was known to venture out and admonish the suppliers, tanker agents, and station owners for allowing gasoline and kerosene to enter the black market. This leadership by exhortation did nothing to solve the underlying structural problem. Price increases were desperately needed but the leftist parties stood ready to block any such increases. Consumption trebled during the 1950s and demand continued to surge in the 1960s, reflecting not only the bargain prices but also hoarding by consumers and black marketeers, and wasteful overconsumption.

With prices held fixed and costs spiraling, by the end of 1963, domestic marketing was a losing proposition. However, the Contracts of Work had shifted the burden from the foreign companies, which were guaranteed cost recovery plus a profit for each phase of domestic operation—crude supply, refining, transportation and distribution—to Indonesia.

When Pertamin assumed the responsibility for domestic marketing, the crush of that financial burden fell on it. There was no way Pertamin could keep afloat financially unless something was done. Migas advanced the position to the Ministry of Finance that by ratification of the Contracts of Work, with its provisions guaranteeing a return of cost and guaranteed profit to the foreign companies on domestic operations, Indonesia had established the policy that any subsidization of the consumer resulting from failure to raise the price of petroleum products should be borne by the government treasury. The Finance Ministry took no exception to this, but like much in the Sukarno period, this agreement in principle was never fully implemented.

In 1965, the difference between cost and receipts was approximately 90,000 million rupiahs of which only 30,000 million were actually paid to Pertamin by the government. Accordingly, Migas intervened, instructing Pertamin to withhold all of the Caltex Contract of Work payments pending a settlement with the Ministry of Finance. From the Caltex payments, Pertamin, among other things, paid the $12.8 million needed to purchase the domestic marketing assets.

The transfer of marketing assets to Pertamin did not end the foreign companies' involvement in domestic marketing; they still retained most of the transport facilities. Sea transportation was principally handled by Shell and Stanvac though Permina was also entering the business. The refineries were also involved, and again this meant principally Shell and Stanvac since Permina and Permigan had very limited capacity. The product yield from Indonesia's domestic requirement share of crude production did not correspond with the product mix required by consumption patterns—generally there was a short fall of kerosene and gasoline and an excess of the heavier fuel oil products. Under the Contracts of Work, Indonesia's excess products were exchanged for products in which there was a shortfall, but there were still shortages. Thus an arrangement was reached with Shell and Stanvac to purchase the needed additional products from their Indonesian refineries at the international price less 15 %. The money owed to Stanvac and Shell under the Contracts of Work formula for crude, refining, and distribution, plus the shortfall sales exceeded the amount payable by the two companies under the Contracts of Work's sixty-forty profit formula and Indonesia became indebted to Shell and Stanvac for the balance. Thus, one consequence of the domestic pricing policy was that Caltex was the only company which continued to yield a surplus of funds to Indonesia.

While blocking all efforts to increase petroleum prices, the *PKI* loudly proposed its own solution. The problem was not the price, they maintained, but the continued presence of the foreign oil companies in Indonesia. Pertamin had merely taken over the "unprofitable" sector. To end the problem, imperialism must be ended. "We have to take over the foreign oil companies and destroy corruptors and capitalist bureaucracy from the financial and economic sectors." (Remarks by the National Branch speaker of the *PKI* labor union federation, July 30, 1965).

Concurrently, the *PKI* did everything possible to frustrate operations. Disruptions of railway transportation through labor agitation and sabotage were common. At the height of the crisis a team chaired by Wijarso and including Drs. Soekotjo of Pertamin, as well as refining and shipping representatives from Shell and Stanvac, met on an almost daily basis trying to cope with the chaotic situation. Tankers were often diverted en route as Wijarso and Soekotjo tried to decide which city could best forego their scheduled shipment.

The solution to the problems of domestic marketing clearly lay beyond the practical power of the oil men responsible for trying to cope with the chaos.

*   *   *

In his direction of Permina, Dr. Ibnu continued to be assisted by Finance Director Geudong in Djakarta while Technical Director Pattiasina remained in charge of field operations in north Sumatra. Lt. Colonel Harijono was assigned to set up Permina's first representative office in Tokyo as provided for in the Nosodeco agreement. Ir. Soedarno and Ir. Soediono constituted the technical staff in Djakarta.

Training programs were undertaken for both Permina's own staff and qualified students interested in joining the industry. Dr. Ibnu stressed the immediate need for upgrading Permina's field staff, since few had ever received formal training and fewer still had any knowledge of post-World War II methods. The company founded the Sekolah Kader Technik (Technical Training School) at Pangkalan Brandan in 1962. Designed as a vocational high school, the school gave refresher courses in oil field and refinery technology as well as various other oil-related subjects. Training programs were also established as an integral part of company employment programs with various incentives given to encourage successful completion of courses. Scholarship programs were established in several Indonesian universities and a number of men were sent abroad for specialized training. Later, in 1962, Permina founded a more advanced school, the Akademi Perminjakan Permina (Permina Oil Academy) in Bandung. The Oil Academy was designed to train young men in all aspects of the oil industry. In the face of criticism that the academy was a waste of money in view of the scarcity of jobs then available, Permina continued to maintain and enlarge it. Dr. Ibnu answered that the school would provide the trained personnel which Permina would need in the future.

Dr. Ibnu also undertook a study program to increase his own knowledge of petroleum, both technically and politically. To accomplish the first, he borrowed and read the books of his young engineers and then asked them for clarification and explanation. Ir. Soediono remembers that these discussions were like taking his final exams all over

again—except the student was quizzing the professor.
Dr. Ibnu held the strong belief that the oil industry
in Indonesia could neither be separated from the nation's
development efforts nor the related politics of international
oil. To study how other developing nations were managing
their oil industries in a market relatively controlled by
several international major oil companies, Dr. Ibnu travelled
extensively in 1961. In Saudi Arabia, Venezuela, Iraq, and
Iran, he discussed petroleum with other national leaders who
saw this resource as a means of aiding their country's
development.

The Japanese employees of Nosodeco began arriving in
north Sumatra during 1961, bringing with them both
equipment and modern technical knowledge. There were
many start-up problems, and many of the Indonesians
found it difficult to work with the Japanese as the memories
of the occupation were still fresh in their minds. There was
also a language barrier and though some Indonesians still
remembered Japanese they were reluctant to use it. Inter-
preters were used but communications remained a problem
until the Japanese acquired a working knowledge of
Indonesian.

There were also differences in approach. Most of the
old hands had gained their knowledge in the "school of
hard knocks" and were reluctant to try new ways. And
though the Japanese engineers had a great deal of theoretical
knowledge, few of them had field experience. This lack
of field experience was not always appreciated by the junior
Indonesian engineers who often regarded the Japanese
with a deference and respect quite unwarranted by the
difference in their knowledge. This deference infuriated
Pattiasina and caused considerable strain between him and
his engineering department.

The problems were, however, transitional and both the
Japanese and the Indonesians approached the job with a
desire to cooperate and to succeed. Experience and technology each gave a little for the sake of harmony and
eventually they were working as a team. Further improvement in relations took place when N. Nakamura arrived
in north Sumatra as part of the Nosodeco team. He

immediately rekindled the friendship with Djohan and thus helped to ease such strains as remained.

Drilling operations were begun with efforts to rehabilitate old wells by redrilling. New discoveries were also made. During the next four years, fifty-four exploration wells were drilled and forty-six old wells were rehabilitated under the Nosodeco contract.

As the north Sumatra fields were brought back into production, Permina's oil exports increased rapidly, and in 1963 ministry approval was requested to build a tanker fleet for handling exports as well as interisland distribution. The request was approved and in 1964 the company began exporting crude in its own ships. At the end of the year they had eleven vessels totalling 55,000 dwt. During 1965, six tankers in the 10,000 dwt. class and two of 5,000 dwt. were purchased. Seven larger tankers were also chartered. By the end of 1965, the fleet had grown to twice the 1964 tonnage.

During 1962, the company took the first step into the development of an air service with the purchase of its first aircraft, an Aero Commander. Captain Repon, a former Garuda pilot, was hired and today he is operations manager of the aircraft services subsidiary, P.T. Pelita.

Also during 1962, a direct communications system was begun between Pangkalan Brandan and Djakarta. Permina purchased a sophisticated telecommunications system which provided both telex and voice communication. This was one of a few such systems in Indonesia, and the first to be manned exclusively by Indonesians. Dr. Ibnu selected Rani Junus, who had been a communications specialist in the army, to head the new division. In April, 1963, Rani was sent to Germany for a two-year study program in telecommunications. The telecommunications network served a dual function characteristic of many Permina projects. It facilitated the company's own operations on the one hand, and on the other hand, served the government as a vital link with the north Sumatran region.

This dual function of facilities was a conscious aim of Permina, which was becoming increasingly involved in local, regional, and national development. The earliest efforts took the form of building and improving roads and bridges, building power plants, public water facilities, schools, and hospitals, all of which could be used by Permina as well as by the community. These projects were generally unpublicized except in the community itself where everybody knew who helped build the mosque, hospital, school, road, or bridge.

Unlike the other two national companies, Permina continued to be successful in enlisting the financial as well as technical support of foreign firms during the first half of the 1960s. Dr. Ibnu continued his earlier relationship with Refican and developed a new one with another Canadian company, Asamera Oil Corporation, Ltd. The Refican contract of June 10, 1961, for the rehabilitation of oil wells in the north Sumatra area was the first to use concepts later incorporated in Production Sharing Contracts and, like the earlier crude oil purchasing contract, was among the shortest, being only two typewritten pages. In August, it was amended to include exploratory drilling and in 1963, amended again to include the area offshore Pangkalan Susu.

Proceeds from rehabilitated wells were to be split sixty-five–thirty-five and from new discoveries sixty–forty, after a 40% allocation for recovery of materials and equipment costs. No extensive mention was made of management except that Refican would provide "the technical aid necessary" and that, "all equipment and services under the contract will be rendered only after approval by Permina." In effect, Permina had control over management and in practice Permina managed the operations with advice from a few Refican expatriate specialists. Unlike the Nosodeco contract, no debt was created; Refican could only look to production to recoup its investment. The Asamera contract of September 1, 1961, followed a similar format for exploration work.

During 1963, Dr. Ibnu conducted extensive negotiations with Union Oil Company for a contract incorporating production sharing, with a final draft agreement being made with Union's attorney, Hank Brandon. This draft agreement was considerably more sophisticated and complete than the Refican and Asamera contracts. However, Union's Board of Directors refused to accept its terms. This may have been, in part, because of the clause requiring Permina's prior approval of work programs, but perhaps the adverse political climate was a more determinative factor. After the demise of the Sukarno government, Union was one of the first of the leading oil companies to show new interest in Indonesia and in 1968, Union signed two Production Sharing Contracts.

The terms of this 1963 Union draft were thereafter incorporated into the Refican contract of March 10, 1964 which consolidated Refican's previous contract and its addenda. Labelled a Production Sharing Contract it merely spelled out in more precise legal terms the agreement of 1961. As compared to the Union draft, the management clause was much stronger and very specific. "Permina shall be responsible for the principal management of the operations contemplated hereunder.... Contractor shall ...be responsible for the execution of work programs."

These early Asamera and Refican contracts had only one drawback—they were not legal, since they were not ratified by Parliament in accordance with the requirements of Law No. 44. The parties believed that approval would be a long, drawn-out procedure so they commenced work with only Ibnu's assurance that everything would work out. Approval was finally obtained many years later.

Until the signing of the Amnesty in 1962 ended the *PRRI* rebellion, operations of Permina and their contractors involved many security problems in the north Sumatra area. After the Amnesty, isolated events continued to occur, but it was then considered safe to return the Sriwidjaja battalion to south Sumatra. The battalion had been providing security service and other aid since 1958. Though the battalion was officially returned, many officers and men were given a choice of remaining in north Sumatra and becoming full-time employees of Permina. The majority decided to stay in north Sumatra and some of them were formed into a paramilitary company security force.

Pressures from Perbum and other communist-affiliated unions continued to grow and cause difficulty in the early 1960s. Perbum had been banned by Pattiasina, but many of the Perbum leaders still remained in the Pangkalan Brandan area and continued their activities. They enlisted members of other communist-dominated unions to help carry out their protests and demonstrations. Usually, Perbum appeared at rallies and demonstrations with the largest banner and with the largest number of people.

In 1963, Marah Joenoes, who is presently head of public relations in Pertamina, was sent to north Sumatra to reduce or eliminate Perbum influence. The courtly Marah enjoyed considerable success. In one instance, he recruited supporters of the contending leftist party, Murba, in order to break up a Perbum rally, inducing them to fight over which was the most authentic communist group. The efforts of Permina to neutralize the influence of Perbum within the company were successful, though the possibility of trouble never disappeared. For example, one night several hundred leftist workers marched to the gates of the Permina compound threatening to burn it down. Pattiasina was not present, and attorney Tirto Utomo spent a long night talking to the mob leaders until everybody got tired and went home.

The staff of Lt. Colonel Pattiasina remained much the same, Husni, Karinda, Sjamsu Radjab, and Rani Junus. On the civilian side, Tirto Utomo and Ir. Astoto were joined by Ir. Harsono, a Migas employee, who after a two-year training stint with Caltex, was assigned to the Nosodeco operations. Ir. Idrus, a 1959 graduate of the Technical Institute of Bandung with three years' experience with Stanvac, joined in 1963 as did London-trained accountant, P. Siregar, who took over accounting administration.

Both Refican and Asamera were in operation under their new contracts by late 1961, and during that year Permina also embarked upon its own development programs. With the end of *PRRI* hostilities, increased efforts were made to repair the pipelines and to put other essential above-ground facilities back into good operating condition. Plans were completed to build an oxygen plant and a lube oil blending plant. Construction was begun at Rantau on carbon-black and LPG plants to utilize gas that had previously been flared. The company also undertook exploratory drilling with their own equipment and crews, and in 1964, Permina engineers and drillers discovered the Semeuntok field that has since become the most productive in North Sumatra.

In October, 1964, an agreement was reached between the stockholders of the Sorong Petroleum Company, formerly *NNGPM*, and Permina to purchase the former's assets in West Irian. Underlying the negotiations was an uncertain legal question: Did Law No. 44 apply to West Irian while it was still a U.N. trusteeship with Indonesia as trustee? Attorney Tirto Utomo argued that it did, but even Tirto had to admit privately that the answer was subject to doubt. In any event, the owners of Sorong Petroleum Company were presumably relieved to place the costly West Irian venture behind them. Thirty years after it first began exploration, and after millions of dollars expended in costly exploration, the company had only very modest production from the Klamono field (about 2,300 barrels per day) to show for its efforts. The assets included a pipeline to Sorong and crude storage and loading facilities there. The purchase price was $600,000. Permina did not have this amount of money available, so it obtained a production loan from the Hong Kong-based company, Ednasa Co. Ltd.

Although dynamic and growing, Permina was still a relatively minor factor in terms of production of crude in Indonesia. In 1965, Permina was producing approximately 21,000 barrels of crude per day out of a total Indonesian production of 480,000 barrels per day. Thus less than 5% of the total Indonesian production came from Permina. Of the crude produced by Permina, almost all was exported, generally varying from 80% to 90% of the total. A good portion of the export proceeds were used to pay off Nosodeco, and as cost recovery to Refican and Asamera. The number of producing fields increased from three in 1961 to nine by the end of 1965, although Rantau still provided over 90% of the entire north Sumatran production.

Lt. Colonel Pattiasina left his position in north Sumatra in 1964 and was sent to study in the United States. He was replaced first by Major Karinda, who later was replaced by Captain Husni. The departure of Lt. Colonel Pattiasina

marked the end of an era in north Sumatra. This is readily
apparent when oldtimers in north Sumatra talk about
Pattiasina. Prior to his arrival, almost nothing had been
accomplished. To them it was Pattiasina who put Permina
on its feet. He is a very rugged and controversial man,
and much criticism was aimed at him during his years of
control in north Sumatra. There are few, if any, however,
who will deny the necessity of having a man of his strength
and determination in that position at that time. His admirers
now include those who were his young engineers, and others
in the organization who had disagreements with him during
the difficult years. As important as his experience in the
oil business was in Permina's development, perhaps even
more vital was his willingness to stand up and fight any
group that threatened Permina's welfare.

The workers of north Sumatra paid tribute to Pattiasina
in a booklet they prepared for the ninth anniversary ceremonies at Pangkalan Brandan:

> He arranged everything in good order ... bravely
> leading the organization and personnel ... with
> the right men according to their experience and
> capability in their fields without looking at their
> party or group.

> Scrap iron and other important equipment which
> had been sold were recollected .... Wages and
> rations given to the *PKI* members who did not
> work were stopped ... undisciplined workers
> were transferred or discharged .... After the
> courageous mopping up of Permina by Pattiasina,
> only workers who liked to work remained here.
> Although most of them were already old and not
> well educated, they had a strong will and applied
> their experiences .... We felt that we were no
> longer workers in the Colonial Period who just
> worked for food without having any responsibilities
> to the company .... We were urged by one
> great idea—to settle the revolution for the glory
> of the nation ... to make progress under the
> leadership of Dr. Ibnu Sutowo and Pattiasina.

*   *   *

Besides the three state oil enterprises, the period 1960–1965 also saw the development of another institution of importance to Indonesia's national oil industry. This was the establishment of a national Institute of Oil and Gas (Lembaga Minjak dan Gas Bumi–Lemigas).

The idea of creating a national research and training center for all oil-related research was advanced shortly after the creation of Migas. As always, there was a financing problem. Omar Hassan, who had been educated in Japan, thought that country might advance the necessary funds, but inquiries were unsuccessful. In January, 1961, they tried another source. Omar Hassan and Wijarso (who was not yet on the oil side) went to Bangkok to present a proposal for assistance to the Committee on Industry and Natural Resources of Ecafe. Unfortunately for Indonesia, Iran was also there with a similar proposal and Iran got the grant. Shortly thereafter, Omar Hassan, who today is the general affairs director at Lemigas, moved on to Pertamin.

Ir. Sjarif A. Loebis, who today is the director of Lemigas, breathed new life into the idea later that year. Ir. Loebis attended the Technical Institute at Bandung on a Stanvac scholarship graduating with a degree in chemical engineering in 1959. He worked briefly for Stanvac before being called to military service during the *PRRI* rebellion. After release, he joined Migas and was instructed to form a refinery section. At Basarudin's suggestion, Ir. Loebis formed a committee to survey the quality of Indonesian crude oil. After Basarudin's ouster, Iskandar Notobroto secured some funds from the government to purchase land for construction of a small research laboratory. The site selected was at Tjipulir, 15 km. (9.3 mi.) southwest of Djakarta. Construction began in 1961.

On November 26, 1962, Iskandar established a team to study the prospects of establishing an oil and gas research laboratory. Besides Loebis, who chaired the committee, it was made up of Hantoro and Harsono from Migas and representatives from each of the state oil enterprises: Soediono and Soedarno from Permina; Dr. Wahjudi and

Sumbarjono from Permigan; and Omar Hassan and Zainal Abidin from Pertamin. The team reported its conclusions on August 19, 1963, recommending the founding of an institute with funds supplied by the national oil companies.

In 1964, a preparatory petroleum institute project was established under the leadership of Ir. Loebis. The institute was officially created on June 11, 1965, by the Ministry of Migas. By September, it had a staff of about sixty people and the first laboratory was in operation.

* * *

One problem which transcended the scope of any one of the state companies was the need to develop a national capacity to market oil abroad.

By far the most important market for Indonesia crude was, and is, Japan—Asia's largest consumer. Indonesian oil has a natural advantage over Middle Eastern competition because of its geographic proximity. By way of comparison, when ocean freight rates are $0.30 to $0.40 a barrel for Indonesia–Japan tanker transport, the rate from the Middle East is about $0.60 to $0.70. In 1965, over 25 % of Indonesian oil exports, about 100,000 barrels per day of crude and 10,000 barrels per day of refined products, were going to Japan and the potential market was much larger.

The Contracts of Work gave Indonesia an opportunity to develop a foreign marketing capability by electing to take up to 20% of gross production in kind. Indeed, it might be said that the Contracts of Work demanded that Indonesia develop the expertise for—unlike the Middle Eastern countries—Indonesia was committed to take not posted prices but realized prices. Unless Indonesia could develop its own marketing outlets, it would remain dependent upon the Big Three's determination of the realized price. And the Big Three's marketing decisions were by no means necessarily equivalent in objective to those of Indonesia. The Big Three sold much of their crude to foreign affiliates, and in these transactions the price set was often strictly an internal bookkeeping matter. The Contracts of Work provided that sales to affiliates would be valued in terms of sales to nonaffiliates. Therefore, if 90% of sales were to affiliates, the foreign company would not be looking after its best interests to press for a high price on the 10% sold to nonaffiliates. The fact that the Big Three had long-established export markets as well as alternative sources of supply also might lead to differences in interest as compared with Indonesia which sought new market penetration. In short, to acquire a real control over oil exports and assure fair prices, Indonesia had to develop its own foreign marketing outlets.

Permina had begun foreign marketing of its own crude in 1958 with the shipments through Refican. In 1963, Pertamin started to ship Bunju crude to Japan. But for the most part, prior to 1964, foreign marketing continued to be a Big Three preserve. In 1964, the national companies began to look for foreign outlets for the crudes received under the Work Contracts. The benefits came quickly. Caltex was selling Duri crude in Japan at $1.49 f.o.b. per barrel. Pertamin found a buyer at $1.63. Discussions between Saleh Siregar and Wijarso of Migas on the one hand, and Caltex officials, on the other, followed. Caltex claimed that a price of $1.63 would ruin the market in six months. But in March, 1965, Pertamin concluded a two-year contract at the $1.63 price. In October, 1965, Wijarso called Caltex offering to buy all its Duri crude. Caltex announced a change to $1.63 retroactive to October 1.

Wijarso sums up the effort this way:

> International marketing outlets are a "must" in exploiting the "realized price" concept, which Indonesia adopted, for the utmost benefit of the country. Permina started its own exports in 1958 and Pertamin in 1963 of their own produced crudes. But within 18 months after ratification of the Contract of Work, Pertamin started to export through its own marketing effort crude produced by its contractor. This crude, taken as payment in kind was sold by Pertamin at a considerably higher price than previously had been claimed by the contractor's Oil Disposal Company

as its worth in the international market. The contractor wisely accepted this fact and began increasing not only its reported realized price but also the real market price. (*Pacific Community,* July 1970, p. 683).

Despite these successes, Pertamin's involvement in Japanese marketing was too small and sporadic to have lasting significance. What was needed was the ability to penetrate the Japanese market on a stable and continuing basis. To do this, Indonesia needed a Japanese partner. Japanese law generally requires that foreign enterprises may do business in Japan only in partnership with Japanese nationals, with the latter having at least a 50% interest.

To Dr. Ibnu, the logical partner for such a marketing organization was Nosodeco with whom Permina had evolved a harmonious working relationship. As things stood in 1964, the Nosodeco management would have nothing to do upon expiration of the extended credit agreement.

Dr. Ibnu saw that the basic concept to be sold was one of mutual interest. Most simply, the concept was to establish a link between Indonesian producer and Japanese consumer avoiding the major oil companies as middlemen. Dr. Ibnu well knew the major companies' dominance in Indonesian oil affairs, and he also knew that the Japanese market was similarly dominated. Indeed, Japan's oil industry was to a large extent dominated by the five parent companies of Indonesia's Big Three, which in Japan appear in a combination known as the Big Four.

Japan's emergence as an oil-dependent country (it supplies only 0.5% of its total consumption) is a postwar development. Before and during World War II, its energy needs were met largely by coal supplemented by hydroelectric power and noncommercial fuels. Thus, its oil needs were largely limited to motor transport and the armed forces. These needs were met by its own indigenous supply plus, during much of the war, from installations captured in Burma and Indonesia. In the postwar occupation period, with the help of the United States, both its hydroelectric facilities and coal industry were rehabilitated and expanded. By 1950, oil still accounted for only 2% of Japan's energy.

But coal resources were insufficient to fuel the rapidly expanding Japanese economy. Necessarily, although reluctantly, and with the encouragement of the U.S. military administration, the Japanese government decided to expand its oil industry. Assistance was given to large industrial users and power stations to convert from coal to oil. To minimize scarce foreign exchange, Japan's old-fashioned refineries were not only rehabilitated, but greatly expanded, while foreign exchange rates were set which favored crude oil imports over finished petroleum products. But expansion of refinery capacity in itself required large amounts of capital, sophisticated equipment, and technical knowledge, that only the United States, at that time, could supply. Consequently, the Japanese government decided to allow the major oil companies to join forces with the local refining companies; the Majors contributed the foreign exchange costs, while the Japanese contributed local currency. The Majors then secured the right to supply all crude oil to the refineries over a period of years. The Majors themselves were not enthusiastic about the arrangement; they would have preferred to form wholly owned refineries, and agreed to the joint venture approach only after pressure from the U.S. military administration.

These arrangements changed Japan from a high cost energy economy to a low cost one. Oil consumption increased by an average of 15% per annum during the 1950–1957 period, and then accelerated further. Oil consumption in 1960 (about 600,000 barrels per day) was double that of 1957, and consumption increased by 25% per annum during the 1960–1964 period. In 1958, Japan was the world's seventh-largest oil consumer; by 1969, it was the third.

In the course of financing this tremendous expansion, every independent refinery in Japan had to rely upon the foreign oil companies for financing. In return, the Majors acquired exclusive supply contracts. Typically, each dollar of financing provided by a Major was "tied" to a commitment to take eight barrels of oil. Moreover, 80% of Japan's oil imports originated from Middle Eastern countries.

In this situation, the Japanese government naturally took a keen interest in oil and was determined to increase

Japanese control and decrease Japanese dependence on the Majors and the Middle East. The policy, begun in 1962, took several forms including efforts to stimulate Japanese-controlled crude oil production both at home and abroad and to diversify supply. However, by 1965, the Japanese had succeeded only in holding their own—the Majors still controlled 80% of Japanese crude sales. Therefore, the Japanese government as well as the management of Nosodeco was receptive to the concept of a joint Japanese–Indonesian marketing company.

Exploratory negotiations began in May, 1964, between Dr. Ibnu, as president of Permina, and Mr. K. Iino, president of Nosodeco. Following Mr. Iino's death, Mr. Kosho Ogasa, a leading Japanese government official, and Mr. T. Imai, the new president, and Mr. Sumio Higashi, managing director of Nosodeco, took over. Dr. Ibnu's original concept had been that Nosodeco should be the vehicle for Indonesia's entry. As, in the course of the negotiations, Dr. Ibnu learned more about the structure of Japanese industry and the needs of the market, he came to realize that it would be of utmost importance to the venture to have public utility companies and independent refineries directly represented as share-holders. These were seen to be the best prospects for market penetration because the more obvious customers, the larger refineries, were already tied up by their affiliations with the Majors. Moreover, many of the public utility companies would be able to burn the Indonesian crude oil in an un-refined state.

As finally agreed in May, 1965, Far East Oil Trading Company, Ltd. was established with 50% of its shares owned by Indonesia through Permina and with the other 50% distributed amongst twenty-one Japanese shareholders including Nosodeco and various Japanese oil independents, utilities, and industrial users. The company's principal purpose is described by its president-director Mr. Sumio Higashi in this way: "Our company intends to serve, so to speak, as a major pipeline between Indonesia and Japan. We hope to contribute in the fiield of petroleum both to Indonesia's economic prosperity and Japan's industrial activities and its battle against air contamination."

To become a major pipeline, Far East Oil would have to develop a market for the Indonesian entitlements to Caltex's production from Minas and Duri. That project lay in the future. Far East Oil began more modestly; for the remainder of 1965, it marketed Permina's north Sumatran crude.

*   *   *

In north Sumatra, the morning of October 1, 1965, was a hectic and disturbing one for Permina's Acting Manager Captain Rani Junus, who had only recently returned from his two-years' study in Germany. He was notified by the marketing office in Medan that the *KODAM* commander, General Darjatmo, was escorting an important motorcade of political officials on their way from Medan to Langsa, in Atjeh; and that they were going to stop at Pangkalan Brandan for some breakfast and sight-seeing. Besides General Darjatmo, the group consisted of First Deputy Prime Minister Subandrio, *PKI* Second Deputy Secretary Njoto, the governor of North Sumatra Mr. Ulungsitepu, the regional commander, General Mokoginta, and a score of cabinet ministers. They were headed for the plantation areas for which Langsa was noted, where Subandrio was expected to speak to assembled union members of the *PKI* plantation workers organization.

The motorcade arrived at Pangkalan Brandan at 9:00 A.M. and immediately Subandrio notified Rani that he had prepared a speech for the oil workers. Rani was not at all in favor of this. The labor situation in the Permina area had been satisfactory for about two years, since Pattiasina's strong pacification tactics had ended Perbum's sway with the workers. Outside the oil area, however, and around Medan, things were not so quiet. The *PKI* and its two large labor and farmer fronts, were at the time stepping up their attacks on the army. The past May, a group of squatters belonging to a *PKI* union at the "Betsy" plantation in the Medan area, urged on by the local "People's Youth" —another *PKI* front group, had beaten to death an army officer who was attempting to evict them from government lands. This "Bandar Betsy Affair" was well-remembered

in Pangkalan Brandan and contributions had been sent
from there to the dead man's family. Pressures were growing
to influence the oil workers and they were subjected to all
sorts of propaganda from the *PKI* fronts when they left
the perimeter of the area. Rani recalls that only two weeks
prior to this, three former *TMSU* work supervisors, all
key Perbum men, had come to him to persuade him to
allow Perbum back into Permina, arguing that under the
principle of *NASAKOM*, the interests of the nation were
being implemented by the left more than by anybody else;
the left was the wave of the future, and so forth. Rani told
them he was satisfied with the present political atmosphere
in Permina, and they left without accomplishing anything.

Now, with somebody of the stature of Subandrio wanting
to speak—and he was known to use all the neo-revolutionary
slogans and appeals of the day—Rani was in a quandary.
He tried to explain that assembling the entire work force
would be impossible; they had already gone to their work
stations. Subandrio was adamant and, in the end, a group
of about eighty work supervisors, section heads, and their
wives, about 120 in all, were gathered in the recreation
room of the Permina guesthouse. There they heard Njoto
play the piano, and listened to a rather curious speech
by Subandrio. While the ministers and other distinguished
guests rambled around the grounds sight-seeing, Subandrio
exhorted the men to remain diligent in their work, and
the wives to remain calm, even in the event of their husbands'
absence. All should be prepared for important developments
in the near future.

It was a short speech of about half an hour. Afterwards
Rani, Subandrio, and all the guests had breakfast in the
guesthouse mess. All conversations centered on the events
of the night before in Djakarta. Nobody had any certain
information but word had reached Medan before the
motorcade left of some sort of action having taken place
involving the top army command. Both Generals Mokoginta
and Darjatmo seemed very worried, more so than Subandrio
and the ministers. Upon arriving, General Darjatmo had
asked Rani to try to contact Djakarta via the Permina
network. When they had left Medan earlier, the police,

army, and public radio systems were unable to get any information. Rani radioed his brother, Masjfar, who was the chief of Permina's radio station at the Permina transmitter in Tjengkareng, some sixteen kilometers west of Djakarta. Masjfar reported that as yet nothing was clear in Djakarta either, except that some top generals had been kidnapped, to where, nobody knew, although it was said that Nasution was not among those missing. Also, there had emerged some sort of revolutionary council to defend Sukarno against CIA plots. The revolutionary council now held the Djakarta radio station. No other source of news was available yet and none of the daily newspapers had been distributed. This was all Rani was able to learn; his brother insisted on cutting the conversation short, fearing that at any moment the Permina station, which seemed to have been overlooked, would come under attack.

Rani brought this news to the mess hall. The generals evinced relief upon hearing that General Nasution had escaped, but Rani recalls that Subandrio and some of the ministers seemed to be thrown off balance, they were "jumpy." In any case, members of the group were at odds whether or not to continue on to Langsa. Subandrio himself could not decide. At this point the minister of Justice, Achmad Astrawinata (an old friend of Rani's from Bandung) insisted that the tour be completed, and this decided the day. In the early part of the afternoon, the motorcade left for Langsa.

It had already been a long day for Rani. The night before he had received word from the *KODIM* (Kommando District Militer–District Military Command) Commanding officer, in the nearby town of Bindjei, that military exercises would be held at 0545 the following morning (October 1). This in itself was not unusual—this was the period of *Konfrontasi*, with emergency drills and maneuvers quite common. In this exercise, Rani was told, Pangkalan Brandan was considered to be occupied by hostile forces, and that *KODIM* troops would maneuver to liberate the area. It was this that was unusual: For the first time, Rani's security forces—about four platoons—were given no part in the operations. Considering this a strange oversight, Rani posted his troops on all-night alert status as was customary during these drills. At around 0530 the *KODIM* troops reached the imagined forward line of the enemy area, in this case the Permina perimeter. At this point, considerable confusion ensued in their ranks when they saw that all of the Permina troops were at their battle stations. Instead of proceeding with the "exercise" however the *KODIM* troops withdrew in some disorder. Everyone thought this strange, but the mystery was soon forgotten with the arrival of the news of the forthcoming Subandrio visit some hours later.

Further information about the events in Djakarta arrived in Pangkalan Brandan that evening. Rani wrote this down and gave it to Lt. Radjab, his security assistant, and instructed him to carry it to Langsa, and deliver the message to either General Darjatmo or General Mokoginta only. These two, upon receiving the report, immediately left Langsa with Governor Ulungsitepu and headed back toward Medan in a driving rainstorm. They stopped at Pangkalan Brandan in the early hours of October 2, and the two generals contacted Rani to learn the latest developments in Djakarta. Ulungsitepu, however would not enter the Permina compound and waited outside for the generals. After Rani told them the latest news he had received, the party proceeded on to Medan.

In Langsa, Subandrio and the ministers decided to cut short their tour and return by boat to Belawan, the harbor near Medan. Upon arriving in Medan, they were put into protective custody by General Darjatmo and General Mokoginta pending their departure back to the capital on the third.

Back in Pangkalan Brandan, Rani detained all workers with a background of leftist labor association and locked them up in a quickly-built enclosure in the middle of the compound, and at the same time he urged the local officials of the surrounding area to do the same, but they were reluctant to do anything on their own initiative. Governor Ulungsitepu, a man of known *PKI* sympathies, had evidently passed the word to stand fast in the ensuing crisis and to follow his instructions alone.

CHAPTER 11

Gestapu and the New Order

In the early morning hours of October 1, 1965, Sukarno's long balancing act between the mutually antagonistic *PKI* and the army came to a grisly end as the *PKI* quite literally attempted to decapitate the army. The targets were seven top men of the Army Central Command who were regarded as staunchly anti-communist. Included were General Nasution, then coordinating minister of defense and chief of staff of the armed forces, the army commander in chief, General Yani and his third deputy, General M.T. Harjono, the man who had once headed the Oil Office under Prime Minister Djuanda. Armed groups consisting of pro-*PKI* troops visited each man's home and awakened him on the pretext of urgent business. Some were killed on the spot and others were abducted to rebel headquarters at Halim Air Force Base on the outskirts of Djakarta. Of the intended victims only General Nasution, with the assistance of his cool-headed wife, escaped by jumping from a high wall to the next door property, breaking his ankle as he fled. However, his aide was abducted to Halim and his five-year-old daughter was shot, and later died. At Halim, the surviving generals and General Nasution's aide were tortured and murdered, and the bodies of all of the victims were mutilated. The killing involved *PKI* irregulars and included the *PKI* women's front. A passing policemen abducted by one of the groups was forgotten and later pointed out the location of the bodies in an abandoned well in a section of Halim called Lubang Buaja, "the Crocodile's Hole."

Meanwhile, other units of the conspiracy seized control of key communications points in the city including the national radio station. The people of Djakarta awoke later to find the large Merdeka Square, opposite the Presidential Palace, occupied by elements of the Central Java Diponegoro Division and the East Java Brawidjaja Division. These, people presumed, had arrived in Djakarta to take part in the annual Armed Forces Day on October 5. However, rumors were already circulating and confusion was further compounded by the 7:20 A.M. radio broadcast by a group identifying themselves as the "September 30 Movement," (The Bahasa Indonesia equivalent of September 30 Movement, "Gerakan September Tigapuluh," soon became the acronym "Gestapu.") and who decreed the formation of a "Revolutionary Council for Indonesia," to supersede the Dwikora Cabinet which they declared dissolved. It was further stated over the radio that the night before a number of generals, members of a "Council of Generals," which had planned a coup, had been arrested. To aid this "cleansing up operation" designed to safeguard the President and the Republic, the people were exhorted to form "Revolutionary Councils." The commander of the September 30 Movement was given as being Lt. Colonel Untung, the batallion commander of the Tjakrabirawa (Presidential) Guards. He was a man little-known by the startled and thoroughly confused populace, but he was known for his radical leftist ideology by at least one important figure in Indonesia, General Soeharto.

*   *   *

By mid-1965, it was clear to many people in Indonesia that the army and the *PKI* were on a collision course and that confrontation of some sort could not be long averted. Though President Sukarno was still acting as intermediary and pacifier between the groups, it was increasingly recognized that he was leaning more toward the *PKI* than to the army.

Sukarno's strong ties with the *PKI* were clearly demonstrated on the forty-fifth anniversary of the Indonesian Communist Party on May 23, 1965. The festivities were practically a state occasion and to many it seemed as if the *PKI* was already in control of the government. In Djakarta, an enormous parade through the streets lined with communist billboards preceded ceremonies before 100,000 roaring spectators in the new Russian-built Senajan Stadium. Here Sukarno embraced *PKI* Chairman Aidit, shouting, "Take pictures of both of us, so that the imperialists can clearly see I embrace the Partai Komunis Indonesia!"

Once Sukarno's patronizing of the Indonesian communists was transformed into what appeared to be a full-scale commitment, the *PKI* embarked on a campaign to extend power and influence in the cities and in the rural areas. In the cities, violent demonstrations were launched against the Western-owned businesses, and, in the name of aiding *Konfrontasi*, the British and American diplomatic communities were harrassed with increasing impunity. The *PKI* also villified the other political parties, Islamic students' groups, the army, and businessmen. All were stigmatized as "traitors to the Revolution of Sukarno."

In the central and east Java countryside, there was great dissatisfaction among tenant farmers and the poor. Crop sharing and land-reform laws had been passed in 1960, but little action had been taken to put them into effect. In 1965, the *PKI* took matters into their own hands and through their "peasant front" began confiscating land. Such actions laid the basis for violent reaction by landowners and other conservatives.

Though the *PKI* had sown the seeds of violence and had created enemies in virtually every area, occupation, and level of society, on the face of it, the future of the party never looked more promising. Already the third-largest communist party in the world, the *PKI*, according to Chairman Aidit, had a membership, in all its groups and affiliations, of nearly 20 million people.

Not only was the hold of communism growing stronger within the country, but internationally Sukarno had strengthened his communist ties and commitments to the point where there was little left of the country's independent foreign policy. In November, 1964, Indonesia recognized

North Korea, North Viet Nam, and the National Liberation
Front of South Viet Nam. In January, 1965, Indonesia
withdrew from the United Nations. Talks followed with
the Chinese on a number of subjects including the formation
of a new world body made up of the New Emerging Forces
countries and headed by Indonesia and China.

The development of closer relations with China encouraged the *PKI* to renew pressure to establish local armed
militias—the so-called fifth-force (the other four were the
army, air force, navy, and national police). This fifth-force
had been a *PKI* objective since the days of the revolution—
though it had always been blocked by the army. If *PKI*
cadres could be armed, then the army's near-monopoly of
military power would be broken. The armed cadres plus
the influence of pro-*PKI* personnel in the four armed
services, would, they believed, be enough to establish
effective *PKI* control over military power. By 1965, the
PKI had obtained many supporters in the armed forces
including, most notably, Air Force Commander in Chief
Omar Dhani and many of his officers. A large number of
navy officers were also pro-*PKI* and, by Aidit's estimate,
25 % of the army was in his camp. With Sukarno's increased
support offering a good prospect of success, the *PKI* began
the fifth-force campaign in earnest.

In January, 1965, *PKI* Chairman Aidit had proposed, in
connection with *Konfrontasi*, that 5 million workers and
10 million peasants be trained and armed to implement the
revolutionary goals of the President. Premier Chou En-Lai
publicly endorsed Aidit's proposal and offered to supply
an initial quantity of 100,000 small arms. This was strongly
opposed by the Army Central Command but by September,
Sukarno appeared willing, given a little more time, to override them.

By September, 1965, the stage was set for escalation of
the long-standing feud. In this unstable environment, it was
the state of Sukarno's health that brought the situation
from threatening to critical. The President had recently
been forced to break off a speech to take medication, and
he was known to have a liver ailment. There were now
widely believed rumors that his death was imminent.

Virtually everyone believed there would be a showdown between the army and the *PKI* following Sukarno's death as it had been only his prestige and intervention that had prevented it earlier.

As the month of September went on, there came to be heard another rumor of equally ominous portent to the ones concerning Sukarno's health. There was, as the rumor went, a cabal, a secret "council of generals," that was preparing to stage a coup and take over the government. Whether the *PKI* leaders seriously believed such a council existed and therefore laid their own plans to pre-empt it, or whether they created the rumor as a cover in preparing their own coup, cannot be determined.

There is no evidence that such a council existed although no doubt the army leadership had made plans for the contingency of Sukarno's death. But that these plans went any further—let alone included an imminent coup attempt—seems highly unlikely· in view of the ease with which the army leadership was taken by surprise.

In any case, based upon fact, fiction, or both, it appears that in late August or early September a special bureau was created within the *PKI* to work with already-converted and leftward-leaning army officers to plan a pre-emptive coup. At the time there were many members of the *PKI* youth front and the women's movement receiving paramilitary training, supposedly related to *Konfrontasi*, at Halim Air Force Base on the outskirts of Djakarta.

The plot took form, as Robert Shaplen has reported it, in two phases:

> It was decided that the top seven generals, headed by General Nasution, should be arrested, abducted, or killed, and, that in order to make it appear that the plot was 'only a movement within the Army,' Army squads would be used for this part of the operation... Once the coup had attained its primary objective–namely, the elimination of the Army generals–a second, political stage would quickly follow. This entailed the creation of a Revolutionary Council, which would take over from the

progressive Army elements which had 'solved the internal struggle' in the military, and which would then dismiss the Cabinet and rule the country as the highest representative of Sukarno's *NASAKOM* policy, which the right-wing generals had allegedly subverted. (Shaplen, p. 93)

The first phase was carried out as planned with the exception of General Nasution's escape.

*   *   *

For General Soeharto, the morning of October 1 marked the beginning of a series of events in which he would emerge from relative obscurity to the position of national leadership.

Soeharto was born, in 1921, to poor and rural parents in the kampung, Kemusu Argamulja, near Jogjakarta in central Java. His father was a minor village official, the "djogotirto" in charge of the water distribution to the rice padis of the village.

When he was two years old, his parents separated and during the next years he lived with relatives in different places in central Java. He received the basic education of the village schools and, when still quite young, determined to make a career for himself in the army. Financial circumstances forced him to leave middle school when he was eighteen and he joined the *KNIL*. In the following year he was accepted into the Military School of the Royal Netherlands Indies Army at Gombong.

After receiving his training, he was assigned to duty at Rampal in east Java and was soon promoted to sergeant. When the Dutch resistance collapsed in early 1942, Sergeant Soeharto returned to central Java. After a stint as a policemen, he joined one of the first *PETA* units in 1943 and became a company leader.

In the revolution, Soeharto distinguished himself as a daring commander, first of Battalion X and then of the regiment which he led in the March 1, 1949 raid on Jogjakarta.

In 1947, Soeharto married Siti Hartinah, the daughter of an upper-class official. Things were changing rapidly in Indonesia at that time and class distinctions were fading as the people united to free themselves from the Dutch.

Soeharto continued his military career after the transfer of sovereignty. He took part in the central government's operations against the various separatist movements in the regions during those early years. By the beginning of the year 1957, he had been promoted to the rank of full colonel, and became the commanding officer of the Central Java Diponegoro Division. During the year 1959, Colonel Soeharto was given orders to attend the Army Staff and Command College at Bandung.

Promoted to brigadier general in 1960, Soeharto was appointed first deputy to Chief of Staff Nasution.

In 1962, Soeharto, then a major general, was assigned as both panglima of east Indonesia and as war theatre commander to undertake the military liberation of West Irian if this should be ordered. Fortunately, United Nation's action prevented a full-scale military operation.

General Soeharto's next assignment was as deputy commander in the *Konfrontasi* against Malaysia. He was also given command of *KOSTRAD*, a combat-ready reserve unit with headquarters in Djakarta.

In 1965, General Soeharto was regarded strictly as a professional soldier. Though he had grave doubts about the future course of his nation he had no political ambitions. He lived a quiet family life in a modest house in Djakarta. No doubt because he seemed so inoffensive and unambitious, Soeharto was left off the assassination list. His own explanation for this omission is, "They probably considered me a minor officer who could be handled later." (Roeder, p. 11)

General Soeharto was awakened by an alarmed neighbor about 6:00 A.M. on October 1, and told that unusual activities had been going on. He immediately drove to *KOSTRAD* headquarters where he was briefed with what little was known of the chaotic events at that time. It was, however, known that General Yani could not be located,

and under standing orders Soeharto became commander in chief in his absence. He recalls: "My officers agreed that I should assume the leadership since I was the only field commander who was in a position to act. I had been commissioned acting commander in chief of the Army previously when General Yani was absent." (Roeder p. 12)

At 7:20 A.M. another piece of information was added when Lt. Colonel Untung spoke over Radio Djakarta. If this broadcast was confusing to most listeners, it was not to General Soeharto. "Being aware of Untung as a man with a radical leftist ideology, it became clear to me that the Revolutionary Council and the September 30 Movement were a coup of the extreme left... My first steps were: to get information about the loyalty or disloyalty of all the troops in Djakarta—Army, Air Force, Navy, and Police—so far as I could contact them. Secondly, I ordered all troops loyal to me to be combat-ready, but confined to barracks. I wanted to avoid bloodshed between them and the soldiers who were just misled by some irresponsible elements. That's why I tried to persuade as many rebels as possible to join us." (Roeder p. 12–13)

Halim Air Force Base was quickly identified at *KOS-TRAD* as the headquarters of the rebels and plans were made and units assigned to undertake its recapture. These plans had to take into account the most peculiar behavior of President Sukarno during these critical hours.

President Sukarno was also informed of events about 6:00 A.M. on October 1. He was at the home of wife Dewi, and immediately left for the Palace. En route he was advised by a security officer to go to wife Harjati's house. There he received further advice that it would be unsafe to go to the Palace or to the homes of his other wives.

He instructed an aide to try to find more information and to seek the advice of the police, the air force, and the navy as to what he should do. Perhaps significantly, neither the President nor any of his staff contacted the army at this time. On the advice of Air Force Commander in Chief Omar Dhani, the President then proceeded to Halim Air Force Base. He explained later that he wanted to be where a plane was available in case flight became necessary.

At 10:00 A.M. the President informed Soeharto that he was safe near Djakarta, but declined to specify his location. Soeharto correctly guessed him to be at Halim. The President again contacted General Soeharto about 7.30 P.M. and Soeharto advised him to leave Halim as he was getting ready to attack the base. Though urged by the rebels to fly to Jogjakarta, the President declined and went instead to the summer palace at Bogor, 65 km. (40 mi.) from Djakarta. Before leaving for Bogor the President, ignoring the position of General Soeharto, appointed Major General Pranoto Reksosamudro to the position of acting commander in chief of the army.

By evening, General Soeharto had the situation reasonably well in hand. The rebel-led troops in Merdeka Square had been induced, by persuasion and threat of force, to give up. There had been no violence. The radio station and other communications facilities that had been seized that morning had also been retaken without combat. The disloyal commanders were rapidly being identified and declarations of loyalty had been received from the commanders of most units. When General Nasution arrived at *KOSTRAD* headquarters General Soeharto briefed him on events and on the action he had taken and offered to turn the command over to Nasution as the senior officer. General Nasution was impressed by the control that General Soeharto had established and declined the offer.

The key to the rebels' success lay in getting an endorsement from President Sukarno, but this they failed to obtain. Well before evening it must have been evident to the President that the army was far from being brought under the control of the rebels and that those who had begun the coup were a small and diminishing percentage of its ranks. A strong endorsement any time on October 1 for either the army or the rebels might well have decided the issue, but Sukarno had learned to balance them one against the other and this he continued to attempt to do. Whether or not President Sukarno was aware of, and had explicitly or implicitly given his blessing to, the Gestapu coup will probably never be known for certain.

By 3:00 A.M. October 2, units led by Colonel Sarwo Edhie

were in position around the Halim base and were ready to
begin the attack. In order to avoid bloodshed, however,
Edhie agreed to meet with the Halim commander at a
conference to be arranged with the President at Bogor.

They did not succeed in seeing the President, for by the
time they reached Bogor, higher ranking officers were
already in conference with Sukarno.

Sukarno attempted to clarify to Soeharto and other
military leaders the meaning of the dual command that
had supposedly been formed with his appointment of
General Pranoto as acting commander in chief. Soeharto
told the President that there was no such thing as two
officers holding simultaneously the same command. The
order was, however, left standing with General Soeharto
commissioned to restore security "in accordance with
Sukarno's policies."

There was, in fact, no dual command. Soeharto was
clearly in charge and had the loyalty of the vast majority
of the army officers.

The shape of events had become evident to the rebels at
Halim even before the Bogor meeting. It was obvious that
the President had not supported their position—or had not
supported it strongly enough to make an operational
difference. And it was also evident that they would have
very little chance against General Soeharto's troops. Aidit
and most of the other rebel leaders then fled and there was
no need for the army to capture the base. Aidit went by
plane to Jogjakarta; Omar Dhani was given asylum by the
President at Bogor.

Throughout their history in Indonesia, the *PKI* had
always managed, in time of crisis, to make the worst of a
bad situation and their handling of Gestapu was no
exception. The killing and mutilation of the generals was a
crime that was to lead inexorably to the death of thousands
of their members. The bodies were discovered on October 4,
and General Soeharto delivered an on-the-scene report over
the radio explaining what had happened. The first reaction
to the information was grief. Then there came another
reaction—an implacable fury against the *PKI* and all they
stood for.

President Sukarno's reaction at that time was to dismiss the coup attempt as just a minor, although unfortunate, incident in the stream of the revolution. At his first post-coup Cabinet meeting, the day after the generals' funeral (which he did not attend), Sukarno playfully joked with his communist and "progressive revolutionary" ministers.

Though the situation for the rebels quickly deteriorated in Djakarta, in central Java, events, at first, went much according to Gestapu plan. The anti-*PKI* commander of the Diponegoro Division escaped, but two of his key officers were murdered, and the division came under *PKI*-sympathetic officers. The mayor of Surakarta issued a proclamation endorsing the movement. The governor of Central Java was abroad, but his deputy was sympathetic to the *PKI*. In Jogjakarta, demonstrations in favor of Gestapu were held on October 1.

But even by the time Aidit arrived in Jogjakarta early in the morning of October 2, it was clear to many that the movement was in trouble. Aidit apparently decided to mark time in Jogjakarta in hopes that Sukarno would at least be able to restore the status quo ante.

In a letter from Aidit to Sukarno (a copy was captured when students sacked the *PKI* headquarters) and later introduced at Deputy Prime Minister Subandrio's trial, Aidit:

> advised the President to equate the September 30 Movement with the Council of Generals ... entrust the restoration of security to the police and the Sukarno-*PKI*-dominated National Front, and authorize "all political organizations, mass organizations, the press and radio to resume operations as prior to the September 30 Movement." (Brackman, *The Communist Collapse in Indonesia*, p. 106)

But it was far too late for this. The discovery of the generals' bodies had already created a national outrage and the vehemance of this reaction caught all leaders unprepared. Rioting against the *PKI* took place in Djakarta where the Chinese Embassy and the *PKI* headquarters, as well as Aidit's home, were sacked and burned. Hundreds were arrested.

On October 19, two battalions of army paracommandos were sent to capture Jogjakarta. Only when immediately threatened by these troops, did Aidit begin to organize for defense. Weapons supplied by rebel army units were distributed to the people and temporary *PKI* authority in the villages was obtained by murdering nearly 250 village leaders. However, when fighting began the *PKI* forces were quickly defeated by the paracommandos and by the end of November, all organized resistance had ceased.

Aidit was pursued for almost three weeks in the Surakarta area, as he traveled from post to post maintaining underground contacts. He was finally captured on the night of November 21. He is reported to have been executed by his captors although this has never been officially announced. A fifty-page confession allegedly made by him prior to his death—in which he assumed full responsibility for both the planning and execution of Gestapu—has also never been officially authenticated. (Brackman, p. 110–112)

During October, November, and December literally thousands of *PKI* members and others were killed throughout the country.

Both army groups and civilians took part in killing *PKI* members and those thought to be their sympathizers. For the army it became an action against an old and hated enemy that had killed their leaders and evidently had plans to kill many more. Violent reactions were further stimulated when raids on *PKI* headquarters yielded "liquidation lists" containing names of many army officers and civilian leaders. The civilian response reflected not only an in-kind response to *PKI* terror tactics but the mental terror which the *PKI* had inflicted upon the Indonesian citizenry as a whole. Throughout the archipelago, the communists had ridiculed religion and the traditional customs and had created fears and anger that only came to the surface with Gestapu. Landlords and wealthy farmers had been in fear of having their lands forcibly taken from them and many took this apparent opportunity to protect their property. The Chinese government was known to have strongly supported the *PKI* and many innocent Indonesians died through a tragic oversimplification of the relation between citizens of Chinese descent and the regime in Peking. Doubtless many

purely personal and family feuds were settled by knives
and spears raised in the name of saving the country.

It has never been possible to make an accurate estimate
of the number of people killed in the months following
Gestapu, and estimates have ranged from a low of about
90,000 to a high of well over a million. A figure of about
150,000 is now increasingly accepted.

*   *   *

As the year 1966 began, a precarious order was restored
to Indonesia. The spasm of spontaneous killing that had
racked the nation was, for the most part, over.

Two new groups became identifiable in the period that
followed Gestapu. On the one side were those supporting
change—for the establishment of a New Order. They saw
that constructive change would only be possible if radical
elements, such as the *PKI*, were controlled and if Sukarno's
extra-constitutional monopoly on state policy was eliminated. They viewed with disgust the consequences of
Sukarno's regime on the quality of Indonesian life—the
stagnation of the economy, the runaway inflation, the
black markets, hoarding, shortages, corruption, and deterioration of virtually all services. For the most part, the
groups supporting a New Order lived in the cities. They
were also from the part of society most dependent on the
money economy and most accessible to information.
Among these groups, there had grown a great contempt
for Sukarno both because of his private life—which was
regarded as a national humiliation—and because of his
disasterous economic leadership of the nation. Many men
in government were included among those who sought a
New Order.

Opposed to these groups were others that sought to
perpetuate Sukarnoism and, in some cases, the *PKI* role
as well. Their leader was, of course, Sukarno, and they
would follow his every wish. These groups included not
only surviving members of the *PKI*, but also many who had
served Sukarno over the years and were not so affiliated.
They believed in Sukarno's priorities—a large role for

Indonesia on the international stage, a national emphasis on Indonesian culture, the need to minimize Western influence, and the drive to establish a socialist economy. Intermixed with conviction, and in some cases apart from it, were considerations of power and career.

For many people it was a time for decision concerning future courses and a time for re-examining past loyalties. Many dedicated and intelligent men were caught in a rending between conviction and career and prominent among these was Chairul Saleh. A former aide recalls that as the years of Guided Democracy passed, Chairul had become increasingly occupied with the problems of economic development, and paid less attention to his own political fortunes. Others would dispute this, contending that Chairul remained first and foremost a politician throughout his life. In any event, in late 1964, Chairul had been among those who had initially encouraged the "Body to Support Sukarnoism," which sought, in the name of Sukarnoism, to forestall Sukarno's and Indonesia's increasing drifts, domestically and also internationally, toward communism. To Chairul's surprise, Sukarno reacted angrily, and ordered this group dissolved shortly after its formation. With his increasingly open opposition to the *PKI*, Chairul became a major target of *PKI* press and pamphlet attacks.

Chairul, in spite of his differences with the *PKI*, remained loyal to Sukarno. It may well have been for this reason that at the time of Gestapu, he had been dispatched out of the country and was in Peking as head of an Indonesian delegation at the sixteenth anniversary of the founding of the People's Republic of China.

When Chairul learned, in Peking, of the murder of the generals and the composition of the Revolutionary Council, which contained Subandrio's name, he reportedly said: "This is the work of Subandrio—either he goes down or I go down." (Brackman, p. 84). One foreign newspaper reported that Chairul planned to set up a government in exile if the Gestapu coup succeeded. (Brackman, p. 227, fn. 14). Whether or not Chairul would have attempted to form an exile government, it was unlikely he would have returned to a *PKI*-controlled Indonesia. A former close associate states that the *PKI* planned to bring Chairul before a public people's court in Djakarta, and hang him in Merdeka Square. After Chairul returned to Djakarta the next week, his first act was to pay his respects at the graves of the slain generals. As evidence of Sukarno's own role in Gestapu mounted, friends advised Chairul to dissociate himself from the President. Chairul, however, did not hesitate—he elected to remain loyal to Sukarno to the end.

Ideologically .between the pro-Sukarno forces and those immediately seeking the New Order, stood General Soeharto. Still politically unambitious, he had, through circumstances and his own willingness to take responsibility, emerged as the man who was responsible for maintaining the precarious public order. At this time his most fundamental concern was to avoid further bloodshed if at all possible. Over the next two years General Soeharto first shared executive authority with Sukarno and, finally, succeeded him as president.

The story of the evolution of the New Order in Indonesian politics is essentially a story of these two men, the one, a flamboyant god-hero to the people and the other an unassuming and quietly competent professional soldier. Their roles and reactions in the events of Gestapu created a highly complex duality of power in the national leadership that had to be resolved. Though there was a great gulf between the positions of the two men, and there had been more than enough violence and acrimony between their supporters, the resolution between the two men was not a violent or brutal one, but rather one that epitomized all that is subtle and toughly gentle in the Javanese character.

General Soeharto was the restraining force on both those groups who sought immediate change and on those who still desired to perpetuate the rule of Sukarno. Recognizing President Sukarno's strong and unique psychological hold on the Indonesian people, Soeharto was concerned over the potential of civil war inherent in any effort to curb Sukarno's powers.

As during the years of Sukarno's Guided Democracy, Indonesian politics were conducted not only through the traditional organs of government, which Sukarno for the most part controlled, but also in the "parliament of the streets." Mass demonstrations, speeches to cheering throngs —these were the testimonials of support on which Sukarno based his rule. In early 1966, both groups—the New Order forces and Sukarno forces—were organized into various action fronts with frequent street clashes between pro-Sukarno and anti-Sukarno student groups.

In his own strategy, Sukarno clung doggedly to the balancing formula of *NASAKOM*. He would not authorize an order banning the *PKI*. He consistently pressed to maintain his own over-large role, and to preserve his entire program of Guided Democracy.

In the first instance, it was in the "parliament of the streets" that Sukarno lost the battle. The concessions he made in his grudging, step by step, relinquishment of power were principally caused by street demonstrations involving groups from many sectors of society, but generally the students—the college students, *KAMI*, and the high school group, *KAPPI*, who emerged as the Generation of '66.

The visible process of decline began on February 24, 1966, when Sukarno made a major mistake. In a Cabinet reshuffle he appointed the "Improved Dwikora Cabinet," later termed by the students the "Gestapu Cabinet." Although General Soeharto was confirmed as minister/chief of staff of the army, General Nasution was dismissed as minister/coordinator of defense, whereas Omar Dhani was added as minister of aircraft industry.

General Nasution was a hero to the students as a revolutionary champion and he was a man reknowned for his integrity. Demonstrations, spearheaded by *KAMI*, began immediately against the reshuffling of the cabinet. Sukarno issued a decree banning *KAMI* and this served only to add fuel to the fire. *KAMI* refused to disband and *KAPPI* moved to add its support.

On March 10, 1966, Sukarno held a meeting of party leaders to whom he offered nothing but a harangue. More of the same followed the next day in a cabinet meeting. In the middle of a rambling speech by Sukarno, in which he demanded that cabinet members either follow him or resign, an aide interrupted the meeting to inform Sukarno that troops from an unidentified army unit were approaching the Palace. Sukarno broke off the meeting, pleading an urgent development, and hurriedly departed to Bogor accompanied by Subandrio and Chairul Saleh. There they met later that day with a delegation of three generals, Basuki Rachmat, Amir Machmud, and Mohammad Jusuf. General Soeharto was not present. After a five-hour meeting, and against the advice of Subandrio and Chairul Saleh, Sukarno agreed to form a new cabinet and reluctantly signed an order under his emergency powers ordering General Soeharto:

> to take all necessary steps to guarantee the security and the stability of the running of the Government and the course of the Revolution while securing the personal safety of, and the authority of, the Great Leader of the Revolution ... for the sake of the Nation's integrity and that of the Republic of Indonesia, and absolutely execute all the teachings of the Great Leader of the Revolution.

The next day, General Soeharto used this order to ban the *PKI*. Three days later, after preliminary meetings on the composition of the new Cabinet involving Sukarno, the Sultan of Jogjakarta, Dr. Leimena, and the three generals among others, Sukarno issued a presidential announcement reminding the Indonesian people of their obligation to put into practice all his teachings and warning those who wanted "to enforce their wish upon the President." He emphasized that "the ministers are appointed by the President alone and by nobody else."

At the receipt of this news, the students again took to the streets and began occupying government buildings. Soeharto placed fifteen of the ministers closest to Sukarno under protective custody and these included Chairul Saleh and Subandrio.

Later in the year several of these ministers were brought to trial. Subandrio's trial established that as head of Indonesia's intelligence organization he had learned generally of the coup plans, but had not informed Sukarno because he thought Sukarno already knew of them. Omar Dhani's trial established his role.

Unlike some of the other ministers arrested, Chairul Saleh was never tried. He was cleared of all political charges but he remained in detention until the time of his death from a heart attack on February 8, 1967. Thus ended the life of one of the most tempestuous and controversial men in Indonesian politics.

A few days after the ministers' detention a new cabinet was announced, the "Once-more-improved Dwikora Cabinet." It again reflected a compromise which satisfied no one. New Order forces were pleased to learn that the fifteen ministers who had been placed under protective custody were all replaced and General Nasution returned to the Cabinet. But the Cabinet's random selection and combination of old and new, left little prospect for decisive policy making.

New Order forces then shifted their attention to the impending meeting of the Provisional Consultative Assembly (*MPRS*). This body was the only organ which could implement the New Order objective to further curb the powers of President Sukarno. Before it met, its membership was reconstituted, and the members of the banned *PKI*, as well as members of other extreme left-wing groups, were dismissed. Also, 142 other members deemed committed to the Old Order were replaced by other representatives of their respective parties and functional groups. In June, the *MPRS* convened and General Nasution was elected chairman. President Sukarno was continued in office, but his role was "reconstitutionalized" by revoking the earlier *MPRS* resolution that had made him "President for Life." President Sukarno's March 11 order to General Soeharto was ratified. It was further provided that in the event of President Sukarno's inability to carry out the duties of president, General Soeharto would assume those duties as acting-president. The order banning the *PKI* was confirmed and the teaching of Marxism-Leninism was restricted.

On June 22, Sukarno was called before the *MPRS* to give a report on the state of the nation. In his speech, which he termed "Nine Points," he seriously misjudged the public temper. The speech was short, truculent, and unyielding. He, Sukarno, was the duly elected mandatory of the *MPRS*, now they must follow him and those policies they had earlier embraced. Moreover, the present *MPRS* was provisional, he stressed, and thus it had no authority to abridge his powers or to make major changes.

Most members of the *MPRS* were outraged at this speech. Angrily they resolved, on July 5, that Sukarno must give a full and detailed report on national issues, including an account of the causes of Gestapu and his explanation for the economic and otherwise visible deterioration of the country.

Three weeks later, President Sukarno was pressured into announcing the formation, "jointly" with General Soeharto, of a new Ampera Cabinet. Although Sukarno retained the title of prime minister, General Soeharto became chairman of the Presidium Cabinet (the inner cabinet of senior or core ministers), and from this time on, the authority over government affairs was exercised primarily by General Soeharto as chairman.

President Sukarno would not accept this change gracefully and he continued to assert his own primacy and to insist that his Guided Democracy program would continue. Thus the Independence Day ceremonies of 1966 saw President Sukarno presiding at the podium in his usual style. His performance was coolly received by General Soeharto and the ministers of the Ampera Cabinet. The confusing dualism in executive authority added further impetus to demands for Sukarno's resignation or, if need be, his involuntary removal. The increased economic deterioration of the nation called for a major change.

Beginning in September, 1966, the first of a series of public trials involving Gestapu participants took place. These trials indirectly focused public attention on President Sukarno's own role in the coup attempt. A movement to investigate the President's role and place him on trial gathered force. As Sukarno's own conduct before and after the event came to the public attention, demands were increasingly heard that he step down from the Presidency, be brought to trial, or both. Clashes between student groups demonstrating for the President's ouster and soldiers charged to maintain order occurred with increasing frequency.

On January 10, 1967, Sukarno complied with the *MPRS* resolution calling for him to supplement his "Nine Points" speech. His response was yet another assertion of his presidential prerogatives, declaring that the *MPRS* lacked the power to inquire into his decisions.

Public outcry against this speech came from virtually all sectors of Indonesian society. The *MPRS* Standing Committee declared it unacceptable, and resolved to demand Sukarno's ouster. By this time Sukarno's own popular base had eroded so greatly that there was then little risk of civil conflict in the event of his dismissal. Still, a voluntary surrender of power was preferable. After discussions with many leaders, and much soul searching, Sukarno surrendered his executive power to Soeharto on February 20, 1967. The *MPRS* reconvened two weeks later and confirmed the action on March 12, 1967, retroactive to February 22. Sukarno was stripped of all powers, but retained the title of president, while Soeharto became acting-president of Indonesia.

This marked the end of President Sukarno as an active force in Indonesian public life. He lived out the remainder of his days in Djakarta, where he died on June 21, 1970. Reportedly he never completely abandoned his hopes for a political comeback, having spent his entire life forming and leading the nation. Sukarno wanted to be remembered as the "spokesman of the people," and to a great extent he was. He gave voice to the hopes of nationalism, and more than any other man it was he who mobilized national resistance against Dutch colonialism. His 1945 speech set forth the principles of Pantjasila. These principles, unlike the ones he later formulated, remain the ideological basis of the Indonesian nation. Thus, today the New Order political system is called Pantjasila democracy. Sukarno is revered for his contribution to the Indonesian independence movement and for forging the modern Indonesian identity. Because of these contributions, his last days were made as comfortable as possible and he was never subjected to the humiliation of public trial. In death he was not forgotten by those who remembered him as their leader and acknowledged their debt for his role in the creation of the Indonesian nation. They came by foot, by bus, by ox cart, by bicycle, and by automobile to Blitar and there his grave lay buried deep beneath a mound of flower petals placed by loving hands.

With the confirmation of Soeharto as acting-president by the *MPRS*, the period of dualism in Indonesian leadership came to an end, and the New Order officially began. While the *PKI* had been eliminated as a legitimate force in Indonesian political life, all the other religious and functional groups remained. Regionalism, religion, the role of the political parties, and the role of the army were all unresolved issues inherited from the past. Now there were new forces as well—the student action fronts, styled the Generation of '66, had earned a claim to participate in the New Order along with the Generation of '45. Their teachers at the university also now sought a more active role.

As surely as Sukarno's personality set the tone of what is now called the Old Order (Orde Lama) President Soeharto's marks are identifiable in the New Order (Orde Baru). The style of the Soeharto government is in stark contrast to that of its predecessor. Careful understatement, candid assessment of progress and failures, and an emphasis on the concrete, are the marks of Soeharto.

In foreign policy, President Soeharto's guidance of the New Order has seen Indonesia's return to the independent non-aligned position of the pre-Guided Democracy period. The foreign policy of the New Order is active and independent but the activity under Foreign Minister Adam Malik is in marked contrast to Indonesia's bellicose activity in the days of Guided Democracy. Today the activity is channelled into mediation of disputes and the promotion of regional cooperation.

This departure was dramatically demonstrated, even before the era of dualism ended in Indonesia, with the termination of the costly *Konfrontasi* with Malaysia in August, 1966. Indonesia pledged an end to *Konfrontasi* and Malaysia pledged to conduct plebiscites consistent with the principle of self-determination in Sarawak and Sabah, the two Borneo states whose cause Indonesia had championed. Also scuttled was the rhetoric of Old Established Forces and New Emerging Forces and the alignment with Peking which accompanied it. In September, 1966, Indonesia returned to the United Nations.

A major rapprochement with the West has also taken place, aided on the Western side by evolution in thinking away from the with-us-or-against-us foreign policies which characterized the 1950's. Indonesia has sought and received major new credits from Europe, the United States, and Japan. Development projects have been resumed and the currency stabilized. But the Soeharto government has stoutly resisted the role of "client state" of the West and has entered no military alliances. Indonesia has not hesitated to deplore the billions of dollars poured into arms races between the great powers while most of the world's peoples struggle to lift themselves out of poverty.

Relations with Communist bloc countries were understandably highly strained in the months following Gestapu. Yet despite restrictions on communist party activity and the teaching of Marxism-Leninism, efforts have been made to maintain or improve relations with the Soviet Union and Eastern Europe. Diplomatic relations with the Soviet Union were maintained and recent improvement is signified by the agreements reached on rescheduling the Indonesian debt to that country. Relations with Peking remain officially "frozen," but Indonesia offered support for that country's admission to the United Nations.

In domestic politics, President Soeharto has followed a moderate course seeking to strike an appropriate balance between civil liberties on the one hand, and the pitfalls of democratic anarchism which prevailed in the early years of the nation.

What kind of government is it? In his biography of President Soeharto, O.G. Roeder answers the questions this way:

> The present political set-up in Indonesia, with the dominating role of the military in most fields

justifies the question. Is the Indonesia of Soeharto
a militaristic state? ... If militarism is defined as
an attitude towards public affairs which conceives
war and the preparation for war as the chief
instrument of foreign policy, then Indonesia is
definitely not a militaristic state... If militarism,
on the other hand, is defined as the predominance of
military power in state affairs, without eliminating
other political forces, this term may be considered
more suitable. There is no doubt that the decisive
power in Indonesia is in the hands of the Armed
Forces, who nevertheless are committed to the
1945 Constitution. (pp. 159-160)

It was the inability to agree upon a new electoral law during
the *MPRS* sessions in 1968 that led to President Soeharto's
elevation to president on March 27, 1968. As acting-
president, Soeharto's tenure had been limited to the period
pending the outcome of next elections which were specified
to be held not later than July 15, 1968. With his appointment
as president, elections were postponed until July, 1971.
The elections of July, 1971, resulted in a sweeping mandate
for his government.

Indonesia has continued under the New Order to grapple
with the problem of finding an appropriate balance between
the desires of the people and the capability of the economy.

The Soeharto government has devoted most of its energies
to the economy and economic development. During the
year 1966, the economic situation had further deteriorated.
Internally, inflation during that year spiraled to 694%.
Externally, the country was virtually bankrupt with only
$8 million in hard currency holdings against current debts
of over $500 million, and with projected gross export
earnings of just $400 million.

To help deal with these pressing economic problems,
President Soeharto appointed an advisory team of six
University of Indonesia economists. Today all of these
men serve as ministers.

To establish the foundations for national development
efforts, the soaring inflation had to be stopped. The primary

cause of inflation had been the government's own printing presses. The economic advisers put together an austere balanced budget that carefully measured government needs in relation to likely government revenues. Concurrently, measures were adopted to stop capital flight abroad and induce domestic saving through the banking system. Annual bank interest rates of up to 72% were announced and a no-questions-asked policy concerning sources of funds was instituted. The complex multiple exchange rate system was gradually dismantled.

The debt inherited from the Sukarno years totalled over $2,000 million. In September, 1966, the Sultan of Jogjakarta and other Indonesian economists met in Tokyo with representatives of the principal Western creditor nations and Japan. Outlining the New Order's commitment to rationalizing the economy, Indonesia succeeded in re-scheduling most of the debts. Moreover, the ten creditor nations established a consortium called the Inter-Govern-mental Group on Indonesia (IGGI). Meeting semiannually the IGGI monitors Indonesian economic performance. It became so impressed with the progress of the Indonesian economy that in subsequent meetings, new credits were extended and these have steadily been increased.

On January 1, 1967, Indonesia adopted a new Foreign Capital Investment Law. To accelerate economic recon-struction, the act invites foreign capital participation in fields and sectors which are not of strategic importance to the state. Approved investments for a maximum of thirty years are authorized, tax holidays during startup for a maximum of five years are permitted, and further exemptions are provided for reinvested profits. In the event that the government interest requires nationalization, compensation is assured according to principles of international law. To date, over $1,000 million dollars has been committed under the new act.

In January, 1969, the blueprint for economic development was unveiled—the New Order's first Five-Year Plan. Pains-takingly conceived by the National Development Planning Council (*BAPPENAS*), it set realistic target increases for national production in all sectors, with priority given to improvement of the badly neglected utilities, transportation and communications, increasing agricultural production (including self-sufficiency in rice), and developing mining and industry. The plan contemplates a development outlay of $3,700 million for the five-year period. Of this amount, nearly 59% is expected to come from foreign aid—a realistic expectation in light of international satisfaction with domestic developments—with another 14% coming from private foreign investment. The remaining 27% is being paid with domestic earnings. Results of the economic program have impressed many economists. The budget has now been balanced, prices have been stabilized, and the Five-Year Plan goals are generally being met on schedule. Private investment has flowed in and domestic savings have improved. Indonesia's reputation for financial responsibility has been firmly established by the New Order.

Characteristically, President Soeharto consistently points out that the road to a better material life and social justice is still a long and hard one for the Indonesian people. The hallmark of his government, as it stands today, is the pursuit of the "just and prosperous society" through the application of tough-minded pragmatism informed by expert advisors, both Indonesian and foreign.

CHAPTER 12

Oil in Transition

Gestapu, that great watershed in Indonesian history, marked the beginning of a new era in the Indonesian oil industry, as it marked the beginning of a new era in the politics and economy of the nation.

When Chairul Saleh went abroad, shortly before Gestapu, he appointed Dr. Ibnu as minister of Migas during his absence. Thus on the morning of October 1, Dr. Ibnu had full charge of the oil sector. As General Soeharto established control in the next few days the process of reviewing the loyalty of persons throughout the nation began. Dr. Ibnu undertook this task in the oil sector and his first act was to ban Perbum and other *SOBSI* related groups in the oil industry. He was apparently the first minister to ban *PKI* affiliated groups in any department of government although early bans were also issued by army commanders.

On October 12, 1965, Dr. Ibnu ordered the directors of Permigan to appear at the Migas office. While they waited in the anteroom, he went to Permigan headquarters accompanied by Lt. Colonel Sudarsono, Sutan Assin, and Suhardi. There Dr. Ibnu announced the dissolution of the existing directorship and the creation of a caretaker board headed by himself as president-director, Lt. Colonel Sudarsono as technical director, Suhardi as administrative director, and Sutan Assin as production supervisor. Dr. Ibnu then returned to the Migas Office to inform Sumarjo Legowo and Kusomo Utojo that their directorships were dissolved. They were arrested later that evening for interrogation. The board secretary, Maladi Jussuf, was also arrested. Ir. Sumbarjono was reassigned to Migas.

The next week, control over field and refinery operations in Tjepu was secured as the army paracommandos swept through central Java. Tjepu, at this time, had about 2,300 workers, 90% of whom were nominal Perbum members. Of this number, however, only about 350 were considered in the cadre, or hard-core, *PKI* status. Members of this group were arrested while the remaining workers were allowed to carry on operations as usual.

The problem immediately arose as to what to do with the Permigan facilities. By strictly business standards the Tjepu operation was marginal at best; the refining facilities were of museum vintage, and the surrounding fields close to exhaustion. Shutdown was then first considered as a possibility but it was quickly recognized that shutdown would only aggravate the economic problems of the area—and poverty had made this part of central Java a major breeding-ground of communism over a period of many years. Both for humanitarian and political reasons, shut-down was therefore ruled out as a possibility.

Dr. Ibnu's solution was to give Tjepu a noncommercial function as well. The area was placed under the jurisdiction of Lemigas, and thus the Academy of Oil and Gas (Akamigas) was founded to supply a modern use for Permigan's old Tjepu facilities. The small Oil Academy, Permina had established in Bandung in 1962 was moved to Tjepu where students could learn in a practical atmosphere surrounded by working oil fields and a refinery. Permigan's marketing facilities were turned over to Pertamin and its production jurisdiction over west Java and Ceram was assigned to Permina.

When Chairul Saleh returned from Peking he resumed his position as minister of Migas. However, as the waves of violence shook the land, it soon became apparent that he would be fully occupied in his position as third deputy prime minister, and in the meantime, oil affairs required attention. The Shell and Stanvac negotiations were still open, domestic distribution was still suffering a financial crisis, and the black marketing in kerosene and gasoline was unchecked. Thus, in November, 1965, Chairul Saleh appointed Dr. Ibnu to administer all daily oil and gas affairs and announced that he would only be concerned with policy matters.

To stave off financial breakdown, an increase in the price of petroleum products was a matter of urgent priority. In the past, strong opposition to price increases had been exerted by the *PKI* and its affiliates and even though these groups were then being eliminated from the national political scene, their influence had been great and strong opposition was still expected. In spite of the outcry from those supporting the low prices, there was little to be said in their defense. It was known that some quantities of refined products were being smuggled out of the country thus aggravating the shortage. The benefits of low prices were largely theoretical in any case, because the service stations were usually out of stock and the users were forced to pay black market prices. Prices had, in effect, been raised but the increase had gone to black marketeers and a few smugglers rather than to the government or the oil companies.

On November 8, Dr. Ibnu, on Chairul Saleh's instructions, signed an order for a price increase, but its announcement was delayed for one week, while its political impact was further debated. The price of gasoline was raised from 4 rupiahs to 250 rupiahs per liter, with equivalent increases in other products. The initial reaction to this increase was muted since the nation was in the midst of the post-Gestapu confusion and people were not, at the time, focusing their attention on economic matters.

In December, 1965, the top ministers of government met at Tjipanas, a mountain retreat south of Djakarta, for five days in around-the-clock sessions in an urgent attempt to salvage the economic situation. Chairul Saleh, as President Sukarno's principal economic architect, presided. Dr. Ibnu and Wijarso represented the oil sector.

Chairul's plan was draconian and oil was its keystone. The rupiah's drastic decline in purchasing power was recognized with the decision to decree a new rupiah—one new rupiah equal to 1,000 old rupiahs. The exchange rate was also adjusted, but, at Ir. Wijarso's suggestion, the export bonus concept was retained. The last official exchange rate had been 250 base rate plus 270 bonus rupiahs to one

U.S. dollar. In new rupiah this would be 0.25 rupiah per U.S. dollar. A bonus rate of 9.75 new rupiahs per dollar would be given to export industries. Under the interpretation established by Wijarso in September, 1964, as to the meaning of the foreign exchange provision of the Contract of Work this could be withheld from the foreign oil companies by simply withholding it from the national oil companies. With the negotiations proceeding with Stanvac and Shell, this had obvious tactical advantages.

Fiscal policy was also rearranged with a clear commitment to balance the budget. A sales tax on domestic petroleum products would be the prime source of revenue. To this end, the price of gasoline, which had been raised to 250 old rupiahs the month before, was quadrupled to 1,000 old rupiahs or one new rupiah. Again, similar increases were made in the prices of other petroleum products. Thus domestic distribution which had previously been a major drain on government revenue was recast as a major revenue source.

The announcement was made on January 3, 1966, and this time there were, as expected, angry popular demonstrations. Chairul Saleh and Dr. Ibnu were singled out for particular abuse. The students joined in earnestly, if naively, championing the "rights of the people."

However, with pro-Sukarno and anti-Sukarno groups already clashing in the streets, President Sukarno felt that he could not afford the personal political risk of pushing through the price increases. The religious holiday, Lebaran, in January, 1966, provided the occasion for reducing the prices by half. They were to remain at this lower level while Sukarno stayed in power.

The retreat on petroleum prices marked a major—and as it turned out, the final—failure in a long series of economic failures of the Sukarno government. Expenditures had already been scheduled on the basis of new earnings from the petroleum sector, and a retreat on the projects so funded would have been as politically hazardous as the maintenance of the price increases. There was thus no possibility of balancing the budget or curbing inflation. In the opinion of some insiders, the retreat on petroleum prices brought about the political end of both Chairul Saleh and President Sukarno—clearly, they could not manage the economy.

While Chairul Saleh was formulating the final economic program of the Sukarno government, Dr. Ibnu was proceeding with the Shell and Stanvac negotiations. Gestapu, and the changes it portended, naturally called for a re-evaluation by the managements of both companies.

Stanvac hesitated. Whereas two days before Gestapu, Dr. Ibnu had advised his negotiating team that an agreement with Stanvac seemed the more likely of the two, after Gestapu discussions bogged down over the price. Negotiations continued into mid-1966, but no final agreement was reached.

Shell, on the other hand, elected to proceed with the sale of its Indonesian holdings. The company had taken a special beating in Indonesia. Following the expulsion of the Dutch, it had been forced to Anglicize its management. No sooner was this done than *Konfrontasi* began with the British cast as the villians, so Americans and Canadians had to be brought in. Although operating conditions in Indonesia could be expected to improve if the army succeeded in curbing the *PKI,* exactly what kind of government would emerge was still unclear. And even if the political situation improved, there remained Shell's disappointing production decline. According to one former Shell executive, more important than any change in the political or economic climate was Shell's conviction that the commitment had been made and that negotiations were too far advanced to be terminated. In these circumstances, they felt it would be better to leave Indonesia in a spirit of goodwill engendered by a cooperative sale. Shell executives hoped the company could return to Indonesia some time in the future, and until that time the company could rely on its Malaysia and Brunei fields for regional production and on its newly constructed refineries at Singapore and at Port Dickson, Malaysia, for refined products.

On the part of Dr. Ibnu, the decision concerning Shell did not involve the purchase as such, but rather whether the assets could be purchased at a price which would enable Indonesia to meet the payments. As negotiations progressed, this was the major point to be resolved. Dr. Ibnu and Shell's managing director, Van Reeven, held a series of meetings in an effort to reach an agreement. Dr. Ibnu's bargaining approach stressed the fact that it was in the interest of both sides to reach a price which Indonesia could realistically be expected to pay. If there was a default both sides would suffer. With this principle in mind, Dr. Ibnu asked Shell to state a price. Shell did so—$150 million. Dr. Ibnu selected an alternative price that he thought Shell might accept and, more importantly, that the negotiating team thought it could repay—$110 million. Shell accepted and the Heads of Agreement was signed on December 31, 1965, effective January 1, 1966.

Payment was to be made over a five-year period. Shell would be repaid from sales of crude oil and refined products from the purchased facilities. Shell would be exclusively entitled to all proceeds of sales until each annual payment was completed. Oil and refined products would be valued by a joint committee established for that purpose.

The Shell purchase did not go uncriticized. Some newspapers attacked it and several cabinet members expressed the view that it was unwise for a country on the verge of bankruptcy to undertake such a commitment. Criticism came from technical quarters as well. One Shell official predicted that, under Indonesian management, the Balikpapan refinery would be shut down within six months.

To Dr. Ibnu and his colleagues, the governmental criticisms missed the point. What was being purchased was not so much a group of facilities, but the opportunity to control and learn by operating them. There was a risk, of course, that operations would not hold up, and repayment could not be made. This was the challenge they dared to meet. The key to repayment was good management of the operations and, as Dr. Ibnu had stressed in discussions on the price, Shell had an interest in this also. Although the entire government of Indonesia stood liable for the debt, if production could not be maintained, payment would be extremely difficult to obtain as the country was nearly bankrupt. To the end of ensuring good management, it was mutually agreed that Shell would provide a small technical assistance team during the course of the agreement.

Chairul Saleh concurred with Dr. Ibnu and appointed Permina as the national company to receive the assets and assume the indebtness. On the Indonesian side, Dr. Sanger, Tirto Utomo, and Ir. Soedarno headed a special team for Permina to oversee the implementation and payments for the Shell purchase. It was agreed that all employees of Shell, numbering over 11,000, would be transferred to Permina, except the members of the Board of Directors who would be given the option of remaining with the Shell organization.

The acquisition of Shell's assets and areas and Permigan's areas changed Permina from a small national oil company to a major enterprise. Where formerly its operations were limited to north Sumatra and West Irian, now it had holdings in south Sumatra, Kalimantan, and Java as well. Where there had been one small refinery, now there were four with Pladju, Balikpapan, and Wonokromo added to Pangkalan Brandan. From an organization of 3,000 employees, it became one of 14,000. As it developed, there arose a host of new problems and many were in areas where there was little previous experience on the part of Permina.

Obviously a transfer of this size presented large organizational problems. Dr. Ibnu became the chairman of the former P.T. Shell Indonesia, but left the actual integration in the hands of the men who had been the members of the Shell supervisory board. This management board worked closely with Suhardi from Permina's personnel section as all of Shell's Indonesian national personnel were transferred over to Permina. The transfer of Shell's operations proceeded by areas beginning with south Sumatra, and followed by Kalimantan and Surabaja in February. The final area of transfer was the Djakarta office where Shell and Permina had maintained a joint headquarters throughout the transfer.

A cooperative atmosphere prevailed during the actual transfer of facilities, with selected members of Shell's expatriate staff remaining on in their normal capacities. As an area was transferred, the first person usually relieved was the area manager. Lower level staff personnel, especially those in technical operations, continued to assist Permina in field work until qualified Indonesian personnel could

take over their jobs. Even after the staff posts were entirely
Indonesianized, a small team of Shell expatriates continued
serving as technical advisors as provided for in the contract.

As part of the national effort to develop new attitudes
and to develop a company esprit de corps, courses were
established which were attended by all employees. These
courses covered general business economics as well as
explanations of the company's working policies. Besides
trying to develop a company spirit, it also included a political
indoctrination of the policies of the New Order, and tried
to dispel the communist oriented philosophy of Sukarno's
Guided Democracy that had become so ingrained among
many of the workers.

Work rules and policies were standardized and basic
retirement benefits were set up. Job security was improved,
and the chances for promotion were greatly increased,
especially in the upper management brackets. Many men
were automatically promoted two grades and given much
more responsibility. A uniform pay system was established,
which included the standardization of the allowance system.

Permina's concerns extended beyond its employees to
their wives and families as well. Mrs. Ibnu Sutowo greatly
expanded the activities of the women's organization that
she had started in 1964. Initially the objective was to develop
more understanding between the families of the workers
and management groups. Its activities still center on helping
to improve family welfare. The organization sponsors
social gatherings, schooling, scouting, cultural courses,
family planning, and guidance. Cooperatives, clinics and
study clubs have been formed under its auspices. For the
wives of oil employees it stresses the importance of their
husbands' jobs in building the nation.

*   *   *

On February 21, 1966, President Sukarno named his
Improved Dwikora Cabinet in which Dr. Ibnu was appointed
minister of Migas, with Chairul Saleh maintaining his core
ministry. Among the fifteen ministers of the Improved
Dwikora Cabinet that were placed under arrest were included

Chairul Saleh and also Minister of Mines Armunanto. On March 27, General Soeharto, in the name of the President, announced the Once-more-improved Dwikora Cabinet. In this cabinet, oil and gas affairs and mining were again recombined with Dr. Ibnu being appointed minister of Mines and Migas. He was also concurrently appointed to the position of deputy minister of Migas, while continuing as president-director of Permina.

In his capacity as minister of Migas, Dr. Ibnu ordered the consolidation of exploration and production activities under Permina, in March, 1966. The field operations were divided into five units. Unit I included the old Permina area of operations in North Sumatra and Atjeh, with headquarters located in Pangkalan Brandan. Unit II covered the Djambi, Lampung, and the south Sumatra area, with Pladju serving as the unit headquarters. Java and Madura made up Unit III, with headquarters in Djakarta. Unit IV included all of Kalimantan plus the islands of Tarakan and Bunju with Balikpapan as the headquarters. Eastern Indonesia including Sulawesi, the Moluccas, and West Irian made up Unit V, with Sorong as the unit headquarters. Today, as operations have expanded, two more units have been added to the original five. Unit VI includes central Sumatra while Unit VII covers the Riau Islands and coordinating activities in Singapore.

Although the consolidation order was issued in March, 1966, it was not fully implemented until Pertamin and Permina were merged two and a half years later.

In the head office, Permina's exploration and production team was drawing together. In 1967, Soediono and four deputy coordinators, all former Shell men, took under consideration the place to drill in the Kuang field, a former *NIAM*/Permindo area in south Sumatra. There had been some shakedown problems in the department and relations between Soediono and his subordinates were still unsettled. The group sat down with the field men from Unit II and considered the seismic data that had been prepared by the Pertamin exploration department. Each made a recommendation. Soediono, a petroleum engineer not a geologist, listened and then picked a compromise location. Drilling began

in 1968, they struck oil, and development of the field began. Unit II proposed bringing in another rig and Soediono ordered a rig relocated from Unit I, north Sumatra. Material to construct an eight-inch pipeline was required and Soediono ordered pipe moved to Unit II regardless of its location. Important things were happening here: Tendencies toward compartmentalization along old lines were being broken down. Unit II—a former Shell Unit—saw Unit I's interests subordinated to its own discovery. Changes in personnel reflected the same theme. Men were placed in new jobs because they met the requirements of the job and without consideration of their former company.

In refining and petrochemicals, the man in charge, Ir. Soedarno, was quite literally a man who had been studying for a job which did not yet exist. Dr. Ibnu, in the early 1960s, told him to study the development of the Japanese refining industry. Concurrently, he handled a number of special assignments for Dr. Ibnu in the secretariat of the *BPU,* as well as studying refining and supply under the Contracts of Work, coordinating the transfer of Stanvac marketing facilities to Pertamin and working on the negotiating team on the Shell purchase. In 1966, he was placed in charge of all the company's refining operations which, in addition to the first refinery at Pangkalan Brandan (7,000 barrels per day) now included the former Shell refineries at Pladju (110,000 barrels per day), Wonokromo (3,200 barrels per day), as well as Balikpapan (75,000 barrels per day).

Contrary to predictions, operations everywhere held up under Indonesian management. Ir. Soedarno was joined in the head office by Ir. Singgih Darsono, Mr. Lucas, and Mr. Jacobs to help administer the national scope of their new operations. The two biggest challenges were Pladju and Balikpapan, where Colonel B.T. Tobing and Ir. Harsono, respectively, were appointed unit general managers. At Pladju, Ir. Soetopo and at Balikpapan, Ir. Indraman Akman and their staffs were moved up two management levels and told to maintain full refinery operations as before the transfer. With minor difficulties they were able to meet their goals. Basically, these men had all been well-trained by Shell and

INDONESIAN ROUGHNECKS LAYING DOWN PIPE.

it was just a matter of having the opportunity to actually run the operations. As they put it, "we had the training, we needed the courage to believe we could do it, and we did."

Important developments were also taking place in Permigan's former area of west Java. During his days in limbo with Permigan, Ir. Sutan Assin used his spare time studying the old Shell data for west Java. Just before World War II, Shell had drilled a number of wells in the Bongas and Djatibarang area. On a few they hit gas and on a few others they hit oil. Reviewing the data, Sutan Assin became interested in the development of a gas supply in west Java

The place of gas in the world energy industry had grown rapidly after World War II with the development of large gas pipelines in the United States and other industrialized countries. At the Indonesian level of development a gas source would have to be near the population center it would serve and this was the case in West Java. If gas could be used in part to replace kerosene, costs of domestic energy would be reduced and gas might even be exported.

From the data it appeared that gas could be tapped merely by drilling between 2,000 and 3,000 feet. "I became obsessed with the idea," Assin says. In 1964, Sutan Assin went to an Ecafe meeting in Teheran to further study the subject. He tried to sell his ideas during the remainder of the Chairul Saleh era. When he explained them to Dr. Ibnu in the spring of 1966, "he was all ears." After completing his duties on the Shell integration in May, 1966, Sutan Assin was named as general manager of Permina's Unit III. He sought and got approval from Dr. Ibnu to do the necessary seismic work, while putting together a team for west Java. From Permigan came Ir. Rumboko and Ben Samsoe. Looking over the data and discussing it, these men had another idea as well—perhaps the Shell drillers had stopped too soon. At 3,000 feet the data revealed volcanic rock, traditionally viewed as an unlikely structure for oil. Against the advice of the Shell advisors who considered deeper drilling as a wasteful "shot in the dark," they decided to try it.

Before they could drill, however, they had to train additional crews. They would, for the first time, take on the job without assistance. Newspaper advertisements were run for oil drilling trainees. One hundred and twenty applicants were screened, and of these, ten were selected and trained. Two drilling rigs were purchased. Because the existing harbor of Tjirebon would not accommodate the ship carrying the rigs, they had to be unloaded at Djakarta's port of Tandjung Priok and then trucked to the Djatibarang project area—over 130 miles to the east. In October, 1968, they began drilling and within two years struck not only the expected gas but oil as well and thus opened a major new field.

As Permina gained momentum, it began to look for new sources of financing in the world oil money markets. The Shell purchase was financed out of the operations of the acquired assets themselves. Previous financing, such as Nosodeco, had been based on loans in exchange for a given amount of production, a form of buyer pre-financing. As Permina began to expand its own activities, Dr. Ibnu needed to expand the scope of his borrowings and credit arrangements. In Tokyo, Far East Oil began arranging construction loans for various projects. To begin operations in the financial center of New York City, Drs. R. Hasmoro opened Permina's representative office there in 1967.

By 1968, the task of raising money was becoming somewhat easier as compared to a decade earlier. Shell's appraisal of Permina's performance was perhaps best indicated by its decision to lend Permina $30 million in that year with no strings or mortgages attached. They based this loan on performance to date on the repayment schedule for their $110 million sale. In December, 1970, that faith was borne out as the final payment on the purchase was made, on schedule. Over 1,000 guests attended a luncheon to celebrate the successful conclusion of the purchase contract. Also in 1968, Hasmoro negotiated a $10 million loan with Union Oil for equipment and fertilizer stock purchases. Equipment suppliers also began extending substantial credits. Permina's credit was considered sound. Most of the financiers interviewed expressed their credit evaluation in four words "Ibnu's signature is good."

CHAPTER 13

Victory for Production Sharing

While functioning as minister of Mines and Migas, Dr. Ibnu had hoped that he would be able to bring about his long-sought objective of creating one national oil company with full responsibility for the management of all Indonesian oil operations. He recognized, however, that the implementation of ideas of such financial and political scope would not be easily done.

The Shell acquisition can, in part, be seen in the context of Dr. Ibnu's objective of ending, by mutual agreement, the Contracts of Work, which he regarded as a "concession in a new cloak." To the same end, negotiations had proceeded with Stanvac. At the same time Pan Am was in the process of terminating its Indonesian operations after a long series of dry holes. However, with the purchase of Stanvac facilities called off and with Caltex not at all interested in selling, Indonesia would have to live with the Contracts of Work until they expired.

If Indonesia would have to continue with the existing Contracts of Work, there was no reason, as Dr. Ibnu saw it, why new contractors should receive the same terms. Dr. Ibnu soon found himself in a major battle over whether or not new companies would receive Contracts of Work which vested management in the hands of the foreign oil companies and gave the national companies only a limited role in marketing.

Since World War II, great technological advances had been made in drilling offshore for oil. In 1966, foreign oil companies' attention began focusing on the continental shelf within Indonesia's territorial waters where the rewards could be extremely high. Geologists believed that the waters of the Java Sea and Makasar Strait covered oil structures that might rival those of Sumatra and Kalimantan. The drilling conditions were almost ideal. The Java Sea lies over the shallowest sea shelf in the world, with an average water depth of only 120 feet. And, unlike other areas such as the North Sea and Gulf Coast, the temperature is warm and constant year round and bad storms are virtually unknown. Other Indonesian waters present almost equally good conditions for offshore drilling.

To secure a new contract structure that vested management in Indonesian hands, Dr. Ibnu had to look not to the Majors, but to the Independents. Among the Independents he could hope to find companies that would look upon his contract provisions in terms of dollars and cents. The Majors, he expected, would regard them on the basis of the precedents they might set for renegotiation of contracts in the Middle East and other areas where they had immense investments.

Before World War II, the international oil business was almost solely the preserve of the seven major oil companies. However, in the United States dozens of independent companies flourished under protection against monopolistic practices provided by the antitrust laws. After the war, many of these companies looked abroad for new areas as extensive exploration within the United States reduced the likelihood of large strikes being made there. In their search for new areas, the Independents were often willing to pay more and to accept terms that would be turned down by the Majors.

In 1966, Dr. Ibnu sought to obtain acceptance of his ideas of production sharing from a small group of American oil men who had pooled their interests in a corporation called Independent Indonesian American Petroleum Company (IIAPCO). The reason for his selection of IIAPCO was simply that they were the first oil company in Indonesia ready to do business after Gestapu.

Donald Todd, Lawrence Barker, and P. J. McDonough, the founders of IIAPCO, are all veteran independent oil operators. Prior to 1964, all three had confined their interest to the United States, particularly in the Rocky Mountain area. In 1964, they were participating in various interests near Billings, Montana, but were getting discouraged with prospects in the United States where prices were falling and costs were rising.

In the course of their work in the Billings area they had learned something of Indonesian oil prospects from Asamera and Shell people who were also in the area. Several of the geologists with Indonesian experience, including Ismet Akil who was then on his Shell training tour, talked optimistically about the areas where they had worked.

McDonough first suggested to Todd and Barker that they explore the possibilities in Indonesia. This was characteristic of McDonough. According to Barker, "McDonough is a mover, the kind of guy who will fly to Caracas for lunch and return the same day." After discussing the idea and gathering more information, they decided to make an initial investigation of the Indonesian prospects, and, if favorable, to try to conclude a contract. McDonough made the first trip in February, 1964, staying in Indonesia only three or four days. During that time he was introduced to Chairul Saleh. McDonough's report to Todd and Barker was optimistic.

In June, 1964, McDonough went back to Indonesia with Todd. The purpose of the trip was to select an exploration area and, hopefully, to conclude a contract. Although they examined several land locations in Java, they decided that they would try to find a promising offshore site. The costs offshore, though higher, were more predictable because operations were less susceptible to labor disruptions, governmental interference, and transport problems.

Donald Todd selected an area off the northwest coast of Java as having the best prospects and they offered to enter a contract for the area based on terms similar to Pan American's Contract of Work. Twice they reworked the contract and submitted it, but no action was forthcoming; most of their time was spent waiting for appointments. Finally, they returned to the United States where more revisions of the contract were made. Meanwhile, in January

1965, another group of Independents, the Carver-Dodge Oil Company, bought in for a percentage of IIAPCO.

In February, 1965, Todd returned to Indonesia in order to try to obtain acceptance of the proposed contract. This time negotiations on the Indonesian side were handled by Chairul Saleh and Lukman Hanafiah. The northwest Java area fell within the domain of Permigan, and Todd was pleased to find that if a contract were negotiated, Sutan Assin, whom he had met previously, would be handling liaison on the technical side. There were, however, problems as Permigan was now dominated by Perbum and, with only a few exceptions, had no experienced oil operators. Thus, when Chairul Saleh and Hanafiah suggested a contract in which IIAPCO would provide the financing only and Permigan would perform all operations, Todd left in disgust. The venture seemed impossible.

The IIAPCO group continued to follow the Indonesian situation, however, maintaining an intermittent correspondence with the commercial attache at the United States embassy in Djakarta. For the first three or four months after Gestapu, Indonesia was simply too uncertain politically to venture any move. In early 1966, they wrote asking the commercial attache whom they should see in efforts to re-explore the possibilities of a contract. The embassy replied that Dr. Ibnu Sutowo was in charge, and that if they were willing to sign a Production Sharing Contract with a sixty-five–thirty-five split they should return. The new percentages were acceptable as were the other general concepts of production sharing. IIAPCO's representatives had not met Dr. Ibnu on their previous trips but they had talked to Harold Hutton who said he believed the principle was workable with Dr. Ibnu. Thus, in early June, 1966, Todd returned to Indonesia with full authority to negotiate a contract. To help finance this new phase, a third group of Independents, Warrior International, based in Denver, bought in for a percentage.

Upon his arrival in Djakarta, Todd was amazed at the change in atmosphere. Although there was still tension, he immediately sensed that the anti-Americanism, so prevalent during his previous trips, had been replaced by the usual Indonesian graciousness. IIAPCO was truly the "early bird"—there were virtually no other foreign businessmen in Djakarta at this time. Todd contacted Permina as soon as he arrived and asked for an appointment with Dr. Ibnu. Based on past experience, he assumed this would take several days, so he left for a resort area on the south coast of Java to spend the weekend. When he returned to Djakarta he was surprised to learn that he had missed an opportunity to see Dr. Ibnu on Saturday. He was perhaps even more surprised when he was promptly given another appointment.

Todd's meeting with Dr. Ibnu confirmed Harold Hutton's assessment. If IIAPCO would agree to five basic principles, a contract could be concluded in short order, Dr. Ibnu said. The principles were:

1. The state enterprise would have management control.
2. The contract would be based on production sharing rather than profit sharing.
3. IIAPCO would bear preproduction risks, and if oil was discovered, cost recovery would be limited annually to a maximum of 40% of the oil produced.
4. The remaining 60% of production (or more when cost amortization was below the 40% maximum) would be split with 65% going to the state enterprise and 35% to IIAPCO.
5. Title to all project-related equipment bought by IIAPCO would pass to the state enterprise upon entry into Indonesia, the cost to be recovered under the 40% formula.

Dr. Ibnu elaborated on his views of what Indonesian management meant. It did not mean, he assured Todd, that IIAPCO would have no say in how their money was used. Rather, it should be conceived of as a partnership with the state enterprise as the senior partner. Both sides obviously had a common interest in making good decisions. It would be expected in the normal course that the state enterprise would agree with IIAPCO's working proposals.

Only in the event of irreconcilable disagreement would Permina's dominant position need to be exercised. Here, too, as a practical matter, the senior partner would have to pay some heed to the fact that it was the other partner's money, knowing that the other partner could, if conditions became unfavorable, terminate the partnership. Finally, Dr. Ibnu added, all government relations would be handled by the state enterprise. The foreign contractor could concentrate strictly on looking for oil.

Todd agreed to the principles outlined by Dr. Ibnu and negotiations began. On the Indonesian side, four men participated in the drafting process—Dr. Sanger, Tirto Utomo, Drs. Sakidjan, and P. Siregar.

For IIAPCO, there was initially only Donald Todd, though Todd did attempt to discuss major decisions with Lawrence Barker, and IIAPCO's legal counsel, Robert Fowler, in Denver. Telephone connections were so poor that frequently communication was impossible and thus Todd had to make many key decisions on his own. Tirto Utomo asked Todd if he had a lawyer and Todd's reaction was, "What for?" Nevertheless, Tirto thought it would be helpful if Todd had a local attorney and therefore he recommended that Todd engage Roger Machmud. Machmud was an ex-Shell attorney with seven years' experience. In the reorganization after the Shell acquisition, he was one of the few "casualties," and rather than accept what he thought was an unfair assignment, he was then in the process of resigning from Permina. Todd agreed it would be good to have someone to consult with, but at the same time was somewhat wary as to possible conflict of interest on Machmud's part. However, as negotiations proceeded his initial doubts vanished, and today Roger Machmud is the administration manager for IIAPCO/ARCO's Indonesian operations.

To embody the principles agreed upon in a written contract, the negotiators began with the draft contract which Permina and Union had negotiated but never executed in 1963. The group met twice a week in working sessions. The cooperative spirit of the negotiations was what most struck Todd: There was little sense of negotiation from opposing sides—it seemed like discussions between partners in a common venture.

Meanwhile, the Japanese had learned that negotiations for offshore areas were open and a group called Kyushu Oil Development Company, Ltd., led by Dr. Minoru Kawamoto, approached Permina. Kyushu reached an agreement in principle with Dr. Ibnu for a large block south of Kalimantan. Progress on the IIAPCO negotiations was slowed somewhat as the Permina team was forced to divide its time between the two groups.

In mid-August, after about ten meetings, the negotiators had a rough draft of the contract worked out. They would not get much further. Dr. Ibnu made one of his infrequent visits to the negotiating conference. "Why is the progress so slow?" he asked, "I want to sign tomorrow." Dr. Ibnu was leaving the country on a business trip and wanted the contract signed before he left. Frenetically, the negotiators put the contract together—close examination of the final product reveals some signs of this haste. If the letter of the contract was not perfect, the spirit of the contract was there. This is most clearly seen in the first sentence of Section I: "... PERMINA shall have and be responsible for the management of the operations contemplated hereunder."

No ceremony attended the signing of the contract which began a new era in Indonesian oil and the inauguration of what is now called in world oil circles, "the Pertamina Production Sharing System." Todd signed for IIAPCO on the evening before Independence Day at a late afternoon meeting. Dr. Sanger, Tirto Utomo, and P. Siregar then took the contract to Dr. Ibnu's house that night. Dr. Ibnu signed it twice, as president-director of Permina, and as director general of Migas. After two and a half months in Indonesia, Donald Todd returned to the United States with a signed contract in hand.

Though the contract with IIAPCO was executed, the battle on the principles involved had just begun. Although Dr. Ibnu had signed in his capacity as director general of Migas, he was no longer minister of Mines and Migas, and he expressly told Todd that additional governmental approval would be required.

On July 25, 1966, in the midst of the IIAPCO and Kyushu negotiations, Dr. Ibnu had stepped down as minister of Mines and Migas. The choice had been his as to whether to give up the ministry or the position as president-director of Permina. Dr. Ibnu made the same choice he had made in 1963 when Chairul Saleh asked him to become one of his deputies. Told that he would have to give up Permina, Dr. Ibnu declined believing he could contribute more to the nation by developing Permina. He retained two positions, however: president-director of Permina and director general of Migas.

Dr. Ibnu's successor as minister was a man fourteen years his junior—Ir. Bratanata. Born in Palembang, Sumatra in 1928, Bratanata was the son of a journalist. He graduated with a degree in mechanical engineering from the Technical Institute at Bandung in 1953. Upon graduation he joined the state railways, and later the Ministry of Land Communications. During his first seven years in government service he held a number of field positions. In 1961, he joined Chairul Saleh's Ministry of Basic Industries and Mining. His first task was to assume management of a new government company that provided industrial engineering and construction services on projects. Chairul Saleh had noticed when foreign loan projects involving construction of factories were implemented that large international construction firms came in and mobilized local labor. But once the project was completed, the laborers would disband and return to their villages. It was Chairul's idea to form a new company that would improve training as well as providing a pool of skilled and trained personnel that could be moved from project to project as required.

In 1965, Bratanata received a new assignment, this one of ministerial rank, as state minister for construction of the Trans-Sumatra Highway. In July, 1966, he became Dr. Ibnu's successor as minister of Mines.

When Dr. Ibnu was consulted on the selection of Bratanata, he replied that he seemed like an able man and one he could work with. Bratanata also expressed his ability to work with Dr. Ibnu as his subordinate. He, like Dr. Ibnu, foresaw no problem. But, in fact, they held very different views for developing the oil industry.

Dr. Ibnu began thinking about the problem of Indonesian relations with the foreign oil companies a few months before he received the Permina assignment in 1957. In his capacity as deputy-operations to General Nasution he was assigned to the Monetary Board which, among other things, oversaw the administration of the 5-A Contracts with Shell Stanvac, and Caltex. Dr. Ibnu was struck by the friction between the government and the three companies—friction which, in his view, was causing loss to both sides. What was needed, he concluded, was to find a form of contract whereby the oil company's interest would be divorced from politics and limited to the technical problems of finding and developing oil. There were three basic sources of discontent at this time, recalls Dr. Ibnu. First was a feeling that Indonesia fairly deserved a larger share of the profits— this was just a matter of bargaining and economics. More important, was the feeling that Indonesia should be more involved in the oil industry and that the government should have more say in the process. Finally, and perhaps most important of all, was the desire to manage not just from the top but at all levels of the business—what was lacking in the existing relationships was a full transfer of know-how—an opportunity to learn the business from top to bottom.

As Dr. Ibnu later learned in his travels to other oil-exporting countries, Indonesia was not the only country with these aspirations and problems; they were shared by all of the underdeveloped oil producing countries, and all have followed their own courses toward attaining the same basic objectives. The creation of OPEC, in 1960, provided an organization in which, among other things, they exchange their respective experiences. Dr. Ibnu's experiences with Permina shaped his own thinking along a unique path. His approach involved basically two changes from the concession system.

The first concerned the ownership of oil and management of operations. The Indonesian Constitution was specific that the people, through the state, owned the oil and other natural resources. This could be easily enough accepted by the foreign companies. The quarrels started once the foreign companies found and began their efforts to extract the oil. At that point they claimed ownership of the oil.

The corollary of ownership was the right to manage the process of extraction. This turned the oil concessions in which they worked into islands of extra-territoriality in the host country, and also led the foreign companies into local politics. If the foreign companies' interest could be limited to, and dictated by, economic and technical considerations, Dr. Ibnu believed, much of the friction would disappear.

The Nosodeco agreement was Dr. Ibnu's first attempt to implement the idea of management control in a contract. The Japanese initially insisted on control of the entire operations, or at least joint management, as a condition of their loan. Controversy over this point caused the negotiations to extend over one year. Dr. Ibnu refused to accede because of his strong conviction that only conflict would result. On the other hand, Dr. Ibnu recognized the Japanese right to assurances that the money would be used for the intended purpose—field development—and that it was used well. A very fine compromise was finally struck. Dr. Ibnu analyzes it this way: "Although the Japanese were not allowed joint management or even any say in management, a kind of joint technical committee was created whose advice was binding. The management of the fields was our right: but their interest in seeing that the money was properly spent was protected through the committee. Thus they did a technical job for which they got paid without having any mining rights or any territorial rights."

Here, then, is the genesis of the allocation of decision making contained in the IIAPCO contract. The IIAPCO contract, of course, goes further, but the tension between the contractor's interest in seeing its money well spent, and Indonesia's interest in full retention of management control still shows in the IIAPCO contract.

The crucial language has been called a masterpiece of ambiguity. If so, this was partly because of the press of time, partly because the negotiators preferred it that way, and partly because the ideas are themselves very subtle. Paragraph 1 begins:

> PERMINA shall have and be responsible for the management of the operations contemplated hereunder.

But Paragraph 2.1 brings more of a consensus idea into play. After repeating the above clause, it adds the following qualification:

> however, PERMINA shall periodically consult IIAPCO with a view to the fact that IIAPCO is responsible for the work program.

The "work program" is defined as the "recommended petroleum operations." It is submitted by the contractor annually four months before the fiscal year begins. The work program is reviewed by Permina which has thirty days to state its objections. If Permina objects, consultation follows, with work proceeding on that part of the program as to which agreement has been reached. No provision is made, however, for resolution of items which remain in dispute, except Permina's general undertaking not to "withhold approval unreasonably." The deletion of any provision as to who decides technically brings the arbitration clause into play, but in fact no arbitration is likely to occur. Dr. Ibnu: "The parties share a common interest; the problems are technical in nature and should be susceptible to reasoned resolution." Provision is made for revisions in light of changed circumstances and unilateral action in the event of emergency. Joint preparation of a budget follows approval of the work program.

The second major source of friction, in Dr. Ibnu's view, concerned that of profit sharing between the host country and the foreign oil company. The first aim was to agree upon a mutually acceptable division. By the end of the 1950s many Indonesians regarded the fifty-fifty profit split as unfair, even though the Indonesian government had agreed to such a split a few years before. Contributing to the sense of unfairness was Indonesia's lack of control over cost and price figures—the two items which determined how much profit there was to be split.

In the 1950s, the Indonesian government was in the position of passively accepting the companies' determinations. Indeed, at that time, access to the accounting records of the Big Three was possible only to a limited extent because the complete books were maintained in the foreign headquarters of the parent companies. Prices, the oil companies contended, were a function of market forces. Ultimately that might be true, but the world oil market was not only oligopolistic (that is, a market where the number of selling units is small enough to destroy the free market precondition that no single seller's conduct will affect the market price), but also one with a history of cartels imposing, or attempting to impose, production and pricing regulations on its members. Furthermore, the companies in Indonesia were all internationally integrated with their local producing companies selling principally to affiliated purchasers. Prices set for crude were, for the most part, a matter of internal company accounting. Thus in 1960, when vast new discoveries of oil in the Middle East created a market glut, the oil exporting nations naturally greeted with hostility the claims of the companies that "market forces" demanded a price reduction. In the Middle East, the companies' decision to lower the price had precipitated the formation of OPEC. Thus banded together, the OPEC countries collectively resisted the proposed reduction in posted prices—that is, the price for purposes of tax calculations. From that date forward, there had been no correlation between prices actually realized on Middle Eastern crudes, and the prices upon which taxes were based.

Dr. Ibnu believed that Indonesia should follow a different course. If price is a source of friction, why not divide production instead? In this way, the question of price could be solved by competition between the national company and the foreign company. Though the Contracts of Work made a move in this direction, the national oil company was entitled to only 20% of the gross production, and the profit sharing basis was retained. The production sharing contract changed this. First, there was no need for profit calculations—although costs must still be calculated and monitored for recovery from the 40% cost production. Second, the national company either keeps its 65% share of profit production or may require the foreign company to market it. If the national company can get a better price it may also market the cost oil unless the foreign contractor meets the price. Much of the basis for friction disappears because the national company asserts real control over the marketing of the oil, and the entire framework for the relationship is anchored in the realities of the market place. In the long run, Dr. Ibnu believed, the ability to market oil and establish its pricing would maximize the return to the nation.

If, to understand Dr. Ibnu's ideas, one must consider the development of his thinking historically, the same is true in the case of Ir. Bratanata. Unlike Dr. Ibnu, Minister Bratanata had little experience in the oil business, but he had over twelve years of first-hand experience in various kinds of Indonesian government enterprises during which time he had developed his own ideas of Indonesia's needs for development.

The management question, the key to Dr. Ibnu's ideas, was of lesser importance to Minister Bratanata. "In the early 1950s," he recalls, "many Indonesians confused the perquisites of management—a directorship, a big office, an automobile—with the act of managing itself. Why keep this illusion? Management has to do with working power, which is ultimately based on shareholding power. The Indonesian managers did not even have any shareholder contact. I prefer to be more modest in our goals. What we need is training and knowhow."

For these reasons, Bratanata had no strong objection to continuation of the management provisions of the Contracts of Work. If Indonesian management was desirable in theory, it had in many cases proved illusory in practice— it was not worth fighting for at the cost of alienating the oil companies whose knowhow and capital were needed to develop Indonesian oil.

Thus, to Bratanata, the important thing was to maximize the financial return to Indonesia from the areas which would be opened for exploration. The best way to do this, in his view, was to divide the territory into relatively small blocks, so as to ensure rapid exploration and exploitation by a large number of companies. Tendering the blocks for bidding by all comers would also provide competition to ensure a maximum return in terms of signature payments. Under this arrangement Bratanata would also serve his regulatory objectives—the chances of undue influence and corruption would be minimized under competitive bidding. However, Bratanata's position assumed the foreign companies would seek the maximum price possible for the oil produced—and this certainly had not proven to be the case in the past.

Besides the differences on the merits of Production Sharing versus the Contract of Work, Ibnu and Bratanata differed on at least two other questions. Dr. Ibnu wanted one integrated national oil company; Bratanata favored two or more. More fundamental was the issue of control. Dr. Ibnu had brought his company through the chaotic Sukarno years and now he wanted full freedom to implement his ideas. Bratanata was equally determined to acquire a greater role in oil affairs for the ministry. It was the question of approval of the Production Sharing Contracts that focused their differences.

On July 25, 1966, the Ampera Cabinet was installed with Ir. Bratanata as minister of Mines replacing Dr. Ibnu. On the evening of August 16, Dr. Ibnu signed the IIAPCO contract and shortly thereafter went on a trip abroad. When he returned, he learned that Bratanata was proposing that Contracts of Work be offered for the development of the offshore areas. In the meantime, Permina's negotiations with Japex were being completed and Dr. Ibnu signed this second Production Sharing Contract on October 6. On October 15, Bratanata sent a letter to the Cabinet recommending regulations and directions for the Contracts of Work. On October 20, Dr. Ibnu executed a third Production Sharing Contract with Refican.

They were clearly proceeding on divergent and independent courses, both believing they had the approval of General Soeharto based on a series of meetings during the month with General Soeharto and his closest advisors. There are conflicting claims about who kept whom informed about what. On November 3, Minister Bratanata issued a policy letter to Director General of Migas, Dr. Ibnu, regarding bids by foreign contractors, and on November 4, sent the same letter to the Cabinet. On November 22, Dr. Ibnu executed another Production Sharing Contract with the Japanese oil company, Kyushu.

Meanwhile, the oil companies, the Japanese Foreign Office, and the U.S. State Department, were aligning behind the two contenders. The Majors and other large companies were appalled at the idea of submitting their operations to Indonesian management, and were concerned about the contracts' precedential effect on their interests elsewhere in the world. Moreover, four small oil companies had secured rights to what they then regarded as the choicest offshore areas. Finally, Caltex and Stanvac, and their parent companies, had a special concern in light of their desire to perpetuate their existing interests in the Contract of Work format.

Most of the maneuvering was behind the scenes. A newspaper article which appeared in the *Malay Mail*, a Singapore newspaper, on November 8, carried the flavor of the attack:

> INDONESIAN GENERAL TO DECIDE ON RIGHTS TO DRILL FOR OIL
>
> JAKARTA, Tues.—Indonesia's offshore oil fight appears to have ended before the opening gong sounded. Three comparatively lightweight oil firms [IIAPCO, Japex, and Refican] and a stubborn Army general seem to have won.
>
> The decision was announced in Jakarta during a closed door meeting when the Army strong man General Suharto told Oil and Mining Minister Bratanata to let deputy minister General Ibnu Sutowo of the Oil and Mining Department make his own decision.

It was another victory for the military and another defeat for the civilians.

Despite the high level order, diplomatic observers and oil men are calling the decision a long term defeat for Indonesia's economic hopes.

They believe General Ibnu may be the man of the hour; that his policies will fall far short of fitting Indonesia's long term needs, though.

Bidding: Sixteen foreign oil firms have been bidding for drilling rights in what Gen. Ibnu believes to be potentially the richest untapped offshore deposit remaining in the world today.

Although no accurate geological surveys have been made, the companies are certain enough of the existence of the offshore deposit, north of Java and east of Borneo, to compete for exploration rights from the Indonesian government.

Gen. Ibnu has virtually promised away all the attractive drilling sites to three relatively small companies.

UPI—The Malay Mail, Nov. 8, 1966

As one example of the big companies' attitude, Shell had an advisor participating in the Kyushu negotiations on an undisclosed backroom basis. As the contract neared conclusion with the hated management clause incorporated, the Shell representative emerged from the Hotel Indonesia in a desperate last-ditch effort to persuade the Indonesian negotiators to delete it. The Indonesians did not yet possess the skill to implement such a clause, he argued. Tirto Utomo's reply was characteristic, "Well, we want to try this new way." When he was unsuccessful, Shell apparently withdrew from further association with the Kyushu venture. A spokesman for another of the Big Three was more direct. He stated bluntly, "My company will never sign a contract based on production sharing."

At least one country's diplomats were not characterizing Dr. Ibnu's ideas "as a long term defeat for Indonesia's economic hopes." The Japanese embassy was vehemently arguing that to disapprove Dr. Ibnu's contracts with the companies—which included Japex and Kyushu—would irreparably discredit Indonesia in the world's financial community.

The American State Department had evidently taken the opposite view. Responding to the major oil companies' views, the embassy in Djakarta made it known that it would welcome affirmation of Bratanata's policies. Also, American oil companies' representatives who sought embassy advice on who to deal with were now advised that Minister Bratanata was the man to see.

At the end of December, Minister Bratanata submitted his final *Rules on the Division of Central Indonesian Off-shore Areas* to the Presidium Cabinet. On January 17, the ministry addressed a letter to interested oil companies offering seven offshore areas but not specifying what type of contract would be used. Included in the areas were those already granted by Dr. Ibnu to Japex, Refican, and Kyushu.

Clearly a showdown had been reached. On January 19, 1967, General Soeharto, in his capacity as chairman of the Presidium Cabinet, advised Minister Bratanata that he approved the Production Sharing Contracts. Minister Bratanata was instructed to accommodate the proposals of the director general of Migas. Twelve days later, the impossibility of any further working relationship between Dr. Ibnu and Minister Bratanata was formally recognized. The Directorate General of Migas was severed from the Ministry of Mines, and placed directly under the Presidium Cabinet. Dr. Ibnu had won the fight.

Dr. Ibnu had an appreciation of the timing and tactics inherent in the situation which none of his countrymen could match. An oil man long affiliated with one of the Majors in Indonesia says: "Ibnu knew the oil industry, the Majors, and how they think. He had experienced contacts with foreign oil men which no one else in Indonesia had. Thus Ibnu knew that the only way to gain acceptance of his principles was to utilize the Independents and proceed on an ad hoc basis."

If a scheme of competitive bidding were employed, Dr. Ibnu would lose his best hope of success—using the Independents to establish the new contractual scheme—which the Majors, concerned with precedents in the Middle East could never accept. If a master plan were presented for review embodying tender bidding based on production sharing, the Majors could more readily mobilize their forces to oppose his concept as a group, as indeed they almost succeeded in doing.

Moreover, such a plan would take time to draft and review. Dr. Ibnu wanted to do business immediately and this in itself gave inducement to the companies to break ranks. As further inducement, he was prepared to give, and did give, first comers more favorable terms, and a pick of areas which late comers would not receive. Competitive bidding would preclude this, although perhaps giving more revenue on the first few contracts. But to Dr. Ibnu, revenue was subordinate until his concept was established. If to secure production sharing meant a few dollars less initially than might result from competitive bidding, in the long run he was certain that production sharing would provide a much surer basis for the development of national wealth.

To succeed, Dr. Ibnu needed a mandate of trust from his fellow Indonesians. To play a strong hand against the international oil industry, he needed a united front behind him at home. President Soeharto's decision must be seen as first and foremost conveying that trust.

Once it was clear that Dr. Ibnu had prevailed, the companies fell into line to work under production sharing, as Dr. Ibnu had predicted they would. Several companies approached Permina concerning the possibility of signing contracts, including such large companies as Continental Oil and Union Oil. Many companies were still wary of the contract, particularly the management clause, and attempted to have it deleted, but to no avail. Dr. Ibnu was insistent on the IIAPCO model, and the terms became tougher for later signers.

The negotiator for a French company claimed to have a mandate directly from President de Gaulle and insisted the management clause be struck. When this was refused, he arose saying, "I am leaving to report this impasse to mon General!" Tirto Utomo's reply was "Please do and I shall report to my General, also." This particular gentleman never returned.

Continental, whose vice-president, Harold Dubuisson, had opted to negotiate with Dr. Ibnu rather than as recommended by the U.S. embassy, became the first of the big companies to sign. Continental obtained the Barito Basin area of southeast Kalimantan in May, 1967. Union signed its first contract in January, 1968. With these two big companies accepting the model, other companies followed suit. A total of fourteen Production Sharing Contracts were signed in 1968.

As of this writing, a total of forty-four contracts have been signed; the companies have committed themselves to a minimum expenditure approaching $500 million in the search for oil in Indonesia. Included in this group are all of the seven Majors. Mobil Oil was the first of the Majors to sign a Production Sharing Contract, buying interests in both Refican and Asamera areas as well as taking a contract in their own right on October 16, 1968. Many of the companies are involved in two or three separate contracts.

As for the original IIAPCO block, it followed a common course of those held by Independents. Sinclair Oil Company bought an interest in 1968. Later, that company merged with Atlantic Richfield which operates the block today. After the assignment of its first block, IIAPCO procured a second adjacent thereto. Shortly thereafter IIAPCO was acquired by the Natomas Company, a U.S. conglomerate. Two of the three original owners of IIAPCO, Donald Todd and Lawrence Barker, are back in Indonesia today participating with a new group called Trend Exploration, which has a contract area in West Irian.

Caltex and Stanvac both continue to operate under their original Contracts of Work in their old areas. Both have interests in Production Sharing Contracts in other areas. In the fall of 1971, Caltex and Pertamina concluded a Production Sharing Contract for its Contracts of Work areas to take effect upon expiration of the Contracts of Work in 1983, as part of a major expansion program on Caltex's part—an expansion program which Caltex would not have willingly undertaken without assurances that it would continue to benefit therefrom after the expiration

of the Contracts of Work. Caltex officials state they are happy to have the matter settled, though they know they paid handsomely to enter a Production Sharing Contract they once scorned.

In late 1967, an Interministerial Negotiating Committee was established reporting to the minister of Mines. Dr. Ibnu was named chairman. He soon found that the committee was doing so well that he increasingly left it on its own, under deputy chairman Ir. Anondo and its secretary, Ir. Trisulo. It includes experts from the Bank of Indonesia, Ministry of Finance, and others concerned. Awards are at the committee's direction. The policy is to keep "a lot of players on the board" thus, if two or more contractors seek a given area, some weight is given to the bidder with the fewest number of existing contract holdings in the interest of diversification.

The Negotiating Committee has developed a number of improvements as the contract has evolved, including large payments for data supplied by Pertamina and production bonuses. Most important, perhaps, is the domestic supply obligation, which was not included in the early contracts. This clause requires the contractor to contribute a pro rata share of its production to be used for Indonesian domestic consumption at a nominal cost of $0.20 per barrel. This changes the split from sixty-five–thirty-five to something closer to seventy-six–twenty-four—the exact figure depending on the size of Indonesia's domestic consumption as related to total production.

*   *   *

Interwoven in the Ibnu-Bratanata dispute was uncertainty as to the legal basis for Production Sharing Contracts. Dr. Ibnu adamantly held that all contracts with foreign companies should be contracts with the state enterprise and nothing more. If Parliament approved the contract, as contemplated by Law No. 44 for Contracts of Work, the contract assumed a higher dignity; it became a law. This was clearly against Indonesia's interest, Ibnu maintained, because in the event of a dispute between the Indo-

IAPCO's CINTA PRODUCTION TESTING PLATFORM IN JAVA SEA.

nesian and foreign company, the Indonesian company could not take action as a party to the contract, rather the government as a whole must act—a most cumbersome and disadvantageous situation. Also, the companies had commonly asserted that Parliamentary ratification of concessions made them irrevocable and unalterable—a dubious legal conclusion but one often used to advantage in negotiations.

Notwithstanding Ibnu's strong feelings about Parliamentary approval, Law No. 44 remained on the books. And Ibnu's negotiators faced the difficult task of finding a way around its requirement of Parliamentary ratification. Since the contents of a Contract of Work were not specified, there was nothing which precluded a Contract of Work from containing the substantive provisions embodied in the IIAPCO contract including Indonesian management and production sharing instead of profit sharing.

But to lable the IIAPCO contract a Contract of Work would subject it to parliamentary ratification. To avoid this, the negotiating team seized upon Indonesia's production sharing regulations. All four of the early contracts contained the prefatory language:

> This Contract is made in accordance with the production sharing laws of and regulations of Indonesia.

Each was also styled a "Production Sharing Contract" rather than a Contract of Work. Legally, the efficacy of this route was, to say the least, far from clear.

The production sharing regulations had been promulgated in 1962 and 1963. They reflected the policy then in favor that foreign capital should not be allowed any equity in the Indonesian economy. Hence, they provided for a system of foreign credits to be paid back with the product being exploited. The classic case for their application was a natural resource like timber, in which there was no preproduction risk of loss as in oil.

Although the production sharing regulations came after the enactment of Law No. 44, there was no expression or implied statement that they were intended to supplement or repeal Law No. 44's exclusive coverage of oil matters.

Moreover, the production sharing regulations were not embodied in either a law or a regulation-in-lieu of a law; they were embodied in a series of policy statements by Sukarno which, though they had the effect of law, may or may not have been superior to prior laws on the subject that had been duly enacted.

The enactment of Indonesia's new Foreign Investment Law on January 1, 1967, gave Dr. Ibnu and his colleagues the opportunity to strengthen their legal basis. In Article 8, the draftsman inserted the following language:

> foreign capital investment in the field of mining shall be based on a joint venture with the Government on the basis of a working contract *or in other form, in line with existing regulations.* (Emphasis added)

The comment to Article 8 provides further support:

> To facilitate economic development, the Government determines forms of co-operation between foreign and national capital which are most profitable for each field of activity. Such co-operation may be in the form of a work contract, joint venture or another type.

Since the preface of the Foreign Investment Law referenced both Law No. 44 and the General Mining Law, it was clear that the phrase "field of mining" must include oil and gas as well as general mining.

The final step was to argue the applicability of the production sharing laws to the IIAPCO and other contracts' financial arrangements. The production sharing regulations did not allow for the foreign creditor to participate in profits. Permina argued that this was because the industries to which it had heretofore been applied involved no risk of loss. In the oil industry, Indonesia could not bear the risk of loss and consequently must induce the foreigner to do so by giving him some profit participation. This policy was approved when the Contracts of Work with the Big Three and Pan American were ratified. Thus it was perfectly proper, Permina's lawyers argued, to interpolate the production sharing regulations to authorize a profit to the foreigners in light of the unique risk assumed.

President Soeharto's legal advisor accepted the argument. The IIAPCO contract was approved by President Soeharto without parliamentary approval. The other contracts were approved thereafter. Two years later, the Wall Street lawyers had their chance; Tirto Utomo lectured a group of twenty lawyers in New York on the legal basis of production sharing. They were persuaded.

Of course, the choice between Dr. Ibnu's and Minister Bratanata's respective approaches did not turn on the legalistic question of what constituted approval. Dr. Ibnu's victory against "legislative ratification" was clearly a subsidiary aspect of the production sharing struggle. Today the problem is of historic interest only. The new Pertamina Law, Law No. 8, 1971, expressly authorizes Production Sharing Contracts with approval by the President.

CHAPTER 14

Pertamina

With the decision of the Presidium Cabinet to sever Migas from the Ministry of Mines during January, 1967, the five month period of dualism in Indonesian oil policy ended; Dr. Ibnu was in charge. It came as a surprise to no one in Indonesian oil circles when three months later, Saleh Siregar and the other board members of Pertamin were replaced.

Pertamin, which had begun with a well-trained organization, two proven fields, and a head start in domestic marketing, also had enjoyed early favoritism in allocations. It was Pertamin which received, first, Pan American, and more importantly, Caltex, under the Contracts of Work, while Permina received Stanvac, the smallest producer of the Big Three. In 1964, again it was Pertamin which was allocated all domestic marketing, mixed blessing though it might be.

But in recent years, Pertamin had been less fortunate. With the establishment of Far East Oil, Permina had begun to market Pertamin's entitlements of Caltex's Minas crude. Pertamin's top management was too conservative to risk undertaking substantial exploration and production programs. Pertamin had no refining facilities, no tankers, and was left only with the domestic marketing—the most problem-riddled area of all.

An Indonesian oil man who was affiliated with neither company at the time compares the two companies this way: "Pertamin was an example of a company which was a good boy. It paid its money on time. It was trusted but it was dying,

305

not just because it lacked production, but more importantly
because it lacked imagination. Permina was just the opposite
—it was doing everything, often against the regulations,
but it was growing."

Permina was a company that was free-wheeling, imaginative,
and dynamic—an organization that was on the move. Permina
would seize the opportunity to grow when the chance was
presented, leaving, when necessary, the organizing until
later. Thus, when the formation of Far East Oil was being
considered, one official gave his opinion that the governing
law for all state enterprises, Law No. 19, prohibited state
enterprises forming subsidiaries. Dr. Ibnu reportedly replied:
"Do we want development or do we follow this outmoded
law?" Approval from President Sukarno followed.

Saleh Siregar and the other directors of Pertamin hoped
to see an improvement in their fortunes with the appointment of Ir. Bratanata as minister of Mines. Indeed, Bratanata favored the concept of multiple companies as a means
of maintaining competition to permit judging comparative
performance. Whatever the merits of this view in the
abstract, however, it had very little relevance to the actual
situation that prevailed in Indonesian oil in 1966. The
two companies were operating in quite different areas of the
business. In fact, the only area in which they competed at
all was in foreign marketing and it was in this area that
the case for competition was weakest because Indonesia
very much needed to make a unified and national entry
into this market.

Also, the three companies had not been developed with
comparable structures that would permit comparison of
their performance through financial data. Early in Chairul
Saleh's ministry, the concept of functional specialization
was introduced although all three companies continued to
engage in exploration and production in their respective
mining areas. Functional roles were created to the extent
that ocean transport was assigned to Permina and domestic
marketing was assigned to Pertamin. Permigan might
logically have been given refining, however their efforts to
build a refinery with Roumanian assistance failed. The

experience with multiple oil company operations had been less than optimal because it presumed a high degree of cooperation between the companies and such did not exist. The coordination board, the *BPU*, which Dr. Ibnu chaired, lacked authority and thus disputes could be resolved only by reference to Chairul Saleh. The competition between the companies was then not of a type to improve performance but rather took the counter-productive form of bureaucratic infighting.

The new president-director appointed to Pertamin was an army man, Brigadier General J.M. Junus. The other directors appointed were; Major Joedo Sumbono, one of Dr. Ibnu's most trusted assistants, as technical director; and Navy Major Hanum Faeni, S.H., from the special staff of Permina, as administrative director. Installed on May 15, 1967, the new directorate was initially designated as the Caretaker Board. Dr. Ibnu in his capacity as director general of Migas, instructed them that their primary assignment was to reorganize and improve Indonesia's domestic marketing of petroleum products. In this task the company made significant and rapid progress under its new top management.

The split between Migas and the Ministry of Mines continued during the remainder of Ir. Bratanata's fifteen month tenure as minister. On October 11, 1967, Acting President Soeharto reshuffled his cabinet. To succeed Bratanata, Soeharto chose the president of the University of Indonesia, Professor Dr. Ir. Sumantri Brodjonegoro. The selection of Dr. Sumantri, a chemical engineer by training, was well-calculated to close the breach between the ministry and the directorate general of Migas. Dr. Sumantri and Dr. Ibnu had known each other for many years and regarded each other with mutual respect. Since 1959, Dr. Sumantri had served informally as an adviser to Permina on various technical matters.

With Dr. Sumantri's appointment, the presidium directive severing Migas from the ministry was rescinded and the Ministry of Mines resumed control over the oil sector. The main decision facing Dr. Sumantri was whether or not

there should be a merger of Pertamin and Permina into a single oil company. Dr. Sumantri personally had long favored the creation of single company units for the efficient development of national resources but he was aware that the creation of such a unit in oil would take time and would involve the solution of problems of both a political and economic nature. During the interim period, members of the Caretaker Board of Pertamin were appointed permanently in November, 1967.

In July, 1968, Dr. Sumantri could finally implement his plan for the oil industry and he recommended to President Soeharto that Pertamin and Permina be merged into one national oil company. That company became Pertamina (Perusahaan Negara Pertambangan Minjak dan Gas Bumi Nasional—the State Company, National Oil and Natural Gas Mining). Minister Sumantri describes his reasoning as follows: "I concluded the better course was to merge the two companies rather than having one company mostly in production and the other mostly in domestic marketing. This would enable us to pool limited manpower, capital, and resources. This shortage of manpower was the single most important factor. I considered the concept of competition, but concluded that this would not override the other considerations."

On August 20, 1968, the decree was promulgated putting the merger into effect. President Soeharto, upon the recommendations of Dr. Sumantri, designated a new board of directors. Dr. Ibnu was appointed as president-director. General Junus was appointed director for domestic marketing and Lt. Colonel Joedo Sumbono was assigned as his deputy.

Ir. Anondo was named director for finance and administration, the position he had held with Permina since 1966. His career recalls the long path which Indonesian national oil had traveled. He began his career in oil with the formation of the oil department during the revolution. During the 1950s, he had served in the Mining Department in various capacities and headed the finance and administrative department of Migas from the mid-1960s, a job in which

WODECO VI DRILLING FOR UNION OIL, OFFSHORE KALIMANTAN—1970.

he has continued to serve concurrent with his Pertamina duties. Today Ir. Anondo is the senior civil servant in Indonesian oil.

Ir. Trisulo was named director for exploration and production. Formerly he had headed exploitation for Pertamin. His career also reflects the many inputs into the new national oil company. He had worked for Stanvac before joining Permindo. In 1965, he served on the OPEC secretariat in Vienna. Thereafter he was assigned as assistant for oil to Minister of Mines Bratanata. Trisulo served Minister Bratanata professionally, formulating many of the ideas that appeared in Bratanata's program. After the severance of Migas from the Mining Ministry, Trisulo was recalled to Migas and later headed the secretariat for the inter-ministerial committee responsible for negotiating Production Sharing Contracts.

The mechanics of the integration of the two companies was relatively simple as compared with the Permina-Shell merger two years before. Structurally, the companies were complementary and Pertamin's marketing organization was simply incorporated intact. In production, Permina's five-unit organization was retained. Under Director Trisulo, two of Permina's engineers, Soediono and Soedarno became deputy directors for exploration and production and refining and petrochemicals respectively.

Permina had already paid tribute to Pertamin's organizational ability by recruiting Suhardi from Pertamin in 1966 to handle the difficult Shell integration. Headed by Suhardi, and his chief assistants; Hanum Faeni, Burhan Danil, and J. L. Wetik, the personnel department expanded its functions in training and development in coordination with Lemigas. In finance, John Abdi, also from Pertamin, was appointed treasurer.

The merger brought together the best of both organizations as the aggressiveness and imagination of Permina were merged with the organizational and financial capability of Pertamin. With the merger came a psychological attitude of unity based on the challenge of running a truly national oil company. Dozens of interviews have revealed the same attitude summed up in, "At last we were one Indonesian company working for the whole nation." Programs that had been established over the past few years by either Pertamin or Permina now gained new force and direction under Pertamina.

*   *   *

In domestic marketing a structural revolution was well on the way to completion, much of it accomplished under the management of Pertamin before the merger. The Soeharto government resolutely carried out a series of price increases in the face of political opposition. Direct attacks on the black market were also instituted and these included such measures as placing barrels of gasoline and kerosene for sale on the street corners while waiting on new station construction. The visible signs of improvement were the disappearance of long lines at service stations and the removal of the signs, "bensin habis" (out of gasoline) that had so characterized distribution in the past.

Equally important were major changes introduced by Brig. General Junus and Colonel Joedo in the relationship between Pertamina and the dealers. In the days of foreign companies, gas stations had been owned by the companies with a nominal rental of one rupiah a month paid by the dealer. Pertamina required dealers to put up 50% of the costs of stations, thus the dealer had to make an investment in the operation. To stabilize distribution, a new contract was negotiated with the various dealers associations which required high minimum daily acceptances. To move to a more economic scale of operations, dealers were merged together, for example, in Djakarta the number was reduced from 170 small agents to 12 large ones. Prohibitions against silent partners were incorporated with termination of the dealership the penalty for violation. Efforts were made to ensure that the dealers would receive a fair return for their investments and labor. As Colonel Joedo, who is in charge of all operations, wryly summarizes, "Domestic marketing was changed to pure business rather than monkey business."

For the first time in years, new gasoline service stations began to be constructed—attractively designed, and with proposed site locations reviewed in advance by Pertamina's marketing staff. By the end of 1968, 52 new stations were completed and 48 upgraded; in 1969, 126 new stations were built and 50 upgraded, with the 1970 plan calling for 146 new and 79 upgraded. A new higher octane gasoline, Super 98, was also introduced. To improve distribution, new storage tank facilities were built and new tank trucks were purchased for resale to the dealers under a dealer assistance program.

On June 30, 1969, Shell's West Irian marketing operations were transferred to Pertamina, increasing Pertamina's domestic marketing responsibilities so that they embraced all of Indonesia. In August, 1970, Brig. General Junus returned to the army and was replaced by Brig. General Soehardiman, formerly Indonesia's consul general in New York City. On his appointment, Soehardiman was charged by President Soeharto and Dr. Ibnu to improve deliveries in all of eastern Indonesia, a social function undertaken pursuant to President Soeharto's efforts to improve the quality of life in these sparsely populated areas.

By the time of the merger, Permina owned or controlled a total of 55 ships having a tonnage in excess of 320,000 dwt. Pertamina continued to expand the fleet both for domestic and international operations. The crucial factor again was to learn by doing, acquiring a knowhow in each area of oil operations. For international tanker operations, Permina established a subsidiary in Hong Kong—the closest international tanker market—Ocean Petrol Ltd. on July 18, 1968.

A consistent increase in domestic consumption, plus the need to increase Indonesian processing of its crude, made necessary an increase in refinery capacity. In 1969, discussions were undertaken with Caltex for building a new refinery under a joint venture. When these proved fruitless, Pertamina made arrangements of its own with Far East Oil and various Japanese companies to construct a new refinery at Dumai, Sumatra with a capacity of 100,000 barrels per day. A second new refinery at Sungei Pakning, Sumatra was completed at the end of 1969 with a first-phase production of 20,000 barrels a day and with a programmed increase to 50,000. Negotiations also were completed for the purchase of the Sungei Gerong refinery from Stanvac. With the purchase, several hundred Stanvac employees joined the ranks of Pertamina, including Ir. Jahja, who now runs the Pladju-Sungei Gerong complex and Ir. Tabrani, who now runs the Balikpapan refinery.

Plans for a petrochemical industry were also underway as well as plans for a fertilizer plant for west Java and a polypropylene project. Plans were made to increase the natural gas feedstock to the *PUSRI* fertilizer plant. A joint venture with Gulf Oil Company for a fertilizer blending and packing operation at Tandjung Priok, Djakarta's port, was negotiated and construction started.

The total crude production of the national companies in 1967 was 36,618,000 barrels. In 1968, this rose to 37,111,000 barrels, but in 1969, it tapered off to 35,290,000 as old wells dried up before new ones could be brought into production. This was, however, within the production forecast and exploration of new areas was going ahead on schedule. Although Stanvac's production also experienced declines in 1968, and again in 1969, Indonesia's production as a whole continued to move upward as Caltex's production rose from 130 million barrels in 1967, to 164 million barrels in 1968, and to 218 million barrels in 1969.

This increase was in no small part related to Far East Oil's and Caltex's successes in promoting Minas low-sulfur crude in the increasingly pollution-conscious Japanese market. In Tokyo, Colonel Harijono was, by 1965, well-acquainted with Japanese business after four years of dealing with the oil suppliers to the Nosodeco group. Colonel Harijono had met Sarwono Sarwohardjono, an Indonesian businessman operating in Japan, who in 1958, after ten years business experience in the Indonesian batik industry, had gone to Tokyo to develop his own business as a supplier to Indonesian companies. Sarwono agreed to become vice-president of Far East Oil. When Harijono returned to Djakarta in 1966, he was replaced by Drs. Soekotjo who had resigned his Pertamin directorship to join Permina.

Thus Soekotjo and Sarwono were the sole Indonesian representatives of the company in Japan as they began to break into Japanese marketing.

The primary task of persuading Japanese industry and policy makers to accept Indonesian oil as marketed by Far East Oil fell to the Japanese side of the partnership headed by president Sumio Higashi and managing director Nagaharu Nakamura. This meant building the market for all types of Indonesian oil exports, but in particular, the bountiful output of the Minas field.

Minas, in direct contrast to the light crudes from Pertamina's own north Sumatran fields, is one of the most viscuous crudes in the world. A sample bottle of Minas oil at room temperature may be turned upside down with no flow. In technical terms, its pour point is about 100° Fahrenheit. To the oil man, Minas' characteristics mean extra costs since it must be preheated before transporting and refining.

The Japanese refineries were not only largely eliminated as purchasers by their "tying contracts" with the Majors, but they also lacked the heating facilities necessary to handle the Minas crude. Thus Caltex had experienced difficulty developing outlets for Minas, despite the company's strong position in the Japanese market. But Minas had another quality, shared with most other Indonesian crudes, which by the mid-1960's presented the possibility of a complete turnabout in market demand—a low sulfur content. Pollution from petroleum combustion is directly related to its sulfur content—the less sulfur content, the less pollution.

Far East Oil's breakthrough came from the electric power companies. They had government permission to directly burn crude oil, but the Japanese-owned Arabian Oil Company had secured an import monopoly for their Middle Eastern crude for this purpose. Their crude had a high sulfur content, however. Higashi hit upon the idea of blending Minas with high-sulfur Middle Eastern crude and sold the idea to the government. Minas was given a special allocation for a small amount of imports to the electrical companies.

Pollution was the issue which eventually enabled the battle to be won and Higashi was the man who knew how to win it. There was a selling job to be done—inertia and conservative technicians worked against change, as did the cost of installing the necessary heating equipment.

In Tokyo, there is a golf course next to the Tokyo Gas Plant. This proximity provided Higashi with a convenient means for bringing to the attention of both the management and other officials concerned, the noxious sulfur dioxide fumes and gases. Higashi did so while playing on the golf course, pointing to the smoke stacks while at the same time pointing out the advantages of Minas crude.

Sales grew slowly at first. In 1966, Far East Oil sold only 3.5 million barrels and in 1967, 5 million barrels. For a time it appeared that the solution to pollution problems was going to be raising the chimney heights rather than switching to Minas. In fact, it took time to convert equipment. In 1968, sales were 13 million barrels, in 1969, they doubled to 26 million barrels and in 1970, they reached 46 million barrels. By 1970, Pertamina, through its Far East Oil affiliate, was established as a strong and active force in the Japanese market.

Sarwono continues as vice-president and director, joined by P. Siregar, director, and Colonel Soedijono who is both a director of Far East Oil and Pertamina's Tokyo representative. The Japanese directors are Sumio Higashi, president-director; Nagahuru Nakamura, managing director; Mr. Kimura, sales director; and senior businessman, Soichi Matsune, director. Tirto Utomo is a Djakarta-based director.

Sarwono explains Far East's market position as follows: "Japanese crude oil purchasing policies are based upon four factors—stability, price, independence, and pollution. All of these factors favor Indonesian crude. Since oil is so vital to Japan's industrial economy, their sources must be secure politically and the Japanese now have great confidence in Indonesia as compared to many troublesome spots in the world. Nowadays price is determined on a worldwide competitive basis and is a function of quality and transportation costs. Since Indonesia is the closest major producing area to Japan, we have a natural cost advantage on transportation. Japan is also seeking to diversify its supply, both among nations and among companies. Here again Indonesia has an advantage because of

our political stability and our independent national oil company. During the past five years a fourth factor has developed strongly in relative importance—pollution control. And here also Indonesia has a natural advantage with one of the world's lowest sulfur content crudes.

"Once we have obtained the confidence of our customers and have established good working relations, the principal task is a technical one to forecast supply and demand requirements. Then a price must be developed which is considered reasonable by both sides in view of world prices. We study the market here and then make our recommendations to Djakarta where the final decision on selling price is determined."

Marketing crude is one part of Far East Oil's activities. The other part is coordinating, with Pertamina's representative office, Japanese financing and equipment purchases for oil development projects. In this regard, over $250 million has been raised by Far East Oil among the large Japanese companies.

While Japan has developed into the major market for Indonesia's low-sulfur crude oil, the West Coast of the United States is also a growing market. It now seems certain that Indonesia can sell all of this type of crude it can produce and this is what has made the area so attractive to the foreign oil companies. One month after the merger of Permina and Pertamin, the first foreign company working offshore spudded in and after six wells, IIAPCO/ARCO struck oil; the boom was on.

As the foreign companies increased operations, Pertamina undertook to set up the liaison offices necessary to assist them in their operations and to monitor their proposed work programs. In April, 1967, the Bureau of Foreign Contractors had been established. In 1968, its name was changed to its present one, Division for Coordination with Foreign Contractors (Divisi Koordinator Kontraktor Asing —*DKKA*). It was originally headed by Brig. General Hartawan with deputy head Ir. Harsono, and Mr. Martalogawa, the senior Shell employee among those who joined Permina after the acquisition. This division provides the vital link in the production sharing concept of a partnership.

TING AN OFFSHORE WELL. THE TEST CRUDE IS BEING FLARED.

Dr. Ibnu announced that the objective of *DKKA* was to free the contractors from all concern except looking for oil. Pertamina would take care of all other matters—government relations, customs, work permits, compliance with safety regulations, etc. *DKKA* would also monitor costs (which would later be reflected in the 40% recovery allocations of cost oil to the foreign contractor if discoveries were made) and the contractors' proposed work programs. Staffed primarily with former Shell managers who were experienced in working with expatriates, the fledging predecessor of today's *DKKA* set about its task. Although these men were all experienced in oil operations, many of the problems were unprecedented, for this was Indonesia's first intensive experience in offshore drilling. Even pirates in the Strait of Malacca were among the problems that had to be coped with.

A special maritime staff within Migas, now headed by Navy Colonel Tjipto Wignjoprajitno, was set up to work with *DKKA* in obtaining flag dispensations, defense permits, and liason officers for the new offshore work.

A team calling upon specialists from the different ministries and headed by a prominent Indonesian attorney, Professor Dr. Mochtar Kusumaatmadja, Dean of the Law School at Bandung, with Ir. Sumbarjono from Migas as secretary, completed the first of over twenty conventions required between Indonesia and neighbouring countries to define the extent of Indonesia's jurisdiction over offshore waters. On October 27, 1969, the first of these was announced, an agreement with Malaysia.

In 1970, Brig. General Hartawan was recalled to the army. As more than twenty-five foreign firms became active, the coordinating problems became considerably more pressing. A diplomat-soldier Brig. General Soekamto Sajidiman was chosen to head *DKKA*. Soekamto was recalled from his post as consul general to South Korea. Previously, he had directed Indonesia's national sports program as part of the post-Gestapu attempt to help provide direction for the youth of the nation. Prior to that, he had directed one of the state trading companies. A diplomat is the ideal choice for *DKKA* since this is the office where Pertamina's management prerogative must be exercised.

Dr. Ibnu's program of providing the infrastructure needed by the foreign oil contractors was important not only for improving the operating efficiency of the companies but also to maximize the economic effects of oil activity on the Indonesian economy. The presence of Singapore thrusting into the very midst of the Indonesian archipelago presented formidable competition.

Dr. Ibnu outlined the various elements of the program: (1) housing; (2) office space; (3) schools; (4) telecommunications; (5) medical; (6) recreation; (7) utilities—water, electricity. In each of these areas, Singapore had a great head start.

Colonel Sarnoebi Said, head of Pertamina's maintenance, was directed to meet the competition. Plans were laid for construction of a $6.5 million office building in Djakarta, (completed in 1971) which would offer suitable space for companies, with *DKKA* located in the same building. Additional plans called for a twenty-one story apartment building for families of the oil men. A project of particular interest to Dr. Ibnu, was the construction of a major 300-bed hospital complex in Djakarta that was completed in 1972. Land was donated for the construction site of a new Joint Embassy School. Further, land was acquired for construction of expatriate housing subdivisions for a projected 300 families under several joint venture agreements. In telecommunications, Pertamina's wholly owned subsidiary P.T. Electronica Nusantara, under Ir. Udaya Hadibroto, was given the assignment to install a system which now links the foreign contractors' offices in Djakarta by both voice and telex communications with any of their drilling sites in Indonesia.

A series of regional supply bases for offshore operations were begun on Batam Island near Singapore, Merak on the west tip of Java, Masalembo Island in the middle of the Java Sea, and at Balikpapan on the east coast of Kalimantan.

During the flurry of Production Sharing Contract signings between 1968 and 1970, Pertamina earned very substantial payments which it used to finance many of these new programs. Funds were also used to build housing for Pertamina workers and for community development projects—a television station in Medan, government office buildings, mosques, schools, utilities, bridges, and roads.

*   *   *

As the year 1969 drew to a close, Pertamina, in the very midst of an economic growth unprecedented in the history of Indonesian business, found itself the object not of praise but of strong attack.

Beginning in late 1969, and continuing for approximately a three-month period, virtually every phase of the organization was attacked in some of the Djakarta newspapers. Spearheading the attack was the *Indonesia Raya*, whose publisher, Mochtar Lubis, is a crusading journalist in the old muckraking tradition. Lubis' credentials for fearless, if not always accurate, journalism were impeccable. In the 1950s his articles had caused one cabinet to fall. In the Sukarno years his attacks led not only to suspension of his paper but to his own house arrest. Released after Gestapu, his paper returned to print on October 29, 1968. In his first issue, Mr. Lubis again sounded the call:

> We are reborn again; our voice comes echoing back. Both the corrupt people and the corrupt, tyrannical regimes which muzzled us are no longer sitting in the throne of their despotism. This daily reemerges, impelled by the determination to carry out its holy war against evil, a war which the Sukarno regime ten years ago forced and abused into extinction ...

Slightly over one year later, Mr. Lubis launched a major campaign against corruption in Indonesian society—a campaign in which Pertamina became the principal target.

No one, least of all the Indonesians, disputes that corruption is a major problem in Indonesian society. Whatever the causes of corruption, and some will trace it back to the system of indirect rule under the Dutch where local village officials were entitled to all that they could extract from peasants of their village, it became epidemic in the Sukarno Guided Democracy era when rampant inflation rendered it very difficult for any public official to live on his salary. This coupled with the bureaucratization of Indonesian life, made "speed money" (bribes paid to get things done), kickbacks, and a host of other illegal practices, a way of life. As the Soeharto government reduced inflation and restored rationality to public affairs and the economy, the functional reason for corruption was certainly greatly reduced. Habits, though, outlive the conditions which create them. Thus President Soeharto's success in promoting economic activity and attracting foreign investment has created additional opportunities for the "invisibles," as corrupt officials are referred to. It is a carryover problem from years past that still remains to be solved.

The *Indonesia Raya* campaign stimulated student demonstrations by *KAMI* and *KAPPI* and other newly formed groups such as the "We Want To Know" student forum. The campaign against Pertamina intensified when, in the midst of the furor, the government, on January 6, 1970, announced further price increases of gasoline and kerosene linked to the need to finance elections, to develop West Irian, and to raise government salaries. Demonstrations at Pertamina's headquarters followed.

The attacks on Pertamina centered principally upon business practices, with the implication that they invited corruption. The company was also criticized for failure to make information public. Indeed, many of the charges made against Pertamina arose from lack of information or gross misinformation. Suggestions that Dr. Ibnu personally owned part of Far East Oil and Tugu Insurance (a Pertamina joint venture insurance company in Hong Kong), were simply false. Other charges related to the use of brokers, particularly for buying tankers and oil field supplies, without also revealing that these brokers financed Pertamina's purchases at a time when international banks would not— and the Pertamina and government treasuries could not— handle the financing. Other charges related to poor buying practices where mistakes were certainly made during the company's rapid expansion.

During the newspaper attacks, Pertamina's head of public relations, Marah Joenoes, undertook to answer some of the dozens of questions which were raised. It was a hopeless task. As Dr. Ibnu notes, "When people are yelling 'Thief! Thief!' it does no good to shout back louder, 'I am no thief!' I told my staff that we would also have our headlines, but our headlines would be about how we accomplish more production, build new refineries, and improve domestic supply. These headlines would let the people know where the money goes. There is no way to answer such charges except by results."

A few days before the price increases were published, President Soeharto announced the formation of a special commission, the Committee of Four, to investigate corruption in government and to make recommendations for its eradication. Specific inquiries into the operations of Pertamina and two other state enterprises were undertaken. The four members of the committee were all respected elder statesmen. The chairman of the committee was former Prime Minister Wilopo. Former Vice-President Hatta added further prestige by agreeing to serve as advisor to the Committee of Four.

The committee's task was a difficult one, and it was given, or took, only five months to perform it. It began in February and completed its report at the end of June. During that time it submitted a report on the attorney general's department, two reports on Pertamina, one report on the state rice procurement agency, one report on the state forestry enterprise, and two further reports on government administration. Although the committee's reports to the President were intended to be secret, in July, a newspaper secured copies of them and published them, and thus they came into the public domain.

President Soeharto, having conducted a thorough review, delivered his own judgment during the dedication ceremonies for IIAPCO's Cinta production platform. He discussed the newspaper attacks and noted that accomplishments in oil are often located far away from where the people can see them. Addressing the employees of Pertamina he told them to ignore such attacks and the rumors that went with them, and to continue with their work and efforts. The President emphasized that the task entrusted to Pertamina in carrying out the nation's production of oil was of urgent importance for the development of the nation, and critical to its very existence. He went on to express his confidence in the management and direction of Pertamina and expressed the nation's appreciation for the perseverence of its engineers, technicians and laborers. As the industry continued to grow there would be changes of course, but not in the fundamental task entrusted to Pertamina.

Although the attacks on Pertamina certainly raised the issue of corruption—almost always indirectly and by implication rather than assertion—the main thrust of the attack was that Pertamina was beyond governmental control and constituted a "government within government." This criticism was widely voiced not only by the public and press but by many in other ministries of government.

Many of the government economists and planners believed that the growth of Pertamina and the Indonesian oil industry was proceeding outside the framework of the Five-Year Plan, indeed outside the framework of any governmental regulation whatsoever. Further, it was believed by many that Dr. Sumantri, the minister of Mines, had but little practical control over Pertamina's activities.

Joining their voices with these domestic critics were men in world governmental banking circles whose credit and continued faith was vital to the success of Indonesia's development effort. Some in this group were critical not only of Pertamina's assertedly excessive financial autonomy, but also of Pertamina's incurrence of foreign indebtedness.

It was, then, the need to establish new regulatory controls over Pertamina that the Committee of Four primarily stressed, although it also enumerated past instances of Pertamina's failure to obey the legal requirements of Law No. 19, regulating state enterprises. A new regulatory framework has been created for Pertamina as an outgrowth of the committee's reports.

In the days of Guided Democracy, the regulation of national oil company affairs was not a matter of high governmental priority. Permina was a small operation producing little revenue beyond what it needed for financing rehabilitation of its fields. In those days of highly personalized

government, Dr. Ibnu complied with the spirit of the times
by reporting, when requested, to the Cabinet, Prime Minister
Djuanda, President Sukarno, Chairul Saleh, and General
Nasution. Economic planning was, at best, handled on
an ad hoc basis.

By the end of 1969, however, an entirely different kind
of government was emerging. A major five-year development plan was in the initial stages, and oil would be looked
to as the primary domestic source of funding for that plan.

Dr. Ibnu was not unhappy with the idea of having a
new governing statute for Pertamina. The company was
still subject to the provisions of Law No. 19 of 1960, which
it had greatly outgrown. He had frankly proceeded with the
establishment of subsidiaries regardless of the constraints
of Law No. 19, albeit always with ministerial and presidential
approval. Lt. General Suprajogi, the draftsman of Law
No. 19, was one of the first to express the view that Pertamina
should seek a law tailored to its own needs. He noted that
a special law had been enacted for regulation of the central
bank, Bank of Indonesia, and Pertamina, he maintained,
was now no less important in the national economy. The
minister of Mines, Dr. Soemantri, also strongly believed
new legislation was necessary and recommended this to
President Soeharto.

Thus, when President Soeharto directed the minister of
Mines to prepare a draft for a Pertamina law, both the
oil sector and the finance and planning sectors favored the
idea of such a law. Each side, of course, had a different
concept of what the contents of the law should be—the
oil people seeking a broad enabling statute, and the finance
and planning people seeking tighter regulations with more
oil money coming into the treasury. Drafting of the law
was entrusted to representatives from the Ministry of Mines,
the National Development Planning Council (*BAPPENAS*),
the Ministry of Finance, and a number of persons from
various other ministries. Their recommendations were
reviewed by the ministers of Mines, Finance, and *BAP-
PENAS*. Their draft proposal was in turn taken under
consideration for almost a year in Parliament where some
modifications were introduced prior to passage.

The resulting law, entitled the Pertamina Law (Law No. 8 1971, effective January 1, 1972), is viewed as a compromise with which all sides profess to be satisfied. Perhaps to clearly mark the beginning of a new era, Law No. 8 establishes a new corporation–Pertamina–in place of P.N. Pertamina. Although the law's provisions treat a large number of different subjects, these can be grouped, for the most part, as they bear on three questions, each a source of difficulty in the past, and each of vital importance to Pertamina's future. These are: (1) Who would participate in the regulation of Pertamina? (2) What would the allocation of funds be between Pertamina and the government? and (3) What growth would be permitted into collateral sectors?

Before Law No. 8, the review of Pertamina's policies, budgets, and financial reports was made first at the Ministry of Mines and ultimately were given to the President. Law No. 8 changes this; it creates a Government Council of Commissioners consisting, ex officio, of the minister of Mines (chairman), minister of Finance (deputy chairman), and chairman of the National Development Planning Council (member). Provision is also made for the addition of two more ministers at the discretion of the President. As before, the President retains the ultimate authority and the Government Council of Commissioners' responsibility to him is recognized. The President may appoint and discharge council members in conformity with the strong presidency provisions of the Constitution of 1945 under which all ministers serve at the pleasure of the President.

The Government Council of Commissioners is empowered to determine Pertamina's general policy and to oversee its undertakings. It further approves annual budgets and all budget alterations and must give prior approval to the establishment of subsidiaries, joint ventures, and various other transactions. However, the exclusive regulatory authority of the Ministry of Mines over petroleum operations is explicitly preserved. The council meets as required and at least monthly. Provision is made for appointment of a secretary (Mr. Gozali, an assistant to the minister of Mines, has been appointed), and the creation of a secretariat to serve the council.

Direction and management of Pertamina, consistent with the general policies laid down by the Government Council of Commissioners, is vested in its Board of Directors consisting of the president-director and five managing directors.

The new Pertamina organization thus has a directorate for each of the five principal activities of the company: exploration and production; refining and petrochemicals; domestic marketing; shipping; and finance and adminstration.

The five directors were named by President Soeharto. Ir. Anonodo remains director of Finance and Administration. General Soehardiman continues in the post of director of Domestic Marketing. Ir. Trisulo continues as the director of Exploration and Production. Ir. Soedarno has been elevated from deputy director to director of Refiining and Petrochemicals. Drs. Soekotjo has also been elevated from division head to director of Shipping. The members of the managing board serve for a term of five years, after appointment by the President upon consultation with the council. The President may discharge a board member prior to expiration of his term at his own request, or for causes specified.

The policy and management provisions of Law No. 8 are in accordance with the general objective of the Soeharto administration to institutionalize decision making as contrasted to the highly personalized methods characteristic of the Sukarno era. In this regard, there was considerable discussion as to whether the president-director of Pertamina should be included on the Government Council of Commissioners. He was not included and this decision went in accordance with the standard Indonesian practice derived from Dutch corporate law of separating active management from the shareholders' representatives in a corporation. Omission will tend to ensure a greater formality of interchange.

If it is accepted that omission of the president-director from the council will tend to improve regulatory control over Pertamina's activities, there remains the question of whether or not this is a good thing. The question is better posed in terms of another part of the law which was hotly debated by the drafting committee, namely the question of prior approvals over specific transactions. Article 27 provides that the council must give prior approval to any transactions which bind the company's assets as a guarantee or involve the establishment of subsidiaries or affiliated companies. It further authorizes the council to establish regulations requiring prior approval over loans, and purchase and sales contracts above a certain amount, as determined by the council. There is, of course, a legitimate state interest in controlling the extent of Pertamina's indebtedness, since the government of Indonesia must allocate its limited credit and capital resources for maximum effectiveness. As for the review of specific sales and purchase transactions, it may be argued that the council, in reviewing large transactions, acts no differently than any other board of directors of a large corporate concern.

The three members of the Government Council of Commissioners are all highly respected in their fields. The chairman of the commissioners is Minister of Mines, Prof. Dr. Ir. Sumantri Brodjonegoro. The deputy chairman is Finance Minister Prof. Dr. Ali Wardhana and the third member is Chairman of the National Development Planning Council Prof. Dr. Widjojo Nitisastro. They are two of the six economists who formed President Soeharto's advisory team in the early days of the New Order. Both men have drawn praise from fellow economists and the world banking community for their contributions to Indonesia's economic turnaround. Widjojo's agency drafted the New Order's first Five-Year plan, and is now working on the second. Wardhana's tenure as minister has seen substantial improvement in tax collection, and the beginnings of needed improvements in tax administration.

The council is seen by most commentators as complementary to the board. As one observer put it, "What could be better for the company than to have the top men from the technical, planning, and finance divisions of the government sitting as its senior board members? The future of

the nation's economy and of Pertamina are to a great extent one and the same so it makes good sense to have these men working together."

The second question with which Law No. 8 deals is the division of profits between Pertamina and the government. To the expressed satisfaction of both sides, the law sets reasonably clear standards where before there was confusion. As before, the entire Indonesian share from the Contracts of Work will be allocated to the government treasury, as will 60% of the net operating income from Pertamina's own operations. The allocation with respect to production sharing requires that with the sixty-five–thirty-five split presently in force, the government will receive 60% and Pertamina 5%, on a seventy–thirty split Pertamina would retain 10%.

The third major question treated by Law No. 8, is the growth of Pertamina beyond the oil sector. Pertamina's drive to serve its contractors, increase its own capacity in subcontracting, increase the secondary effects in the Indonesian economy, and perhaps just to grow, have taken it into many collateral fields. These include not only operationally related activities such as telecommunications, aircraft services, and supply base operations, but also activities somewhat further afield including housing, office buildings, hotels, and a steel plant.

In Indonesia, Pertamina is big. It is one of the largest employers in the nation, and it has operations spanning the entire Indonesian archipelago. There is a saying in Djakarta, "Throw a stone and it will strike a Pertamina building." If there is a touch of pride in this statement, there is also resentment and envy at Pertamina's obvious wealth and influence. Since the 1968 merger which created it, Pertamina has held a monopoly in the field of oil undertakings that cover exploration, exploitation, refining, and processing, transportation and marketing. By international oil company standards, Pertamina is still small. It is frequently strapped for funds and it pays salaries to its employees that are considerably below those paid by its own contractors to their Indonesian employees. But in

ERTAMINA'S GOVERNMENT COUNCIL OF COMMISSIONERS WITH DR. IBNU. LEFT TO RIGHT: PROF. DR. ALI WARDHANA, DR. IBNU, PROF. DR. IR. SUMANTRI BRODJO-NEGORO, PROF. DR. WIDJOJO NITISASTRO.

Indonesia's struggling and growing economy many see
it as the foundation of Indonesia's modern economy.

In many instances, Pertamina may be the only Indonesian
enterprise capable of supplying the capital investment
necessary in a new venture. In these cases, the argument
is not whether or not it is a proper undertaking for Pertamina,
but whether Pertamina or a foreign company will take
advantage of a new opportunity. The other side of the
coin is the assertion that Pertamina is not only big but a
monopolist, and that it should not be allowed to discourage
development of other indigenous enterprises.

With these considerations in mind, Law No. 8 treats the
problem by giving the President and the Council of Commissioners broad powers to determine whether or not Pertamina should enter collateral fields. The law provides for
expansion of Pertamina's fields of operation beyond oil
and natural gas only (1) with the consent of the President
and only (2) as long as such activities are still connected
with oil and mineral gas operations. The official clarification
makes clear that the Government Council of Commissioners'
approval will also be required for such expansions before
a request reaches the President's desk. If the expansion
takes the form of a subsidiary, or it involves the participation
of another entity, the Government Council of Commissioners'
prior approval is also required, as it is for the establishment
of all subsidiaries and all participations whether or not
an expansion is involved.

The possibility of creating subsidiaries and participating
in joint ventures is indirectly authorized. It is considered
an important concession for Pertamina which had heretofore
proceeded in this area in possible violation of the provisions
of Law No. 19. Law No. 19 does not expressly prohibit
the creation of subsidiaries. Those who contend that it
does, apparently ground this view on the doctrinaire proposition that state enterprises, by their very nature, should
not own shares in other companies. Henceforth, the question
whether to operate a given activity in the form of subsidiary
or to participate with a private partner through a corporation
or some other mode, may be based on practical business
consideration—the need for a Japanese partner in the case
of Far East Oil, the need to develop a greater sense of

independence in managers, or the desirability of limiting liability as in case of Tugu Insurance.

There are a number of subissues involved in the matter of Pertamina's expansion into other sectors, and many of the competing considerations are just beginning to surface. Take, for example, the question of Pertamina's relationship with subcontractors that supply goods and services to its production sharing contractors and to Pertamina's own operations. Over one hundred and fifty companies are involved in supplying drilling mud, steel pipe, seismic surveys, catering services, and helicopter services, to name just a few. Although some of the companies maintain local subsidiaries, they are virtually all foreign-owned and the goods and services they sell are predominantly of foreign origin. Indonesia has two different objectives to be balanced. First, like any business enterprise, Pertamina must attempt to get the maximum in services for the least cost—an objective best served by fostering competition among the different companies. But, as a national oil company devoted not only to profit, but to development of the Indonesian economy as well, Pertamina must also strive to create a capacity to produce as many of these goods and services as possible in Indonesia, thereby increasing the multiplier effect upon the Indonesian economy.

To achieve the second objective, Pertamina may itself enter a given field as it has in aircraft services. Alternatively, it might join with one of the foreign companies in a joint venture with it as it has in the area of food catering. Finally, the government might give preferential status to the product of a company that establishes a local assembly or manufacturing plant for the product concerned.

The effects of these different courses of action on the objective of maintaining competition varies. For example, Pertamina may without question serve its own operations through its aircraft subsidiary, but if it attempts to pre-empt serving its production sharing contractors as well, private airline companies seeking to compete will be foreclosed.

If, instead of entering the field itself, Pertamina elects to proceed by means of a joint venture, then the other foreign competitors may be locked out of access to Pertamina's own market by a foreign competitor who has achieved a monopoly—or something near it—at a bargain price.

If all companies could be induced to base operations in Indonesia, the problem of seeking competition versus development would be reduced. However, often the market is not large enough to justify more than one or two local operations. The issues here are not easy to resolve in general terms. An effort is presently being made to draft general guidelines which will outline current official thinking on the subject. In any event, the Ministry of Mines now requires that all firms doing business in the oil industry in Indonesia register with Migas and maintain a registered office in Indonesia.

Pertamina's expansion has not always been a result of its own desire, but rather because of its reputation as an enterprise that can get things done. This was the case in the Tjilegon Steel Project in West Java which was begun in the early 1960s as a Russian-sponsored project upon which work was suspended after Gestapu. Pertamina was asked to participate in government efforts to resume construction and has complied. As a result, Pertamina is a participant in the project, now known as P.T. Krakatau, on a sixty-forty basis with the Ministry of Industry holding the 40%.

It is often the foreign firm that seeks out Pertamina as a partner, regardless of the nature of the enterprise, simply because strong, well-managed Indonesian firms are hard to find for joint ventures. In this regard, Pertamina has been presented proposals ranging from shipbuilding and construction to tourist services. Certainly in oil-related activities, Pertamina is the first choice for a partner and often the only choice. In many cases, if Pertamina refuses to participate there will be no Indonesian participation.

These examples merely provide a brief glimpse of the overall complexities that Pertamina management, the Government Council of Commissioners, and the President will face in deciding the proper pace of Pertamina's development and the scope of its activities. Though the Pertamina Law establishes a general framework for reaching decisions it leaves much for determination on a pragmatic basis.

* * *

While the new law was being formulated, oil activities continued at an even faster pace. In west Java, the Djatibarang project got underway and oil was struck in November, 1969. Five rigs were brought in to do delineation and development work. In late 1970, Dr. Ibnu negotiated credit arrangements for over $120 million for the development of this project with Far East Oil and other Japanese companies. Construction was started on gathering systems, a block station, pipelines, and a single-buoy mooring system for loading tankers offshore.

Further oil discoveries were made by Pertamina in north Sumatra and east Kalimantan. Recent gas discoveries, particularly those in north Sumatra, are currently being evaluated and plans are being made for a potential $1,000 million development program. President Soeharto has shown his confidence in these projects by personally directing the negotiation of a government-to-government loan with Japan for $200 million which is required by Pertamina for exploration and development programs.

During 1970, Pertamina took over the operations of the Sungei Gerong refinery (75,000 barrels per day) purchased from Stanvac. In 1971, the expansion of the Sungei Pakning refinery (50,000 barrels per day) was completed and later that year construction was finished on the new Dumai refinery (100,000 barrels per day).

In Tokyo, Far East Oil was continuing to increase its sales volume from 45.8 million barrels in 1970 to over 60 million barrels expected in 1972. Negotiations were underway for a series of price increases which have almost doubled the price of Indonesia's oil in the Japanese markets.

Offshore, up to ten rigs were operating at an aggregate cost of over $250,000 per day. Discoveries were announced by IIAPCO, Atlantic Richfield, Union, and Total. Seven Production Sharing Contracts were signed during 1970, and five more in 1971. Together with the thirty contracts signed before 1970, more than 90% of Indonesia's offshore waters are now under Production Sharing Contracts.

The Indonesian oil business is, in fact, an international one, and Pertamina has won its place in the world oil community. On any given day, Pertamina representatives, like their counterparts with the Majors, may be found in the world oil centers—London, Houston, Geneva, New York City, Tokyo, Vienna and The Hague. The present position of Pertamina is the result of the development and implementation of an entirely new set of legal and working relationships, which Shell and Pertamina called "the new partnership" in their joint booklet commemorating the signing of one of Shell's Production Sharing Contracts. The process of adjustment has naturally been a source of conflict, but to the credit of both the Indonesian leadership and that of the international oil industry, resolutions and compromises have been achieved.

Today, the oil leaders of other countries are looking to Pertamina as a source of ideas for building their own national industry. Thus in June, 1972, Dr. Ibnu headed a delegation to Malaysia to consult with that country on the Pertamina approach to building a national oil industry.

This is the tempo of the 1970s. Those who started their oil careers in the late 1950s often marvel at the pace of this progress. Those starting their careers in the 1970s accept this pace as the norm. The idea of fighting guerilla bands in order to repair a pipeline is beyond their experience, as is building a refinery out of scrap-iron. For the young engineers and technicians of Pertamina, the challenges are modern—the application of new technology, new techniques, new equipment. Yet talking with them in the fields, laboratories, refineries and offices reveals that they very much share the spirit of those who fought the revolution. They too view their work as part of the national effort to build the nation.

In a world where the consumption of oil is expected to double in the next fifteen years, there are great challenges for Pertamina and its new generation of employees.

There are still many problems to be solved—technical problems of pollution, development of the petrochemical industry and application of computer technology, and management problems of implementing the new Pertamina

Law, solving partnership problems under Production Sharing Contracts, and defining the role of oil in the further development of the nation.

As the Indonesian oil industry enters its second century, all of these problems and more will be on the agenda of Indonesia's oil men and policy makers. The most fundamental accomplishment of Dr. Ibnu and his colleagues is that the solutions to these problems will be determined by Indonesians, upon the advice of men who have developed experience in all phases of the oil industry. This was not the case in 1957; it is the case today.

For Pertamina's future progress, Dr. Ibnu believes the fundamental principles remain the same. "We now control and are responsible for the future of our nation's oil. Djakarta has become our oil capital. We shall continue working and shall continue learning—this is our responsibility for Indonesia."

APPENDIX A

SAMPLE PRODUCTION SHARING CONTRACT

SECTION 1
SCOPE AND DEFINITIONS

1.1 SCOPE

1.1.1   This Contract is a production sharing contract in accordance with the provisions herein contained. Pertamina shall have and be responsible for the management of the operations contemplated hereunder.

1.1.2   Contractor shall be responsible to Pertamina for the execution of operations contemplated hereunder in accordance with the provisions of this Contract, and is hereby appointed and constituted the exclusive legal entity to conduct the Petroleum Operations contemplated hereunder.

1.1.3   Contractor shall provide all the financial and technical assistance required for such operations.

1.1.4   Contractor shall carry the risk of Operating Costs required in carrying out operations. Such costs shall be included in Operating Costs recoverable as provided in Section 6 hereof.

1.1.5   During the term of this Contract the total production achieved in the conduct of such operations shall be divided between the Parties hereto in accordance with the provisions of Section 6 hereof.

1.2 DEFINITIONS

In the text of this Contract, the Words and Terms defined in Article 1 of Law No. 44/1960 shall, unless otherwise specified herein, have the meaning in accordance with such definitions.

1.2.1   *Contract Area* means the offshore area within the statutory mining territory of Indonesia covered by the "Authority to Mine" which is the subject of this Contract, which Contract Area is described in Exhibit "A" and outlined in Exhibit "B" attached hereto and made a part hereof; it being understood that areas surrendered by Contractor pursuant to Section 3 hereof shall thereupon be excluded from the Contract Area and references herein to Contract Area shall thereafter refer to the area as so reduced.

1.2.2   *Contractor* means OIL COMPANY and any assignee or assignees of any interest of OIL COMPANY under this Contract provided the assignment of any such interest is accomplished pursuant to provisions of Sections 5.1.12, 5.1.13 or 5.1.14 hereof.

1.2.3   *Petroleum* means mineral oil and gas, hereinafter called Crude Oil and Natural Gas, as defined in this Contract and in Law No. 44/1960.

1.2.4   *Crude Oil* means crude mineral oil, asphalt, ozokerite and all kinds of hydrocarbons and bitumens, both in solid and in liquid form, in their natural state or obtained from Natural Gas by condensation or extraction.

1.2.5   *Natural Gas* means all gaseous hydrocarbons produced from wells, including wet mineral gas, dry mineral gas, casing-head gas and residue gas remaining after the extraction of liquid hydrocarbons from wet gas and non-hydrocarbon gas which is in natural association and produced with gaseous hydrocarbons.

1.2.6   *Petroleum Operations* means all exploration, development, extraction, producing, transportation, and marketing operations authorized or contemplated under this Contract.

1.2.7   *Operating Costs* means expenditures made and obligations incurred in carrying out Petroleum Operations hereunder determined in accordance with the Accounting Procedure attached hereto and made a part hereof as Exhibit "C".

1.2.8   *Effective Date* means the date of the approval of this Contract by the Government of the Republic of Indonesia in accordance with the provisions of applicable law.

1.2.9   *Barrel* means a quantity or unit of oil, forty-two (42) United States gallons at the temperature of sixty (60) degrees Fahrenheit.

1.2.10 *Work Programme* means the programme of the Petroleum Operations to be carried out in the Contract Area as set forth in Section 4.

1.2.11 *Budget* means a cost estimate of all items included in the Work Programme.

1.2.12 *Foreign Exchange* means United States Dollars or other currencies other than that of the Republic of Indonesia but acceptable to Pertamina and to the Republic of Indonesia and to Contractor.

1.2.13 *Calendar Year* means a period of twelve (12) months commencing with January 1 and ending on the following December 31 according to the Gregorian Calendar.

1.2.14 *Contract Year* means a period of twelve (12) consecutive months according to the Gregorian Calendar counted from the Effective Date of the Contract or from the anniversary of such Effective Date.

1.2.15 *Associated Company* or *Associate* in relation to Contractor means any other company, wherever it may be established, in which OIL COMPANY possess directly or indirectly, by means of one or more other companies, at least 50% of the shares which carry the right to exercise voting rights in respect of the appointment of members of the board.

1.2.16 *Non-Associated Company* or *Non-Associates* or *"Third Parties (Party)"* means a company or other entity (other than Pertamina and Contractor) that is not an Associated Company or an Associate.

SECTION 2
TERM

2.1 The term of this Contract shall be thirty (30) years as from the Effective Date.

2.2 If Petroleum is discovered in any portion of the Contract Area within ten (10) years as from the Effective Date, which in the judgement of Contractor after consultation with Pertamina can be produced commercially, based on consideration of all pertinent operating and financial data such as the size and location of the reserves, the depths and number of wells required to be drilled and the transport and terminal facilities needed to exploit the reserves, then as to that particular portion of the Contract Area Contractor will commence development. On other portions of the Contract Area exploration may continue concurrently without prejudice to the provisions of Section 3 regarding the exclusion of areas.

2.3 If at the end of the tenth (10th) year as from the Effective Date no Petroleum is discovered within the Contract Area which can be produced commercially, as determined pursuant to Section 2.2 above, this Contract shall automatically terminate in its entirety, unless agreed otherwise.

2.4   For any subsequent discovery of Petroleum within the Contract Area after ten (10) years as from the Effective Date the provisions of Section 2.2 above shall also apply.

SECTION 3
EXCLUSION OF AREAS

3.1   Not later than the end of the initial three (3) Contract Years' period as from the Effective Date, Contractor shall surrender _____ per cent of the original total Contract Area.

3.2   Not later than the end of the sixth Contract Year, Contractor shall surrender an additional area equal to _____ per cent of the original total Contract Area, and not later than the end of the eighth Contract Year, Contractor shall surrender an additional area equal to _____ per cent of the original total Contract Area, provided such relinquishment will not reduce the retained area to less than _____ square kilometers.

3.3   Not later than the end of the tenth Contract Year, Contractor shall surrender such additional area that the Contract Area thereafter retained and covered by this Agreement shall not be in excess of _____ square kilometers of the original total Contract Area.

3.4   Contractor's obligation to surrender parts of the original Contract Area under the preceding provisions shall not apply to any part of the Contract Area corresponding to the surface area of any field in which Petroleum has been discovered.

3.5   With regard to the Contract Area remaining after the above mandatory surrenders, Contractor shall maintain such reasonable exploration efforts as in the judgement of Pertamina and Contractor is warranted, having regard to sound engineering principles, relevant economic and competitive factors, and the extent of previous exploration efforts. If in respect of such remaining Contract Area Contractor does not during two (2) consecutive years submit an exploration programme, Pertamina and Contractor shall consult as to whether any such part of the Contract Area should be surrendered or whether exploration thereon should be resumed at a later date.

3.6   Upon thirty (30) days written notice to Pertamina prior to the end of the third Contract Year and prior to the end of any succeeding Contract Year, Contractor shall have the right to surrender all or any portion of the Contract Area. In the case of surrendering all of the Contract Area Contractor shall be relieved of its obligation pursuant to this Contract, except such rights and obligations as related to the period prior to such surrender.

3.7   Contractor shall advise Pertamina in advance of the date of sur-
       render of the portion to be surrendered. For the purpose of such
       surrenders, Contractor and Pertamina shall consult with each other
       regarding the shape and size of each individual portion of the areas
       being surrendered, provided, however, that so far as reasonably
       possible, such portions shall each be of sufficient size and convenient
       shape to enable Petroleum Operations to be conducted thereon.

SECTION 4
WORK PROGRAMME AND EXPENDITURES

4.1   Contractor shall commence Petroleum Operations hereunder not
       later than six (6) months after the Effective Date.

4.2   The amount to be spent by Contractor in conducting Petroleum
       Operations pursuant to the terms of this Contract during the first
       eight (8) Contract Years following the Effective Date shall in the
       aggregate be not less than hereinafter specified for each of these
       eight (8) years as follows:

First Contract Year	US $
Second Contract Year	US $
Third Contract Year	US $
Fourth Contract Year	US $
Fifth Contract Year	US $
Sixth Contract Year	US $
Seventh Contract Year	US $
Eighth Contract Year	US $

4.3   All Operating Costs incurred by Contractor for Petroleum Opera-
       tions hereunder shall be included in the amounts referred to above.

4.4   If during any Contract Year, Contractor should expend more than
       the amount of money required to be so expended, the excess may
       be subtracted from the amount of money required to be so ex-
       pended by Contractor during the succeeding Contract Years; and
       should Contractor, due to unforeseen circumstances or with the
       consent of Pertamina expend less during a Contract Year than
       the amount of money required to be so expended, the deficiency
       has to be added to the amount of money required to be so ex-
       pended by Contractor during the succeeding Contract Years.

4.5   At least three (3) months prior to the beginning of each Contract
       Year or at such other times as otherwise mutually agreed by Per-
       tamina and Contractor, Contractor shall prepare and submit for
       Pertamina's agreement a Work Programme and Budget for the
       Contract Area setting forth the Petroleum Operations which Con-
       tractor proposes to carry out during the ensuing Contract Year.

When considering Work Programmes and Budgets proposed by Contractor, Pertamina will give due consideration to the fact that Contractor carries the risk of and provides the necessary funds for the petroleum operations hereunder.

4.6   Should Pertamina wish to propose a revision as to certain specific features of said Work Programme, it shall within thirty (30) days after receipt thereof so notify Contractor specifying in reasonable details its reasons therefor. Promptly, thereafter, Pertamina and Contractor will meet and endeavour to agree on the revisions proposed by Pertamina. In any event, any portion of the Work Programme as to which Pertamina has not proposed a revision shall in so far as possible be carried out as prescribed herein. If Pertamina shall fail to so notify Contractor, the said Work Programme and Budget shall be deemed to be agreed.

4.7   It is recognized by Pertamina and Contractor that the details of a Work Programme may require changes in the light of changing circumstances and nothing herein contained shall limit the right of Contractor to make such changes, provided they do not change the general objective of the Work Programme.

4.8   It is further recognized that in the event of emergency or extraordinary circumstances requiring immediate action, any Party may take all actions it deems proper or advisable to protect its interests and those of its respective employees and any cost so incurred shall be included in Operating Costs.

4.9   Pertamina's agreement to a proposed Work Programme and Budget will not be unreasonably withheld.

SECTION 5
RIGHTS AND OBLIGATIONS OF THE PARTIES

5.1   Subject to the provisions of sections 5.1.12, 5.1.13 and 5.1.14 Contractor shall:

5.1.1   Provide all necessary funds and purchase or lease all material, equipment and supplies required to be purchased or leased pursuant to the Work Programme;

5.1.2   Furnish all technical aid, including foreign personnel required for the performance of the Work Programme;

5.1.3   Furnish such other funds for the performance of the Work Programme, including payment to foreign Third Parties who perform services as a contractor;

5.1.4   Be responsible for the preparation and execution of the Work Programme which shall be implemented in a workman-like manner and by appropriate scientific methods. Contractor shall take the necessary precautions for the protection of navigation, fishing and the prevention of extensive pollution of the waters;

5.1.5   Retain control of all leased property paid for with Foreign Exchange and brought into Indonesia and be entitled to freely remove same therefrom;

5.1.6   Have the right of ingress to and egress from the Contract Area and all adjacent areas and to and from facilities wherever located at all times; have the right to use contractors and sub-contractors in its operations;

5.1.7   Have the right to use and have access to, and Pertamina shall furnish all geological, geophysical, drilling, well, production and other information held by Pertamina or by any other governmental agency or enterprise, relating to the Contract Area including well location maps;

5.1.8   Have the right to use and have access to, and Pertamina shall make available, so far as possible, all geological, geophysical, drilling, well, production and other information now or in the future held by it or by any other governmental agency or enterprise relating to the areas adjacent to the Contract Area;

5.1.9   Submit to Pertamina copies of all such original geological, geophysical, drilling, well, production and other data as it may compile during the term hereof;

5.1.10 Prepare and carry out plans and programmes for industrial training and education of Indonesians for all job classifications with respect to operations contemplated hereunder as provided in Section 11 hereof;

5.1.11 Appoint an authorized representative for Indonesia with respect to this Contract who shall have an office in Djakarta;

5.1.12 Have the right to sell, assign, transfer, convey or otherwise dispose of all its rights, interests and obligations under the Contract to any Associated Company without the prior written consent of Pertamina or the Government of the Republic of Indonesia; provided that Pertamina and the Government of the Republic of Indonesia will be notified of the same in writing beforehand;

5.1.13 Have the right to sell, assign, transfer, convey or otherwise dispose of any undivided part of its rights, interests and obligations under the Contract to parties other than Associated Companies with the prior written consent of Pertamina which consent shall not be unreasonably withheld;

5.1.14 Have the right to sell, assign, transfer, convey or otherwise dispose of all its rights, interests and obligations under the Contract to parties other than Associated Companies with the prior written consent of Pertamina and the Government of the Republic of Indonesia, which consent shall not be unreasonably withheld;

5.1.15 Have the right during the term hereof to freely take, receive, lift, dispose of, export and carry away its share of Crude Oil as well as the share of the Crude Oil for the recovery of Operating Cost subject to the penultimate paragraph of Section 6.1.6 and to Section 7.4 of this Contract;

5.1.16 Be entitled to retain abroad the proceeds of the sale of all Crude Oil, except for the proceeds of any portion of Pertamina's share pursuant to Section 6.1.3 hereof sold by Contractor;

5.1.17 Be authorized to import all equipment, materials and supplies required for carrying out the Work Programme;

5.1.18 Give preference to such goods and services which are produced in Indonesia or rendered by Indonesian nationals provided such goods and services are offered at equally advantageous conditions with regard to quality, price, availability at the time and in the quantities required.

5.2   Pertamina shall:

5.2.1   Periodically consult with Contractor with a view to the fact that the Contractor is responsible for carrying out the Work Programme adopted pursuant to Section 4 of this Contract;

5.2.2   As respects Contractor and Petroleum Operations reasonably envisaged hereunder (including any joint venture relationship through which Petroleum Operations are conducted), except as provided in Section 6 hereof and except for taxes on tobacco and liquor and personnel (employees') income taxes, and income taxes or other taxes, duties/exactions not listed below of contractors and sub-contractors (which will be non-discriminatory and for which contractors and sub-contractors shall be solely responsible), Pertamina shall pay and assume and hold Contractor harmless from all present and future Indonesian taxes and exactions of any Government, Regional, Municipal or other public authority and including without limitation: transfer taxes, import and export duties on materials, equipment and supplies brought into or taken out of Indonesia by Contractor or its contractors or sub-contractors, and exactions in respect of property, capital, net worth, operations, remittances or transactions, all including any tax, levy or exaction on or in connection with Petroleum Operations performed hereunder by Contractor, its contractors or sub-contractors. The obligation of Pertamina hereunder shall be deemed to have been complied with by the delivery to Contractor within one hundred and twenty (120) days after the end of each Calendar Year of documentary proof in accordance with the Indonesian fiscal laws that there exists at the end of such Calendar Year no liability for any of the above-mentioned taxes. In the event, whether for the purpose of expediency or otherwise, Contractor or another person on Contractor's behalf pays any amount on account of any of the aforementioned taxes from which such Contractor is entitled hereunder to be held harmless, Pertamina shall reimburse the person paying such tax within sixty (60) days after receipt of the invoices therefor. Pertamina should be consulted prior to payment of such taxes by Contractor or by another party on Contractor's behalf;

5.2.3 Otherwise assist and expedite Contractor's execution of the Work Programme by providing, at Contractor's request, facilities, supplies and personnel including, but not limited to, supplying or otherwise making available all necessary visas, work permits, transportation, and security protection and surface rights as well as rights-of-way and easements as may be requested by Contractor and made available from the resources under Pertamina's control. In the event such facilities, supplies or personnel are not readily available, then Pertamina shall promptly secure the use of such facilities, supplies and personnel either onshore or offshore in Indonesia, from alternative sources. Any expense incurred pursuant to this Section 5.2.3 by Pertamina at Contractor's request shall be included in the Operating Costs and shall be reimbursed to Pertamina by Contractor to the extent not covered by advances as hereinafter set forth. Contractor will advance to Pertamina funds for the purpose of enabling Pertamina to meet Indonesian Rupiah expenditures incurred pursuant to this Section 5.2.3. Such advances to Pertamina shall be made and accounted for as follows:

(a) Prior to the commencement of each annual Work Programme period, the sum of _____ ($ U.S.);

(b) If at any time during the annual Work Programme period, the amount advanced under paragraph (a) of this Section 5.2.3 has been fully expended, separate additional amounts as may be necessary to provide for Indonesian Rupiah expenses estimated by Contractor and Pertamina to be incurred by Pertamina during the balance of such annual Work Programme period;

(c) If any amount advanced hereunder is not expended by Pertamina by the end of an annual Work Programme period, such unexpended amount shall be credited against the amount to be advanced pursuant to paragraph (a) of this Section 5.2.3 for the succeeding annual Work Programme period;

(d) Pertamina shall submit detailed quarterly statements of Indonesian Rupiah expenditures to Contractor within thirty (30) days after the end of each quarterly period of the annual Work Programme period, and at the time of a change, if any, in the exchange rate applicable to any Petroleum Company carrying on business in Indonesia;

5.2.4   Ensure that at all times during the term hereof sufficient Indonesian Rupiah funds shall be available to Contractor to cover the Rupiah expenditure necessary for the execution of the Work Programme;

5.2.5   Have title to all original data resulting from the Petroleum Operations including but not limited to geological, geophysical, petrophysical, engineering, well logs, completion status reports and any other data as Contractor may compile during the term hereof; provided, however, that all such data shall not be disclosed to Third Parties without informing Contractor and giving Contractor the opportunity to discuss the disclosure of such data if Contractor so desires and further provided that Contractor may retain copies of such data;

5.2.6   Permit the use of the equipment, title to which is placed in Pertamina by virtue of this Contract, solely for the Petroleum Operations envisaged under this Contract; if Pertamina wishes to use such equipment for any alternative purpose it may do so to the extent it does not interfere with Contractor's performance of Petroleum Operations, subject to Contractor's concurrence not to be unreasonably withheld;

5.2.7   Not surrender all or part of its Mining Authority covering the Contract Area in derogation of the rights of Contractor.

SECTION 6
RECOVERY OF OPERATING COSTS AND HANDLING OF PRODUCTION

6.1 CRUDE OIL

6.1.1   Contractor is authorized and obligated to market all Crude Oil produced and saved from the Contract Area, subject to Section 14.9 hereof and to the provisions hereinafter set forth, except that Contractor shall not be obligated in any Calendar Year to market from Pertamina's portion of Crude Oil (as defined in Section 6.1.3

hereof) the amount of Crude Oil calculated under the following formula:

$$\frac{a}{b} \times c$$

In the above formula
a = the quantity of crude oil to which Pertamina is entitled under Section 6.1.3
b = the quantity of crude oil to which Contractor is entitled under Section 6.1.3
c = the quantity of crude oil which Contractor is obligated to sell and deliver under Section 14.9 hereof.

6.1.2 In each Calendar Year Contractor will recover Operating Costs by taking that portion of total production, up to a maximum of forty percent (40%) of total Crude Oil produced and saved hereunder in such year and not used in Petroleum Operations, which, when valued under Section 7 hereof is equal in value to such Operating Costs for such year, and except as provided in Section 7.4 hereof Contractor shall be entitled to freely take, receive, lift, dispose of, export, and carry away such portion of Crude Oil. If in any Calendar Year the Operating Costs exceed the value of the forty percent (40%) of production calculated as stated above, then the unrecovered excess shall be recovered in succeeding Calendar Years.

6.1.3 Of the balance of the Crude Oil remaining, Pertamina shall be entitled to take and receive sixty-five percent (65%) herein sometimes referred to as Pertamina's portion of Crude Oil) and Contractor shall be entitled to take and receive thirty-five percent (35%), provided, however, that as to the quantity of daily production of Crude Oil which is in excess of seventy-five thousand (75,000) Barrels per day up to and including two hundred thousand (200,000) Barrels per day, Pertamina shall be entitled to take and receive, sixty-seven and one half percent ($67\frac{1}{2}$%) and Contractor shall be entitled to take and receive thirty-two and one half percent ($32\frac{1}{2}$%), and provided further that as to the quantity of daily production of Crude Oil which is in excess of two hundred thousand (200,000) Barrels per day, Pertamina shall be entitled to take and receive seventy percent (70%) and Contractor shall be entitled to take and receive thirty percent (30%). For this purpose the quantity of Crude Oil to be taken by Contractor for recovery of operating cost under Section 6.1.2 shall be allocated to the production of Crude Oil up to and including seventy-five thousand (75,000) Barrels per day and to the production in excess of seventy-five thousand (75,000) Barrels per day up to and including two hundred thousand (200,000) Barrels per day and to production in excess of two hundred thousand (200,000) Barrels per day on the basis of said production quantities.

6.1.4   Title to Crude Oil which Contractor is entitled to take or sell pursuant to the terms of this Contract shall pass the Contractor upon delivery to vessel at point of export.

6.1.5   Contractor will use its best reasonable efforts to market the Crude Oil as provided in Section 6.1.1 hereof to the extent markets are available.

Pertamina and Contractor shall each be entitled to take and receive their respective portion in kind. If additional facilities are required by Pertamina's election to take its portion of Crude Oil in kind over and above those which would be required under normal industry practice if Contractor were to market all Crude Oil then Pertamina shall bear the cost of such additional facilities provided, however, the cost of additional facilities normally necessitated by increased production shall not be so borne by Pertamina.

If Pertamina elects to take any part of its portion of the Crude Oil in kind the production level under the Work Programme shall be based on the market requirements of both Pertamina and Contractor, however, as long as Pertamina does not elect to take its portion in kind such production level shall be based on Contractor's marketing requirements only.

6.1.6   Pertamina shall advise Contractor of its election specifying quantity and quality in due time in writing but not later than two (2) months prior to the date on which Contractor has to submit the Work Programme pursuant to Section 4.5 of this Contract. However, Pertamina may also make such election at any time during the Calendar Year by advising Contractor in writing not less than ninety (90) days prior to the date of lifting provided that the additional quantities can be produced with existing facilities. Failure to give such notice shall be conclusively deemed to evidence Pertamina's election not to take in kind.

Pertamina's election to take all or part of its portion of Crude Oil in kind shall not interfere with the proper performance of any Crude Oil Sales Agreement for Petroleum produced within the Contract Area which Contractor has executed prior to the notice of such election.

Any sale of Pertamina's portion of Crude Oil by Contractor shall not be for a term of more than one (1) year without Pertamina's consent, such consent not to be unreasonably withheld.

Should the sum of the requirements of both parties be in excess of the production rate allowable under good oilfield practice Contractor shall subject to Section 7.4 hereof be entitled to satisfy its requirements over and above its Contractual share pursuant to Section 6.1.3 hereof out of the portion of Crude Oil for the recovery of Operating Costs and any balance left shall be allocated to Pertamina which shall account to Contractor for such quantity at a price not less than the weighted average realized export price determined pursuant to Section 7.2 hereof during the period involved.

Should Pertamina's election to take its portion of Crude Oil in kind result in a production rate in excess of Contractor's market requirements then Pertamina shall sell for Contractor's account such quantity of Crude Oil for the recovery of Operating Cost which is in excess of Contractor's market requirements at a price which shall not be less than the weighted average realized export price determined pursuant to Section 7.2 hereof during the period involved.

Payments to be made by Pertamina to Contractor under this Section 6.1.6 shall be made within thirty (30) days following the end of the month in which delivery of each is made to Pertamina or may at Contractor's option be effectuated by assignment of the payment of purchaser to Contractor.

6.1.7   Contractor shall be subject to the Indonesian income tax laws with respect to its income and shall comply with the requirements of such laws in particular with respect to filing of returns, assessment of tax and keeping and showing of books and records. Contractor's taxable income for Indonesian income tax shall be an amount equal to the sums received by Contractor from the sale or other disposition of its share of the Crude Oil pursuant to Section 6.1.3 hereof plus an amount equal to Contractor's Indonesian income tax. The sums Contractor receives from the sale or other disposition of the Crude Oil which Contractor shall be entitled to take and receive under Section 6.1.3 shall be considered Contractor's net income after Indonesian income tax.

6.1.8   The portion of Crude Oil which Pertamina is entitled to take and receive hereunder shall be inclusive of all of Contractor's Indonesian income taxes. Pertamina shall assume, pay and discharge on behalf of Contractor Contractor's Indonesian income taxes and shall furnish Contractor with proper official receipts evidencing the payment thereof. Such receipts shall be issued by the Minister of Finance or other duly constituted authority for the collection of Indonesian income taxes provisionally within ninety (90) days and finally within one hundred and eighty (180) days following the commencement of the next ensuing Calendar Year and shall state the amount and other particulars customary for such receipts.

As used herein Indonesian income taxes shall be inclusive of all taxes on income payable to the Government of Indonesia and any Regional, Municipal or other public authorities such as but not limited to corporation tax, income taxes or taxes based on income or profits including all dividend, withholding and other taxes imposed on the distribution or remittance of income or profits by Contractor.

6.2 NATURAL GAS

6.2.1   Any Natural Gas produced from the Contract Area to the extent not used in operations hereunder, may be flared if the processing or utilization thereof is not economical. Such flaring shall be permitted to the extent that gas is not required to effectuate the maximum economic recovery of Petroleum by secondary recovery operations, including repressuring and recycling.

6.2.2   Should Pertamina and Contractor consider that the processing and utilization of Natural Gas is economical and choose to participate in the processing and utilization thereof, in addition to that used in secondary operations, then the construction and installation of facilities for such processing and utilization shall be carried out pursuant to an approved Work Programme. It is hereby agreed that, while it is the intention of Pertamina and Contractor to enter into further contractual arrangements to implement the foregoing, all costs and revenues derived from such processing, utilization and sale of Natural Gas shall be treated on a basis equivalent to that provided for herein concerning Petroleum Operations and disposition of Crude Oil.

6.2.3   In the event, however, Contractor considers that the processing and utilization of Natural Gas is not economical, then Pertamina may choose to take and utilize such Natural Gas that would otherwise be flared, all costs of taking and handling to be for sole account and risk of Pertamina.

6.3 SEGREGATION OF CRUDE OIL

6.3.1   In the event the Petroleum Operations involve the segregation of Crude Oils of different quality and/or grade and if the Parties do not otherwise mutually agree:

   (a) any and all provisions of this Contract concerning evaluation of Crude Oil shall separately apply to each segregated Crude Oil;

(b) each Crude Oil produced and segregated in a given year shall contribute to:

   (i)   the 'total quantity' up to forty percent (40%) destined in such year to the recovery of all Operating Costs pursuant to Section 6.1.2 hereof;

   (ii) the 'total quantity' of Crude Oil to which a Party is entitled in such year pursuant to Section 6.1.3 hereof;

   (iii) the 'total quantity' of Crude Oil which Contractor agrees to sell and deliver in such year for domestic consumption in Indonesia pursuant to Section 14.9 hereof, out of the share of Crude Oil to which it is entitled pursuant to Section 6.1.3;

   with quantities, each of which shall bear to the respective 'total quantity' (referred to in (i) or (ii) or (iii) above) the same proportion as the quantity of such Crude Oil produced and segregated in such given year bears to the total quantity of Crude Oil produced in such year from the Contract Area.

6.4   During any given Calendar Year, the handling of production (i.e. the implementation of the provisions of Section 6 hereof) and the proceeds thereof shall be provisionally dealt with on the basis of the relevant Work Programme and Budget and based upon estimates of quantities of Crude Oil to be produced, of internal consumption in Indonesia, of marketing possibilities, of prices and other sale conditions as well as of any other relevant factor. Within thirty (30) days or a longer agreed period after the end of said given year, adjustments and cash settlements between the Parties shall be made on the basis of the actual quantities, amounts and prices involved, in order to comply with the provisions of this Contract.

SECTION 7
VALUATION OF CRUDE OIL

7.1   For the purpose of this Section the following terms shall have the meaning as defined:

Governmental Crude Oil Sale means a barter transaction or a sale by Pertamina related to a barter or government-to-government transaction, sale to another state enterprise or government, or a sale to a customer controlled directly or indirectly by a government which is on terms not competitive with or comparable to arm's length purchases and sales by commercial buyers and sellers.

Crude Oil Sales to Associated Companies means any sale by Contractor to an Associate of Contractor as defined in Section 1.2.15.

Third Party Sales means sales by Contractor to purchasers independent of Contractor, that is purchasers with whom (at the time the sale is made) Contractor has no contractual interest involving directly or indirectly any joint interest relating to such sale, or purchasers which are not Associated Companies of Contractor.

7.2   Subject to the provisions hereinafter set forth in this Section 7 the weighted average per barrel net realized price f.o.b. point of export (including therein that received by Contractor pursuant to Section 7.4 hereof and received either by Contractor or Pertamina for sales pursuant to Section 6.1.6 hereof but excluding therefrom that received either by Contractor or Pertamina for sales pursuant to Section 14.9 hereof and excluding that received by Pertamina in any Government Crude Oil Sale, except in the case of a sale by Pertamina pursuant to Section 7.4 hereof) for all sales by Contractor and Pertamina in each Calendar Year of Crude Oil produced from the Contract Area shall be used as the basis for valuing Crude Oil for the recovery of Operating Costs in such year.

All Crude Oil Sales to Associated Companies in any Calendar Year will be valued at the weighted average net realized price f.o.b. point of export determined in respect of other sales (excluding any sale which is on terms not competitive with or comparable to arm's length purchases and sales between commercial buyers and sellers) without any reduction for commissions or brokerage paid on such other sales, provided, however, that if there are no such other sales during the semester of the Calendar Year for which Crude Oil is to be valued, then for the purpose of this Contract the value of such sales to Associated Companies shall be determined in a commercial manner taking into account prices at which comparable types and quantities have been sold in competing exports markets, bearing in mind in that connection possible differences in quality and in transport costs.

Sales by Contractor of Pertamina's portion of Crude Oil will be accounted for to Pertamina at the net realized price received by Contractor for such Crude Oil.

7.3   Subject to redetermination and adjustment on an annual basis for and after each Calendar Year, a weighted average per barrel net realized price shall be calculated at the end of each of the first and second semesters of the Calendar Year, based on sales of Crude Oil in the semester just finished and such net realized price will be used in the ensuing semester as the crude valuation basis.

7.4   Subject to any existing Crude Oil Sales Agreement of Contractor, as respects Crude Oil to be taken by Contractor for the recovery of Operating Costs, if a net realized price more favourable than that obtainable by Contractor is available to Pertamina for Crude

Oil sales for a contract term of one (1) year or longer, then Pertamina shall advise Contractor in writing not less than ninety (90) days prior to the commencement of deliveries under Pertamina's proposed sales contract. Forty-five (45) days prior to the commencement of deliveries under Pertamina's proposed sales contract Contractor shall notify Pertamina regarding its election to account to Pertamina for such Crude Oil to be taken by Contractor for the recovery of Operating Costs (to the extent of the quantity available at such more favourable price) on the basis of the more favourable net realized price at the commencement of deliveries under Pertamina's proposed sales contract, or to deliver said quantity of Crude Oil to Pertamina for a price equal to the more favourable market price secured by Pertamina, provided that payment therefor shall be made to Contractor within thirty (30) days following the end of the month in which delivery of each cargo is made to Pertamina or by mutual agreement of the Parties that payment by purchaser shall be assigned to Contractor. The amount of Operating Costs recoverable by Contractor under Section 6.1.2 by the delivery of oil in any year will be reduced by the amount of any such payment by Pertamina to Contractor under this Section 7.4 in respect of such year.

7.5   Any commission or brokerage paid in connection with sales to Third Parties hereunder shall not exceed the customary and prevailing rate. No commissions or brokerage shall be deducted on any sales to any Associated Company.

7.6   Pertamina shall be duly advised before sales to Third Parties of Crude Oil except sales of Contractor's share of Crude Oil.

SECTION 8
PAYMENTS AND CURRENCY

8.1   All payments which this Contract obligates Contractor to make to Pertamina shall be made in United States Dollars currency at New York, at a bank to be designated by Pertamina and agreed upon by the Central Bank of Indonesia, or other currencies acceptable to Pertamina, except that Contractor may make such payments in Indonesian Rupiahs to the extent that such currencies are realized as a result of the sale of Crude Oil or Natural Gas. All such payments shall be translated at a rate no less favourable to Contractor than that accorded to any other petroleum company carrying on exploration and production operations in Indonesia.

8.2   All payments due to Contractor shall be made by Pertamina in United States Dollars or, at Pertamina's election, other currencies acceptable to Contractor, at the BANK, or at another bank to be designated by Contractor.

8.3   Contractor shall, during the term of this Contract, have the right, without the imposition of any controls except as otherwise imposed by the terms of this Contract, to make any payments and to maintain, and operate bank accounts in whatsoever currency and wheresoever situated and freely to retain or dispose of any funds therein. The foregoing is limited to bank accounts maintained outside of Indonesia. However, it is recognized that Contractor may operate and maintain US Dollar or other foreign currency bank accounts within Indonesia subject to Indonesian laws in effect from time to time.

8.4   In respect of other matters of Foreign Exchange arising in any way out of its connection with this Contract and not specifically mentioned herein, Contractor shall be entitled to receive treatment no less favourable to Contractor than that accorded to any other petroleum company carrying on exploration and production operations in Indonesia.

8.5   Contractor, in the exercise and performance of its rights and obligations as set forth in Sections 5.1.1 through 5.1.18, shall be authorized to pay abroad, in any currency it may desire, without conversion into Indonesian Rupiahs, for the goods and services it may require, and to defray abroad, in any currency it may desire, any other expense incurred for Petroleum Operations under this Contract.

8.6   Any payments which Pertamina is required to make to Contractor and which Contractor is required to make to Pertamina pursuant to this Contract shall be made within thirty (30) days following the end of the month in which the obligation to make such payments occurs.

SECTION 9
EQUIPMENT

9.1   The landed cost of equipment purchased by Contractor pursuant to each Work Programme shall be included in Operating Costs. Contractor shall finance the cost of purchasing equipment required for each Work Programme. Such equipment shall become the property of Pertamina when landed at the Indonesian port of import. In consideration thereof Contractor shall have the sole use of such equipment for the Petroleum Operations hereunder so long as it may require, subject to Section 5.2.6 hereof. Rental payments on readily movable equipment as defined in Exhibit "C", Article II, shall begin on the date of commencement of normal marketing of production, and shall be at a rate commensurate with the useful life of the relevant asset but not to exceed ten percent (10%) per annum of the landed cost price until such rental payments equal such price. Such rental payments shall be included in Operating Costs. It is understood that readily movable equipment purchased in Calendar Years prior to the Calendar Year during which the rental payment obligation first arises shall be considered for computation of the rental only as being purchased in the Calendar Year during which the rental payment obligation first arises.

9.2 The provisions of Section 9.1 hereof shall not apply to equipment leased to Contractor or leased or belonging to foreign Third Parties who perform services as a contractor, which equipment may be freely imported into and exported from Indonesia.

SECTION 10
CONSULTATION AND ARBITRATION

10.1 Periodically Pertamina and Contractor shall meet to discuss the conduct of the Petroleum Operations envisaged under this Contract and will make every effort to settle amicably any problem arising therefrom.

10.2 Disputes, if any, arising between Pertamina and Contractor relating to this Contract or the interpretation or performance of any of the clauses of this Contract, and which cannot be settled amicably, shall be submitted to the decision of arbitration. Pertamina on the one hand and Contractor on the other hand shall each appoint one arbitrator and so advise the other Party and these two arbitrators will appoint a third. If either Party fails to appoint an arbitrator within thirty (30) days after receipt of a written request to do so, such arbitrator shall, at the request of the other Party, if the Parties do not otherwise agree, be appointed by the President of the International Chamber of Commerce. If the first two arbitrators appointed as aforesaid fail to agree on a third within thirty (30) days following appointment of the second arbitrator, the third arbitrator shall, if the Parties do not otherwise agree, be appointed at the request of either Party by the President of the International Chamber of Commerce. If an arbitrator fails or is unable to act his successor will be appointed in the same manner as the arbitrator whom he succeeds.

10.3 The decision of a majority of the arbitrators shall be final and binding upon both Pertamina and Contractor.

10.4 Except as provided in this Section 10, arbitration shall be conducted in accordance with the Rules of Arbitration of the International Chamber of Commerce.

10.5   The provisions of this Section relating to arbitration shall continue
        in force notwithstanding the termination of this Contract.

10.6   In the event the arbitrators are unable to reach a decision, the
        dispute shall be referred to Indonesian Courts of Law for settle-
        ment.

SECTION 11
EMPLOYMENT AND TRAINING OF INDONESIAN PERSONNEL

11.1   Contractor agrees to employ in its operations qualified Indonesian
        personnel with qualifications acceptable to Pertamina and Con-
        tractor and, after commercial production commences, undertake
        the schooling and training of Indonesian personnel for all positions
        including administrative and executive management positions. At
        such time Contractor shall also consider with Pertamina a pro-
        gramme of assistance for training of Pertamina's personnel.

11.2   Costs and expenses of training Indonesian personnel for employ-
        ment by Contractor in Petroleum Operations shall be included in
        Operating Costs. Costs and expenses of a programme of training
        for Pertamina personnel shall be borne on a basis to be agreed
        by Pertamina and Contractor.

SECTION 12
TERMINATION

12.1   This Contract cannot be terminated during the first three (3) years
        as from the Effective Date, except by provision as stipulated in
        Section 12.3 hereunder.

12.2   At any time after the end of the third year as from the Effective
        Date, if in the opinion of Contractor circumstances do not warrant
        continuation of the Petroleum Operations, Contractor may, by
        giving thirty (30) days written notice to that effect to Pertamina
        and after consultation with Pertamina, relinquish its rights and
        be relieved of its obligations pursuant to this Contract, except such
        rights and obligations as related to the period to such relinquishment.

12.3   Without prejudice to the provisions stipulated in Section 12.1
        hereinabove, either Pertamina on the one hand or Contractor on
        the other hand, shall be entitled to terminate this Contract in its
        entirety by a ninety (90) days written notice if a major breach of
        contract is committed by the other provided that conclusive evidence
        thereof is determined by arbitration or final court decision to exist
        as stipulated in Section 10 hereof and the Party proved to be in
        breach fails to remedy the breach within the time specified by
        arbitration or by court decision as the case may be.

SECTION 13
BOOKS AND ACCOUNTS AND AUDITS

13.1 BOOKS AND ACCOUNTS

Pertamina shall be responsible for keeping complete books and accounts reflecting all Operating Costs as well as monies received from the sale of Crude Oil, consistent with modern petroleum industry practices and proceedings as described in Exhibit "C". Until such time as normal marketing and production commences and thereafter if Pertamina so requests, however, Pertamina hereby delegates its obligation to keep such books and accounts to Contractor. The books shall be kept in US Dollars on which the recovery of Operating Costs pursuant to Section 6.1.2 hereof shall be based.

13.2 AUDITS

Pertamina or Contractor, as the case may be, shall have the right to inspect and audit the books and accounts relating to this Contract for any Calendar Year within the one (1) year period following the end of such Calendar Year. Any such audit will be completed within twelve (12) months after its commencement. Any exception must be made in writing to the other within sixty (60) days following the end of such audit and failure to give such written exception within such time shall establish the correctness of the books and accounts.

SECTION 14
OTHER PROVISIONS

14.1 NOTICES

Any notice required or given by either Pertamina or Contractor to the other shall be deemed to have been delivered when properly acknowledged for receipt by the receiving Party.

All such notices shall be addressed to:
P.N. PERTAMBANGAN MINJAK DAN GAS BUMI NA-SIONAL,
Djalan Perwira 2,
Djakarta
Indonesia

OIL COMPANY
(Address)

Pertamina and Contractor may substitute or change such address on written notice thereof to the other.

14.2 LAWS

The Laws of the Republic of Indonesia shall apply to this Contract.

14.3 FORCE MAJEURE

14.3.1 The non-performance or delay in performance by Pertamina or Contractor, or either of them, of any obligation under this Contract shall be excused if and to the extent that such non-performance or delay is caused by force majeure. The period of any such non-performance or delay, together with such period as may be necessary for the restoration of any damage done during such delay, shall be added to the time given to this Contract for the performance of such obligation and for the performance of any obligation dependent thereon and to the term of this Contract. However, it is understood that Pertamina may not invoke as force majeure any action (or failure to take action) on the part of the Government of the Republic of Indonesia, or any of its agencies, instrumentalities or subdivisions.

14.3.2 "Force majeure", within the meaning of Section 14.3 of this Contract, shall except as provided in Section 14.3.1 above, include any order, regulation or direction of any government whether promulgated in the form of a law or otherwise, or any act of God or the public enemy, perils of navigation, fire, flood, hostilities, war (declared or undeclared), blockage, labour disturbances, strikes, riots, insurrections, civil commotion, quarantine restrictions, epidemics, storms, earthquakes, accidents or other causes beyond the control of Pertamina or Contractor, or either of them, whether similar to the causes hereinabove specified or not; provided nothing herein contained shall require Pertamina or Contractor, or either of them, to accede to the demands of labour unions or their respective employees which either, as the case may be, considers unreasonable.

14.3.3 The Party whose ability to perform its obligations is so affected shall notify the other Party thereof in writing, stating the cause and both Pertamina and Contractor shall do all reasonable within their power to remove such cause.

14.4 CONTINUED EXPLORATION OF EXPLOITATION EFFORTS

With respect to any areas that have been surrendered, or if at the end of the term of this Contract, Contractor may wish to make a request for continued exploration or exploitation efforts regarding one or more parts of the Contract Area, particularly with respect to any part thereof which has been surrendered, then Pertamina shall give sympathetic consideration to such requests.

14.5   TEXT

This Contract is drawn up in the English and Indonesian language. If any question as regards the interpretation of the two texts arises, then the English text shall prevail.

14.6   MUTUALITY

Pertamina and Contractor undertake to carry out the terms and provisions of this Contract in accordance with the principles of mutual good will and good faith and to respect the spirit as well as the letter of said terms and provisions.

14.7   SUCCESSION

If the functions of Pertamina shall be transferred to another agency, instrumentality, or subdivision under the control of or responsible to the Indonesian Government, Pertamina shall ensure that such agency, instrumentality, or subdivision assumes all of the obligations of Pertamina under this Contract. The terms, undertakings, and conditions of this Agreement shall inure to the benefit of and be binding upon the Parties hereto and their respective successors and assigns. In the event of the dissolution or termination of the existence of Pertamina or the non-assumption of its obligations as aforesaid, the Government of the Republic of Indonesia shall assure that an appropriate entity assumes such obligations.

14.8   BONUS

Contractor shall pay to Pertamina a bonus of U.S. Dollars _____ after daily production from the Contract Area exceeds an average of _____ Barrels per day for a period of one hundred and twenty (120) consecutive days and another bonus of U.S. Dollars _____ after daily production from the Contract Area exceeds an average of _____ Barrels per day for a period of one hundred and twenty (120) consecutive days. Payment of these bonuses shall be made within thirty (30) days following the aforementioned qualifying periods. Such payments shall not be included in Operating Costs.

14.9   CRUDE FOR DOMESTIC CONSUMPTION

Contractor agrees to sell and deliver a portion from its share of the Crude Oil to which it is entitled pursuant to Section 6.1.3 for domestic consumption in Indonesia on the following terms and conditions:

(*a*) For the purpose of this paragraph 14.9 "Contractor's Percentage Interest" shall mean the quantity of Crude Oil to which Contractor is entitled pursuant to Section 6.1.3 expressed in a percentage of the balance of Crude Oil remaining, divisible under said Section.

(*b*) The amount of Crude Oil which may be required to be sold and delivered under this paragraph in any Calendar Year shall not exceed Contractor's proportionate share of the total amount of Crude Oil consumed for domestic market in Indonesia in such year. Such proportionate share shall be the same percentage of the total amount of Crude Oil consumed in Indonesia for domestic market in such year as Contractor's Percentage Interest of the total amount of Crude Oil produced and saved from the Contract Area in such year is of the total amount of Crude Oil produced and saved in all of Indonesia in such year. The amount of Crude Oil Contractor shall be required to sell and deliver hereunder during such Calendar Year shall be initially computed from the estimated amounts of Crude Oil to be produced from the Contract Area and all of Indonesia during such Calendar Year and the estimated amount of Crude Oil to be consumed and used in Indonesia during such Calendar Year in which deliveries are to be made. Adjustments will be made on actual production and consumption amounts. It is understood that deliveries hereunder will be made and received in approximately equal monthly quantities.

In no event, however, shall Contractor be obligated to sell and deliver hereunder in any Calendar Year an amount of Crude Oil which exceeds an amount equivalent to twenty-five percent (25%) of Contractor's Percentage Interest of the Crude Oil produced and saved from the Contract Area in such year.

(*c*) The price at which such Crude Oil shall be delivered and sold hereunder shall be twenty U.S. cents (U.S. $0.20) per Barrel at point of export.

(*d*) Payment shall be made to Contractor in U.S. Dollars within thirty (30) days after the end of each Calendar Month for sales and deliveries made hereunder during such month.

(*e*) Deliveries of Crude Oil shall be made at point of export. Contractor shall not be obligated to transport such Crude Oil beyond said point, but upon request Contractor will assist in arranging for the transportation of such Crude Oil but such transportation shall be without cost or risk to Contractor.

14.10 PROCESSING

Contractor shall be willing to consider to come to another contract or loan agreement for the local processing of any product derived from the Petroleum Operations hereunder, on mutually agreeable terms.

Within the framework of the preceding principle, Contractor would agree on the conditions stated below to have refined in Indonesia ten percent (10%) of the share of Crude Oil to which it is entitled pursuant to Section 6.1.3 hereof and should no refining capacity be available therefor to set up a corresponding refining capacity for that purpose. The conditions above referred to are that:

(*a*) Pertamina has first requested Contractor thereto;

(*b*) Contractor's share of Crude Oil pursuant to Section 6.1.3 hereof be not less than _____ Barrels per day; and

(*c*) if refining capacity has to be erected the setting up and use of such refining capacity be economical in the judgement of the Parties.

It is further agreed that Contractor may in lieu of setting up such refining capacity but subject to the same conditions make an equivalent investment in another project related to petroleum or petro-chemical industries.

Petroleum to be delivered to such facilities would be sold by Contractor at a price not less than the net realized price f.o.b. Indonesia received by Contractor established pursuant to Section 7 hereof and would be payable in U.S. Dollars or any other mutually acceptable currency.

SECTION 15
PARTICIPATION

15.1 Pertamina shall have the right to demand from Contractor that a five (5) percent undivided interest in the total rights and obligations under this Contract be offered to either a limited liability company to be designated by Pertamina the share holders of which shall be Indonesian Nationals, or to an Indonesian

Government entity to be designated by Pertamina (both hereinafter called "The Indonesian Participant").

15.2 The right referred to in Subsection 1 of this Section shall lapse unless exercised by Pertamina not later than three (3) months after Contractor's notification by registered letter to Pertamina of its first discovery of Petroleum in the Contract Area, which in the judgement of Contractor after consultation with Pertamina can be produced commercially. Pertamina shall make its demand known to Contractor by registered letter.

15.3 Contractor shall make its offer by registered letter to the Indonesian Participant within one (1) month after receipt of Pertamina's registered letter referred to in Subsection 2 of this Section. Contractor's letter shall be accompanied by a copy of this Contract and a draft Operating Agreement embodying the manner in which Contractor and the Indonesian Participant shall cooperate. The main principles of the draft Operating Agreement are contained in Exhibit "D" to this Contract.

15.4 The offer by Contractor to the Indonesian Participant shall be effective for a period of six (6) months. If the Indonesian Participant has not accepted this offer by registered letter to Contractor within the said period, Contractor shall be released from the obligation referred to in this Section.

15.5 In the event of acceptance by the Indonesian Participant of Contractor's offer, the Indonesian Participant shall be deemed to have acquired the undivided interest on the date of Contractor's notification to Pertamina referred to in Subsection 2 of this Section.

15.6.1 For the acquisition of a five (5) percent undivided interest in the total of the rights and obligations arising out of this Contract, the Indonesian Participant shall reimburse Contractor an amount equal to five (5) percent of the sum of Operating Costs and the compensation paid to Pertamina for information referred to in Section 16 of this Contract, which Contractor has incurred for and on behalf of its activities in the Contract Area up to the date of Contractor's notification to Pertamina mentioned in Subsection 2 of this Section.

15.6.2 At the option of the Indonesian Participant the said amount shall be reimbursed:

(i) either by a transfer of the said amount by the Indonesian Participant within three (3) months after the date of its acceptance of Contractor's offer referred to in Subsection 3 of this Section, to Contractor's account with the banking institution to be designated by it, in the currency in which the relevant costs have been financed; or

(ii) by way of a "payment out of production" of fifty (50) percent of the Indonesian Participant's production entitlements under this Contract valued in the manner as described in Section 7.2 of this Contract, equal in total to one hundred and fifty (150) percent of the said amount and commencing as from the beginning of commercial production.

15.6.3 At the time of its acceptance of Contractor's offer the Indonesian Participant shall state whether it wishes to reimburse in cash or out of production in the manner indicated in Subsection 6.2 under (i) and (ii) of this Section.

16.1 This Contract shall come into effect on the Effective Date.

16.2 Pertamina shall be paid the sum of U.S. Dollars _____ within fifteen (15) days after the Effective Date as compensation for information now held by Pertamina. Such payment shall not be included in Operating Costs.

16.3 This Contract shall not be annulled, amended or modified in any respect except by the mutual consent in writing of Pertamina and Contractor.

APPENDIX B

PERTAMINA ORGANIZATION

Pertamina's activities are divided into two basic categories, head office organization and field organization. These organizations in turn are directly responsible to the Board of Directors. This board consists of a president-director, and a maximum of five managing directors. The managing directors are drawn from Pertamina's five directorates: (1) Exploration and Production; (2) Domestic Marketing; (3) Finance and Administration; (4) Refining and Petrochemicals; and (5) Shipping.

The Board of Directors is responsible via the president-director to the Government Council of Commissioners for all of Pertamina's activities, as well as to the Ministry of Mines regarding the management aspects of the company. The members of the Board of Directors are appointed by the President. The term of appointment is five years, and members can be reappointed. According to Law No. 8, the decisions of the board are reached on the basis of deliberation, and if this fails, by voting. If the voting does not yield a decision, the decision is made by the president-director. The president-director represents the company in all affairs and has authority to delegate this responsibility to other employees of the company.

The tasks of the Board of Directors are designated in Article 20 of Law No. 8. Briefly, these tasks are to implement general company policy as determined by the Government Board of Supervisors, and to prepare the annual budget and work programs. The board is responsible for managing and maintaining company property, determining the organization structure of the company and its subsidiaries and branches, hiring and firing personnel, and determining salaries and other benefits. The board is also obligated to provide all necessary information to the Government Council of Commissioners and to the Ministry of Mines.

The five directorates form the base of the head office organization, although there are seventeen divisions and service departments which provide staff support. Whether an organ is entitled a division or service depends on the type of activity it is engaged in, and has no meaning in terms of rank or status. Each of the service and division heads is responsible for all activities within his respective division or service and reports to the president-director. Some of these divisions and services coordinate their activities through the office of the General Assistant.

The organization of field operations falls into four separate categories. The largest of these categories is the operational unit of production. Pertamina's exploration and production operations are divided into seven geographical areas, and all of the operations conducted within each region fall under the authority of a unit general manager. The unit general manager is responsible for all of Pertamina's activities within that unit, and reports directly to the president-director.

Domestic marketing operations are divided into seven areas, although they do not correspond with the seven operational units of production. All marketing operations within one of the prescribed areas fall under the authority of the area marketing manager who in turn reports directly to the president-director.

The final two categories of field operations are the general foreign representatives and the foreign shipping representatives. They are responsible to the president-director and look after Pertamina's interests abroad, both general and shipping interests.

The relationship between the field managers and the president-director is referred to as a "direct line" relationship. Each field manager is responsible for all operations within his particular area, and all branches within that area report to him, and he in turn reports directly to the president-director. This does not imply, however, that the units operate independent of the head office organization. The relationship between field managers and their head office counterparts is called a "functional relationship." In each of the various field organizations, a close functional relationship is maintained with Djakarta. One of the primary functions of many of the head office organs is to monitor and coordinate the activities in the field. Not only do the respective head office branches coordinate and monitor unit branch activities, they are in many cases given the responsibility of determining work programs and budgets and given the power to rotate personnel. The nature of the activity involved determines somewhat the extent of the functional relationship. A highly technical field section, such as exploration and production, would tend to maintain a closer functional relationship with the head office than would the public relations section, for example.

There are other bodies within Pertamina that fall outside the realm of the individual organizational bodies. The subsidaries and joint and profit-sharing ventures are organizations that are outside the standard organizational structure. Although they work hand-in-hand with many of the company's organs, they are independently administered and report directly to the president-director.

A common feature of Pertamina's organization is the team approach in handling various tasks. For example, in the Directorate of Exploration and Production teams might be made up of strictly E & P personnel, and other times they might include representatives from various other directorates, divisions, and services. The Budget Committee is another example of the team approach. This consists of members from various company organs, and is charged with the responsibility of screening budget requests and submitting a budget to the Board of Directors.

The team approach reaches out beyond the organization itself. The body given the responsibility of negotiating Production Sharing Contracts is an example. This negotiating team is chaired by Dr. Ibnu with Ir. Anondo and Ir. Trisulo as the chief negotiators. The committee also has representatives from the Ministry of Mines, Ministry of Defense, Ministry of Finance,

Ministry of Foreign Affairs and the Bank of Indonesia. The same joint government approach was used to draft the Pertamina Law.

Within Pertamina the lines of authority and responsibility are not nearly as clear-cut as they might appear on the chart. It is very common to find one division chief intimately involved in the activities of another division, or to find a man within a particular directorate or division who has the authority to deal with certain matters without consulting his immediate superior; in this case being responsible directly to the president-director. All of the duties given to a particular organ might not correspond with what might ordinarily be assumed to be the duties of that organ. For example, one of the chief functions of the Division of Economics and Development is to operate a fertilizer marketing system.

DIRECTORATES:

DIREKTORAT EKSPLORASI DAN PRODUKSI (E & P)
(Directorate of Exploration and Production)

The chief function of the Directorate of Exploration and Production is to prepare work programs and assure the proper implementation of such programs in the field of exploration and production. The director of E & P is Ir. Trisulo, and the deputy director is Ir. Soediono. The directorate is divided into four major branches. The Geology Branch is headed by Drs. Ismet Akil and is in charge of coordinating all geological data. The branch works very closely with Lemigas. The Technical Coordinating Body is headed by Ir. Gondani Sam, and serves as a trouble-shooting body which handles technical problems that might arise throughout the organization. The third branch is the Logistics Branch (LOGEP), headed by Mr. Mangun-wardojo. This branch is in charge of all material acquisition, and works closely with the individual units and the Purchasing Division.

The biggest of the four branches is the Exploration and Production Branch, headed by Deputy Director Ir. Soediono. This branch is charged with the responsibility of planning and carrying out exploration and production activities. It is divided into six sections. The Exploration Section is headed by Drs. A. Pulunggono and his deputy, Mr. Soeparjadi, and is in charge of geology, geophysics, paleontology, topography, and road building. The Exploitation Section is headed by Mr. Soetowireno, and handles production engineering and economics, reservoir engineering, production geology, and petrophysics. The Administration Section handles the directorate's administrative activities, and is headed by Mr. Mustawa. The Budget Section is headed by Mr. Z. Abindin and is in charge of budget planning and evaluation, statistics, analysis, and price control. The Production Section is headed by Mr. H.C. Lahenda, and is in charge of operations, pipelines, materials, equipment evaluation, and production statistics. The final section is the Drilling Section which is headed by Mr. A. Frederik and his assistant, Mr. Mursito. It is charged with handling all facets of the drilling activities. Each one of these sections maintains a close functional relationship with its counterparts in the field.

There are several teams within the directorate of E & P in charge of certain projects, such as the development of the Djatibarang Field. Deputy Director Soediono, for example, is in charge of a gas conservation team, as well as a task force which can be put to work wherever needed on short notice.

DIREKTORAT PEMBEKALAN DALAM NEGERI (PDN)
(Directorate of Domestic Marketing)

The primary function of the Directorate of Domestic Marketing is to operate all domestic marketing activities for oil and gas based products, as well as petrochemical products. Brig. General Soehardiman is the director of PDN, and Colonel Drs. Joedo Sumbono is the deputy director. Besides the director's staff and a Research and Analysis Section, the directorate is divided into four separate branches. The largest of these is the Marketing Branch, headed by Deputy Director Joedo Sumbono. This branch is divided into a Sales Section, which in turn is subdivided into a Fuel Products Section, Lube and Greases Section, Special Products Section, Military Service Section, Technical Marketing Service Section, and Sales Administration Section. Shipping and Supply is the second major section in the Marketing Branch and it is in charge of supply and distribution, airfield services, and coordinating domestic shipping operations. Retail merchandising, marketing and trade promotion, make up the third major section of the Marketing Branch. Another branch within PDN is Technical Marketing, which is in charge of technical maintenance, fire and safety, and office engineering. Manufacturing is the third branch, and it is responsible for production, development, and plant coordination. The fourth branch is Administration, which includes personnel, finance, communication, health, and office supply. PDN maintains a close functional relationship with each of the domestic marketing areas, as well as the Directorate of Shipping.

DIREKTORAT ADMINISTRASI DAN KEUANGAN
(Directorate of Finance and Administration)

The function of the Directorate of Finance and Administration is to administer and coordinate all of Pertamina's financial activities. This includes handling all of the day-to-day financial transactions, monitoring the budget of the individual organs, preparing the yearly budget and other financial reports, and monitoring the financial transactions of the foreign contractors. Ir. Anondo is in charge of this directorate. The three primary branches of the directorate are Treasury, Comptroller, and Internal Audit. The treasurer is presently John Abdi, who is responsible for all funds received or paid out, as well as insurance and the payment of taxes. The Internal Audit Branch is headed by Drs. Sugarba, and is responsible for the internal control of funds. Drs. Pulungan is the company comptroller, and his branch is in charge of all accounting as well as overall budget control. There is also a Budget Committee consisting of the directors and other selected members and has the responsibility of screening the various budgetary requests and drawing up the final budget. The Directorate of Finance and Administration also maintains a close functional relationship with the units and those directorates and divisions which maintain their own financial sections.

DIREKTORAT PENGOLAHAN DAN PETROKIMIA (P & P)
(Directorate of Refining and Petrochemicals)

The primary function of this newly formed directorate is to plan and administer all of Pertamina's refining and petrochemical operations. This directorate had formerly been under the Directorate of Exploration and Production, but was recently elevated to the status of a directorate. The director is Lt. Colonel Ir. Soedarno. The directorate is divided into five branches, General Assistant, Operations, Special Projects, Logistics, and Development. With petrochemicals in an embryonic stage, a great stress is placed on planning. Although the refining operations are directly responsible to the particular unit manager, each refining installation maintains a close function relationship with the Directorate of Refining and Petrochemicals, which programs all refining operations.

DIREKTORAT PERKAPALAN
(Directorate of Shipping)

The primary function of the Directorate of Shipping is to handle all of Pertamina's sea transportation requirements, both interisland and international. This includes operating representative offices throughout Indonesia and certain foreign ports. Colonel Drs. Soekotjo is the director of shipping, and Mr. Soempeno is his deputy. The director's staff takes care of all security matters, financial control, legal and insurance matters, and research and development. The directorate is divided into seven branches. The Armada Branch handles nautical matters, technical, survey, telecommunications, equipment, and supply. The Dock Service and Maintenance Branch handles technical dock matters, administration, and logistics. Operations coordinate the interisland shipping operations, and the operations of P.T. Pertamina-Tongkang and Ocean Petrol Ltd. The Finance branch handles bookkeeping and budget. Personnel includes training and public relations as well as other personnel matters. The last two branches are Domestic Shipping Area Representatives, and the Foreign Shipping Representatives. In Hong Kong this is Ocean Petrol Ltd., in Singapore, Tunas Ltd., while agents are also located in Pertamina's offices in New York and Tokyo.

DIVISIONS AND SERVICES

ASISTEN UMUM
(General Assistant)

The primary function of this office is to aid the president-director in coordinating the activities of the Divisions of Personnel, Health, Telecommunications, Purchasing, Maintenance, Public Relations, Security Services, and the General Secretariat. It also acts as a general control body for the president-director as well as serving as his personal staff. It may also be put in charge of new or special projects, and given any other duties as the president-director may assign. The man who heads the General Assistant Office is Hadji Achmad Thahir.

DIVISI PERSONALIA DAN ORGANISASI (DIPO)
(Division of Personnel and Organization)

The chief responsibility of the Division of Personnel and Organization is to take care of all personnel matters within Pertamina. These include labor relations, organization and administration, development planning, remuneration, education and training, as well as establishing personnel regulations which the foreign contractors and sub-contractors must follow. The division Head is Mr. R. Suhardi. The division itself is divided into three major branches. The first of these branches takes care of personnel and industrial relations, and is headed by Lt. Colonel H. Burhan Danil. The second major branch is Personnel Development, Training, Organization and Method, and is headed by Hanum Faeni. The third major branch is UKKA (Urusan Kepegawaian Kontraktor Asing) which is in charge of making policy for the employees, both expatriate and Indonesian, of the foreign contractors. In the case of UKKA, its function is one of policy formulation, while the actual implementation falls under the responsibility of DKKA. Mr. J.L. Wetik is in charge of UKKA.

DIVISI KESEHATAN
(Division of Health)

The Division of Health is responsible for all aspects of Pertamina's rather extensive health program. This includes preventive and curative medicine, medical logistics, and sanitation engineering. This division is responsible for maintaining a series of hospitals and clinics throughout Pertamina's units. Recently the Division of Health has become involved in family planning. Lt. Colonel Dr. R.M. Soetidjo is the head of the health division, while Lt. Colonel Dr. Hardjanto acts as the deputy head of the division. The new Pertamina General Hospital in Djakarta is under this division.

DIVISI TELEKOMUNIKASI
(Telecommunications Division)

Under the auspices of the Government of Indonesia's Board of Tele-communications, Pertamina has been given the responsibility to handle all facets of telecommunications for the oil industry in Indonesia. Initially, the division was primarily responsible for inter-unit communications. With the entrance of foreign contractors, the division's task was greatly expanded. At present, servicing the foreign contractors is a responsibility shared with Pertamina's subsidiary, P.T. Elnusa, although it is planned that Elnusa will eventually take over all the operations connected with the foreign contractors, limiting the division's activities to servicing Pertamina's own communications operations. Lt. Colonel Rani Junus heads up this division. It is divided into two primary branches. The Operations Branch coordinates all communication and operates the Communications Center, and is headed by A. Masjfar. The Technical Branch is headed by Ir. Amri S. Lubis and is in charge of all maintenance and project engineering. There is also an Administration and Personnel Section, a Traffic Section, and a Materials Section.

DIVISI PEMBELIAN
(Purchasing Division)

The chief function of the Purchasing Division is to handle the purchasing of materials both from foreign and domestic suppliers. It works very closely with the Logistics Branch of the Directorate of Exploration and Production. Most purchases need the approval of the Logistics Branch, but the actual buying is handled by the Purchasing Division. Aside from determining prices and deciding on distributors, the Purchasing Division also takes care of bureaucratic procedures, such as import permits, customs, etc. The Purchasing Division maintains sections at both Tandjung Priok and Kemayoran Airport to handle the influx of materials. The Purchasing Division also maintains warehouses for storage, and is responsible for making claims for lost and damaged material as well as expediting and checking deliveries. The Purchasing Division is headed by Colonel A.H. Kastubi.

DIVISI PERMELIHARAAN
(Maintenance Division)

The primary function of the Maintenance Division is to provide maintenance for Pertamina's operations in Djakarta and the surrounding area. This includes the maintenance of all Pertamina-owned housing and office facilities in the Djakarta area. It is responsible for operation and maintenance of Pertamina's vehicles, and also arranges for transportation of Pertamina's employees in the Djakarta area. The Maintenance Division also arranges company recreation programs and provides the necessary transportation and facilities. The division is headed by Lt. Colonel Sjarnoebi Said, with J.I. Widjaja acting as his administrative assistant and Drs. M.M.J. Pattiasina serving as his assistant in charge of operations.

DINAS HUBUNGAN MASJARAKAT (HUMAS)
(Public Relations Service)

The Public Relations Service runs an extensive program to keep the public informed of Pertamina's activities. The service regularly publishes brochures and information sheets in both Indonesian and English. Marah Joenoes is the head of the Public Relations Service and the deputy head is Colonel R. Ambardy.

DINAS SECURITY
(Security Service)

The Security Service assures the security of company property and classified information and provides the security guards for the different operations of the company. The Security Service is also in charge of screening prospective employees and in this activity it works closely with the Personnel Division. Colonel Sainan Sagiman is in charge of the service and his deputy is Lt. Colonel R. Achmad.

SEKRETARIAT UMUM
(General Secretariat)

There are two primary functions of the General Secretariat. It acts as secretary to the Board of Directors and also as general secretariat for the organization of inter-office communications and administration. In its capacity as secretary to the Board of Directors it provides information, arranges meetings, handles correspondence, and compiles the company reports. Its internal function covers company mail, reproduction, filing and maintenance of official records. This section also operates a printing section and coordinates protocol with the Public Relations Service. Brig. General Iwan Soepardi is the acting secretary to the Board of Directors and head of the General Secretariat. Lt. Colonel Soewito Wardojo is the deputy head of the General Secretariat.

DIVISI EKONOMI DAN PENGEMBANGAN
(Division of Economics and Development)

The function of the Division of Economics and Development is to provide overall corporate planning and ensure maximum efficiency in the company's development. In theory it serves the function of a research and development division. Although this division does engage in these activities, at present it is also charged with the responsibility of operating Pertamina's fertilizer marketing operation. Fertilizer is marketed under a separate marketing system, totally independent from the domestic fuel marketing system. The Division of Economics and Development presently administers this system, although it is planned that this responsibility will be transferred to a new subsidiary, P.T. Pupuk. Mr. Sumarno is the division head.

DIVISI HUKUM, HUBUNGAN DAN PEMASARAN LUAR NEGERI (H-HPLN)
(Legal, Foreign Relations, and Foreign Marketing Division)

The primary functions of H-HPLN are to handle Pertamina's legal matters and its foreign relations and marketing. The division head is Dr. E. Sanger and the deputy head is Tirto Utomo, S.H. The division

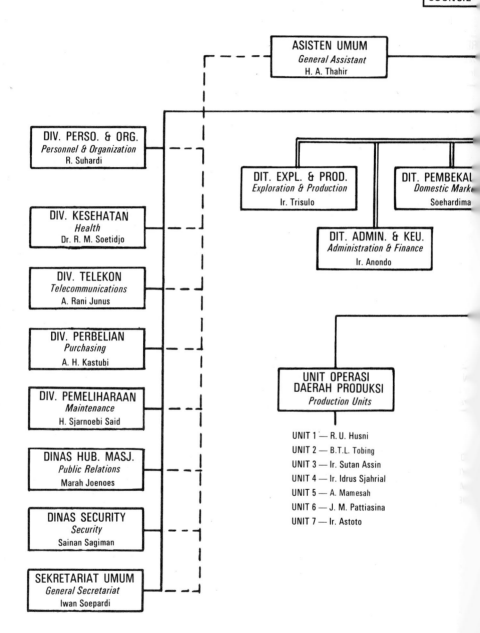

DEW
COUNCIL

ASISTEN UMUM
General Assistant
H. A. Thahir

DIV. PERSO. & ORG.
Personnel & Organization
R. Suhardi

DIV. KESEHATAN
Health
Dr. R. M. Soetidjo

DIV. TELEKON
Telecommunications
A. Rani Junus

DIV. PERBELIAN
Purchasing
A. H. Kastubi

DIV. PEMELIHARAAN
Maintenance
H. Sjarnoebi Said

DINAS HUB. MASJ.
Public Relations
Marah Joenoes

DINAS SECURITY
Security
Sainan Sagiman

SEKRETARIAT UMUM
General Secretariat
Iwan Soepardi

DIT. EXPL. & PROD.
Exploration & Production
Ir. Trisulo

DIT. PEMBEKAL
Domestic Mark
Soehardima

DIT. ADMIN. & KEU.
Administration & Finance
Ir. Anondo

**UNIT OPERASI
DAERAH PRODUKSI**
Production Units

UNIT 1 — R. U. Husni
UNIT 2 — B.T.L. Tobing
UNIT 3 — Ir. Sutan Assin
UNIT 4 — Ir. Idrus Sjahrial
UNIT 5 — A. Mamesah
UNIT 6 — J. M. Pattiasina
UNIT 7 — Ir. Astoto

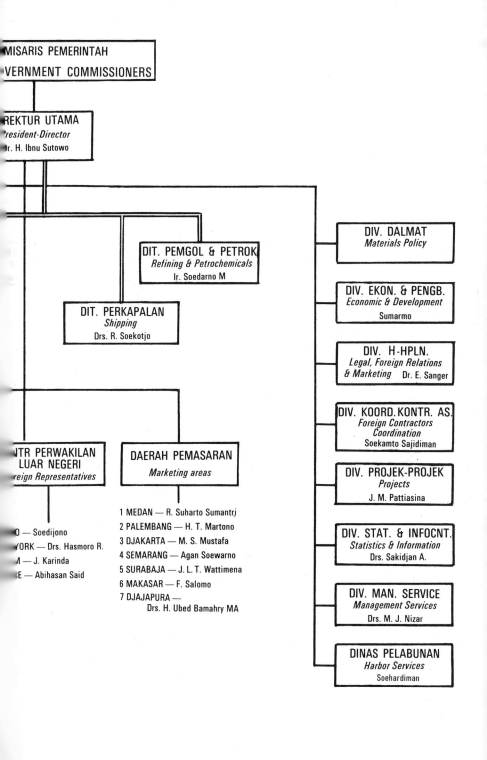

MISARIS PEMERINTAH
VERNMENT COMMISSIONERS

REKTUR UTAMA
President-Director
Ir. H. Ibnu Sutowo

DIV. DALMAT
Materials Policy

DIT. PEMGOL & PETROK
Refining & Petrochemicals
Ir. Soedarno M

DIV. EKON. & PENGB.
Economic & Development
Sumarmo

DIT. PERKAPALAN
Shipping
Drs. R. Soekotjo

DIV. H-HPLN.
Legal, Foreign Relations
& Marketing   Dr. E. Sanger

DIV. KOORD. KONTR. AS.
Foreign Contractors
Coordination
Soekamto Sajidiman

TR PERWAKILAN
LUAR NEGERI
Foreign Representatives

DAERAH PEMASARAN
Marketing areas

DIV. PROJEK-PROJEK
Projects
J. M. Pattiasina

O — Soedijono
YORK — Drs. Hasmoro R.
A — J. Karinda
E — Abihasan Said

1 MEDAN — R. Suharto Sumantri
2 PALEMBANG — H. T. Martono
3 DJAKARTA — M. S. Mustafa
4 SEMARANG — Agan Soewarno
5 SURABAJA — J. L. T. Wattimena
6 MAKASAR — F. Salomo
7 DJAJAPURA —
    Drs. H. Ubed Bamahry MA

DIV. STAT. & INFOCNT.
Statistics & Information
Drs. Sakidjan A.

DIV. MAN. SERVICE
Management Services
Drs. M. J. Nizar

DINAS PELABUNAN
Harbor Services
Soehardiman

is divided into five basic branches. These are Legal, Right of Ways, Insurance, Foreign Relations, and Foreign Marketing. There is also a special staff. H-HPLN maintains close relations with the foreign representatives. Dr. Sanger also handles most of Pertamina's OPEC dealings, while Tirto Utomo is a director of Far East Oil Trading Company and involved in all aspects of foreign marketing.

DIVISI KOORDINATOR KONTRAKTOR ASING (DKKA)
(Division for Coordination with Foreign Contractors)

The primary function of DKKA is to coordinate all activities of the foreign contractors employed by Pertamina, as well as acting as a general liaison between the foreign contractors and the government of Indonesia. In this capacity, practically all matters that might come up between Pertamina and the contractors are handled by DKKA. The division is headed up by Brig. General Soekamto Sajidiman, with Ir. Harsono acting as the deputy head of the division. The organization of the division is divided into five primary branches:

(1) The Operations Branch deals primarily with all activities relating to the technical side of the production operations of the contractors. This includes the supervision of the production phase of the operation. Ir. Wishnu Hidajat is in charge of this branch.

(2) The Exploration and Exploitation Branch deals primarily with the non-production end of the contractors' activities. This branch is in charge of work programs and the collection of all technical data. In this regard, they work very closely with E & P, which provides the real technical knowhow in evaluating the data and the work programs. This branch is headed up by Ir. D. Zahar.

(3) The Logistics Branch deals primarily with obtaining material permits, flag dispensations, and communications permits. It handles all activities relating to the acquisition of passports, visas, etc. In this regard, the Logistics Branch acts merely as a liaison, for it is Migas that actually deals with the other Ministries involved to obtain the permits, etc. Mr. Dick S. Sapi-ie is in charge of this branch.

(4) Finance deals with the financial end of the contractors' operations. It is chiefly responsible for reviewing budgets, performing accounting, and coordinating tax payments by the contractors. The man who heads this branch is Mr. R. Soendoro.

(5) The General Affairs Branch is in charge of internal DKKA personnel, legal relations, public relations, government relations, and also acts as a secretariat for DKKA. Mr. Djoemardi Djoekardi heads up this branch.
Besides maintaining their headquarters in the Oil Centre Building in Djakarta, DKKA maintains two regional offices, one in Makasar and

one in Tandjung Pinang, which act as field liaison between the contractors and the head office.

It must be noted that DKKA acts very much as a liaison unit between the contractors and Pertamina. Much of the evaluation and decision-making regarding the operations of the contractors is done by the appropriate head office organ, but is passed on to the contractors via DKKA.

DIVISI PROJEK-PROJEK
(Projects Division)

The primary function of the Projects Division is to plan, administer, and supervise the construction of projects determined by the Board of Directors to be too broad to be handled by an individual company organ, or because it is a separate part of the company's budget. Refinery and pipeline construction are usually administered by the Projects Division. The division is a completely integrated unit with its own Planning, Technical, Logistics, Financial, and Administrative branches. The Sungei Pakning refinery, the Tjiltjap-Maos-Jogjakarta pipeline, and the Semarang submarine pipieline, are being administered by the Projects Division. Brig. General J.M. Pattiasina is the division head.

DIVISI STATISTIK DAN INFORMATION CENTRE
(Division of Statistics and Information)

The chief responsibility of the Division of Statistics and Information is to gather and collect all statistical data concerning Pertamina's operations. This data is distributed both internally and externally. This division also provides statistical analysis to management on a variety of topics such as pricing. The division is also responsible for the technical library. This division publishes quarterly oil statistics, annual statistics, and a monthly management information service. Drs. Sakidjan is in charge of the division.

NEW DIVISIONS

Recently, Pertamina has established three new divisions. These are the Divisi Dalmat (Materials Policy Division), Dinas Pelabuhan (Harbor Service), and the Divisi Management Services (Management Services Division). The primary function of the Materials Policy Division is to determine purchasing and materials control policies at all levels of the organization. The division is temporarily headed by Dr. Ibnu. The Harbor Service is responsible for the operations of Pertamina's harbor facilities. Brig. General Soehardiman is temporarily in charge. The Management Services Division is in charge of all data processing and computer services. It also has the responsibility for monitoring organization and management effectiveness and providing reports and recommendations to the Board of Directors. Drs. M. J. Nizar is in charge of the Management Services Division.

PRODUCTION UNITS:

Pertamina's production operations are divided into seven geographical units.

UNIT	AREA	HEADQUARTERS	MANAGER AND DEPUTY
I	North Sumatra	Pangkalan Brandan	Lt. Colonel H. U. Husni Ir. Ashari Wargadalam
II	South Sumatra	Pladju	Colonel B. T. Tobing Ir. R. I. J. Soetopo
III	Java and Madura	Djakarta	Ir. Sutan Assin Lt. Colonel H. Sudarsono
IV	Kalimantan	Balikpapan	Ir. Idrus Sjahrial
V	Eastern Indonesia and West Irian	Sorong	A. Mamesah
VI	Central Sumatra	Dumai	Brig. General J. M. Pattiasina*
VII	Singapore and the surrounding islands	Singapore	Ir. Astoto

*temporary

Each of these units operates as a separate operational entity. The general manager is responsible for all operations in the area, and reports directly to the Board of Directors. Because the operations vary somewhat from unit to unit, there are differences in the individual organization of each unit, although there is a basic organizational format.

The general manager generally has a deputy general manager. Operations are divided into several branches, depending on the extent of the local operations; Exploration and Production, Refining, Technical, Logistics, Security, Finance, Personnel, Health, and General. It is also common to have a man in charge of major fields or other specific operations within the unit, such as refineries. Each of the men in charge of these branches is directly responsible to the general manager, although they have a functional relationship to their counterpart division in Djakarta.

The units are responsible for supervising and servicing the foreign contractors working in their areas. They work closely with DKKA and the head office in monitoring and servicing the foreign contractors.

MARKETING AREAS:

The Marketing Operations are divided into seven areas:

AREA	LOCATION	HEADQUARTERS	MANAGER
I	North Sumatra	Medan	R. Suharto Sumantri
II	South Sumatra	Palembang	H.T. Martono
III	West Java	Djakarta	M.S. Mustafa
IV	Central Java	Semarang	Agan Soewarno
V	East Java, Kalimantan and the Moluccas	Surabaja	J.L.T. Wattimena
VI	Sulawesi	Makasar	F. Salomo
VII	West Irian	Djajapura	Drs. H. Ubed Bamahry

Because of the difference in the extent of the individual operations, there are slight differences in the organizations of the units. The basic format is the marketing manager being in charge of all operations, with operations being divided into Sales, Distribution, Technical, Financial, and Personnel branches. Operations are further divided into regions which are the responsibility of the regional managers. They report directly to the area marketing manager. The area managers report directly to the Board of Directors, and also maintain close functional relationships with *PDN*.

KANTOR PERWAKILAN LUAR NEGERI & KANTOR PERKAPALAN LUAR NEGERI
(Foreign Representative Office & Foreign Shipping Office)

The function of the foreign representatives is to handle all activities that might arise between Pertamina and other concerns in these regions. The function of the foreign shipping office is to plan tanker operations, maintain the tankers, and arrange for maritime facilities in the respective areas. At present, the foreign representatives in New York and Tokyo handle shipping as well, while in Hong Kong and Singapore shipping is under separate management. The managers of each respective office report directly to the Board of Directors.

OFFICE	ADDRESS	REPRESENTATIVE
New York	United Nations Plaza 866	Drs. Hasmoro R.
Tokyo	9th Floor Mori Bldg 18 No. 20 Nishikubo Akefune-cho Shiba Minato-ku Tokyo	Colonel R. Soedijono
Amsterdam	Carlton House Vijzelstraat 2-18	J. Karinda
Singapore .	Wisma Indonesia 3rd Floor Orchard Road	Colonel Abihasan Said

SHIPPING

Hong Kong	Room 1502-6 Union House	P.T. Ocean Petrol
Singapore		Tunas Ltd.

SUBSIDIARIES:

P.T. Pelita

P.T. Pelita is a wholly owned subsidiary that is in charge of aviation. It was established on January 24, 1970. It had grown out of the old Permina and later Pertamina aviation department. P.T. Pelita is a special company, for by the terms of its charter, it is only allowed to charge at cost and cannot return a profit. Furthermore, it can only provide service to oil companies, more specifically, the director general of Civil Aviation has approved service to only Pertamina personnel and dependents, contractors, and persons connected with oil.

Colonel Harijono is the president-director of P.T. Pelita, and Capt. Repon is in charge of operations. Pelita's fleet consists of thirty-three aircraft, which includes 19 helicopters, five DC 3's, six Fokker 27's, one new Jet Fokker F 28, one Aero Commander, and one Hawker Siddeley 125. Recently Pelita has expanded its operations by accepting contracts to provide aviation service to some of Pertamina's contractors.

P.T. Pertamina Tongkang

P.T. Pertamina Tongkang is a wholly owned subsidiary of Pertamina which was formed on September 9, 1969. Its function is to manage all of Pertamina's non-tanker shipping. Included are a number of dry cargo vessels, tugs, barges, and small craft. Many of these vessels are owned outright by Pertamina and others are obtained on charter. Tongkang is the general agent for all vessels chartered to Pertamina except tankers. Colonel P.T. Affan is head of P.T. Pertamina Tongkang, and Mr. A. Safarudin is in charge of operations.

Ocean Petrol Ltd.

Ocean Petrol is a wholly owned subsidiary of Pertamina and is in charge of scheduling, management, and maintenance of the vessels in the company's international tank ship fleet. The company was established on July 18, 1968 and has its head office in Hong Kong. In addition to carrying much of Pertamina's oil exports the company provides a valuable service in teaching Indonesians all aspects of the shipping business and ship operations. Ir. M.S. Hutasuut is managing director of Ocean Petrol.

P.T. Electronika Nusantara (Elnusa)

P.T. Elnusa is a wholly owned subsidiary of Pertamina which works in the field of telecommunications. It was established on January 25, 1968, with the idea that it would handle all maintenance, service, and installation of communications equipment for the shipping fleet. It later expanded by providing this service for other companies as well. In its beginning stages, it worked closely with Radio Holland. Recently, its activities have been expanded by being given the responsibility for handling the telecommunications requirements of the offshore contractors. Ir. Udaya Hadibroto is the general manager of P.T. Elnusa.

P.T. Patra Djasa

P.T. Patra Djasa is a wholly owned subsidiary which grew out of the former Shell owned Company, N.V. Puntjak. Presently, it is in charge of managing bungalows at the Puntjak mountain resort area near Djakarta, several houses and apartments in Djakarta which are rented to foreign contractors, and a fleet of automobiles which are also rented to the foreign contractors. P.T. Patra Djasa is in charge of the Pertamina Oil Centre Office building, and also is responsible for the management of Pertamina's two hotels in Djakarta. Mr. Ibrahim Martalogawa is the manager of P.T. Patra Djasa.

JOINT VENTURES:

Tugu Insurance

Tugu Insurance is a fifty-fifty joint venture between Pertamina and several private investors which handles a great deal of Pertamina's own insurance as well as that of its contractors. It is based in Hong Kong and was founded in 1965. It offers several different types of insurance, and its activities are not limited to Pertamina and its contractors. In fact, the majority of its insured ventures are in no way related to oil or to Pertamina. Dr. Ibnu represents Pertamina's interest on the Board of Directors, and Tugu is managed by non-Pertamina staff. Tugu was established to allow Pertamina to retain a percentage of its insurance premiums, yet not accept the risks of self-insurance.

P.T. Krakatau Steel

P.T. Krakatau Steel is a sixty-forty joint venture between Pertamina and the Ministry of Industry. It was established on October 22, 1969 at the request of the government. P.T. Krakatau Steel is in charge of completing the Tjilegon Steel Plant which was started by the Russians in the Sukarno era but has never been completed. After unsuccessfully attempting to attract foreign investors to come in and take over the development, the government decided to take over the operation itself, and thus P.T. Krakatau Steel was formed. Pertamina presently has a good deal of activity going in the west Java area and it is expected to become one of the major users of steel to be produced at Tjilegon.

P.T. Pertamina Gulf Industrial Processing

This is a fifty-fifty joint venture between Pertamina and Gulf Oil Company which was formed on October 25, 1969. P.T. Pertamina Gulf operates a fertilizer packaging plant at Tandjung Priok, packaging almost all of the fertilizer that Pertamina markets in the west Java area. The operation is under joint management. Ir. Sudarno and Drs. Sakidjan represent Pertamina as directors.

Far East Oil Trading Company Ltd.

Far East Oil is a fifty-fifty venture between Pertamina and Japanese companies including JPDC, Nosodeco, electric power companies, and oil refining companies. It specializes in the supply of Indonesian crude and heavy oil to the Japanese market. The company was established on May 15, 1965. At present, it has an authorized capital of 480 million yen. Besides trading all of the Indonesian government's crude sold in Japan, Far East also acts as a general trading company and is authorized to import and export and buy and sell oil and gas products, petrochemical products and machinery, and equipment and supplies necessary for the development of oil production. Far East is also a partner in the Kansai Minas Kosan Co., a company specializing in crude storage.

Presently Mr. S. Higashi is the president of Far East, while S. Sarwono serves as vice-president and N. Nakamura acts as managing director. Mr. P. Siregar, Soichi Matsune, Tirto Utomo, and Colonel R. Soedijono are directors of Far East.

KEMENTERIAN PERTAMBANGAN
(Ministry of Mines)

The Ministry of Mines is responsible for all mining activities within the Republic of Indonesia. The ministry is divided into three basic departments, the Directorate General of General Mining, the Secretary General, and the Directorate General for Oil and Gas (Migas). At present, the minister of mines, Prof. Ir. Sumantri Brodjonegoro concurrently serves as both director general of General Mining and director general of Migas. Ir. Kurnadi Kartaatmadja is the secretary general. The function of the secretary general is to coordinate the administration of the ministry as a whole. The Directorate General of General Mining is in charge of all mining activities other than oil and gas and is divided into three branches, the Geology Branch, the Mining Branch, and the State Enterprise Branch.

The Directorate General of Migas is also divided into three branches. The first of these is the Directorate of Migas, which is in charge of handling the technical aspects of Migas. Ir. Wijarso serves as director of the Directorate of Migas. The directorate is further divided into four sections. Exploration and Production, headed by Ir. E.E. Hantoro, is in charge of obtaining all government permits, making reports on drilling activities, and geological reports, as well as gathering other pertinent data. The Economy and Finance Section, headed by Mr. Nilwan Munir, is in charge of handling all external financial matters, and the registration of foreign companies working in the oil and gas sector. Mr. Oetojo Boenjamin is in charge of the Safety and Calibration Section. Ir. Sumbarjono is in charge of the Planning and Development Section, which coordinates general development and handles everything not covered in the other sections.

The second branch of Migas is the Secretariat of Migas. This branch is headed by Ir. Anondo, and is in charge of all internal administration, programming, and financial matters. The branch is divided into four sections, whose titles explain the nature of their activities. General Affairs is headed up by Mr. Adimir Adin, Personnel and Organization is the responsibility of Mr. Nurdin. The Legal Section is headed by Mr. Suharto, and Mr. Soejono is in charge of the Administrative Section.

The third branch of the Directorate General of Migas is Lemigas, the petroleum institute. This body is headed by Ir. Sjarif Lubis, and is in charge of technical research and development. It also runs the Academy of Oil and Gas at Tjepu.

APPENDIX C

PRODUCTION SHARING CONTRACTS
AS OF SEPTEMBER 1, 1972

COMPANY	DATE OF SIGNING	LOCATION
1. REFICAN	10-6-1961	Onshore north Sumatra
2. ASAMERA	1-11-1961	Onshore north Sumatra
3. IIAPCO	18-8-1966	Offshore N.W. Java
4. JAPEX	6-10-1966	Offshore Bunju/Majakam Area, Kalimantan
5. REFICAN	20-10-1966	Offshore southeast Kalimantan
6. KYUSHU	22-11-1966	Offshore south Kalimantan
7. AUSTRALIAN DRILLING COMPANY	1-4-1967	Off-/Onshore northeast Java, Madura
8. CONTINENTAL OIL	12-5-1967	Onshore Barito Basin S. Kalimantan
9. UNION OIL	26-1-1968	Off-/Onshore northwest Sumatra
10. INTERNATIONAL OILS	8-4-1968	Off-/Onshore Timor, Roti, Savu Island
11. PHILLIPS/SUPERIOR PETROLEUM CO.	28-5-1968	Off-/Onshore southwest West Irian
12. COMPAGNIE FRANCAISE DES PETROLES	6-7-1968	Off-/Onshore Djambi (Sumatra)
13. VIRGINIA INTL./ ROY HUFFINGTON	8-8-1968	Deep-drilling south Sumatra southeast Kalimantan
14. IIAPCO	6-9-1968	Offshore southeast Sumatra
15. AGIP	10-10-1968	Offshore Kepala Burung, West Irian
16. REDCO	15-10-1968	Onshore Sumatra, Java, Kalimantan

17. MOBIL OIL	16-10-1968	Offshore north Sumatra
18. CONTINENTAL OIL	16-10-1968	Offshore Block B, South China Sea
19. UNION OIL	25-10-1968	Off-/Onshore east Kalimantan
20. FRONTIER	1-11-1968	Offshore Block C, South China Sea
21. GULF	17-12-1968	Offshore Block D, South China Sea
22. AGIP	19-12-1968	Offshore Block A, South China Sea
23. SOUTH EAST ASIA OIL	14-6-1969	Offshore south Sulawesi
24. JENNEY MANUFACTURING COMPANY	8-8-1969	Offshore Mentawai
25. JENNEY MANUFACTURING COMPANY	8-8-1969	Offshore Karimata
26. ASIA OIL	9-8-1969	Offshore Lampung & Banten
27. DEARBORN COMPUTER & MAR. CORP.	9-8-1969	On-/Offshore Halmahera
28. GULF & WESTERN IND.	1-11-1969	On-/Offshore the Islands of Sula, Buru, Ambon & Ceram
29. SHELL	6-12-1969	Onshore east Kalimantan
30. TOTAL	9-12-1969	Onshore Tebo Area Sumatra
31. WENDELL PHILLIPS	4-2-1970	On-/Offshore north West Irian
32. CALASIATIC/TOPCO	9-2-1970	Offshore Antara Djawa & Sulawesi
33. BRITISH PETROLEUM	2-3-1970	Offshore Kalimantan Timur Laut
34. KONDUR PETROLEUM SA	5-8-1970	Offshore Riau
35. TREND EXPLORATION	15-10-1970	Onshore Kepala Burung, West Irian

36. WHITESTONE INDONESIA	24-10-1970	Onshore West Irian
37. GULF	24-10-1970	On-/Offshore west Sulawesi
38. SHELL	15-1-1971	Offshore Tjilatjap
39. CALTEX	9-8-1971	Onshore Sumatra Tengah
40. CALASIATIC/TOPCO	9-8-1971	Onshore Coastal Plains Sumatra Tengah
41. ATLANTIC RICHFIELD	9-8-1971	Onshore Sekitar Tarakan Kalimantan Timur
42. CONTINENTAL OIL	28-10-1971	Onshore West Irian (Mimika)
43. INDONESIA OFFSHORE OPERATORS, INC.	3-3-1972	Offshore south West Irian
44. TOTAL	27-7-1972	Onshore Mantulik and Panai areas

APPENDIX D

ORAL INTERVIEWS

NAME	POSITION
PERTAMINA & SUBSIDIARIES	
Abdi, John	Finance
Affan, Colonel	P.T. Pertamina—Tongkang
Ambardy, R. Colonel	Public Relations
Anondo, Ir.	Director–Finance and Administration
Anton, Setianto, Drs.	H-HPLN
Astoto, Ir.	Unit VII—Manager
Basri, M. Hasan, Major	Unit II
Broto	Retired
Burhan Danil, Colonel	Personnel
Cores de Vries, J.O.	Wonokromo
Darmo Wardojo	Unit I
Darpanto, R.M.	Unit V (Marketing)
Djohan, H.	Retired
Djoemardi Djoekardi	DKKA
Frederik, A.	E & P
Geudong, S.M., Colonel	Finance
Gooandi	Retired
Hanum Faini, S.H.	Personnel
Hardjanto, Lt. Colonel Dr.	Health Division
Harijono, Colonel	P.T. Pelita
Harsono, Ir.	DKKA
Hidajat, J.	Personnel
Husni, Lt. Colonel	Unit I—Manager
Hutabarat, K.D.	E & P
Hutapea, Ben, Drs.	Unit II

Ibnu Sutowo, Lt. General Dr.	President-Director
Mrs. Ibnu Sutowo	
Idrus Sjahrial, Ir.	Unit IV—Manager
Indraman Akman, Ir.	P & P
Ismet Akil, Drs.	E & P
Iwan Supardi, Brig. General	General Secretariat
Judo Sumbono, Colonel Drs.	PDN
Kariodimedjo, J.	Personnel
Karudin Nasution	Retired
Kastubi, Colonel	Purchasing
Korompis	Unit VII (Marketing)
Lahenda, H.C.	E & P
Latumahina	Wonokromo
Legiman	Retired
Lumempouw, M.J.	E & P
Machmoed	Retired
Mamesah, A.	Unit V—Manager
Marah Joenoes	Public Relations
Martalagowa, I.	P.T. Patra Djasa
Mursito, W.	E & P
Nizar, M.J.	Management Services Division
Panggabean	Retired
Pattiasina, J.M. Brig. General	Projects Division
Pulungan, Drs.	Finance
Pulunggono, A., Drs.	E & P
Rahim, A.	Retired
Rani Junus, Lt. Colonel	Telecommunications
Repon, Captain	P.T. Pelita
Rumboko	Unit III
Safarudin, A.	P.T. Pertamina—Tongkang
Sagiman, Sainan	Security
Sajid Sujud	Unit IV

Sakidjan, Drs.	Statistics & Information Division
Samandi	Retired
Sanger, E., Dr.	H-HPLN
Sapi-ie, Dick	DKKA
Siallagan, R.M.P.	Unit I
Singgih Darsono, Ir.	P & P
Sitomurang, B.S.	Unit I
Sjamsu Radjab	Projects Division
Soebardi, Ir.	E & P
Soedarno, Ir.	Director—P & P
Soedarsono	Retired
Soedijono, Colonel	Tokyo representative
Soediono, Ir.	E & P
Soehardi	Retired
Soehardiman, Brig. General	Director—PDN
Soekamto Sajidiman, Brig. General	DKKA
Soekotjo, R. Drs.	Director—Shipping
Soendoro, R.	DKKA
Soeparjadi, R.A., B.S.	E & P
Soepropto	Retired
Soetopo, Ir.	Unit II
Soetowireno, H.S.	E & P
Soewito Wardojo, Lt. Colonel	General Secretariat
Subagio, Ir.	Personnel
Subijanto	Unit IV
Suhardi, R.	Personnel
Suharto Sumantri	Unit I (Marketing)
Sumantri	Retired
Sutan Assin, Ir.	Unit III—Manager
Suwarto, Ir.	Wonokromo
Tabrani Ismael, Ir.	Unit IV

Tirto Utomo, S.H.	H-HPLN
Tobing	Retired
Tobing, B.T., Colonel	Unit II—Manager
Trisulo, Ir.	Director—E & P
Ubed Bamahry, Drs.	Unit VII (Marketing)
Udaja Hadibroto, Ir.	P.T. Elnusa
Urip	Retired
Usman	Wonokromo
Wattimena, J.L.T.	Unit V (Marketing)
Wetik, J.L.	Personnel
Widjaja	Wonokromo
Wimarto, Ir.	Unit III
Wishnu Hidajat, Ir.	DKKA
Zahar, Ir.	DKKA

PERTAMINA AFFILIATED COMPANIES

Higashi, S.	Far East Oil Trading Co., President
Nakamura, N.	Far East Oil Trading Co., Managing Director
Sarwono, S.	Far East Oil Trading Co., Vice-President
Siregar, P.	Far East Oil Trading Co., Director

OTHER INTERVIEWS

Adin	Former Secretary to Chairul Saleh
Bachtoel Chatab	P.T. Caltex Pacific Indonesia, Exploration Manager
Barker, Lawrence	Former President of IIAPCO
Basarudin Nasution	Former Head of Migas
Bratanata, Ir.	Former Minister of Mines
Danda Tasrip	P.T. Stanvac Indonesia, Director
Diah, B.M.	Chief Editor "Merdeka"
Englehart, C.E.	IIAPCO, Vice-President
Gozali	Secretary to the Government Board of Supervisors

Gillert, M.P.	P.T. Stanvac Indonesia, President & General Manager
Gohier, Joseph C.	Refican, Director
Hanafiah, L., S.H.	Former Advisor to Chairul Saleh
Hantoro, E.E., Ir.	Migas
Hutton, Harold	Refican, President
Hutton, Betty	
Kartamihardja, T.	P.T. Caltex Pacific Indonesia, Employee Development
Kawamoto, Minoru, Dr.	Kyushu Oil Development Co., Managing Director
Kishi, N.	Former Prime Minister of Japan
Koch, Herman	Geophysical Services International
Loh, Robin	Industrialist
Machmud, Roger, S.H.	ARCO, Manager-Administration
Magee, D.T.	P.T. Caltex Pacific Indonesia, Managing Director
Mamesa	Lemigas
Mohammad Isa, Dr.	Former Governor of South Sumatra
Nasution, A.H., General	Former Chief of Staff
Nishijima, S.	Managing Director of Nosodeco
Nugroho Notosusanto	Army Historian
Okada, I.	Toyo Menka Kaisha, Managing Director
Okubo, S.	Maruzen Oil, General Manager, International Operations Dept.
Omar Hassan Asaari, Ir.	Lemigas
Perkins, Charles	Union Oil, Advisor to the President
Roeslan Abdulgani	Former Cabinet member
Saleh Siregar	Former President-Director of Pertamin
Sajono, R.I.	P.T. Stanvac Indonesia, Public Affairs Manager
Soeriatmadja, A.	P.T. Caltex Pacific Indonesia, Manager-Administration

Soewarno	Lemigas
Sukartono	P.T. Caltex Pacific Indonesia, General Affairs
Sumantri Brodjonegoro, Prof. Dr. Ir.	Minister of Mines
Sumbarjono, Ir.	Migas
Tahija, Julius	P.T. Caltex Pacific Indonesia, Chairman of the Board of Management
Todd, Donald F.	Former Vice-President of IIAPCO
Wahjudi Wisaksono, Dr.	Lemigas
Walton, J.I.	Mobil Oil, Regional Vice-President
Whitehouse-Vaux, W.V.	Lawyer and Advisor
Wijarso, Ir.	Director of the Directorate of Migas

NOTE: This is a listing of formal interviews. We are also indebted to many others whom we visited with on our trips and visits throughout Indonesia. We are also indebted to several others who were formally interviewed but chose to have their names left off the list. They all contributed much to our overall understanding of the development of oil in Indonesia.

APPENDIX E

SELECTED BIOGRAPHIES

NAME	CURRENT POSITION
Abdi, John	Treasurer
Agan Soewarno	Head of 4th Marketing Area
R. Ambardy	Deputy Head of Public Relations
Anondo, Ir.	Director of Finance & Administration
Astoto, Ir.	General Manager of Unit VII
Hadji Achmad Thahir	General Assistant to President Director
Harsono Hadipoetro, Ir.	Deputy Head of Division of Coordination of Foreign Contractors
Umar Husni, Lt. Colonel	General Manager of Unit I
Ibnu Sutowo, Lt. General Dr., H.	President-Director
Idrus Sjahrial, Ir.	General Manager of Unit IV
Iwan Soepardi, Brig. General	Head of General Secretariat
A.H. Kastubi, Colonel	Head of Purchasing Division
Mamesah, A.	General Manager of Unit V
Marah Joenoes	Head of Public Relations
H.T. Martono	Head of 2nd Marketing Area
M.S. Mustafa	Head of 3rd Marketing Area
Nizar, M.J., Drs.	Head of Management Services Division/Special Assistant to President-Director
Pattiasina, J.M. Brig. General	Head of Projects Division/Acting Manager of Unit VI
A. Rani Junus, Lt. Colonel	Head of Telecommunication Division
Sainan Sagiman, Colonel	Head of Security Division
Sakidjan, Drs.	Head of Central Statistics and Information Division
F. Salomo	Head of 6th Marketing Area
Sanger, E., Dr.	Head of Legal, Foreign Relations and Foreign Marketing Division

H. Sjarnoebi Said, Lt. Colonel	Head of Maintenance Division
Soedarno, M., Lt. Colonel, Ir.	Director of Refining and Petrochemicals
Soediono, Ir.	Deputy Director of Exploration and Production
Soehardiman, Brig. General	Director of Directorate of Domestic Supply
Soekamto Sajidiman, Brig. General	Head of Division of Coordination of Foreign Contractors
Soekotjo, Colonel, Drs.	Director of Shipping
R.M. Soetidjo, Lt. Colonel, Dr., H.	Head of Health Division
R. Suhardi Prawironoto	Head of Personnel and Organization Division
R. Suharto Sumantri	Head of 1st Marketing Area
Sumarmo, Drs.	Head of Economic and Development Division
Judo Sumbono, Colonel, Drs.	Deputy Director of Directorate of Domestic Supply
Sutan Assin, Ir.	General Manager of Unit III
Tirto Utomo, S.H.	Deputy Head of Legal, Foreign Relations and Foreign Marketing Division
Tobing, B.T., Colonel	General Manager of Unit II
Trisulo Djokopurnomo, Ir.	Director of Exploration and Production
H. Ubed Bamahry, Drs.	Head of 7th Marketing Area
J.L.T. Wattimena	Head of 5th Marketing Area

ABDI, JOHN; Treasurer; b. October 30, 1926, Samarinda; BBA Akademi Perniagaan Indonesia; 1942–1959 banking; September 14, 1959 Permindo financial department, Pertamin financial department 1961–1968, 1968—Present position.

HADJI ACHMAD THAHIR; General Assistant to President-Director; b. November 12, 1912, Palembang, Sumatra; Middle Commercial School (Palembang); 1945—Quartermaster Major of the Sumatran Command in Palembang; 1949—Colonel, Head of Financial Staff of the Sumatran Command in Bukittinggi, Central Sumatra; 1968—Present position.

AGAN SOEWARNO; Head of 4th Marketing Area (Semarang); b. February 28, 1922, Medan, Sumatra; Technical High School, 1945–1948— PTMN (Jogjakarta); 1950—P.T. Shell, Engineering Assistant Instructor, Surabaja; 1964—P.T. Shell, Head of Tandjung Priok Installation, Djakarta; 1966—P.N. Pertamin, Head of Distribution, Surabaja Commercial Area; 1968—Present position.

R. AMBARDY; Deputy Head of Public Relations; b. June 5, 1925, Modjokerto, Java; 1943—SMT-Technical High School; 1950—Lieutenant Republic of Indonesia Navy; 1956—Naval Officer's School, Surabaja, Java; 1961—U.S. Army/Navy Information Course for Officers, special warfare school, U.S.A.; 1968—Supervisor, Technical and administration P.N. Dok; 1970—Board of Directors, P.T. Tongkang; 1971—Present position.

ANONDO, IR.; Director of Administration and Finance; b. June 23, 1912, Salatiga, Java; 1938—Engineering Degree, Bandung; 1959—B.A. in Economics, University of Indonesia; 1965—National Defense Institution, Djakarta; 1968—Management Courses, Canberra; Secretary General VI/F of the Trade/Industrial Department, Jogjakarta; Directorate of Mining; Ministry of Basic Industry/Mining; Ministry of Mining & Migas; 1966— Director P.N. Permina; 1968—Present position.

ASTOTO, IR.; General Manager of Unit VII; b. September 7, 1926, Semarang, Java; 1957—Faculty of Technology, University of Indonesia/ Bandung; 1959—P.T. Permina; 1967—Home Staff Employee at P.N. Permina's agency in Tokyo; May, 1970—Legal/Foreign Marketing Division; August—Present Position.

HARSONO HADIPOETRO, IR.; Deputy Head of DKKA; b. January 16, 1932, Pemalang, Java; 1957—Engineering Degree, Institute of Technology at Bandung; 1957—Head of Agraria Section, the Tandjung Enim (South Sumatra) coal mines; 1961—Head of Nosodeco-Permina Project, North Sumatra; 1963—Head of Petroleum Exploitation and Financial and Economic Section of Migas; 1966—General Manager Unit IV; 1968— Present position.

HUSNI, UMAR, LT. COLONEL, H.; General Manager Unit I; b. July 9, 1929, Java; HBS (Dutch Senior High School); SMA (Indonesian Senior High School); Country Central College, U.S.A.; 1945—Indonesian National Army (TNI); 1958—P.T. Permina, Head of Material Section, Pangkalan Brandan, Sumatra; 1964—Manager Exploitation Area; 1966—Present position.

IBNU SUTOWO, LT. GENERAL, DR., H.; President-Director; b. September 23, 1914, Grobogan Semarang, Java; NIAS (Medical School) 1940; Doctor of the Belitung colony; Indonesian National Army (TNI); Deputy II of the Chief of the Army; 1957—President Director of P.T. Permina; 1961—Chairman of the BPU Minjak dan Gas Bumi, President Director of P.N. Permina; 1965—Minister of State; 1966—Minister of Mining, Director General of Migas; 1968—President Director Pertamina.

IDRUS SJAHRIAL, IR.; General Manager of Unit IV; b. January 24, 1924, Lolo; Institute of Technology at Bandung, 1959; 1945—Joined irregular forces during revolution; 1966—P.N. Permina, Manager of Rantau fields; 1968—Deputy General Manager of Unit II; 1970—Present position.

IWAN SOEPARDI, BRIG. GENERAL; Head of General Secretariat; b. July 7, 1917, Gombong, Java; 1945—Indonesian National Army (TNI); 1953—Army Staff College Bandung; Business and Industrial Top Management Courses; 1960—Appointed Deputy Governor, West Kalimantan; 1967—Secretary to Bureau of Directors (Permina) and Head of the Secretariat.

A.H. KASTUBI, COLONEL: Head of Purchasing Division; b. December 20, 1919, Bandung, Java; B.A. Sociology, University of Indonesia; Finance School 1959–1960 (Fort Benjamin Harrison, Indianapolis, Indiana, U.S.A.); 1935—Higher Indies School teacher, Djakarta, Java; 1945—Indonesian National Army (TNI); 1966—Financial Director of P.T. Oceanic Ship Company (PT/PP) Berdikari; 1968—Present position.

MAMESAH, A.; General Manager of Unit V; b. February 29, 1916, Menado, Sulawesi; Dutch Junior High School, Shell Surveying Course, Balikpapan; 1935—Assigned to N.V. NNGPM-Sorong; 1938—Surveyor for Development of Sele, Klamono, Wasian and Mogoi; 1950—Managing Employee for Topographic Works, West Irian; 1959—P.T. Permindo, Head of Topography/Roadbuilding Djambi (loan from Shell); 1966—P.N. Permina.

MARAH JOENOES; Head of Public Relations; b. November 1, 1925, Padang, Sumatra; Indonesian Senior High School, Economic Section (SMA-C); 1945—Indonesia National Army (TNI); 1958—General Manager of Binuang Shipping Co.; 1964—P.N. Permina, Acting Head of Industrial Relations; 1967—Deputy Head of Public Relations; 1969—Present position.

H.T. MARTONO; Head of 2nd Marketing Area (Palembang); b. February 10, 1929, Kebumen; Upper Indonesian High School (SMA); 1953—Caltex Oil Co. (Pekanbaru); 1955-P.T. Stanvac (Surabaja); 1964-P.N. Pertamin (Surabaja); 1971—Present position.

M.S. MUSTAFA; Head of 3rd Marketing Area (Djakarta); b. February 7, 1932, Tandjung Morawa, Sumatra; Upper Indonesian High School (SMA); 1959—P.T. Shell, Sales Inspector, Medan; 1964—P.N. Pertamin, Head of Sales, 1st Commercial Area, Medan; 1968—P.N. Pertamina, Head of Sales, 2nd Marketing Area, Palembang; 1971—Present position.

NIZAR, M.J., DRS.; Head of Management Services Division/Special Assistant to President-Director; b. November 25, 1924, Mageland, Java; B.A. Economics, University of Indonesia, 1957; August, 1967—Assigned to Tugu Insurance Co. Ltd., Hong Kong; November, 1970—Special Assistant to President-Director in Admin. and Financial Affairs; 1972—Present position.

PATTIASINA, J.M. BRIG. GENERAL; Head of Projects Division/Acting Manager of Unit VI; b. September 12, 1912, Makasar, South Sulawesi Technical School for 3 years, 1930; Shell Technical Assistant at Pladju; Permiri; 1958—Managing Director of P.T. Permina; 1961—Exploration and Technical Director of P.N. Permina; 1965—Director of P.N. Permina and Manager of Irian Barat operation; 1968—Present position.

A. RANI JUNUS, LT. COLONEL; Head of the Telecommunication Division; b. August 8, 1925, Medan, Sumatra; 1939–1942—vocational school (communications); December 1959–June 1960—Courses at Siemens Schuckert, Germany; 1943—Member of the Indonesian Army (TNI); 1953—Netherlands Mission; 1956—Air Liaison Office; 1957—P.T. Permina; 1963—Head of Telecommunications Section, P.N. Permina; 1965— Appointed Deputy Manager of P.N. Permina Pangkalan Brandan, North Sumatra; 1968—Present position.

SAINAN SAGIMAN, COLONEL; Head of Security Division; b. February 22, 1922, Palembang, Sumatra; Indonesian Senior High School (SMA); Faculty of Business Economics; ZPDI, Course B, Ecole Superieure de Guerre, Paris; 1946—Indonesian National Army (TNI); 1972—Present position.

SAKIDJAN ATMOSUDIGO, DRS.; Head of Central Statistics and Information Division; b. March 30, 1926, Jogjakarta; B.A. Gadjah Mada U. University of Indonesia—Faculty of Economy; International Marketing Institute, Harvard, Cambridge (1970); World Bank Course in Economic Development Institute 1957–1958; 1950—State Planning Bureau; 1951— World Bank Economic Development; 1962—OPEC Secretariat; 1965—P.N. Permina Staff; 1970—Present position.

F. SALOMO; Head of 6th Marketing Area (Udjung Pandang); b. August 5, 1932, Tjimahi; Technical High School; 1959—P.T. Shell, 2nd Engineering Supervisor, Medan Branch; 1961—P.T. Shell, District Superintendant, Panang Branch; 1969—P.N. Pertamina, Head of 7th Marketing Area, Djajapura; 1971—Present position.

SANGER, E., DR.: Head of H-HPLN (Legal and Foreign Marketing Division); b. January 14, 1927, Gorontalo, Sulawesi; Faculty of Law and Social Sciences, University of Indonesia; Faculty of Legal Sciences at University of Bonn, Germany; 1966—Appointed as Director of P.N. Permina; 1967, February—Head of DKKA; October, 1968—Appointed Secretary General of OPEC; 1970—Present position.

SJARNOEBI SAID, LT. COLONEL, H.: Head of the Maintenance Division; b. January 18, 1927, Subang Djerigi/Palembang, Sumatra; Senior High School, Economic Department (SMA-C), 1957; Faculty of Law, University of Indonesia, 1959; Indonesian National Army (TNI); 1967— Assistant to President-Director of P.N. Permina; 1968—Head of Technical/ Transportation Division; 1969—Present position.

SOEDARNO, M., LT. COLONEL, IR.; Director of Petrochemicals and Processing; b. February 11, 1926, Purbolinggo, Java; Institute of Technology at Bandung; 1959—Kantor Minjak; 1960—Assistant to President-Director P.N. Permina for petrochemical and processing affairs; 1968—Deputy Director of Exploration and Production in charge of Petrochemicals and Processing; 1972—Present position.

SOEDIONO, IR.; Deputy Director of Exploration and Production; b. April 8, 1932, Pati, Java; Technical Institute at Bandung; Tulsa University, Oklahoma, U.S.A. 1959–1961; Institut de Petrol, Paris, France, October-December 1962; 1958—Economic and Financial Bureau of State Planning Bureau, Assigned to P.T. Permina; 1961—Acting head of E & P sector; 1965—Deputy Director E & P, P.N. Permina.

SOEHARDIMAN, BRIG. GENERAL; Director of PDN; b. March 19, 1922, Surabaja, Java; Aviation Academy of Indonesia 1954–1956; United States Transportation Officer Course, Virginia, USA; Application Infantry, Fort Benning, U.S.A.; SESKOAD (Army's General Staff and Command School); Ministry of Production; Ministry of Distribution; Supreme Command's Economic Operations section; 1961—President-Director P.N. Tulus Bhakti; 1965—Consul General, Amsterdam, Netherlands; 1965—Consul General, New York, U.S.A.; 1969—Assistant to President-Director P.N. Pertamina; 1970—Present position.

SOEKAMTO SAJIDIMAN, BRIG. GENERAL; Head of the DKKA; b. March 8, 1927, Surabaja, Java; Academy of Military Law; Faculty of Law, University of Indonesia; Faculty of Economics, University of Indonesia; Indonesian National Army (TNI); Military Judge; President-Director of P.N. Juda Bhakti; Director General of Sports; Consul General of Indonesia in Seoul, Korea; 1971, January—Advisor to the President-Director P.N. Pertamina; June—Present position.

SOEKOTJO, COLONEL, DRS.; Director of Shipping; b. July 27, 1927, Surabaja, Java; Economics Degree, University of Indonesia; TNI; 1963—Director of P.N. Permigan for Administration; 1964—Director of P.N. Pertamin; 1966—Representative P.N. Pertamina Tokyo, Japan; 1971—Chief of Shipping Division; 1972—Present position.

R.M. SOETIDJO, LT. COLONEL, DR., H.; Head of Health Division; b. February 12, 1912; NIAS (Medical School), 1938; 1942—Regency Doctor of the Japanese Occupation; 1946—Indonesian National Army (TNI); 1966—P.N. Permina, Head of Health Section; 1967—Appointed Head of Director General Migas Health Service in addition to prior function.

R. SUHARDI PRAWIRONOTO; Head of Personnel and Organization Division; b. March 9, 1926, Ponorogo, Java; High School, Madiun, Java; Military Intelligence School, Sarangan, 1945–1946; Top Management Seminar, Lembaga Management Indonesia; Ministry of Defense; Army Headquarters; 1958—NIAM; 1959—P.T. Permindo; 1961—P.N. Pertamina; 1965—Caretaker Director of P.N. Permigan; 1966—Present position.

R. SUHARTO SUMANTRI; Head of 1st Marketing Area (Medan); b. October 21, 1929, Surabaja, Java; Indonesian Upper High School (SMA/B); 1964—P.T. Shell; 1966—Central Java Marketing Manager; 1966—P.N. Pertamin, Head Representative in Surabaja; 1968—Head of Lubes and Grease Bureau, Domestic Supply Office, Djakarta; 1970—Present position.

SUMARMO, DRS.; Head of Economic and Development Division; b. May 13, 1921, Klaten; Degree in Economics; 1954—NIAM; 1959—P.T. Permina; 1961—Assistant to the President-Director of P.N. Permina; 1963—Coordinator for Nosodeco-Permina agreement while continuing prior function; 1966—Commercial advisor to President-Director and Manager of Unit II (interim); 1968—Head of Commercial Division; 1969—Present position.

JOEDO SUMBONO, COLONEL, DRS.; Deputy Director of PDN; b. August 17, 1929, Pare-pare; Navigation Academy (AIP); Degree Social Politics, Djajabaja University; Republic of Indonesia's Student Army (TRIP); Indonesian National Army (TNI); State Shipping Line PELNI; Armed Forces Staff; 1964—P.N. Permina; 1967—Technical Director of P.N. Pertamin; 1968—Deputy Director of PDN.
SUTAN ASSIN, IR.; General Manager of Unit III; b. February 4, 1930, Madiun, Java; Degree in Mining Engineering, Delft, Netherlands, 1957; 1958—P.T. Shell, Exploitation Engineer, Pladju; 1963—Director of P.N. Permigan; 1966—Present position.

TIRTO UTOMO, S.H.; Deputy Head of H-HPLN; b. March 8, 1930, Wonosobo, Java; Faculty of Law & Social Sciences, University of Indonesia, 1961; 1952—Editorial staff *Java Post*, Surabaja; 1955—Editor *Pantjawarta/Pantjawarna*; 1962—P.N. Permina; 1968—Advisor to the Head of DKKA; 1969—Present position.

TOBING, B.T., COLONEL; General Manager of Unit II; b. May 4, 1926, Medan, Sumatra; 1942–1945—Gizitsu Heiho Oil School, Pladju, Sumatra; 1960—International Development/Business Administration (Syracuse Unisity, N.Y., USA); 1945—Indonesian National Army (TNI); 1966—P.N. Permina, Acting General Manager of Unit II; 1967—Present position.

TRISULO DJOKOPURNOMO, IR.; Director of Exploration and Production; b. April 15, 1932, Bandung, Java; Technical Institute at Bandung (1956); 1957—Petroleum Engineer with Stanvac; 1960—P.T. Permindo Djambi; 1960—P.N. Pertamin, Chief of Exploitation Department; 1965—Member of Indonesia's delegation to OPEC; 1966—Ministry of Mines; 1968—Present position.

H. UBED BAMAHRY, DRS.; Head of 7th Marketing Area (Djajapura); b. April 1, 1932, Ambon; Graduated August 17 University, Djakarta; B.A. Dartmouth College, USA; 1961–1965—P.T. Stanvac, General Salesman in Surabaja and Djakarta; 1966—P.N. Pertamin, Sales Supervisor,

West Java; 1966–1968—P.N. Pertamin, Sales Supervisor in Medan; 1968–1971—P.N. Pertamina, Head of 6th Marketing Area (Udjung Pandang); 1971—Present position.

J.L.T. WATTIMENA; Head of 5th Marketing Area (Surabaja); b. September 6, 1932, Djakarta; Dutch Senior High School (H.B.S.); 1952— Sales Inspector, Medan; 1954—P.T. Shell/Netherlands; 1961—P.T. Shell, Sales/Division Director, Domestic Supply, Djakarta office; 1969—Head of Aviation Supply, Domestic Supply, Djakarta office; 1970—Present position.

GLOSSARY

Adat law—the customary law of the rural villages.

AKAMIGAS—Akademi Minjak dan Gas Bumi—Oil and Gas Academy.

Angkatan '45—The "Generation of '45".

Bahasa Indonesia—(lit. "Indonesian Language")—the national language of Indonesia.

bangsa Indonesia—"Indonesian race".

BAPPENAS—Badan Perantjanaan Pembangangunan Nasional—national Development Planning Council, post—1965.

Batavia—the name given to the first permanent trading post of the United East Indies Company, later the adminstrative capital of the Netherlands East Indies; now Djakarta.

Bhinneka Tunggal Ika—"Unity in Diversity" (the National Motto of Indonesia—from Sanskrit).

BPM—De Bataafsche Petroleum Maatschappij—Shell's production company in the N.E.I.

BPU—Badan Pimpinan Umum—General Management Board.

Budi Utomo—Highest Endeavor—early Indonesian cultural Javanese group formed May 20, 1908, now celebrated as National Awakening Day.

Depernas—Dewan Perantjang Nasional—National Planning Council during Guided Democracy.

Dewan Perusahaan—Council of labor leaders installed in all Indonesian state enterprises 1964–65.

DI—Darul Islam—State of Islam—an Islamic extremist movement opposing the separation of State and Religion.

DKKA—Divisi Koordinator Kontractor Asing—Division for coordination with foreign contractors.

DPR—Dewan Perwakilan Rakjat—Parliament (literally, "Council of the People's Representation").

Drs.—Doctorandus—denotes university degree in liberal arts or sciences.

Dwi-Funksi—the "Dual Role" of the Indonesian National Army in society, embracing both civic and military undertakings—formulated by General Nasution.

Dwi-Tunggal—the Diumverate of Sukarno and Hatta, 1945–1956.

FDR/PKI—Front Demokrasi Rakjat/Partai Komunis Indonesia—a leftist coalition between the Indonesian Communist Party and the People's Democratic Front, culminated in the Madiun Affair of 1948.

GESTAPU—Gerakan September Tigapuluh—September 30th Movement (1965).

Gotong-rojong—"mutual help", "cooperation".

H.—Hadji—a Muslim who has made the pilgrimage to Mecca.

IIAPCO—Independent Indonesian American Petroleum Company.

Indonesia Raya—"Greater Indonesia", the Indonesian National Anthem.

Ir.—Insinjur—"Engineer".

ISDV—Indies Social Democratic Association, a Marxist organization founded in 1914 which became the basis for the *PKI*.

KAMI—Kesatuan Aksi Mahasiswa Indonesia—Indonesian (University) Students Action Front.

KAPPI—Kesatuan Aksi Pemuda Peladjar Indonesia—Indonesian (High School) Student Youth Action Front.

KNIL—Royal Netherlands Indies Army.

KODAM—Regional Military Command.

KODIM—District Military Command.

Konfrontasi—"Confrontation" (usually refers to the 1963–66 "Crush-Malaysia" campaign).

KOSTRAD—Komando Strategik Ankatan Darat—Army Strategic Command.

ladang —(literally, "dry field") the "slash-and-turn" technique of rice farming.

Lasjkar minjak—groups of oil workers who became "oil freedom fighters" during the Indonesian revolution.

Lemigas—Lembaga Minjak dan Gas Bumi—Oil and Gas Institute, under the jurisdiction of the Ministry of Mines.

Manipol—Political Manifesto of Sukarno's 1959 Independence Day speech.

Masjumi—Madjelis Sjuro Muslimen—The major Islamic party during Parliamentary Democracy; dissolved 1960.

Merdeka—literally "Free", freedom, independence.

Migas—Direktorate Minjak Dan Gas Bumi—Oil and Gas Directorate.

MPR(S)—Madjelis Permusjawaratan Rakjat (Sementara)—(literally, "Assembly of Popular Consultation")—People's Consultative Assembly (Provisional).

NASAKOM—Nasionalisme, Agama, Komunisme—Nationalism, Religion, Communism—Sukarno's concept of the three major ideas in Indonesian Society.

NEFO/OLDEFO—New Emerging Forces/Old Established Forces.

N.E.I.—Netherlands East Indies.

NIAM—Nederlandsche Indische Aardolie Maatschappij—Netherlands Indies Oil Company (fifty-fifty joint venture between the N.E.I. and Shell), 1921–1958.

N.I.A.S.—Netherlands Indies Medical School at Surabaya.

NKPM—Nederlandsche Koloniale Petroleum Maatschappij—Netherlands Colonial Petroleum Company. Standard of New Jersey's Netherlands incorporated subsidiary operating in the Dutch East Indies, 1912–1947. Jointly owned with Mobil after 1933.

NNGPM—Nederlandsche Nieuw Guinea Petroleum Maatschappij—Netherlands New Guinea Petroleum Company—three company joint venture (Caltex, Stanvac, Shell), formed in 1935.

Nosodeco—North Sumatra Oil Development Company, Ltd.

NPPM—Nederlandsche Pacific Petroleum Maatschappij—Netherlands Pacific Petroleum Company—Standard of California's Netherlands incorporated subsidiary operating in the Dutch East Indies, 1930–1951.

NU—Nahdatul Ulama—Muslim Scholars Party.

OPEC—Organization of Petroleum Exporting Companies.

Pangeran—prince (Javanese).

Panglima—Military territorial commander.

Pantjasila—(literally "the Five-fold Way"—from Sanskrit) the State ideology; formulated by Sukarno in 1945, consisting of:
(1) Belief in God
(2) Nationalism
(3) Humanitarianism
(4) Social Justice
(5) Representative government

Pemuda—Youth.

Perbum—Persatuan Buruh Minjak—Oil Workers' Union (now banned)

Permigan—Pertambangan Minjak dan Gas Nasional—National Oil and Gas Mining. Established as state company (P.N.) on June 5, 1961. Dissolved on March 9, 1966.

Permina—Perusahaan Minjak Nasional—National Oil Company; Pertambangan Minjak Nasional—National Oil Mining. Established as a government-owned P.T. (private company) December 10, 1957. Reorganized as a state company (P.N.) on June 5, 1961. Merged with P.N. Pertamin to form P.N. Pertamina by decree promulgated August, 1968.

Permindo—Perusahaan Minjak Indonesia—Indonesian Oil Company (replaced NIAM in 1959). 1959–1960. Replaced by P.N. Pertamin.

Permiri—Perusahaan Minjak Republik Indonesia—Republic of Indonesia Oil Company—revolutionary company in south Sumatra.

Pertamin—Pertambangan Minjak Indonesia—Indonesian Oil Mining. Established as a state company (P.N.) on February 13, 1961. Merged with P.N. Permina to form P.N. Pertamina by decree promulated August 20, 1968.

Pertamina—Pertambangan Minjak dan Gas Bumi Nasional—National Oil and Natural Gas Mining. P.N. Pertamina was formed from a merger of P.N. Permina and P.N. Pertamin by decree promulated August 20, 1968.

As a result of Law No. 8, effective January 1, 1972, P.N. Pertamina became Pertamina.

PETA—Sukarela Tentara Pembela Tanah Air—Volunteer Army of the Defenders of the Fatherland; sponsored by the Japanese in 1943.

PKI—Partai Komunis Indonesia—Indonesian Communist Party.

P.N.—Perusahaan Negara—State Company, State Enterprise.

PNI—Partai Nasional Indonesia—Indonesian Nationalist Party.

PRRI—Pemerintah Revolusioner Republik Indonesia—The Revolutionary Government of the Republic of Indonesia. 1958–61.

PSI—Partai Socialis Indonesia—Indonesian Socialist Party. Dissolved 1960.

P.T.—Perseroan Terbatas—Ltd., Inc.

P.T. ETMSU—P.T. Exploitasi Tambang Minjak Sumatera Utara—North Sumatra Oil Exploitation Mining, Ltd. The name under which P.T. Permina was established in 1957.

PTMN—Perusahaan Tambang Minjak Nasional—National Oil Mining Company.

PTMRI—Perusahaan Tambang Minjak Republik Indonesia—the Republic of Indonesia Oil Mining Company. 1951–1957.

R.I.S.—Republik Indonesia Sarekat—the Federal Republic of Indonesia 1950.

sawah—(literally "wet rice field") irrigated rice cultivation.

SBM—Sarikat Buruh Minjak—Union of Oil Workers—an oil workers' labor union during the revolution and the early fifties.

S.H.—Sardjana Hukum—the Degree of Law in Indonesia.

SOBSI—Sentral Organisasi Seluruh Indonesia—All Indonesia Federation of Labor Organizations (now banned).

sukus—ethnic classes or groupings.

SVPM—Standard Vacuum Petroleum Maatschappij (title changed from NKPM)—Standard Vacuum Petroleum Company.

TMKL—Tambang Minjak Kabupaten Langkat—The Langkat Area Oil Mining. 1951–1954. Replaced by TMSU in 1954.

TMNca.—Tambang Minjak Nglobo ca.—Nglobo Oil Mines—Replaced PTMRI in 1957. Reorganized as P.N. Permigan in 1961.

TMSU—Tambang Minjak Sumatera Utara—North Sumatra Oil Mining. 1954–1957. Replaced by P.T. Permina.

TNI—Tentera Nasional Indonesia—Indonesian National Army.

USDEK—(1) *U*ndang-Undang Dasar '45—Constitution of 1945; (2) *S*ocialism a la Indonesia; (3) *D*emokrasi Terpimpin—Guided Democracy; (4) *E*konomi Terpimpin—Guided Economy; (5) *K*epribadian Indonesia—Indonesian Indentity.
Volksraad—People's Council, set up the N.E.I. Government in 1917.

BIBLIOGRAPHY

BOOKS

Adams, Cindy. *Sukarno, An Autobiography.* Bobbs-Merill, New York, 1965.

Benda, Irikura, & Kishi. *Japanese Military Administration in Indonesia: Selected Documents.* Southeast Asian Studies, Yale University, 1965.

Brackman, Arnold C. *Indonesian Communism.* Praeger, New York, 1963.

_____*The Communist Collapse in Indonesia.* Donald Moore for Asia Pacific Press, Singapore, 1969.

Coast, John. *Adventure and Politics in Indonesia, Recruit to Revolution.* Christophers, London, 1952.

Feith, Herbert; Castles, Lance, eds. *Indonesian Political Thinking 1945–1965.* Cornell University Press, Ithaca, New York, 1970.

Feith, Herbert. *The Decline of Constitutional Democracy in Indonesia.* (Published under the auspices of the Cornell Modern Indonesia Project) Ithaca, New York, 1962.

Fifield, Russell Hunt. *Southeast Asia in United States Policy.* (council on Foreign Relations) Praeger, New York, 1963.

Fischer, Louis. *The Story of Indonesia.* Harper & Brothers, New York, 1959.

Frankel, P.H. *Mattei, Oil & Power Politics.* Faber & Faber, London, 1966.

Geertz, Clifford. *Religions of Java.* Free Press of Glencoe, Illinois, 1960.

Geertz, Hildred. *Indonesian Cultures and Communities.* HRAF Press, New Haven, 1963.

Gerretson, Dr. F.C. *History of Royal Dutch, Vol. I-IV.* E.J. Brill, Leiden, 1958.

Golay, Anspach, et. al. *Underdevelopment and Economic Nationalism in Southeast Asia.* Cornell University Press, Ithaca, 1969.

Gould, James. *Americans in Sumatra.* Martinus Nijhoff, Hague, 1961.

Grant, Bruce. *Indonesia.* Melbourne University Press, Carlton, 1964.

Hanna, Willard. *Bung Karno's Indonesia.* American Universities Field Staff, New York, 1961. (revised edition)

_____*Eight Nation Makers—Southeast Asia's Charismatic Leaders.* St. Martin's Press, New York City, 1964.

Hartshorn, J.E. *Oil Companies and Governments.* Faber & Faber, London, 1962.

Higgins, Benjamin. *A Case Study of Stanvac in Indonesia.* National Planning Association, New York, 1957.

_____*Indonesia: The Crisis of the Millstones.* D. Van Nostrand Co., Princeton, New Jersey, 1963.

Issawi & Yeganeh. *The Economics of Middle Eastern Oil.* Praeger, New York, 1962.

Jones, Howard Palfrey. *Indonesia: The Possible Dream.* Harcourt, Brace, Jovanovich. New York, 1971.

Kahin, G. M., ed. *Major Governments of Asia.* (section on Indonesia) Cornell University Press, Ithaca, New York, 1958.

_____ *Nationalism and Revolution in Indonesia.* Cornell University Press, Ithaca, New York, 1952.

K'tut Tantri. *Revolt in Paradise.* Harper & Row, New York, 1960.

Legge, J.D. *Indonesia.* Prentice Hall, Englewood Cliffs, New Jersey, 1964.

Longhurst, Henry. *Adventure in Oil, the Story of British Petroleum.* Sidgwick and Jackson, London, 1959.

Lutfi, Ashraf. *OPEC Oil.* The Middle East Research & Publishing Center. Beirut, 1958.

Martinez, Anibal. R. *Our Gift, Our Oil.* Vienna, 1966.

Mossman, James. *Rebels in Paradise.* Jonathan Cape, London, 1961.

Multatuli, Eduard Dowes Dekker. *Max Havelaar or the Coffee Auctions of the Dutch Trading Companies.* trans. Baron Nahuys. Edmunston & Douglas, Edinburgh, 1968.

Nasution, A.H. *Fundamentals of Guerrilla Warfare.* Seruling Masa Djakarta, 1970.

Odell, Peter R. *Oil and World Power.* Penguin Books, Ltd., London, 1970.

Palmier, Leslie. *Indonesia.* Thames and Hudson, London, 1965.

Polomka, Peter. *Indonesia Since Sukarno.* Penguin Books, Middlesex, 1971.

Porter, Stanley P. *Petroleum Accounting Practices.* McGraw-Hill, New York, 1965.

Rastin & Benda. *A History of Modern Southeast Asia.* Prentice-Hall, Inc. 1968.

Robertson, J.B., Spruyt, J. *A History of Indonesia.* Macmillan, Melbourne, 1967.

Roeder, O.G. *The Smiling General.* Gunung Agung, Djakarta, 1970.

_____*Who's Who in Indonesia.* Gunung Agung, Djakarta, 1971.

Shaplen, Robert. *Time out of Hand—Revolution and Reaction in Southeast Asia* (section on Indonesia) Harper Row, New York, 1969.

Sjahrir, Sutan. *Our Struggle*, trans. Benedict R. O'G. Anderson. Modern Indonesia Project, Ithaca, N.Y., 1968.

Steinburg, David Joel, ed. *In Search of Southeast Asia.* (sections on Indonesia by John Smail) Praeger, New York, 1971.

Sudjarwo, ed. *Illustrations from the Revolution 1945–1950, From Unitary State to Unitary State.* Department of Information, Djakarta, 1954.

Sutter, John O. *Indonesianizasi Politics in a Changing Economy 1940–55.* Ithaca, 1959.

Tarling, Nicholas. *A Concise History of Southeast Asia.* Donald Moore Press, Singapore, 1967.

Tugendhat, Christopher. *Oil, the Biggest Business.* Eyre & Spottiswoode, London, 1968.

van der Kroef, J.M. *Indonesia Since Sukarno.* Donald Moore for Asia Pacific Press. Singapore, 1971.

Zainu'ddin, Ailsa. *A Short History of Indonesia.* Cassel, Australia, 1968.

ARTICLES AND REPORTS

Arce, Roberto. "Conclusions and Recommendations Based on the Statistics of the Indonesian Petroleum Industry." March, 1959.

Bank Negara Indonesia Annual Reports for the Financial Year (Formerly known as Java Bank [1950] and Bank Indonesia [1951–1965]).

Bratanata, Ir. "Tjatatan Seorang Bekas Menteri" (Notes from a former Minister). Suara Pembaruan, 1970.

Castles, Lance. "Socialism and Private Business: The Latest Phase." *Bulletin for Indonesian Economic Studies*, June, 1965, 13–45.

Catten, H. "The Evolution of Oil Concessions in the Middle East and North Africa."

————*"The Law of Oil Concessions in the Middle East and North Africa."*

Commission of Four Report, as published in Sinar Harapan.

Duxbury, David. "IIAPCO Accepted the Challenge of Indonesia." May 1, 1971. (an unpublished report)

Finch & Lev. "Republic of Indonesia Cabinets 1945–1965." *Interim Reports Series.* Modern Indonesia Project, Ithaca.

Hanna, Willard. "Petroleum as Panacea." American University Field Service Report, August, 1971.

Hindley, Donald. "The 1965 Coup in Indonesia." *Journal of Asian Studies*, XXVI, 2, February, 1967.

Hopper Richard H. "Petroleum in Indonesia: History, Geology and Economic Significance." *ASIA*, XXIV, Winter 1971/72.

Hunter, Alex. "Indonesian Oil; A New Generation of Explorers." *Bulletin of Indonesian Economic Studies*. October, 1967, 85–91.

————"New Prospects in Indonesian Oil." *Bulletin of Indonesian Economic Studies*. February, 1967, 89–91.

————"Oil Developments." *Bulletin of Indonesian Economic Studies*. March, 1971, 96–113.

————"The Future of Indonesian Oil." *Bulletin of Indonesian Economic Studies*. June, 1968, 56–61.

————"The Indonesian Oil Industry." *Australian Economic Papers*. June, 1966. 59–106.

————"The Oil Industry: The 1963 Agreements and After." *Bulletin of Indonesian Economic Studies*. September, 1965, 16–33.

"Indonesia's Oil." *Indonesia Magazine*. No. 9, 1971.

Joenoes, Marah. "The Growth of Pertamina in the Indonesian Society."

Knowles, Ruth S. "A New Look at Indonesia's Potential." *World Petroleum*. January, 1968, 38–40.

Mabbet, John. "Cabinet Changes Confirm the Development Drill." *Insight*, November, 1971.

Mackie, J.A.C. "The Report of the Commission of Four on Corruption." *Bulletin of Indonesian Economic Studies*. November, 1970, 87–101.

McVey, Ruth. "Post Revolutionary Transformation of Indonesian Army, Part I." Cornell Indonesia Project Series. No. 11, April 1971.

Nakamura, Mitsuo. "General Imamura and the Early Period of the Japanese Occupation." Cornell Modern Indonesia Project, Number 10, 1970.

NIAM, Yearly Reports, 1953–57.

N.V. De Bataafsche Maatschappij, Pladju, Djakarta, October, 1955.

Oei, Hong-lan. "Petroleum Resources and Economic Development: A Comparative Study of Mexico and Indonesia." Austin, Texas, 1964. PhD. thesis. University of Texas.

"Oil: Indonesia Strikes it Rich," *Asian Industry*, August, 1971, 32–42.

Panglaykim, J. and Palmer I. "Entrepreneurship and Commercial Risks: The Case of a Schumpterian Business in Indonesia." Institute of Business Studies. Occaisonal Papers 2, Nanyang University, Singapore 22.

"Projek Badja Tjilegon." *Indonesia Magazine.* No. 12, 1971.

P.T. Shell Indonesia. "Oil in Indonesia." 1961.

Quah Swee Lan. "Oil Discovery and Technical Change in Southeast Asia, A Preliminary Bibliography." Institute of Southeast Asian Studies, October, 1971.

Smail, John. "The Military Politics of North Sumatra." Cornell Modern Indonesia Project, Number 6, October, 1969.

Todd & Pulunggono. "The Sunda Basinal Area." (pamphlet)

————"Wildcatters Score in Indonesia." *The Oil and Gas Journal.* June 14, 1971, 104–110.

Wijarso. "Oil in Indonesia: In Review and Prospect." *Pacific Community.* July 1970, 672–686.

CONTRACTS, REGULATIONS, AND LAWS FREQUENTLY REFERRED TO:

Indonesian Constitution of 1945

5-A Contract, BPM, 1948, No. 212.

Decree No. 1906/15/PSU/1954—formation of TMKL

Collective Labor Agreement Law, Official Gazette No. 69/1954

Government Regulation No. 34/1956—asserting central government authority over the oil fields in Atjeh and North Sumatra, designated North Sumatran oil fields

Decree of the Minister of Industry No. 3177/M dated October 15, 1957 —transferring authority of North Sumatran oil fields to the Army

Ordinance of the Military Authority No. Prt/PM/017/1957—revocation order for North Sumatran oil fields

Articles of Association, P.T. ETMSU, October 16, 1957

Articles of Association Addendum, renaming P.T. ETMSU as P.T. Permina, December 10, 1957

Refican Crude Sales Agreement, 10/12/57

Kobayashi Group Credit Agreement, (Nosodeco), 2/9/59

Law No. 19/1960—formation and regulation of State Enterprises

Law No. 44/1960—Oil Mining & Natural Gas Law

Government Regulation No. 3/1961—formation of P.N. Pertamin

Government Regulation No. 198/1961—formation of P.N. Permina

Government Regulation No. 199/1961—formation of P.N. Permigan

Rehabilitation Agreement & Addenda, Refican, 10/6/61

Rehabilitation Agreement, Asamera, 1/9/61

Presidential Decree No. 476/1961—status of foreign oil companies during transition

Contract, Pan American Indonesia Oil Company, 15/6/62

Government Regulation No. 18/1963—transition period ultimatum to foreign oil companies prior to Work Contract

Work Contract, P.T. Stanvac Indonesia, 23/9/63

Work Contract, P.T. Caltex Pacific Indonesia, 24/9/63

Work Contract, P.T. Shell Indonesia, 25/9/63

Law No. 14/1963—approval of Work Contracts

Heads of Agreement, Sale of P.T. Shell Indonesia, 30/12/65

Law No. 1/1967—Foreign Investment Law

Government Regulation No. 27/1968—merger of Permina and Pertamin

Law No. 8/1971—Pertamina Law

INDEX

The Authors:

ANDERSON GORDON BARTLETT III

Mr. Bartlett, from Tulsa, Oklahoma, received his AB from Dartmouth College, JD from Harvard Law School, with additional work as a post-graduate at Harvard Business School. Mr. Bartlett has five years' experience in the oil industry as an executive with an international offshore drilling firm, serving as Regional Director, S.E. Asia, in 1969/1970. In 1971 he formed a business development and consulting firm with offices in Djakarta and Singapore.

ROBERT JOHN BARTON

Mr. Barton, from Denver, Colorado, received his AB from Dartmouth College, then served four years as an officer in the United States Navy. Thereafter he received his JD from Harvard Law School. He practiced international law for two years in San Francisco before joining Mr. Bartlett as co-director of the project.

JOE CALVIN BARTLETT

Mr. Bartlett, (brother of Anderson) from Tulsa, Oklahoma, is an international relations student on a year's leave of absence from Dartmouth College. Two years ago he was an American Field Service student to Sweden. He is fluent in Bahasa Indonesia.

GEORGE ANDERSON FOWLER, JR.

Mr. Fowler, from Sharon, Connecticut, is a linguist and S.E. Asia student. He studied classics for two years at the University of Toronto, then joined the United States Marine Corps, serving two tours in Vietnam. Prior to joining the project he studied languages for a year at Nanyang University, Singapore and is fluent in Bahasa Indonesia.

CHARLES FRANCIS HAYS

Mr. Hays, from Albert, Kansas, is a graduate from the Asian studies program of the University of Kansas where he developed fluency in Japanese. He served three years in the United States Army where he studied Malay for a year. He is fluent in Bahasa Indonesia.